D1292180

Cost
Considerations
in
Systems
Analysis

# Cost
# Considerations
# in
# Systems
# Analysis

### GENE H. FISHER
*The Rand Corporation*
*Santa Monica, California*

## American Elsevier
## Publishing Company, Inc.
NEW YORK · 1971

AMERICAN ELSEVIER PUBLISHING COMPANY, INC.
52 Vanderbilt Avenue, New York, N.Y. 10017

ELSEVIER PUBLISHING COMPANY, LTD.
Barking, Essex, England

ELSEVIER PUBLISHING COMPANY
335 Jan Van Galenstraat, P.O. Box 211
Amsterdam, The Netherlands

International Standard Book Number 0-444-00087-9

Library of Congress Card Number 76-133272

*Printed in the United States of America*

# CONTENTS

v

x

# FOREWORD

The last few years have seen a plethora of books on the theory and practice of systems analysis. This is the first text, however, that concentrates on the cost analysis aspects of systems analysis. In a real sense it is long overdue. Our experience at the Defense Department indicates that appropriate conceptual treatment of cost and cost estimation accuracy are the two areas where past systems analyses have most frequently come to grief. We have seen carefully structured system studies, on which hundreds of analyst hours have been expended, arrive at what, in retrospect, are totally invalid conclusions, simply because of major deficiencies in the cost analyses on which they were based.

The study and analysis of the costs of defense are important not only for the obvious budgeting and accounting reasons, but also because costs are a measure of other defense capabilities foregone. The size of the defense budget limits the amount we can spend on defense. Monies spent on one program, obviously, are not available to spend on another. Therefore, properly constructed cost estimates and cost analyses are essential because an accurate assessment of the cost of individual programs is the first necessary step toward understanding the comparative benefits of alternative programs and capabilities. Thus, without proper analysis of *costs*, defense decisionmakers will not understand the alternative *forces* and *capabilities* available to them and will be deprived of flexibility in planning.

Our sponsorship of this book is a recognition of the Defense Department's need for people trained to perform the cost analysis function properly. We realize that the performance of this function is more than a matter of cost accounting, more than the preparation of cost estimates for short-term operating decisions; that it, in fact, requires structuring and analysis of resource alternatives in a full planning context. The capability to carry out these tasks requires an extensive familiarity with the total systems analysis process. Thus, the various chapters of this book address specific cost analysis problems, but always within the total systems analysis framework. This is a text for the teaching of force planning cost analysis as it should properly be taught, as a subset of systems analysis.

While the primary objective of this book is to assist in the training of analysts in the national security area, and all the case problems posed are defense oriented, its spillover value should be considerable. The methods and techniques of systems analysis that were developed to cope with defense problems have been found extremely useful in transportation, health, public housing, and environmental protection resource planning. The approach to cost analysis described in this text should be equally transferable.

DONALD B. RICE
Deputy Assistant Secretary of
Defense (Resource Analysis)

*Washington, D.C.*
*Spring 1970*

# ACKNOWLEDGMENTS

Many people share in the conception and execution of a book of this nature, too many to permit individual mention of them all. However, I want, in particular, to acknowledge my indebtedness to David Novick, former head of The Rand Corporation's Cost Analysis Department, under whose leadership the subject of "cost considerations in systems analysis" was developed over a twenty-year period at Rand, and to whom this book is dedicated. For having conceived of the idea for the book, my thanks go to Alain Enthoven, former U.S. Assistant Secretary of Defense (Systems Analysis). I am also grateful to all those staff members of Rand's Resource Analysis Department who provided much help and encouragement along the way – too long a list to enumerate here (essentially the entire Department); and to many other staff members at Rand who provided advice, comment, and criticism, especially, G. R. Hall, M. W. Hoag, E. W. Paxson, and E. S. Quade.

In addition, I am much indebted to Donald B. Rice, Deputy Assistant Secretary of Defense (Resource Analysis), who helped in the original structuring of the book and whose advice and encouragement were gratefully received at many points in its preparation; to R. E. Bickner, University of California (Irvine), who prepared Chapter 3, and served as a helpful reviewer and critic of the rest of the book; to Wayne Boucher, who did the final editing, but who is much, much more than the usual editor (the substantive nature of the work was improved by many of Wayne Boucher's suggestions); to J. Y. Springer, who read and edited the original draft manuscript and provided much help throughout the preparation of the final manuscript; and to L. H. Wegner and M. G. Weiner of Rand's Systems Sciences Department who provided the air-ground trade-off example in Chapter 9.

Even this partial list would be incomplete if I did not acknowledge my gratitude to Olive Hook, of Rand's Resource Analysis Department, who typed the entire manuscript – more than once – and splendidly each time; to Elizabeth Ridgman and Mary Jane Park of Rand's Resource Analysis Department, who competently performed the numerous activities that attend the development and production of a work of this kind; and to numerous individuals outside of Rand who served as critics and reviewers of all or parts of the manuscript, especially Richard Burton and W. A. Mauer, both of the Naval Postgraduate School, Monterey, California; Marvin Frankel, University of Illinois; and Arthur Smithies, Harvard University.

xiii

In addition to these individuals, I am especially grateful to the Office of the Secretary of Defense (Systems Analysis) for sponsoring this book as part of The Rand Corporation's continuing effort to further the development of analytical concepts, methods, and procedures and to extend their application to important public policy problem areas.

G. H. FISHER

# Chapter 1

# INTRODUCTION

## The Setting

Modern governments have to devote considerable time and effort to planning for the future. Inevitably, since resources are limited, the central issues in most planning problems concern resource allocation decisions.

Making major resource allocation decisions is difficult for many reasons. Objectives are not always clear-cut, and, typically, numerous alternative ways may be possible for attaining a given set of objectives. Moreover, uncertainties are likely to be abundant and pervasive particularly in those cases where lead time – the time from program initiation to the beginning of operations – spans a number of years. In the Department of Defense, for example, the lead time for a new military capability can be as long as 10 or more years. Long lead times invariably make planning more difficult, mainly because uncertainties are compounded as time horizons extend farther into the future.

Ultimately, most major long-range planning decisions have to be made primarily on the basis of the experience and judgment of the decision-makers. But resource allocation problems have become increasingly complex; and more and more it has come to be recognized that for decisionmakers to exercise their judgment effectively, ways must be found to assist them in dealing with complicated and interrelated issues. The result has been that attempts have been made to develop analytical concepts, methods, and skills to be used in generating information which will be useful in the planning process. One of the most important of these aids to decisionmaking is called *systems analysis*.

Systems analysis is discussed at some length in the next chapter. For the purposes of the present discussion it may be viewed as an analytical approach to, or way of looking at, a complex problem of choice under varying conditions of uncertainty. A fundamental characteristic of the approach is the systematic examination of objectives in a given area and of the alternative ways of achieving these objectives. Accordingly, systems analysis has many facets, but most of them can be associated directly or indirectly with an attempt to determine both the effectiveness (utility, benefit) of alternatives and their cost (or disutility).

## What This Book Is About

This book is concerned with *cost* considerations in systems analysis. While

1

effectiveness or utility considerations are thus not the prime focus, the discussion of cost analysis concepts and methods is always presented in the systems analysis context.

The following chapters are concerned primarily with questions like:

1. What concepts of cost are appropriate for dealing with resource considerations in systems analyses of long-range planning problems?
2. What analytical methods should be used in assessing the resource impact of proposed future alternatives for meeting objectives in a given problem area? How might uncertainties be taken into account explicitly in such analyses?
3. How should the results of cost analyses be presented in order to be most useful in the larger systems analysis and hence to the decision-makers?

At this point it is important to recognize what this book is not. It is not about cost accounting, cost estimating for current operations, cost analysis in support of detailed engineering design activities, cost estimating for next fiscal year's operating budget, and the like. No doubt portions of the material would be of some use in efforts like these, but the main concern of this volume is major resource allocation decisions in the long-range planning context,[1] and the basic concepts stem from the field of economics.

Moreover, this book limits its attention to questions of national security. Thus, in discussing specific concepts and methods of analysis, the concern is primarily with assessing the cost implications of alternative future military capabilities. However, most of the basic ideas are applicable, at least in part, to other realms: for example, health, education, transportation, public order, and the like.

Finally, the objective here is not to present a "cookbook" of detailed procedures. Nor is it to deal only with abstract concepts. The main thrust is toward the middle ground, with a view to promoting understanding of how cost analysis concepts and methods can substantively support the systems analysis process. Examples are used to illustrate key points.

## Organization of the Remainder of the Book

The initial chapters contain the background material necessary to provide an appropriate setting for the subsequent detailed treatment of military

---

[1] The specific meaning of "long-range" is, of course, context dependent and can range from 10 years or more (in the case of alternative proposals for *new* capabilities) down to a much shorter period (if, for example, the problem concerns the modification of existing systems).

cost analysis. Chapter 2 is designed to give the reader a general understanding of systems analysis. Chapter 3 turns to economic theory and discusses various concepts of cost, including problems associated with time. These chapters, together with the present one, comprise the basic conceptual setting, and the discussion then turns to military cost analysis *per se*. The transition is provided in Chapter 4, which outlines the main characteristics of the framework within which military cost analysis must be performed, given the basic concepts set forth in Chapters 2 and 3.

Chapter 4 is oriented primarily toward the cost analysis of the output or end-product side – that is, potential military capabilities which are in some way related to the achievement of future national security objectives. In Chapter 5 the orientation switches to the input side, the dimension in which most of the basic work of cost analysis must be carried out. Here, types of inputs to the cost analysis process are discussed, and input structures are presented. The discussion of input structures sets the stage for a vitally important subject: the derivation and use of estimating relationships. Estimating relationships, which are devices that relate various categories of cost to key cost-generating variables, form the heart of a cost analysis capability. Chapter 6 is devoted to this subject.

The input and output dimensions are combined in Chapter 7, which deals with cost models. Types of cost models and illustrations of their uses are presented and discussed.

Chapter 8 covers special topics, some of which – such as the treatment of uncertainty and problems associated with time – will have been alluded to previously but not discussed in the necessary depth.

Chapter 9 goes back to the beginning – to systems analysis. Here the objective is to present several examples of systems analysis studies and to show how the cost considerations are handled. Finally, Chapter 10 contains a summary and offers some speculations about the future of cost analysis.

## Summary

The main points in this chapter may be summarized as follows:

1. There is widespread and justifiable interest in developing improved approaches to handling resource allocation problems associated with major program decisionmaking processes in the context of long-range planning.

2. Systems analysis is one such approach. A systems analysis is a study designed to aid decisionmakers by systematically investigating the relevant objectives in a given problem area and the alternative ways of achieving these objectives. Two important facets of systems analysis are: (a) effectiveness (utility) considerations and (b) cost (disutility) considerations.

3. This book is concerned with *cost* considerations in systems analyses of long-range planning problems. The basic concepts stem from the field of economics.

4. Attention focuses on problems concerning the national security. However, most of the basic ideas are applicable to nonmilitary realms.

### Suggested Supplementary Readings

1. Charles J. Hitch, *Decision-Making for Defense*, Chap. II, "Planning-Programming-Budgeting," (Berkeley and Los Angeles: University of California Press, 1965), pp. 21–39.
2. William A. Niskanen, "The Defense Resource Allocation Process," in Stephen Enke (ed.), *Defense Management* (Englewood Cliffs, N.J.: Prentice-Hall, Inc., 1967), pp. 3–22.
3. T. Arthur Smith, "Economic Analysis and Military Resource Allocation," in *Economic Analysis and Military Resource Allocation* (Washington, D.C.: Office, Comptroller of the Army, 1968), pp. 3–18.

Chapter 2

# WHAT IS SYSTEMS ANALYSIS?

**Introduction**

The spectrum of resource allocation problems is very broad. At one extreme, the ideal prescription for resource allocation in a society is to maximize a weighted sum of all objectives by an efficient allocation of resources. But such an ideal is, and will remain, unattainable. We cannot know how to weigh one objective against all others, nor could so huge a policy analysis be undertaken even if we knew the appropriate weights to place upon objectives.

The central conceptual problems in policy studies stem from these inevitable analytic deficiencies. We are driven to "sub-optimizations" that are much narrower, but more tractable, policy analyses.[1] As a result, "spillover" benefits and costs will not be automatically taken into account, although they may be very important. Therefore, the policy analyst must carefully structure his study to make appropriate, although necessarily imperfect, allowances for spillover benefits and costs, which raises difficult conceptual and practical issues.

From the viewpoint of this book, one particular region of sub-optimization is of special interest: the region just a few steps down from the "grand optimum." Examples of Department of Defense resource allocation problems in this area are:

1. Seeking preferred general war policies or strategies, and the preferred mix of future strategic offensive and defensive forces to implement such policies or strategies.
2. Seeking the preferred mix of future military airlift, sealift, and prepositioning of supplies and equipment.
3. Determining the preferred configuration and armament of a future long-endurance antisubmarine aircraft to patrol and destroy enemy submarines.

Systems analysis is concerned primarily (though certainly not exclusively)

---

[1] Generally speaking, all resource allocation decisions below the "grand optimum" level are referred to as "sub-optimizations." As Hitch and McKean put it, "At the highest level, the decision-makers seek a grand optimum. At lower levels, they *sub-optimize*." See Charles J. Hitch and Roland N. McKean, *The Economics of Defense in the Nuclear Age* (Cambridge, Mass.: Harvard University Press, 1960), p. 396.

with these kinds of problems. At its present state of development, systems analysis cannot now help very much in dealing with the grand optimum.[2] In the other direction, at relatively low levels in the decision hierarchy, a full systems approach is usually not required; narrower context techniques like those used in the management sciences may suffice.[3]

**Definition of Systems Analysis**

Attempting to define systems analysis is difficult for several reasons. First of all, the term itself already has several established meanings, which vary from person to person. To make things worse, numerous other terms are in current usage which in some contexts have a systems analysis connotation, but which in others have a somewhat different meaning. Some examples are: cost-benefit analysis, systems engineering, cost-effectiveness analysis, operations research, and operations analysis. No attempt will be made here to resolve this terminological problem or to differentiate among the subtleties of meaning of these words.[4] Rather we shall proceed with a definition of systems analysis as we shall use it in this book and then discuss some of its more important characteristics.

> Systems analysis may be defined as inquiry to *assist* decisionmakers in choosing preferred future courses of action by (1) systematically examining and *reexamining* the relevant objectives and the alternative policies or strategies for achieving them; and (2) comparing quantitatively *where possible* the economic costs, effectiveness (benefits), and risks of the alternatives.[5]
>
> It is more a research strategy than a method or technique;[6] and in its present state of development it is more an art than a science, although scientific methods are utilized wherever possible. In sum, systems analysis may be viewed as an approach to, or way of looking at, complex problems of choice, usually under conditions of uncertainty.

The italicized words in the above definition deserve special comment. The word "assist" is italicized to emphasize that systems analysis is not

---

[2] To the knowledge of the present author, no other research strategy can help much either, and none is likely to be superior to systems analysis.

[3] For example, problems associated with determination of stock level policy can best be tackled through the use of presently developed inventory management techniques.

[4] A good discussion of the semantics problem may be found in Edward S. Quade (ed.), *Analysis for Military Decisions* (Chicago: Rand McNally & Company; Amsterdam: North-Holland Publishing Company, 1964), pp. 2–12; and E. S. Quade and W. I. Boucher (eds.), *Systems Analysis and Policy Planning: Applications in Defense* (New York: American Elsevier Publishing Co., Inc. 1968), pp. 1–5.

[5] This definition is very similar to that contained in Quade, *op. cit.*, p. 4. It stresses the *analytical* usage, where the boundaries of the "system" extend or contract significantly, depending upon the particular problem at issue. This contrasts with the *administrative* usage, where it is convenient to define the boundaries of a "system" in a fixed way so as to relate it to an administrative task (for example, to coordinate logistics support for the B-52 force).

[6] See Quade and Boucher, *op. cit.*, p. 2.

designed to replace the judgment of the decisionmakers. Rather, the objective is to provide a better basis for exercising that judgment through the more precise statement of problems, the discovery and outlining of alternatives, the making of comparisons among alternatives, and the like.[7] In practically no case should it be assumed that the results of the analysis will "make" the decision. The really critical problems are too complex, and there are too many incommensurables (for example, political, psychological, and sociological considerations) that cannot be taken fully into account in the analytical process, especially in a quantitative sense. In sum, the analytical effort should be directed toward assisting the decisionmaker in such a way that this basis for judgment is better than it would be without the results of the analysis. And in many instances even a modest amount of incisive analytical work can have a high payoff.[8]

The word "reexamining" is italicized in the definition to stress the fact that systems analysis typically involves an iterative process of formulation, testing, reformulation, retesting, and so on. The initial structuring of the problem rarely turns out to be adequate. The original set of alternatives may be incomplete and may not even contain those that are most relevant. Additional alternatives usually have to be generated (oftentimes invented) and investigated. Even the original objectives usually have to be modified as the analysis unfolds and as suggestions for interesting new objectives are uncovered. Moreover, it should be pointed out that the iterative process may never generate a "preferred" set of objectives and alternative means for attaining them. Nevertheless, the results may be very useful to the decisionmaker – for example, in helping him to reexamine and clarify his objectives.

Finally, the words "where possible" are italicized to suggest that although systems analysis does stress quantitative methods of analysis, it

---

[7] A former Assistant Secretary of Defense (Systems Analysis) puts the matter this way: "Ultimately all policies are made . . . on the basis of judgments. There is no other way, and there never will be. The question is whether those judgments have to be made in the fog of inadequate and inaccurate data, unclear and undefined issues, and a welter of conflicting personal opinions, or whether they can be made on the basis of adequate, reliable information, relevant experience and clearly drawn issues. In the end, analysis is but an aid to judgment. . . . Judgment is supreme." (A. C. Enthoven, quotation contained in an article in *Business Week*, November 13, 1965, p. 189.)

[8] Former Secretary of Defense Robert S. McNamara sums it up as follows: "They [the systems analysis staffs] provide the top level civilian and military decision makers of the Department [of Defense] a far higher order of analytical support than has ever been the case in the past. I am convinced that this approach leads not only to far sounder and more objective decisions over the long run, but also maximizes the amount of effective defense we obtain from each dollar expended." (*Statement of Secretary of Defense Robert S. McNamara Before the Senate Armed Services Committee on the Fiscal Year 1969–73 Defense Program and 1969 Defense Budget*, January 22, 1968, p. 194.)

does not attempt to push quantification to meaningless extremes. Many aspects of complex long-range planning problems cannot be reduced to numbers, and systems analysis does not try to do so.[9] Placing emphasis on the use of quantitative methods does not imply that incisive qualitative analysis is ruled out. In fact, most examples of good systems analysis studies contain an appropriate combination of quantitative and qualitative methods. As a minimum, systems analysis should try to isolate and sharpen the key qualitative issues for the benefit of the decisionmakers.

## Some of the Major Considerations Involved in Systems Analysis

From the definition of systems analysis, it is apparent that the subject has many dimensions. All of these cannot possibly be explored in a single chapter. Since the objective here is merely to provide a stage setting for the discussion of military cost analysis in subsequent chapters, it will suffice to list and briefly describe a few of the more important considerations.[10]

### The Analytical Process

The analytical process typical of systems analysis is similar to that employed in serious inquiry or investigation of problems in a wide range of situations. The analysis usually proceeds by a series of iterations or re-cyclings through something like the following phases:[11]

FORMULATION
(The Conceptual Phase)

Clarifying the objectives, defining the issues of concern, limiting the problem, searching out good criteria for choice.

SEARCH – INCLUDING THE DEVELOPMENT OF HYPOTHESES
(The Research Phase)

Looking for data and relationships, as well as alternative programs of action that have some chance of solving the problem.

EVALUATION
(The Analytic Phase)

Building various models, using them to predict the consequences that are likely to follow from each choice of alternatives, and then comparing the alternatives in terms of these consequences.

---

[9] See Alain C. Enthoven, "The Systems Analysis Approach," in *Planning-Programming-Budgeting*, Selected Comment, prepared by the Subcommittee on National Security and International Operations, Committee on Government Operations, United States Senate, 90th Cong., 1st Sess., (Washington, D.C.: U.S. Government Printing Office, 1967), p. 4.

[10] For a more thorough treatment, see Quade, *op. cit.*, Chaps. 2, 8, and 17; and Quade and Boucher, *op. cit.*, pp. 11–14, Chaps. 3 and 22.

[11] These phases are suggested by Quade and Boucher in *ibid.*, p. 33, and are discussed in detail in *ibid.*, pp. 34–53.

INTERPRETATION
(The Judgmental Phase)

Using the predictions obtained from the models and whatever other information or insight is relevant to compare the alternatives further, derive conclusions about them, and indicate a course of action.

VERIFICATION
(The Testing Phase)

Testing the conclusions wherever possible.

Which of these phases is most important is difficult to say. However, the first should receive particular emphasis.[12] Many analyses flounder right here, simply because of the failure to devote enough of the total time available for a study to deciding what the problem really is. Indeed, this is perhaps the most common pitfall in systems analysis.

Let us now turn to a discussion of several important subjects which bear on the conduct of the phases outlined above, with special emphasis on evaluation, or the analytical phase.

### Building the Models

The heart of the evaluation phase involves the assessment of the likely consequences of the various alternative courses of action being examined. This usually requires the development and use of an analytical model or series of models.[13]

Here the term "model" is used in a broad sense. Depending upon the nature of the problem at hand, the model used in the analysis may be formal or informal, very mathematical or not at all, heavily computerized or only moderately so, and so on. However, the main point is that the model need not be highly formal and mathematical to be useful. And there are several other important points that should be kept in mind:

1. Model building is an art, not a science. It is often an experimental process.
2. The main thing is to try to include and highlight those factors which are most relevant to the problem at hand, and to suppress

---

[12] Quade puts the matter this way: "It is difficult to overemphasize the importance of a careful formulation. It should identify the subproblems involved, isolate the major factors, develop a vocabulary for dealing with them, sketch out the relationships between the variables as they appear, and even arrive at a tentative set of conclusions. The idea is to make clear the structure of the analysis. But more importantly, it offers a concrete hypothesis for others to probe." (E. S. Quade, *Analysis for Military Decisions, op. cit.*, p. 307.)

[13] See R. D. Specht, "The Nature of Models," in Quade and Boucher, *ibid.*, Chap. 10.

(judiciously!) those which are relatively unimportant. Unless the latter is done, the model is likely to be unmanageably large.

3. The main purpose in designing the model is to develop a meaningful *set of relationships* among the objectives, the relevant alternatives available for attaining the objectives, the costs of the alternatives, and the utility of each of the alternatives.

4. Provision must be made for the explicit treatment of uncertainty – a subject we will consider in detail later.

5. Since by definition a model is an abstraction from reality, the model must be built on a set of assumptions. These assumptions must be made explicit. Failure to do so is a defect of the model design.

### The Conceptual Framework for Making Comparisons

Another important part of the evaluation phase is the comparison of alternatives in terms of the consequences generated by the model or models.

In making such comparisons there are two principal conceptual approaches:

1. *Fixed effectiveness approach.* For a specified level of effectiveness to be attained in the accomplishment of some given objective, the analysis attempts to determine that alternative (or feasible combination of alternatives) which is likely to achieve the specified level of effectiveness at the lowest economic cost.

2. *Fixed budget approach.* For a specified cost level to be used in the attainment of some given objective, the analysis attempts to determine that alternative (or feasible combination of alternatives) which is likely to produce the highest effectiveness.[14]

---

[14] In Chapter 1, it was suggested that systems analysis derives many of its concepts from economic theory. Here is a case in point. The fixed budget situation is somewhat analogous to the economic theory of consumer equilibrium. For a given level of income (budget) the consumer is assumed to behave in such a way that he maximizes his utility. From a wide range of alternative goods and services (and their prices) available to him, he will choose a set of quantities of goods and services such that the ratios of marginal utility to price for all items in the set are equal. See, for example, Paul A. Samuelson, *Economics: An Introductory Analysis* (New York: McGraw-Hill Book Company, 1967), pp. 421–422, 429–432.

The "fixed effectiveness" approach also has an analogy in micro-economic theory – for example, in the selection of the optimal (minimum cost) resource mix for a given level of output of the firm. Here, given the market prices of the factors of production (the inputs) the entrepreneur will minimize cost by hiring the productive factors until he has equalized the marginal-physical-product per last dollar spent on each factor of production. (Samuelson, *ibid.*, pp. 519–20.)

We should, however, point out a difference between economic theory and systems

Either (or both) of these approaches may be used, depending upon the context of the problem at hand. In any event, the objective is to permit *comparisons* to be made among alternatives, and for this purpose something has to be made fixed.[15]

At this point a comment on the use of ratios – for example, effectiveness-to-cost ratios – seems in order. Very often such ratios are used to evaluate alternatives. The use of ratios usually poses no problem as long as the analysis is conducted in the framework outlined above – that is, with the level of effectiveness or cost fixed. However, it is common to encounter studies where this has not been done, with the result that the comparisons were essentially meaningless. For example, consider the following illustration.

|               | *Effectiveness* (E) | *Cost* (C) | E/C |
|---------------|:-------------------:|:----------:|:---:|
| Alternative A | 20                  | 10         | 2   |
| Alternative B | 200                 | 100        | 2   |

If the analyst is preoccupied with ratios, the implication of this example is that he can be indifferent regarding the choice between A and B. But *should* the analyst be indifferent? Most probably not, because of the wide difference in scale between A and B. In fact, with such a great difference in scale, the analyst might not even be comparing relevant alternatives at all.[16]

### Treatment of Uncertainty

Most important decision problems involve major elements of uncertainty, and a systems analysis of such problems must provide for explicit treatment of uncertainty. This may be done in numerous ways.

---

analysis in practice. For example, in many instances in economic theory, given a set of market prices and a set of resource transformation relationships, it does not matter whether the decisionmaker minimizes costs or maximizes utility. One problem is essentially the equivalent of the other. The environment in which systems analysis is usually applied differs, however, from that assumed by conventional economic theory. In the defense systems analysis environment there is no simple operational criterion of effectiveness that has the role of profit or utility maximization in economic theory. Consequently, systems analysis of necessity uses a sub-optimization framework and exogenously fixes either a budget or a level of effectiveness. Under these conditions the two approaches will not necessarily yield the same results.

[15] Very often several levels, as we shall see in a moment, may be used to investigate the sensitivity of the ranking of the alternatives to effectiveness or budget level.

[16] For a further discussion of the possible pitfalls of using ratios, see Roland N. McKean, *Efficiency in Government Through Systems Analysis* (New York: John Wiley & Sons, Inc., 1958), pp. 34–37, 107–113. See also C. J. Hitch and R. N. McKean, *The Economics of Defense in the Nuclear Age* (Cambridge, Mass.: Harvard University Press, 1960), pp. 166–167.

For purposes of discussion, two main types of uncertainty may be distinguished:

1. Uncertainty about the state of the world in the future. Major factors here are technological uncertainty, strategic context uncertainty, and uncertainty about the enemy and his reactions.
2. Statistical uncertainty. This type of uncertainty stems from chance elements in the real world having a more or less objective or calculable probability of occurrence. It would exist even if there were no uncertainties of the first type.

Uncertainties of the second type are usually the least troublesome to handle in systems analysis studies. When necessary, Monte Carlo,[17] sensitivity analysis, or other techniques may be used to deal with statistical fluctuations. But these perturbations are usually dwarfed by uncertainties of the first type, which are dominant in most long-range planning problems.

Uncertainties of the first type are typically present, and they are most difficult to take into account in a systems analysis. Techniques which are often used are sensitivity analysis, contingency analysis, and *a fortiori* analysis.[18]

*Sensitivity Analysis.* Suppose in a given analysis there are a few key parameters about which the analyst is very uncertain. Instead of using mean values for these parameters, the analyst may successively use several values (say, high, medium, and low) in an attempt to see how sensitive the results (the ranking of the alternatives being considered) are to variations in the uncertain parameters.

Enthoven talks about sensitivity analysis in the following way:

> If it is a question of uncertainties about quantitative matters such as operational factors, it is generally useful to examine the available evidence and determine the bounds of the uncertainty. In many of our analyses for the Secretary of Defense, we carry three estimates through the calculations: an "optimistic," a "pessimistic," and a "best" or single most likely estimate. Although it is usually sensible to design the defense posture primarily on the basis of the best estimates, the prudent decision-maker will keep asking himself, "Would the outcome be acceptable if the worst possible happened, i.e., if all the pessimistic estimates were borne out?" Carrying three numbers through all of the calculations can increase the workload greatly. For this reason, a certain amount of judgment has to be used as to when the best guesses are satisfactory and when the full range of uncertainty needs to be explored. If there are uncertainties about context, at least one can run the calcula-

---

[17] For a discussion of Monte Carlo techniques see Herman Kahn and Irwin Mann *Monte Carlo*, P-1165 (Santa Monica, Calif.: The Rand Corporation, July 1957); and Quade, *op. cit.*, pp. 80, 241–243.

[18] See Albert Madansky, "Uncertainty," in Quade and Boucher, *op. cit.*, Chap. 5.

tions on the basis of several alternative assumptions so that the decision-maker can see how the outcome varies with the assumptions.[19]

If a certain alternative is superior in all of these sensitivity investigations, it is referred to as a *dominant* solution. Dominance is a characteristic that the analyst is always seeking, but its existence is rare in the types of problems of concern in this book.

*Contingency Analysis.* This type of analysis investigates how the ranking of the alternatives under consideration holds up when a relevant change in criteria for evaluating the alternatives is postulated, or a major change in the general environment is assumed. If, for example, in a military context, the enemy is assumed to be countries A and B, we might want to investigate what would happen if C joins the A and B coalition.

*A Fortiori Analysis.* Suppose that in a particular planning decision problem the generally accepted judgment favors alternative A. However, the analyst feels that A could turn out to be a poor choice and that alternative B might be preferred, particularly if certain assumptions about uncertainty are postulated. In performing an analysis of A versus B, the analyst may choose deliberately to resolve the major uncertainties in favor of B and see how A compares under these adverse conditions. If A still looks good, the analyst has a very strong case to support its selection.

While these three techniques may be useful in a direct analytical sense, they may also contribute indirectly. For example, through sensitivity and contingency analyses the analyst may gain a good understanding of the really critical uncertainties in a given problem area. On the basis of this knowledge he might then be able to come up with a newly designed alternative that will provide a reasonably good hedge against a *range* of the more significant uncertainties. This is often difficult to do; but when it can be accomplished, it offers one of the best ways to compensate for uncertainty.

### Treatment of Problems Associated with Time

More likely than not, a problem will be posed in a dynamic context, or at least it will involve some dynamic aspects. While a "static" analysis keyed to a particular future point in time can go a long way toward providing the decisionmaker with useful information, very often this has to be supplemented by analytical work which takes explicit account of the flow of time. A case in point is the treatment of the estimated costs of the alternatives for a stipulated level of effectiveness over time. Once these costs have been

---

[19] Alain Enthoven, "Decision Theory and Systems Analysis," *The Armed Forces Comptroller*, Vol. IX, No. 1, March 1964, pp. 16–17.

time-phased, the result will be cost streams through time for each of the alternatives.

The time-phasing of the costs of alternatives offers several advantages. In the first place it gives the decisionmakers an explicit picture of the points in time when the heaviest resource impacts of the various alternatives might occur. Also, as we shall see in later chapters, the estimates of cost are likely to be better. And finally, developing cost streams through time for the various alternatives provides a good basis for a definitive treatment of time preference.[20]

The problem of time preference is discussed in subsequent chapters. The key point, however, is that the assumptions underlying the treatment of the problem in the analysis should be made explicit. And in most cases the impact of alternative assumptions on the decision should be calculated and portrayed. For example, it is not always clear what rate of discount should be used to equalize cost streams through time. In this instance the analyst should calculate upper- and lower-bound rate cases to see whether it really makes a significant difference in the final outcomes (the ranking of the alternatives being considered).

### Checking for Validity

In the preceding paragraphs we have discussed building the analytical model, "exercising" the model (sensitivity and contingency analysis), and the like. Another important consideration – often slighted – is testing the validity of the model. Since the model is only a representation of reality, it is desirable to do some sort of checking to see if the analytical procedure used is a reasonably good representation, within the context of the problem at hand. This is difficult to do, especially in dealing with systems analysis problems having a time horizon 5, 10, or more years into the future

In general we cannot test models of this type by controlled experiments. However, the analyst might try to answer the following questions:[21]

1. Can the model describe known facts and situations reasonably well?
2. When the principal parameters involved are varied, do the results remain consistent and plausible?

---

[20] As used throughout this book, the term "time preference" refers to the fact that decisionmakers are usually not indifferent to the timing of a certain gain or cost. An outlay of $100 next year is not equivalent to $100 five years from now, even if there is no risk. (This is the reason for the existence of positive interest rates.) Later we shall discuss in detail how the two amounts may be made equivalent, with respect to time preference, by computing their present values through use of a discounting procedure.

[21] E. S. Quade, *Military Systems Analysis*, RM-3452-PR (Santa Monica, Calif.: The Rand Corporation, January 1963), p. 20.

3. Can it handle special cases where we already have some indication as to what the outcome should be?
4. Can it assign causes to known effects?

### Qualitative Supplementation

We have already stressed the importance of qualitative considerations in systems analysis – particularly qualitative supplementation of the quantitative work. Introduction of qualitative considerations may take several forms:

1. Qualitative analysis *per se*, as an integral part of the total analytical effort.
2. Interpretation of the quantitative work.
3. Discussion of relevant nonquantitative considerations that could not be taken into account in the "formal" analysis.

The third approach can be particularly important in presenting the findings of a study to the decisionmaker. The idea is to present the results of the formal quantitative work, interpret these results, and then to say that this is as far as the formal quantitative analysis itself will permit us to go. The important qualitative considerations that the decisionmaker should try to take into account, such as certain key political factors, could then be listed and discussed.

### Some of the Pitfalls

In discussing some of the major considerations in systems analysis, the important subject of possible pitfalls should always be taken into account. No analysis, whether it is a systems analysis or not, can be a panacea; and the practitioners – and users – of analysis should be aware of the numerous traps into which even an experienced analyst can fall.

A few of the more common pitfalls are the following:[22]

1. Failing to allocate and to spend enough of the total time available for a study deciding what the problem really is.
2. Examining an unduly restricted range of alternatives.
3. Trying to do too big a job.
4. Determining objectives and criteria carelessly.
5. Using improper costing concepts.
6. Becoming more interested in the details of the model than in the real world.

---

[22] For an excellent discussion of the pitfalls and limitations of analysis, see Quade and Boucher, *op. cit.*, Chap. 19.

7. Forcing a complex problem into an analytically tractable framework by overemphasizing ease of computation.
8. Failing to take proper account of uncertainty.
9. Treating the enemy threat too narrowly – for example, considering only the "expected value" cases or only the "worst possible" case.

## Some Examples of Past Applications

In Chapter 9 we will consider three extended examples of systems analysis. Some brief illustrations might be useful at this point, however, to give substance to the preceding (and perhaps too abstract) discussion and to indicate some of the problems systems analysts have actually addressed.[23]

### Military Examples

*General War Alternatives.* In planning the strategic offensive and defensive forces of the future, many issues have to be examined systematically. Obviously, particular attention must be paid both to objectives or strategies and to the alternative ways for attaining them.

A primary objective is the deterrence of general thermonuclear war through the maintenance of a "highly reliable ability to inflict an unacceptable degree of damage upon any single aggressor, or combination of aggressors, . . . even after our absorbing a surprise first strike."[24] This is called an "assured destruction capability," and provides one means of ensuring deterrence of general war. But in addition there are many other types of capabilities that might be considered; for example:[25]

1. Damage-limiting capabilities to limit damage if deterrence fails and war breaks out.[26]
2. Coercion and bargaining capabilities to be used in an escalation process stemming from a crisis situation (to the extent that these capabilities are not automatic from damage-limiting).

---

[23] Although the discussion here is confined to the public sector, this in no way is meant to minimize the importance of work done in private industry. In the automobile industry, for example, something similar to systems analysis has been used for many years. Lead times for the development and production of new car lines are fairly long – about 4 or 5 years – and much advanced planning activity is engaged in by firms in the industry. In the process of planning for the future, many alternative configurations of a given proposed vehicle are systematically examined, and various "mixes" of future car lines are explored.

[24] Robert S. McNamara, in a speech to the Editors of United Press International in San Francisco, September 18, 1967. Text published in *The New York Times*, September 19, 1967.

[25] This is a very short list. For a more complete discussion, see Herman Kahn, *On Escalation: Metaphors and Scenarios* (New York: Frederick A. Praeger, Publishers, 1965), especially Chap. 2.

[26] For example, see *ibid.*, pp. 153–154.

3. Capabilities for intrawar deterrence of countervalue exchanges.[27]
4. Capabilities for war termination.

Thus the range of strategic capabilities that the planners have to consider is very wide. Even wider is the range of alternative instrumentalities that may be used to attain various sets of these capabilities in the future. Examples of alternatives for the offense are: manned bombers; fixed, land-based ballistic missiles; mobile, land-based ballistic missiles; sea-based ballistic missiles; missiles based on satellites in outer space; and so on. Examples of defensive alternatives include: manned interceptor aircraft; land-based antiballistic missiles; airborne platform-based interceptor missiles to defend against enemy submarine-launched ballistic missiles; a satellite fleet of boost-phase intercept missiles; civil defense measures; and so on. To complicate matters even further, each of these offensive and defensive instrumentalities can have a number of plausible hardware configurations, weapon or warhead options, and operating concepts. Moreover, a range of alternatives for sensors and command and control systems usually has to be considered.

Clearly, decisionmakers are confronted with an incredibly large number of interrelated, complex considerations in determining future strategic objectives and the "preferred" future force mix to meet these objectives. How can they make these choices on the basis of judgment unaided by analytical support? The answer is that they cannot and they have not. Particularly in the nuclear age, long-range planning of the strategic forces has always been assisted by analysis of some sort. However, in recent years such support has been more extensive and much more systematic than ever before. This is particularly true in the case of the work done concerning future assured-destruction and damage-limiting capabilities, offensive and defensive.

With respect to other areas (coercion and bargaining in a controlled general war environment, intrawar deterrence of countervalue exchanges, and so on) the analytical effort to date has been limited – and understandably so, since the emphasis falls heavily on the exceedingly difficult task of attempting to analyze gradual interactions of intentions and capabilities, rather than on extreme situations where the adversaries' intentions may be to use their full capabilities. Controlled general war is harder to deal with analytically than "all-out" general war, primarily because of the relatively greater importance of political and psychological factors in a dynamic, multisided decision process. Here, use of traditional methods of analysis

---

[27] Countervalue exchanges involve salvos launched against cities. See *ibid.*, p. 183.

alone is not likely to be sufficient. New approaches and perhaps new combinations of existing approaches will have to be developed.

Much effort is presently being spent to develop the necessary analytic capabilities. Some of these are mainly mathematical. Others involve attempts to devise methods for systematically taking into account factors which up until now have been little understood, yet which are critical to national security decisions: for example, various organizational, political, psychological, and social considerations.[28]

In sum, in the general war area, systems analysis has been used many times in the past, it is being used extensively today, and attempts are currently under way to develop new approaches for examining a wide range of strategic problems in the future.

*Mobility of the General Purpose Forces.* The central issue here is planning for the rapid deployment of forces – especially ground forces – to trouble spots around the world in the future.

Mobility may be attained in a number of different ways. The main alternatives are airlift, prepositioning of men and equipment (or of equipment only), and sealift. Each of these in certain respects is competitive with the others. In some instances, however, the alternatives are more complementary than competitive. In any case, they all have different relative advantages and disadvantages. For example:

1. Airlift offers the advantages of very rapid response time and flexibility of response, provided appropriate air bases are available in or near the combat area in the overseas theater. The necessity of having available air bases can be eased considerably through the use of very large payload aircraft with advanced power plants and landing gear to permit operations from relatively short runways at primitive forward air bases.[29] (This increment in capability is attained, of course, at the expense of an increase in the cost of the aircraft system.) In general, the main disadvantage of airlift is that it is costly.

2. Prepositioning of stocks and equipment around the world has the

---

[28] In some instances the search for new approaches is taking the form of attempting to combine several complementary techniques which, when taken together, might produce a whole greater than the sum of the individual parts: for example, a combining of gaming, current systems analysis concepts, new computer technology (especially on-line, time-sharing systems), and techniques to systematize the interactions of a group engaged in a joint judgmental endeavor in the context of a dynamic sequential decision process. The latter is essentially an outgrowth of the Delphi Method. For a discussion of the method itself, see Olaf Helmer, *Analysis of the Future: The Delphi Method*, P-3558 (Santa Monica, Calif.: The Rand Corporation, March 1967); and N. C. Dalkey, *Predicting the Future*, P-3948 (Santa Monica, Calif.: The Rand Corporation, October 1968).

[29] The new C-5A transport aircraft will utilize these improvements.

advantage of low cost per site. Its disadvantages include problems involved in obtaining real estate in foreign countries, and the risk that the real estate (if acquired) and the prepositioned stocks will be in the wrong location in the world when war threatens. There is also the risk, in some countries, that a lack of internal stability may pose a security threat to the pre-positioning area.

3. Conventional sealift has the advantage of low cost. The main disadvantage is slow response time for initial deployments. Sealift, how-ever, can offer some very interesting possibilities when combined with the notion of prepositioning supplies and equipment not on land, but on ships. The result is fast deployment logistics ships (FDLS) located at various points in the world and ready to steam to a trouble spot within a particular FDLS's region of responsibility. This combination of sealift and prepositioning produces a new alternative which tends to minimize the main disadvantages of sealift and prepositioning taken separately.[30] The combination can be made even more attractive by replacing conventional ships with newly designed craft called Roll-on/Roll-off ("Ro-Ro") ships. These ships have the capability to load and unload army vehicles very quickly, even at ports having primitive docking facilities. They also have a cruising speed considerably above that of conventional transport ships. The net result is an alternative for fast deployment which is potentially competitive with airlift – at least in some situations. If this should turn out to be the case, the mix of airlift, sealift, and prepositioning can be less heavily weighted with expensive airlift than would otherwise be the case. The result might be the attainment of rapid deployment objectives at a lower total force mix cost.[31]

This discussion of the mobility of the general purpose forces is brief, but it should be sufficient to convey some of the key considerations involved in the problem. Several alternatives are available for considera-tion, each having different costs and utilities. While the alternatives are competitive in some cases, in others the complementarities are very strong.

---

[30] This is a good example of the invention of a new alternative in the systems analysis process. See Charles J. Hitch, *Decision-Making for Defense* (Berkeley and Los Angeles: University of California Press, 1955), p. 54.

[31] Here, however, as in all systems analysis studies, great care and attention must be given to the formulation of the problem to be examined – particularly with respect to relevant questions about mobility and response. Such issues include, for example: (1) How are the fuels and lubricants, food, and other supplies to be obtained for the equip-ment and men to be moved? (2) What are the conditions that would require a large supply of material rapidly? (3) What are the dangers of escalating a conflict by an overly quick response? (4) Where are the personnel to use the equipment to come from, how are they to be moved, and how quickly will they get there? (5) What would we find to do with the equipment after we get it to the destination?

Where they are significantly strong, the planning problem takes the form of determining the preferred force mix to meet the desired rapid deployment objectives. Obviously, a large number of alternative mixes is possible. Moreover, as is often the case, examination of numerous mixes may result in changing the initially specified objectives.

Again, as in the general war example discussed previously, it is difficult to see how the force planners could grapple with the airlift, sealift, and prepositioning force-mix problem without having some kind of analytical support. And again, they in fact have had a great deal of analytical help to assist them in making their planning decisions. Models have been developed which can rapidly calculate estimates of the cost and of certain effectiveness measures for alternative force mixes. While these analytical models cannot determine *the* "optimum force mix," they can generate information which provides insights about break-even points, regions of sensitivity, and the like.[32]

### Non-Defense Examples

For many years, systems analysis, or something similar to it, has been applied to numerous non-defense problems. Since the summer of 1965,[33] however, the number of such applications has increased markedly, and the range of problems subjected to analytical treatment has been extended.

A classic example of an important problem area where systems analysis of a sort has been attempted for a number of years is water-resource development: dams, drainage of marshlands, subsurface storage, water reclamation, and a host of other types of water-resource projects.[34] While budgets for water-resource projects have typically been fairly large, they have never been large enough to permit undertaking all the new projects proposed in any particular planning period. One of the basic problems, therefore, has been to try to choose a preferred mix of projects that could be obtained from available budget levels. Since water-resource allocation problems involve numerous complex considerations, including indirect or "spillover" effects, it is not surprising that economists, engineers, and others have endeavored to develop methods of analysis which might help in choosing preferred mixes of water-resource projects.[35]

---

[32] Hitch, *Decision-Making for Defense, op. cit.*, p. 55.

[33] In August 1965, the President directed all Federal agencies and departments to establish Planning-Programming-Budgeting Systems (PPBS). Systems analysis is a key component of PPBS. See David Novick (ed.) *Program Budgeting: Program Analysis and the Federal Government* (Cambridge, Mass.: Harvard University Press, rev. ed., 1967).

[34] See Roland N. McKean, *Efficiency in Government Through Systems Analysis, op. cit.*, pp. 16–20.

[35] Efforts have also been devoted to the individual project – its content and ingredients and the allocation of the project budget among them.

Beyond the classic example of water-resource development, the list of problem areas where systems analysis has been attempted is indeed a long one. The following list, while reasonably representative, is far from complete; and the particular ordering in no way is intended to suggest the relative importance of the problems, or the quality of the work done. Its purpose is simply to serve to impress upon the reader that the application of systems analysis has not been confined to national security problems.

1. Analysis of health programs by the Department of Health, Education and Welfare: Examination of the estimated costs and benefits of alternative programs in several areas – cancer control, arthritis control, syphilis control, tuberculosis control, motor vehicle injury prevention, and child health care measures.[36]

2. Analysis of the future transportation problems of the Northeast corridor (from Boston to Washington, D.C.), sponsored by the Department of Transportation: Systematic examination of the costs and utilities of possible alternative mixes of private cars, public buses, rail networks (surface and subsurface), airplanes, and so on, in order to get some notion about what the preferred mix might be for the 1970s and 1980s.[37]

3. Examination of alternative ways to deal with urban transportation problems in large cities: Comparisons of estimated costs and benefits of freeways (surface, below surface, above surface), rail rapid transit systems (surface, below surface, above surface), buses, and so on, and of various mixes of these means of transportation.[38]

4. Studies of problems in education: For example, analysis of the costs and benefits of various alternative ways of preventing high school dropouts.[39]

5. Studies of the commercial aviation problem in the 1970s and 1980s: Analysis of the estimated costs and benefits of alternative air transport systems; for example, various configurations of supersonic systems versus second generation subsonic jet aircraft systems.[40]

---

[36] For an excellent summarization and critique of these studies, see Elizabeth B. Drew, "HEW Grapples with PPBS," *The Public Interest*, No. 8, Summer 1967, pp. 13–22.

[37] For example, see *The Northeast Corridor Transportation Project: Study Design*, Office of High Speed Ground Transportation, Washington, D.C., June 1966.

[38] For a general discussion of the urban transportation problem, see J. R. Meyer, J. F. Kain, and M. Wohl, *The Urban Transportation Problem* (Cambridge, Mass.: Harvard University Press, 1965).

[39] See Burton A. Weisbrod, "Preventing High School Dropouts," in Robert Dorfman (ed.), *Measuring Benefits of Government Investments* (Washington, D.C.: The Brookings Institution, 1965), pp. 71–116.

[40] Most of these studies were sponsored by the Federal Aviation Agency and are not available for general distribution.

6. Analytical study efforts in support of long-range planning in the National Aeronautics and Space Administration: Systematic examination of the estimated costs and utilities of alternative space goals and missions in the future; and analyses of preferred ways to accomplish a given future mission – for example, a Mars landing.

## Summary

The main points contained in this chapter may be summarized as follows:

1. Systems analysis may be viewed as an approach to, or way of looking at, complex problems of choice under conditions of uncertainty.

2. It attempts to assist decisionmakers in choosing preferred courses of action by (a) systematically examining and reexamining the relevant objectives and the alternative policies or strategies for achieving them; and (b) comparing quantitatively where possible the economic costs, effectiveness (benefits), and risks of the alternatives.

3. Systems analysis usually proceeds by a series of iterations or re-cyclings through something like the following phases:

   (a) Formulation (the conceptual phase)

   (b) Search (the data gathering or research phase)

   (c) Evaluation (the analytic phase)

   (d) Interpretation (the judgmental phase)

   (e) Verification (the testing-of-conclusions phase)

4. Assessment of the likely consequences of the various alternatives being examined usually requires the development and use of an analytical model or series of models.

5. In making comparisons among alternatives there are two principal conceptual approaches: (a) fixed effectiveness (for a specified level of effectiveness, seek the minimum-cost alternative); and (b) fixed budget (for a specified level of cost, seek the alternative that maximizes effectiveness).

6. Uncertainties must be treated explicitly in systems analysis studies.

7. Sensitivity analysis is vitally important in the search for dominant solutions.

8. The analyst must always be aware of the pitfalls of analysis.

9. Systems analysis has been applied to many problem areas in both military and nonmilitary contexts.

**Suggested Supplementary Readings**

1. Alain C. Enthoven, "The Systems Analysis Approach," in *Planning-Programming-Budgeting*, prepared by the Subcommittee on National Security and International Operations, Committee on Government Operations, U.S. Senate, 90th Cong., 1st Sess. (Washington, D.C.: U.S. Government Printing Office, 1967), pp. 1–10.

2. Charles J. Hitch, *Decision-Making for Defense* (Berkeley and Los Angeles: University of California Press, 1965), Chap. III, "Cost-Effectiveness."
3. Charles J. Hitch and Roland N. McKean, *The Economics of Defense in the Nuclear Age* (Cambridge: Harvard Univerity Press, 1960), Chap. 7, "Effectiveness in Military Decisions."
4. E. S. Quade and W. I. Boucher (eds.), *Systems Analysis and Policy Planning: Applications in Defense* (New York: American Elsevier Publishing Co., Inc., 1968), Chap. 1, "Introduction," Chap. 3, "Principles and Procedures of Systems Analysis."
5. Bernard H. Rudwick, *Systems Analysis for Effective Planning* (New York: John Wiley & Sons, Inc., 1969), Chap. 1, "Introduction and Overview."

# Chapter 3

# CONCEPTS OF ECONOMIC COST[1]

**What Is "Economic Cost"?**

Systems analysis, as outlined in Chapter 2, is an approach to complex problems of choice. To help us make the best possible choice we try to *identify* and, wherever feasible, to *measure* and *evaluate* the pros and cons of our alternatives. That is, we try to assess their "costs" and "benefits." What do we mean by "costs"?

Like many common words, the word "cost" is used differently by different people, and vaguely by most. Consequently, we must take pains first to clarify the concept and second to become alerted to the various modifications of the concept that will, unless we watch out for them, confuse or mislead us.

To illustrate the various ways in which the word "cost" might be used, consider the "cost" of stopping by the neighborhood bar on the way home from work tomorrow. This might "cost" you (a) an expenditure of several dollars, (b) a chance to watch your favorite newscast and stockmarket report, and (c) a hangover. What would be the "cost" of stopping by the bar?[2]

We will return to this elemental question about the meaning of "cost," and to this simple illustration, again. Meanwhile it should be emphasized that:

1. If we define "cost" to mean only dollar expenditures, then obviously we will not be able to make rational choices simply by comparing cost, in this restricted sense, with benefits.
2. Determining the cost of most government programs will be much more complicated, not less, than determining cost in the example given.

---

[1] This chapter was prepared by R. E. Bickner of the University of California, Irvine.

[2] The reader may be in haste to simplify the concept of "cost" by distinguishing "dollar cost" from "nondollar cost," for example, or by distinguishing "economic cost" from "noneconomic cost." Any of the three cost items mentioned could involve "dollar costs," however, and distinctions between "economic cost" and such things as "psychological cost" or "social cost" or "political cost" will not survive serious scrutiny. The example given does introduce one simplifying distinction, however. It distinguishes costs to *you* from costs to *other people*, such as your wife, the bartender, and local law enforcement agencies. For many government programs, the decisionmaker may be uncertain about whose costs he wants to consider and whose costs to ignore.

3. No decisionmaker can sensibly claim to be comparing the cost and benefits of his decisions unless he has a clear and defensible notion about the meaning of "cost."

## An Economic Cost Is a Benefit Lost

If we choose to use some of our resources to develop and produce a certain new military capability, then those resources are obviously not available for the production of some other, perhaps superior, capability. If we assign our best available engineers to research and development, then they are not available for quality control – or vice versa. If we assign a number of ships or aircraft or men to one combat theater, or to one military operation, then they will not be available for alternative assignments. An estimate of the cost of any such choice or decision is an estimate of the benefits that could otherwise have been obtained. *"Economic costs" are benefits lost*. It is for this reason that economic costs are often referred to as "alternative costs" or "opportunity costs." It is in *alternatives*, it is in forgone opportunities, that the real meaning of "cost" must always be found. The only reason that you hesitate to spend a dollar, incidentally, is because of the *alternative* things that it could buy.[3]

Since economic costs are simply benefits lost, it follows that costs and benefits have the same dimensions. If this were not so, incidentally, it would be impossible to compare costs and benefits. It would be meaningless to say that the benefits of a certain program exceed its costs if these two concepts had different dimensions.

## Which Is Easier to Measure, Costs or Benefits?

Since costs and benefits have the same dimensions, it might seem that they would be equally difficult, or equally easy, to measure. It will help us develop a better insight into the meaning of cost, and a better awareness of the difficulty of measuring cost, if we consider for a moment the question: Which is easier to measure, costs or benefits?

It is very true that the benefits of a certain planned government program are likely to be very difficult to measure, but at least the decisionmaker and the cost analyst will know what the planned program looks like. The costs, on the other hand, are to be found in the benefits of some unspecified and dimly perceived alternatives to the program. Surely, then, in the final analysis, it must be much more difficult to identify and measure costs than benefits.

---

[3] For an example of the concept of opportunity cost applied to a simple case from the microeconomic theory of the firm, see Appendix A.

Nonetheless, it is commonly asserted that costs are easier to measure than benefits. Why?

There are two very different reasons for this common assertion. First, for reasons that will be discussed shortly, dollars can be a very useful measure of both costs and benefits, but we are more often able to get a reasonable dollar estimate of costs than of benefits.[4] It must be emphasized immediately, however, that not all dollar estimates really add up to a valid and comprehensive measure of costs.

Second, from long tradition and careless habit, it is our custom to dismiss all those costs which we cannot conveniently measure in dollars as "non-cost considerations," or as "qualitative factors." We arbitrarily and unconsciously modify the concept of cost to mean *only* those costs that can be readily evaluated in dollars, and then we confidently assert that we can measure costs. We could easily measure benefits if we permitted ourselves the same convenient modification of the concept.[5]

In sum, we can make the problem of cost estimation as easy as we like, by either (a) restricting our attention to decisionmaking problems in which costs happen to be easily measured, preferably in dollars, or (b) restricting our definition of costs to mean only those things which are easily measured, preferably in dollars.

## To Ignore Costs Is to Ignore Benefits

There are two different ways to ignore costs, both of them common. The first is characteristic of poor decisionmakers, who dismiss them by fiat; the second is characteristic of poor cost analysts, who dismiss them out of ignorance.

Since costs are often difficult to measure, some decisionmakers give them only minor importance, at best. But benefits are also difficult to measure, and we could just as well ignore them as ignore costs. As a matter

---

[4] This difference between costs and benefits is easily exaggerated, however. If the government builds a power dam in the Grand Canyon, or diverts military personnel from training exercises to the construction of roads, or condemns a neighborhood playground for use as a Post Office site, it may be much easier in every case to develop a reasonable "dollar" estimate of benefits than of costs. To press this point further, note that any tentative government decision can be reversed. It follows that, if we can estimate the cost of a tentative decision more easily than the benefits, then we can estimate the benefits of *reversing* that decision more easily than we can estimate the costs.

[5] Essentially, what we customarily do is transfer any costs that are difficult to measure in dollars over to the benefit side of the cost/benefit equation. Such costs become "negative benefits," and are left for the benefit analyst, rather than the cost analyst, to evaluate. Interestingly, however, if there happen to be any benefits readily measured in dollars, they are likely to be transferred over to the cost side of the equation as "credits against costs" or "cost savings." There can be no doubt that, after all such transfers, costs are easier to measure than benefits.

of fact, to ignore costs *is* to ignore benefits. One thing we *should* ignore is advice that ignores cost!

Consider a very simple decision and a simple cost/benefit analysis. You have a number of fighter bombers and a number of B-52 heavy bombers available, and a few bridges to be destroyed and a large number of air bases to be attacked. Which aircraft do you assign to destroy the bridges? We could use other examples, with dollars or men or material as our resources and the procurement of ships or the construction of runways, or whatever, as our objectives, but the problem would be the same in concept.

Suppose that 1 B-52 or 2 fighter bombers can destroy a bridge, and that 1 B-52 accomplishes as much destruction as 10 fighter bombers when attacking an air base. Then, *provided there are no other costs to be considered,* you would surely assign fighter bombers to destroy the bridges. To assign B-52s to the bridges will either *increase the cost* of achieving a given level of destruction, or *reduce the benefits* achieved with a given inventory of aircraft.

This simple example highlights the interrelation of costs and benefits. Given the objectives and the resources stated, the benefit of using a B-52 to destroy a bridge can be expressed in terms of the number of fighter bombers that can then be released for alternative assignment, i.e., 2. The cost of using the B-52 must be found in the forgone benefits of its alternative use, attacking air bases. This cost can also be expressed in terms of the number of fighter bombers released, i.e., 10. In other words, considering the alternatives, the cost of using B-52s to destroy bridges exceeds the benefits.[6]

If the decisionmaker ignores this relation of cost to benefits, and if he assigns B-52s to destroy bridges, then it will inevitably follow that (a) less destruction will be achieved than was possible, given a fixed number of B-52s and fighter bombers, or (b) more aircraft must be used than are really necessary, given the level of destruction achieved.

In sum, costs and benefits are alternate sides of the same coin, and to ignore one is to ignore the other. After all, as we stressed at the beginning, costs are benefits lost. No responsible decisionmaker can afford to ignore either.

Nor can a responsible cost analyst. In the example, we were careful to emphasize that the conclusion to use fighter bombers followed "provided there are no other costs to be considered." It is very likely that there would have been other costs requiring attention, however, such as crew losses,

---

[6] This example can also be discussed in terms of the concept of "comparative advantage." (For an example, see Appendix B.)

aircraft losses, ammunition and fuel expended, and so on. Should the cost analyst ignore such costs?

It is well that a cost analyst realize his limitations and that he restrict his ambitions to practicable objectives. He may not know how to estimate crew losses, for example, or how to evaluate such losses. But he goes beyond the bounds of modesty in restricting his attention to just that *part* of the cost which he can easily measure and then presuming that he has measured the whole. Nor is there any great merit in making cost/benefit comparisons on the basis of painstaking and precise estimates of some very uncertain fraction of total cost.

Cost analysts can ignore costs just as surely as decisionmakers can. Indeed, it is often the analyst's temptation to oversimplify or ignore costs that tempts the decisionmaker, in turn, to be skeptical of the significance of cost.

### Identifying, Measuring, and Evaluating Costs

In a sense, it would seem that we cannot evaluate alternatives unless we can first measure them, and we cannot measure them without first identifying them. Cost analysis is essentially a sequential process: identification, measurement, and then evaluation of alternatives. And yet, as we will see, the three steps are often accomplished almost simultaneously, especially when we use dollars to facilitate the cost analysis process.

A close look at the problem of measurement will help us understand the relationships among the three steps of the process. Fortunately, we have the option of measuring the costs of a program in several different ways. We also have the option of using dollars as a general-purpose measure of many of the costs and benefits of a program.

Suppose that we are trying to decide whether or not to procure and deploy a certain new proposed military capability. How might we measure the cost? Consider the following four possible procedures and note the relationships among them:

1. We could estimate and list the *resources required* for the proposed new capability: the manpower of various types, the real estate, the production facilities, the transportation services, the fissionable materials, and so on.

2. We could identify and describe some of the *alternative uses* of these resources. For example, we could determine what alternative military capabilities could be produced with the same resources. If the required resources are flexible enough, there may be a very wide variety of alternative uses. The resources could be used, not just to produce other capabilities

to be used directly in combat, but perhaps to produce warning and intelligence systems, or passive defenses, or training facilities. It may be relevant to note that the resources could even be used to produce public schools or hospitals or automobiles or television sets.

3. We could attempt, if we were ambitious enough, not only to identify some of the alternative uses of the required resources, but to estimate the *value of the alternatives*. For example, we could estimate the effectiveness of the alternative combat capabilities, or the probable increase in warning time from the new warning system, or the consequences that would result from the additional warning time, or the value of the hospitals or automobiles that could be produced with the resources. In other words, we could attempt to evaluate the benefits forgone.

4. We could estimate the *dollar expenditures* that will be entailed by the procurement and deployment of the proposed capability.

In short, we can attempt to estimate (1) the resources required, (2) the alternative uses of these resources, (3) the value of these alternatives, or (4) the dollars spent. Which of these four things should we try to do when we analyze costs? An easy and reasonable answer to this question, in light of our definition of "costs," is "all four." Yet each of the four procedures implies a somewhat different notion about the exact meaning of "cost." Because all four notions are closely interrelated, however, it may be a helpful preliminary to much that follows to make a number of observations about these four different but related procedures before we try to answer the question in depth.

- If we do a good job of applying any of the four procedures, the results will be very useful to the decisionmaker.
- The ultimate meaning of "cost" must be found, as we have emphasived repeatedly, in estimating the value of the alternatives (that is, the third procedure). The other procedures are useful only insofar as they contribute to the challenging task of evaluating alternatives.
- There is no way to evaluate alternative uses of resources, however, unless someone can first identify the alternative uses (the second procedure). This point cannot be overstressed.[7]
- But before we can identify the alternative uses of resources, we must estimate the resources required (the first procedure). This is the easiest of the four procedures. The list of required resources, however, will

---

[7] It should also be stressed that the alternative uses depend upon both the ingenuity and the authority of the decisionmaker. In other words, "cost" has no meaning independent of the assumed options and constraints facing the relevant decisionmaker or decisionmaking organization. This important point will be elaborated later.

be very long; it will contain many different items; it will include a large number of optional choices between substitute resources; and, in comparison with the results from applying the other procedures, it will be of only limited usefulness to the decisionmaker. Rarely if ever would such a list satisfy a decisionmaker's expectations from his cost analyst.

● The last procedure, estimating dollar expenditures, is significantly different in nature from the other three. Compared with them, the significance of dollar expenditures will probably appear less obvious to many readers, and more obvious to some. It may even seem like the least ambitious of the four different procedures, and in a limited sense this is true. On the other hand, if we present an estimate of dollar expenditures as an estimate of cost, then we are simultaneously using dollars to accomplish *all three* of the other procedures. It is really *the most ambitious* of the four procedures whenever dollar expenditures are translated to mean cost. Needless to say, of course, great care should always be exercised in deciding whether or not an estimate of dollar expenditures represents a reasonable estimate of cost.

### Dollars as a Measure of Cost

Any important decision or program involves many different costs, and these costs can be investigated at three different analytic levels, as we have just noted. That is, we can estimate the resources required, the alternative uses of these resources, or the value of these alternatives. If we choose the first, and simply list resources, our list will include many disparate items, such as tons of aluminum, manhours of labor, numbers of skilled military personnel, kilograms of plutonium, acres of land, and so on. Usually, we try to do something more than simply list these items. We try to convert most or all of them into some common unit of measure, dollars for instance, so we can add them up.[8]

It may seem odd to think of dollars as a substantive, meaningful, consequential element of cost. It is difficult to compare such transcendent values as the defense of freedoms or the preservation of lives, on the one

---

[8] Whether or not our decisions are actually improved by converting all of the many different elements of cost into a single unit of measure is sometimes problematical. It depends upon whether or not the common denominator we choose is really meaningful, and whether or not most of the consequential costs can be sensibly translated into this single dimension. It is often reported that dollars can buy anything – but it is also true that there is often legitimate dispute over the proper price.

hand, with the trivial inconvenience of printing more dollar bills, or even the more serious inconvenience of collecting more taxes, on the other. Furthermore, it is clear that our defensive capabilities are fabricated out of aluminum, plutonium, and skilled manpower, rather than out of paper money. Are dollars a meaningful measure of cost?

To help us answer this important question we will need to understand dollars better. A dollar, as a unit of measure, is not exactly equivalent to a dollar in your pocket that you can spend, any more than 12 inches is equivalent to your left foot, although of course they are related. It will be very important as we proceed to keep these two meanings of a dollar clearly separate.[9]

Dollars, as a medium of exchange, are often elaborately engraved pieces of paper. More often they are simply entries in the accounting books of our treasury and banking and audit system. These dollars do not, of course, have any intrinsic value. Their only importance derives from their use as accounting devices for allocating purchasing authority among government departments, industrial firms, individual consumers, foreign creditors or beneficiaries, and so on. In our politico-economic system, it is customary to allocate dollars to various government departments rather than to allocate resources directly such as manpower, materials, or transportation facilities. This procedure gives the departments more flexibility, and permits them to choose those resources that can accomplish their mission at least cost, that is, at least sacrifice of other possible benefits. Alternatively stated, the procedure permits the departments to maximize their accomplishments given a certain level of sacrifice of other benefits. (The essential equivalence of "minimizing cost" for a given level of accomplishment and "maximizing accomplishment" for a given level of cost will be emphasized later.)

In order for this ingenious system to work, of course, it is necessary that dollar prices be attached to the various resources available to the department, and that these dollar prices reflect the value of the benefits that could otherwise be produced with the resources. This is the function that our free competitive market system accomplishes for us.[10] Individual con-

---

[9] We have carefully spoken of different *meanings*, rather than different *functions*, of dollars. In economic mythology there is some unique and distinguishable thing, called "money," which simultaneously functions as a "measure of value," a "commonly used medium of exchange," a "good store of value," and so forth. There is really no such thing in today's economy – although much discourse in monetary theory is generated by the implicit denial and then the inevitable discovery of this fact.

[10] For a description and analysis of the free competitive market mechanism the reader should consult any of the standard textbooks in economic principles. An excellent discussion will be found in Paul A. Samuelson, *Economics: An Introductory Analysis*, 7th

sumers, or producers, or other government departments that can derive benefit from the resources "bid" for them with their dollars. The resultant prices are a measure of the value to them of these resources.[11] "Dollars" help us *measure* costs because, and only because, and only to the extent that, they help us *identify* and *evaluate* alternatives.

## The Variety of Costs

The cost analyst's lexicon includes a multitude of terms distinguishing one variety of cost from another. Some of these terms are useful in distinguishing *relevant* from *irrelevant* costs. The distinction, of course, will always depend very precisely upon the specific choice or specific decision under analysis. Illustrative of these terms are: *fixed* costs, *variable* costs, *sunk* costs, *incremental* costs, *recurring* costs, *nonrecurring* costs, *internal* costs, *external* costs, and so on.

The cost analyst also has a very long, actually unlimited, list of adjectives with which he may divide relevant costs, in many different ways, into convenient categories for separate analysis. Examples of such terms would be: *labor* costs, *material* costs, *procurement* costs, *operating* costs, *maintenance* costs, *manpower* costs, *current-year* costs, *next-year* costs, *direct* costs, *indirect* costs, and so on *ad infinitum*. Such convenient categorizations will be used throughout this book.

Finally, the cost analyst uses a number of terms, like *marginal* costs, *average* costs, and *total* costs, which are very useful for various analytic purposes. We will make use of these concepts later. First, we will discuss the important problem of distinguishing relevant from irrelevant costs. To introduce the subject, let us consider the question of the relevance of past costs.

## Past Costs and Future Costs

Do the costs of an aircraft carrier lie in the future or in the past? If we think of costs in terms of the resources used in its production, it will seem that costs lie in the past. If we think of costs in terms of the alternative uses of the aircraft carrier, costs will appear to lie in the future. In which direction does the cost analyst look, backward or forward?

While we are posing this somewhat paradoxical question, we might as

---

ed. (New York: McGraw-Hill Book Company, 1967), Chap. 3 and pp. 609–18. Also, for a very brief statement, refer to our discussion of general competitive equilibrium in the latter portion of Appendix A.

[11] To be very precise, dollar bids indicate a family's, or a corporation's, or a department's, *estimate* of the *relative* value to *it* of acquiring additional units of *alternative* goods or services.

well add another: How *far* backward into history, or how far forward into the future, must the cost analyst look? The propulsion machinery aboard an aircraft carrier is produced with materials and parts that were, in their turn, produced by other machinery, and so on in an infinite regress. How far backward should the cost analyst trace this endless (or rather, beginning-less) sequence? Or if the cost analyst looks into the future to compare alternative uses of the carrier, how far into the future must his clairvoyance take him?

To answer the easy question first: *Relevant costs lie in the future, not in the past.*

If, for example, we are estimating the cost of using an aircraft carrier that has already been constructed, the construction cost is no longer relevant.[12] Similarly, if we are estimating the cost of constructing a carrier that has already been designed and engineered, the engineering and design cost is no longer relevant. And, if we are estimating the cost of designing the carrier, the cost of sending the design engineers through college is no longer relevant.

Costs that have already been incurred are costs resulting from *past* decisions. They are not costs of any conceivable current or future decision. The cost of using a carrier once it has already been commissioned can only be found by evaluating the alternative uses of the carrier and of the man-power and support facilities and consumable supplies that will be necessary to sustain the carrier in operation.[13] It is not the past alternatives that matter, for those alternatives no longer exist.

For these reasons, economists stress the fact that past costs are *sunk* costs. The cost analyst must be careful not to include any sunk costs in his cost estimates or he will only confuse rather than illuminate the decisionmaking problem. Sunk costs no longer represent meaningful alternatives, and, hence, they are no longer real costs. By contrast, economists stress the

---

[12] The construction cost *was* relevant, of course, at a time in the past when the decision to build was still under consideration. Construction cost is no longer relevant, however, except possibly to (a) a historian trying to decide whether or not the decision to build was a mistake; (b) an accountant trying to determine which expenditure accounts should be tapped to pay the bills; or (c) a cost analyst trying to learn, for future reference, how to estimate the cost of constructing other carriers.

[13] For reasons that will be explained in any economics text, the *production cost* of an item, say petroleum, may be commensurate with its *price* in a free competitive market, and this price in turn may be commensurate with the marginal *value* of its alternative uses, that is, with its current real *cost*. Hence, the current real cost of an item may often be equal in value to its past production cost. Nonetheless, it is only the current real costs, the value of alternative uses, that are relevant to current decisions. For such items as an aircraft carrier, the value of alternative uses may be widely different (either higher or lower) than its production costs.

importance of *future* costs or *incremental* costs. What matters in deciding whether or not to complete a half-built carrier is not the past costs already incurred, but the additional or incremental costs necessary for its completion. These costs still represent meaningful alternatives; they are real costs.

Now let us consider the more difficult question that was posed: How *far* into the future must the cost analyst look?

The only really legitimate answer to this question is: As far as he can. However, the fact that the future is unlimited and uncertain does not mean that the cost analyst's task is hopeless. As a matter of fact, whenever you buy or sell a piece of property, you must inevitably estimate the value of its use in the uncertain and unending future. Furthermore, in order to determine whether or not "the price is right," you must also reduce this unending and uncertain stream of value to a single, finite, estimate of *current value*. We will discuss this problem at length later. At the moment we will simply note that a free market economy will automatically provide the cost analyst with such estimates for a great many of the items that he must evaluate – though unfortunately not all.

This leads us to one of the continuous challenges facing a cost analyst: The task of distinguishing those items for which the marketplace generates reliable value, or cost, estimates from those other items for which such estimates are either spurious or altogether lacking. For example, the military departments have no satisfactory mechanism for generating reliable dollar estimates of the value of trained military personnel assigned to various duties. The dollar pay and allowances of a staff sergeant undoubtedly understate his value in alternative assignments, and hence his cost. Even if we added training costs to his pay, the resultant dollar estimate would probably grossly understate his real cost.[14]

Whether or not a meaningful dollar estimate of the future value, or cost, of an item is automatically provided to the cost analyst depends upon whether or not there is a *free, competitive, well-informed market for the item*.[15] The existence of such a market depends, in turn, on many things, such as the commonness and producibility of the item. There is not likely to be a meaningful market price for an aircraft carrier or a staff sergeant.

---

[14] His real cost is probably understated both from the point of view of the military department and from the point of view of the economy, or the society, as a whole. The relevance of the point of view in estimating cost is an extremely important issue, often overlooked, which we will explore later. As we have mentioned before, there is no meaning to the concept of cost independent of some chosen point of view. The reader should also take notice that the absence of reliable estimates of the cost of military personnel means that they are continuously susceptible to misallocation in assignment and in duty.

[15] For a description of the characteristics and the working of a competitive market economy, see Paul A. Samuelson, *op. cit.*, Chap. 3.

On the other hand, if we turn our attention to the steel hull plates and the skilled shipyard workers that could produce a carrier, we may find fairly meaningful market prices. If we turn our attention further backwards in the production sequence to the very common and basic ingredients of the carrier, such as iron ore and coke, or labor that is still untrained, we will be able to find even more meaningful market prices.

For this reason, it is usually easier to develop meaningful dollar cost estimates for programs that are still in the conceptual or developmental stage, since the ingredients of such programs are still in a common form for which market prices are readily available. This is not, by any means, equivalent to saying that it is easier to develop *reliable* dollar cost estimates for programs in their earlier stages of development. On the contrary, the reliability of such estimates will improve as development proceeds. We must also emphasize that it is the existence or nonexistence of a well-functioning market, not the length of time into the future through which we must gaze, that actually determines the availability of meaningful dollar cost estimates.

### Distinguishing Relevant Costs from Irrelevant Costs

All costs are relevant to some decision or other, past or future, for otherwise they would not be costs. The responsibility of the cost analyst, however, is not simply to add up any and all costs indiscriminately, but rather – as we have seen – to identify and measure that particular collection of costs that are contingent upon a specific decision or choice under consideration. He must distinguish the relevant from the irrelevant costs.[16] Any cost that will be incurred no matter what choice we make, any cost that must be borne regardless of the decision at hand, is not a cost of that particular choice or decision.

The distinction between past and future costs is simply one example of the more general problem of distinguishing relevant from irrelevant costs. We will introduce several other examples, along with the pertinent terminology of cost analysis, and then we will present a generalized statement of the problem.

Consider first the distinction between *fixed* costs and *variable* costs. A defense contractor who decides to increase his production rate by 20 per cent will find that some of his costs (those, for example, of production materials or assembly line workers) will increase significantly while other costs (such as top management salaries, rental of real estate, advertising

---

[16] Perhaps the term "irrelevant" is too strong. Even *past* costs or sunk costs are relevant to the question of whether or not there is any money left in the budget, and whether or not the cost analyst should be fired.

and public relations, basic research) will hardly increase at all. The former costs are called *variable* costs, since they tend to vary directly with the production rate, while the latter costs are called *fixed* costs, since their magnitude is relatively independent of changes in the production rate.

If the cost analyst is helping the defense contractor estimate the cost of expanding the production rate by 20 per cent, he should not include even a pro rata share of fixed costs in his estimate, for fixed costs are not affected by the decision at hand. Only the increase in variable costs is relevant to that decision.[17]

Another example is the distinction between *recurring* and *nonrecurring* costs. Each additional year that we decide to keep a certain aircraft squadron in operation we will find various costs recurring. Periodic maintenance inspections, flight pay, aviation gasoline, spare parts, and so on, are all recurring costs. By contrast, the design, development, testing, and procurement of the aircraft, the initial training of the aircraft crews and maintenance personnel, the purchase and installation of auxiliary operations and maintenance equipment, and so on, are essentially *nonrecurring*. If the cost analyst is estimating the costs of extending the operational period of the squadron for a year, he should include only *recurring* costs. It would be misleading to include even some proportionate share of the *nonrecurring* costs in his cost estimate, because the decision to extend or not to extend the operational period will make no difference in these costs.[18]

The concepts of sunk and incremental costs, fixed and variable costs, and recurring and nonrecurring costs illustrate the necessity, and also the occasional difficulty, of distinguishing relevant costs. In essence, we have simply noted that costs are inevitably and precisely related to the *time*, the *scope*, and the *horizon* of the decision under analysis. That is to say, the costs of continuing a certain program (and the dividing line between sunk and incremental costs) depend upon the precise *time* of the decision. The costs of expanding a program (and the dividing line between fixed and variable costs) depend upon the initial and the revised *scope* of the program. The costs of extending a program (and the dividing line between recurring

---

[17] The reader should note that the dividing line between fixed and variable costs is not absolute and invariant. On the contrary, it depends upon the scope of the planned change in production rate. If the contractor considers an expansion of 100 or 200 per cent, many costs that were *fixed* in regard to small rates of expansion will now become *variable*.

[18] As in the case of fixed and variable costs, it is important to note that the dividing line between recurring and nonrecurring costs is not absolutely firm. The cost of flight crew training, for example, might be considered a *nonrecurring* cost if we are considering only a 6-month extension in the phase-out date for a certain aircraft type, but this training might be a *recurring* cost if we were planning a 5-year extension.

and nonrecurring costs) depend upon the initial and the revised termination dates, or *horizon*, of the program.

We need to generalize the basic idea which we have been illustrating. How, in general, can we distinguish relevant costs from the irrelevant? The answer must be found by giving very careful attention to the specific decision or choice being analyzed. We must find the answer by identifying clearly the specific choices available to the decisionmaker and the specific consequences of his choice. *Relevant costs are those costs that depend upon the choice made, given the choices available.* This important point will be developed further, after we have introduced the reader to some of the other varieties of cost.

### External Costs and Internal Costs

Easily confused with the question of *relevance* is the question of *concern*. Some costs may concern us and others may not. The Navy may, or it may not, be concerned about those costs of a military program that happen to be borne by the Army or the Air Force rather than by the Navy. It may choose to ignore, or at least to give less weight to, costs that are external to the Navy Department and to concern itself primarily with costs that are internal to the Department.

Presumably, a cost analyst for the Defense Department would be concerned equally with costs borne by any of the three services and somewhat less interested in those borne by other governmental agencies such as the Atomic Energy Commission, National Space and Aeronautics Administration, or the Post Office Department. The Bureau of the Budget and Congress may be concerned with all costs borne by Federal agencies and perhaps costs borne by state or local government agencies as well, or by private citizens.

"External" costs are those costs of a decision or program that fall beyond the boundaries of the decisionmaker's organization or beyond the scope of interest of the cost analyst's customer. Obviously, whether a given cost is external or internal depends upon how high up in the decisionmaking hierarchy the decisionmaker happens to be or how comprehensive his concern.

It may appear that the cost analyst, unlike the decisionmaker, should accept no limits to his own concerns. To him, we might think, a cost is a cost – no matter who bears the burden. A little reflection will assure us, however, that even the best intentioned or most ambitious cost analyst must draw some boundaries. For example, even if costs to every governmental and nongovernmental agency and every person in the country are considered a matter of concern, it is likely that cost burdens falling on allied nations will be considered less important. Certainly, burdens falling upon hostile nations will not concern us in the same way as burdens falling upon our own population. As a matter of practicality and of choice, therefore, the cost analyst must determine the effective boundaries of his concern – and these boundaries will be less than worldwide and everlasting.[19]

In essence what we are saying is that the cost analyst, like the systems analyst, must inevitably sub-optimize. He has neither the responsibility nor the capability to pursue an indefinable "ultimate good." We are also saying that there is no obvious, unique, commonly acceptable meaning of *the* cost of a government program or policy. The cost analyst must give meaning to *the* cost of a program by deciding what costs are of concern and how they are to be weighed and evaluated.

### Minimizing Costs or Maximizing Benefits

In addition to estimating the costs of proposed programs, the cost analyst has a responsibility to help discover ways to minimize costs or maximize benefits of a program. Indeed, this is often the major purpose of cost analysis. To help with this task the cost analyst will find it convenient to distinguish among *marginal* costs, *average* costs, and *total* costs. Before proceeding it should be emphasized, in the unlikely case that the reader is not well aware of it, that *minimizing costs* and *maximizing benefits* are alternate sides of the same coin. The housewife who has learned how to get a given quality and quantity of groceries for the least money has also learned how to get more groceries of better quality with a given shopping budget. She has learned how to improve the ratio of costs, on the one hand, to quality and quantity, on the other.

Neither the expert housewife nor the cost analyst has much in common with the two prevalent forms of naïvety represented by the miser and the spendthrift. Neither the *cheapest* nor the *most expensive* is always the best. Neither the miser nor the spendthrift has learned how to get the most military effectiveness out of the resources available.

It should be emphasized, of course, that neither the expert housewife

---

[19] We should also stress that the cost analyst must decide what relative weights to assign to costs that fall upon different agencies or individuals. For convenience, if for no other reason, the cost analyst is very likely to give *unequal* weights to the interests of different agencies and people. This is what he does in fact whenever he uses the dollar bids in the marketplace as his measure of costs, since the distribution of purchasing power among people and agencies is not in any obviously meaningful sense "equal." The appropriateness of using the weights that are automatically assigned by the distribution of purchasing power depends in part upon whether or not all costs are going to be reimbursed or compensated.

nor the professional cost analyst ever simply "minimizes costs," or simply "maximizes benefits." The aim is either to "minimize the costs of accomplishing a certain mission or of maintaining a certain program," or to "maximize the benefits achieved with a certain level of resources or at a certain level of cost." When we use the phrase "minimize costs" or "maximize benefits," we are using a commonly understood shorthand for the longer, more meaningful phrases. The two longer phrases are essentially equivalent.[20] If we are *minimizing* the cost of attaining a certain level of output, it inevitably follows that we are *maximizing* the level of output attainable for that given level of cost.

In order to minimize the total costs of our military defenses or to maximize our military capabilities for a given defense budget, we must do a great deal more than simply choose the optimal force mix. We must choose the optimal number of units of each element in the mix, the optimal rate of production of each, the optimal frequency of maintenance inspections for each, the optimal combination of production materials for each, the optimal configuration of each, and so on. A whole host of difficult cost analysis problems still remain even after the basic choice among competing programs has been made.

To help guide the decisionmaker with this host of problems, the cost analyst focuses attention on *marginal* costs, rather than directly on *average* costs or *total* costs, although it is these latter costs that are his ultimate concern.

Marginal costs are those costs incurred as we make *marginal changes* in a program.[21] If we add one more quality inspection during the production process, for example, this will add a marginal increment to the quality inspection costs and, also, it should add some marginal improvement in the reliability rate of the end product. Since there will be hundreds of such alternative ways to increase the effectiveness of a program, we will need to estimate the marginal costs of these competing alternatives so we can allocate our resources to the best of them. We need to know the *marginal ratio* of benefits (increases in effectiveness) to costs for each of these numerous alternatives. Only then can we be sure of getting the greatest effective-

[20] The relationship of the two phrases was discussed in Chapter 2. In addition to maximizing the ratio of benefits to costs for a given scale of effort or a given size of a program, there is the separate problem of choosing the scale or size. If we try to choose the scale by simultaneously specifying *both* the level of benefits and the level of costs, these two specifications may very likely be inconsistent.
[21] Marginal cost can be thought of as the "first derivative" or "the rate of change" of the total cost of a military program as the scale of the program (or the schedule, or the readiness level, or the performance capability, or the reliability, or whatever) is being slightly altered.

ness with the resources available, or of achieving a given level of effectiveness for the least cost.

Effectiveness is maximized, or costs are minimized, only when the marginal ratios of benefits to costs are *equal* for all of the competing alternative ways available for making marginal improvements in a program. For example, if we *reduce* the effective payload of an aircraft by 1 pound in order to save $100 in the materials cost of the fuselage, then we should not simultaneously spend $200 more on the construction costs of the ailerons in order to *increase* payload by 1 pound. The marginal ratio of cost to benefits should be the same for all the various ways of increasing payload or of increasing any other performance characteristic. Similarly, we should not spend $1,000 to hasten the delivery date of a missile by one week and, at the same time, delay delivery by a week in order to save $500.[22]

This is the reason that the cost analyst and the decisionmaker must be continuously concerned with marginal costs. We must be sure that our dollars, or our manpower, or our facilities are used in ways that give us the greatest marginal increase in benefits. Unless we equate cost-effectiveness or cost-benefit ratios at the margin we can be sure that we are not getting the greatest effectiveness from the resources committed to a program.[23] No responsible decisionmaker can afford to be mindless of this simple and fundamental principle.

### Comprehensive Coverage of Costs

There is one way to minimize costs that we should not allow the decisionmaker or the cost analyst. We should not allow either of them to minimize costs by *overlooking* them!

Anyone can provide the decisionmaker with precise and reliable estimates of some of the costs of a program. That service alone, however, is not really as helpful as we sometimes suppose. It is very difficult to make a rational choice between proposed military capabilities A and B, for instance, no matter how detailed and precise and dependable the cost figures, if the figures represent some uncertain fraction of the total cost of each. The decisionmaker needs to compare, as well as he can, their total costs.

---

[22] The examples we have used each include dollars as the measure of cost, but this is not at all necessary. We could be sacrificing aircraft payload to increase aircraft speed, for example, and if so, it is important that the marginal trade-off ratio between payload (cost) and speed (benefit) be equal for all possible trade-off opportunities between the two. Incidentally, the reader should note that whether payload is the *cost* and speed the *benefit*, or vice versa, depends simply on the direction of the exchange.

[23] Again, we may illustrate these points directly from economic theory. An example from the theory of the firm is presented in Appendix C.

Consequently, the real challenge facing the cost analyst is to be comprehensive in his analysis of costs. Often we focus our attention only on those parts of total cost that can be conveniently identified, measured, and evaluated, and then give little attention to the remaining costs.

Earlier, we mentioned some of the many convenient cost categorizations that are used in an effort to be comprehensive in our data collection and cost-estimating efforts. For example, costs of a new military capability are sometimes divided into development costs, investment costs, and operating costs. *Development costs* would include all those costs that must be incurred simply to develop the technological know-how that permits us to produce the new capability. *Investment costs* would include all those costs involved in producing the needed equipment and in setting up the new program, and these costs, of course, would depend upon the size of the program and upon production rates and schedules. *Operating costs* would include all the additional costs involved in using the new capability or in keeping it operationally ready. These costs would depend, of course, upon utilization rate or readiness level. If these three categories are interpreted broadly enough, the three combined should be comprehensive enough to include all the relevant costs. The appropriate set of categories will naturally vary depending upon the particular military capability, or item, or policy, or decision being analyzed, and a number of useful categorizations will be illustrated in later chapters of this book. The important thing is that the categories be comprehensive as well as convenient.

### The Difference Between Dollar Expenditures and Total Cost

To be comprehensive it is essential that our categorizations of costs are not restricted to money expenditures or to budgetary commitments. It may occasionally be the case that our only concern is with dollar expenditures, but in such cases we should use the label "dollar expenditures," not "total costs." As we have stated before, great care should always be exercised in deciding whether or not an estimate of "dollar expenditures" represents a reasonable estimate of "total costs." To emphasize the need, and also the difficulty, of being comprehensive, it is often desirable to distinguish costs according to their measurability, for example,

1. Dollar expenditures,
2. Other costs that can be evaluated in dollars,
3. Other costs that can be quantified,
4. Other, nonquantifiable, costs.

The first category, dollar expenditures, is largely self-explanatory. Some reminders are perhaps appropriate, however. A program or policy may alter the dollar expenditures of many different organizational divisions within, say, the Department of the Army. Moreover, even the dollar expenditures of the other military departments may be altered, and quite possibly the expenditures of still other Federal agencies, local governments, and nongovernmental units. The extent to which all these expenditures are included in a cost estimate will depend upon the cost analyst's skill and upon his client's interests. In his efforts to be comprehensive the cost analyst must, of course, avoid double counting as dollars spent are subsequently re-spent by the initial recipients. Similarly, the cost analyst must take pains to include only those dollar expenditures which are altered by the decision at hand, and exclude all expenditures that will be incurred regardless of the decision.

The second category includes the consumption or utilization of many resources which might not affect dollar expenditures immediately or directly but which can be conveniently evaluated in dollars. Two subcategories should be distinguished. One includes those common expendable items withdrawn from accumulated stores, such as ordnance or petroleum or spare parts, that can often be measured and aggregated in dollar terms more conveniently and more meaningfully than in terms of, say, pounds or cubic feet. The consumption of such items is likely to require, sometime in the future, the expenditure of dollars to replenish stocks, and this provides us with a meaningful dollar evaluation of these resources. It is important to realize that the appropriate dollar measure to use in evaluating these resource costs is the anticipated future dollar expenditures, not the actual past dollar expenditures. All items in this subcategory could be covered in the first category, actual dollar expenditures, if the cost analyst chose a sufficiently long-run time horizon for his analysis. The cost analyst faces many serious difficulties, however, as he attempts to look into the distant future, and consequently, he will undoubtedly select some more manageable short-run time horizon.

The second subcategory differs in nature from the first. If we are ingenious enough, manpower requirements, or office space needs in the Pentagon, or the utilization of air base facilities can all be evaluated, more or less meaningfully, in terms of dollars. The dollar evaluation, however, need not be a simple reflection of dollar expenditures even in the long run. To evaluate such items the cost analyst will need to discover the best, or the most likely, alternative use for these resources and then discover a plausible way of evaluating these alternative uses in terms of dollars. Of course, this task will rarely be easy, and it will often be better simply to measure these resources in some other terms than dollars and to list them separately. They would then fall under the third category listed earlier.

The third category includes all of those quantifiable costs that cannot be reasonably or confidently evaluated in dollars. In addition to some of the items mentioned in the last paragraph, this category may include a number of extremely important costs – for example, lives lost. In the example presented at the very beginning of this chapter, consider the hours that were spent, in addition to the dollars that were spent, at the neighborhood bar.

Finally, the fourth category includes those elements of costs that we are unable to quantify in any helpful way. A program or policy may dissipate some of the limited reservoir of public good will, or staff esprit, or political influence, or international credibility, for example. A program may increase the risks of accidents, or restrict the flow of information, or reduce the effectiveness of training programs, and so on. Of course, if a cost analyst is clever and presistent, he may often find a way to shift items from this fourth category into the third category, or possibly even into the second. If he is simply ambitious, however, rather than ingenious, his efforts to quantify costs, and then to convert them all into dollars, may prove utterly misleading to the decisionmaker. Often, it may be better simply to cite the considerations and leave them unquantified.

The reader has probably noted that the last two categories of costs may very likely include a different sort of costs than those we have previously discussed. We have focused most of our attention on the benefits obtainable from an *alternative use of resources*. It is clear, however, that the *direct consequences* from any particular use of resources can include both beneficial and noxious elements. The latter should probably be included among the costs of a decision, but they are usually considered "negative benefits" rather than costs, in keeping with our tendency to transfer all of the difficult measurement problems over to the "benefit" side of our cost-benefit analyses.[24] The reader should also note that, just as the costs of a decision are benefits lost, so also the benefits of a decision can include costs avoided. The important thing, however, is not how we label costs and

---

[24] An example of this form of cost was also included at the beginning of this chapter when we considered "stopping by the neighborhood bar," that is, the resultant hangover. The difference between these two forms of cost is not always clear, and we do not intend to stress the distinction. The high salary paid a test pilot, for instance, is partly a recompense for his *alternative* employment opportunities and partly a compensation for the hazard that is a *direct consequence* of his employment. The cost of building an airport or a supersonic transport includes damages (which may or may not lead to dollar expenditures) to residents living near landing and take-off patterns. Fundamentally, though, direct consequences are simply a special form of alternatives. The test pilot's premium salary must recompense him for giving up his alternative to live safely as well as his alternatives to earn money elsewhere.

benefits, nor even which side of the equation they are on. The important thing is that all of the significant consequences of our decisions appear somewhere in our cost-benefit analyses and that they are neither forgotten nor double-counted.

## Costs Are Consequences

Before proceeding we need to reconcile the two seemingly different concepts of cost that have just been mentioned: "cost" as the value of forgone alternatives and "cost" as the undesirable direct consequences of a policy or program. In either case, costs are consequences of our decisions. This rather simple observation introduces several important points that deserve some reflection.

First, since costs are consequences, we must note and remember that only decisions or choices have costs. Nuclear submarines don't have costs. The decision to build them, or not to build them, has costs, and the choice of one design rather than another has costs. The distinction may seem like a fine point, and it may not be necessary in common parlance to correct our habits of speech. Nonetheless, the professional cost analyst and the senior decisionmaker must always be aware that they are analyzing decisions, or choices, and that the meaning of cost depends precisely on the specific decision under consideration. We have already stressed this point.

Second, it is important to note that we cannot estimate the consequences, or the costs, of any decision without presupposing some alternative decision, or choice. This statement may appear trite and obvious to some readers and heretical to others. Since it is fundamental to cost analysis, it may warrant elaboration and emphasis.

How can we estimate the consequences of a decision? A moment's reflection will assure us that we can only do so by comparing two alternative states of the world.[25] We must estimate what will happen if we make a certain decision and, also, what will happen if we do not, or if we make some other decision. *The costs and benefits of a decision lie in the differences between two alternative worlds.* Even in retrospect, even after a certain decision has been made and implemented, we cannot fully determine its actual costs or benefits without estimating the different state of the world that would otherwise have ensued. The careful definition and comparison

---

[25] In case a moment's reflection hasn't done the trick, consider the question of whether or not the rising of the morning sun is a consequence of the cock's crowing. The answer depends upon whether or not the sun would rise even if the cock remained silent. Only *differences* that result from *different* decisions can be properly counted as consequences, or as costs or benefits.

of alternatives (alternative decisions and alternative worlds) is the essential nature of the challenge facing a cost analyst.

There is really nothing heretical in these statements. The only purpose of cost analysis is to help guide decisions, and the only purpose of making a decision is to choose among different worlds. After all, a decisionmaker is a man who changes the world. If a decision doesn't change the world we dismiss it as inconsequential by saying, "It doesn't make any *difference*!" Differences between worlds are the essence of decisions and choices, and of costs and benefits.

## Costs Depend Upon the Choice and the Chooser

Since the costs of a decision can only be found by a comparison of alternatives, what alternatives should we compare?

Suppose we are asked to estimate the cost of using several square miles of land on the outskirts of Washington, D.C., for a military air base. The cost depends upon the alternative uses of the land, but what alternatives are relevant? It could be used as a military transportation depot, or as a commercial air base, or as a public park, or as a new shopping center, or for private housing, or it could simply be bought and sold in a free competitive market with no zoning restrictions at all. Should the cost analyst attempt to guess what the *actual* alternative use will be? Or should he estimate the *best* alternative use? Or should he assume a *commercial* use, since this would give him a convenient dollar valuation of the alternative?

The answer to this question depends upon the interests and the authority of the decisionmaker and his cost analyst. A very simple example will illustrate this dependence and emphasize its importance.

Colonel Smith is trying to decide whether or not to use a company of airmen, temporarily assigned to his command, to police the grounds around the barracks. What will it cost him to use these men for this purpose? A novice at cost analysis might suggest that it costs nothing, but Colonel Smith knows better. He could also use these men to repair the auxiliary runway, which may save the Air Force considerable money, or he could assign them to training exercises. He knows the cost of policing the grounds is to be found in *his* alternatives. But note that his alternatives for employing these airmen are very circumscribed. The commanding General of the air base has a much broader range of alternatives, the Secretary of Defense has a still broader set of choices, and Congress has an even broader set.

The cost of using these airmen depends upon the decisionmaker – or upon the decisionmaking level that the cost analyst has in mind. The higher up the decisionmaker is on the ladder of authority, the higher the costs are certain to be, because there are more and more competing alternative uses for these men.

Similarly, if we focus our attention on the cost of accomplishing a specific mission (like repairing a runway) rather than on the cost of using a certain resource (like the airmen), we will find that this cost also depends upon the decisionmaker. In this case, as we go higher up on the decisionmaking ladder we can consider more alternative ways of doing the job, and hence the *lower* the cost is likely to be.

It is clear that costs depend upon the decisionmaking level under consideration. If we are analyzing alternative means to a given end, the higher the decisionmaking level the lower the cost – because we have a larger choice of means. If we are analyzing alternative ends for a given means, the higher the decisionmaking level the higher the cost – because we have a larger choice of ends. But what decisionmaking level should the cost analyst consider?

To answer the preceding question the cost analyst must remember, or decide, who his client is. If he focuses his attention at too low a decisionmaking level, if he overlooks some of the relevant alternative uses of resources or some of the relevant alternative means of accomplishing a mission, his estimates of costs will be incorrect. On the other hand, if he focuses attention at too high a level, his cost estimates will be irrelevant.

It might seem that a cost analyst should focus on the highest conceivable decisionmaking level, and that this focus will permit a "true" estimate of cost. This may be a laudable ambition and a useful theoretic exercise, but we are likely to find it exceedingly difficult to define the "highest decisionmaking level," and even more difficult to make cost estimates that are relevant for that undefinable decisionmaker. Even a cost analysis undertaken for a congressional committee should take for granted *most* of the numerous constraints on decisionmaking and the numerous boundaries on alternatives that are incorporated into Federal and local laws and into the contemporary framework of the economy and the social order. In estimating costs we always choose some restricted level of decisionmaking. The extent of authority and influence assumed for the decisionmaker, however, can vary over a wide and deep range, and the meaning of cost will vary accordingly.

As we mentioned earlier, cost depends not only upon the decisionmaking level but also upon the imagination and ingenuity of the decisionmaker. Every time Colonel Smith, for instance, discovers a new and better alternative use for his airmen, the cost of using them to repair a runway increases. Similarly, of course, every time he thinks of some more ingenious new way to repair the runway, the cost of repairing it decreases. But what level of imagination should the cost analyst assume?

Again, it might seem that the cost analyst should assume, for purposes of estimating costs, that the decisionmaker has no limit of ingenuity. This procedure may also be laudable, but it is no more practicable than the procedure of assuming unlimited authority. There is always certain to be a better use of resources than the use which we select – if only we were ingenious enough to find it. *If we define cost as the best possible alternative use of resources, the cost of any practicable program will exceed its benefits.* The cost analyst will have to content himself with those very limited alternative uses that the decisionmaker, or the cost analyst, can readily discover. Helping the decisionmakers discover and evaluate alternatives is the function of cost analysis. It is also the function, incidentally, of our competitive free-market economy.

We have been stressing that costs depend upon the choices available and that, consequently, they also depend upon the authority and the ingenuity of the decisionmaker. We are not suggesting that costs are undefinable, however, or that we have no way of estimating them. On the contrary, we are simply stressing that any meaningful estimate of costs must inevitably be related to alternatives. Costs depend upon alternatives. Costs *are* alternatives.

### Comparing Alternatives

We are now in a position to put much of what has been said in simple perspective, after which we will discuss further the two particular aspects of cost analysis which most often puzzle the layman: the relation of dollar costs to other costs and the value of time.

The problems presented to the cost analyst and the systems analyst can appear in varied forms. For example, should we implement a certain proposed program or not? Should we choose program A or program B? Is there a better way to implement the proposed program? These are questions that could be stated in cost terms if we wished: Will the benefits of a certain proposed program exceed its costs? Will program A accomplish more for a given cost, or cost less for a given capability, than program B? Is there a less costly way to implement the proposed program? All of these questions are reducible to the basic problem of comparing alternatives.

There are three component elements of an alternative to any program: the common component; the specified differences; the remaining, unspecified differences. The cost analyst must carefully delineate these three components. They are illustrated in the following example.

Consider the question of whether to strengthen our defenses by adding another wing of strategic bombers or by increasing the alert status of bomber wings already operational. It may be that neither manpower nor currently authorized expenditures permits the Defense Department to do both, so the two possibilities are being analyzed and reviewed as alternatives. Before we could begin to estimate the resource requirements of the additional wing or of the increased alert status we would need to know the currently planned program: the number of wings currently operational, for example, and the support facilities currently in existence, the current readiness levels, the trained flight and maintenance crews presently available, and so on. That is to say, we would need to identify the factors that are *common* to both alternatives. In other words, we would need to identify those factors concerning which the decision at hand makes no difference. These factors will be considered as "given" or as "cost-free."

We then need to identify *specified differences* among the alternatives. In our example, one alternative includes an additional wing of bombers, while the other alternative has a higher alert status. There are likely to be other differences, however, such as a difference in manpower requirements or dollar expenditures. These are the *unspecified differences*, and the identification, measurement, and if possible, evaluation of these differences is the challenge facing the systems analyst and the cost analyst.

If the specification of differences between alternatives were truly complete, of course, there would be no remaining unspecified differences for the analysts to be concerned with. At the other extreme, the alternatives to a program may not be specified at all, so the entire burden of identifying alternatives and their consequent differences rests with the analysts. In any case, the analysts must fulfill these two responsibilities:

1. The decision or choice to be analyzed must be clarified either by delineating the range of alternatives to be compared or, equivalently and more easily, by delineating the common component of all acceptable alternatives – that is, by specifying the "givens."

2. A comprehensive accounting of all the important differences, specified and unspecified, that will result from making one decision or choice rather than another, must be developed and presented to the decisionmaker. These differences should not only be identified, but wherever feasible measured and if possible evaluated.

*No cost analysis problem has been meaningfully stated until the first task has been done with reasonable clarity. No cost analysis is truly completed until the second task has been done with reasonable comprehensiveness.*

**The Relation of Dollar Costs to Other Costs**

It is often said that money isn't the only thing in life – but that it is well ahead of whatever comes second. The reader could probably think of several close competitors, but actually the statement is deceiving. Money is not first, or second, or third in a list of the important things in life. Money is a means for attaining some of the important things. To the extent that it actually can procure them, money can be a proxy for them, and dollar costs can then be used as a meaningful measure of real costs. But, as we have already stressed, dollar costs may be neither a complete nor an accurate measure of costs. We hasten to add, however, that simply because dollars aren't everything, it does not follow that we, as individuals or as decisionmakers, can afford to dispense them casually or to ignore dollar costs. Responsibility requires an awareness of both their importance and their limitations.

Recall the example of Colonel Smith and his problem of choosing the best assignment for his airmen. We saw that the dollars paid to the airmen are not a complete or accurate measure of their real costs. It is worth noting, incidentally, that their pay would be an inaccurate measure of costs no matter whether we were concerned with "costs" in the very narrow sense of *dollar expenditures* or in the deeper economic sense of *meaningful alternatives*. Since the airmen must be paid regardless of how, or whether, they are productively employed, the additional dollar expenditure entailed by using them is zero. And the value of the meaningful alternatives their present activity may preclude could be far greater than that suggested by their pay. The dollars paid to these men are a very inaccurate measure of their actual cost.

Granted the limitations, what meaning do dollars have? What significance arises from knowing that two different items, for example, a truck and a radio transmitter, have the same dollar cost? It can mean several different, but closely related things, as we suggested earlier. It can mean that the two items are considered of equal marginal value in the marketplace, provided, of course, that the two items are actually traded in the market. Or it can mean that the two items could be produced with the same resources or, more likely, that the resources required to produce one of them could be exchanged in the marketplace for just enough of the right resources to produce the other. In any of these cases, it means essentially that society considers the sacrifices involved (the alternatives forgone) to be of equal measure. This is the essential meaning, but the practical meaning to the decisionmaker is much simpler and more direct. It means that whenever he allocates some of his budget to procure one of the items he is sacrificing an option to procure the other.

In sum, the immediate significance of dollar costs – to you, to me, to a decisionmaker, to any government department with a given mission and a fixed budget – is that dollar costs help to indicate our choices among alternative *means*. The broader significance of dollars is that they help to indicate the relative value of alternative *ends*, as determined by society as a whole operating through the marketplace and by the government through the budget allocation process. In either case, dollars are only a help, though a very great help.

We stress that dollars are only a help no matter whether we are trying to discover alternative means or trying to evaluate alternative ends. With respect to choosing means, we have already mentioned that a full accounting of costs must cover not only dollar expenditures but other costs measurable in dollars, other quantifiable costs, and nonquantifiable costs as well. We should also mention that there are other ways to compare means, other measures of costs, than dollars. Many special analyses can be simpler and more meaningful when costs are measured in terms of, say: flying hours, days, available payload, men, manhours, lives lost, floor space, missiles ready, pounds of fuel, cubic feet, and so on.

With respect to evaluating alternative ends, dollar measures are often simply not available, as we have mentioned, and even when they are available their validity is not always beyond reasonable dispute. Dollars are not really any smarter than engineers and production managers and inventors and reporters and city planners and systems analysts. Dollars reveal alternative uses of a resource only to the extent that large numbers of people and government departments are bidding for the resource in a free market and they are aware of the availability and possible uses of the resource. For many important resources, this is simply not the case.[26] Moreover, there are other ways to discover and evaluate alternatives than through the use of dollars and the marketplace. Public opinion surveys are one way. Political processes are another. These varied procedures differ, not only in the methods of analysis they suppose, but also in the relative weights they attach to the competing interests and judgments of different individuals. Such procedures have obvious limitations, but each has a claim to validity. Of course, economists, sociologists, psychologists, political scientists, businessmen, politicians, and, these, have differing preferences among them.

One final comment on dollar costs must be made. Dollars are not all

---

[26] Even where dollar prices of resources are available, they represent values only at the margin, and they may consequently be inapplicable for the analysis of *very large* government programs.

alike. It matters a good deal whether the dollars spent for a given program come from your pocket or someone else's. It also matters whether the dollars saved by a government department are available to that department or whether they will revert back to the Treasury. Where dollars will come from and where they will go is a reasonable and inevitable concern of the decisionmaker. It is also very true that a dollar spent overseas is not equivalent to a dollar spent at home and that a dollar in this year's budget is not at all equivalent to a dollar in next year's. This last important difference will be discussed further in the next section.

### Time Is Money: The Concept of Discounting

Time is valuable. Indeed, few things are more valuable, whether we are thinking about our personal lives, or a military compaign, or business investments, or farming, or the development of new military capabilities, or national economic and social programs. And yet the value of time is often forgotten, particularly whenever someone compares dollar expenditures this year with those of next year and the year after, as if all of the dollars were equal.

They are not. No military officer would suggest that a reserve infantry battalion arriving at the front line next week is equivalent to a battalion arriving today. No shipbuilding contractor would admit that construction materials arriving next month are equivalent to those arriving this week. Resources on hand today are usually worth more than identical resources deliverable tomorrow. Consequently, dollars with which we can buy resources today are worth more than dollars available tomorrow. Thus, before we can meaningfully add together dollars spent or received in different periods, we must "discount" future dollars, for they are worth less than current dollars.

The procedure for discounting is simple, although the choice of a discount rate is often difficult. If a local savings bank will give us 1 dollar next year for every 90 cents we deposit this year, or if the bank will give us 90 cents today in return for a promise to pay 1 dollar next year, then we might reasonably adjudge a dollar next year to be worth only 90 cents on hand today. We might "discount" future dollars at a rate of 10 percent per annum. What we mean is this: A dollar available next year will be judged as worth only 90 percent as much as a dollar available today. Similarly, a dollar available 2 years from today will be judged as worth only 90 percent as much as a dollar available next year (or 90 percent × 90 percent of a dollar on hand today) and so on. By discounting the value of future dollars in this way we can reduce all dollars into their "present value" equivalent, and then we can compare these dollars sensibly.[27]

We have stated that future dollars are worth less than currently available dollars, but how much less? To argue that time has value is easy; to measure the value of time, however, is anything but easy. How much is it worth to the Marine Corps to have another million dollars in this year's budget rather than next year's? How much is it worth to the DOD to be able to postpone a certain expenditure for a year? What "discount rate" should be applied to future dollars so that they can be sensibly compared with current dollars?

**Other Problems Related to Time**

Before attempting to answer this question, we must take pains to identify and distinguish several closely related problems that often become intermingled and confused with the problem of estimating the value of time. First, we are not concerned here with the problem of inflation or the diminishing purchasing power of the dollar. This is a different problem and is handled by "deflating" dollars, that is by dividing dollars by some appropriate index of prices. The procedure itself is very simple, although finding an appropriate index can often be a problem.[28]

Second, we are not concerned here with the problem of shifting burdens onto future generations. We often choose to avoid making sacrifices today and, as a consequence, impose additional costs on the general public in future years. As we exploit our natural resources, for instance, we tend to diminish the resources available in the future. If we fail to solve the problems of urban ghettos in this generation, we leave these costs to the next. This problem of balancing our current interests with the interests of future generations is very real, but it is not the problem of the "value of time" that we are discussing here. Although the two are inextricably intertwined, conceptually they are distinguishable. The problem of allocating the burden of a government program (that is, deciding who will pay the cost) is distinguishable from the problem of estimating the cost.

---

[27] For the reader who is unfamiliar with the basic mechanics of "discounting" and the use of discount rates, a specific illustration is included in Chapter 8.
[28] Actually, the cost analyst can usually escape this problem altogether. If he is estimating future costs of a program he is probably assuming, for purposes of his cost estimates, that prices will remain at current levels. In other words, he does not have to take price changes *out* of his estimates because he has not put any such changes *into* his estimates. His unadjusted cost estimates represent an estimate in "constant dollars" – that is, in dollars that are all equivalent in purchasing power. Only if he wants to estimate actual dollar expenditures, for financial planning purposes, will he need to become concerned about general price changes. If he wants to compare *real costs* of alternative programs, general price level changes due to monetary phenomena may be ignored.

The reader should be warned, however, that it is much easier to distinguish these two problems in theory than in practice. Any decisionmaker is concerned with *both* problems. Any voter wants to know whether the real burden of a program is going to fall on him or on someone else. When a cost analyst says that two programs are equal in "cost," he is usually asserting only that they require equivalent resources – resources that either are identical or can be exchanged equally in the marketplace. The decisionmaker and the voter, however, are inevitably concerned not only with this estimate of total cost, but also with the question of who will pay the cost. Similarly, they are concerned not only with total benefits, but with the question of who will receive the benefits.[29]

Third, in discussing "discounting" here we are not concerned with uncertainty, although this, too, is a very real and important problem, as we have stressed elsewhere. Our estimates of both the costs and the benefits of a proposed program become increasingly uncertain as we attempt to look further and further into the future. The decisionmaker cannot afford to overlook this. His decisions must take into account the fact that cost and benefit estimates 5 or 10 or 20 years into the future have much less reliability than estimates for the next year or two. In a very different sense of the word, he must "discount" distant future estimates as being less reliable than near future estimates. But this is not the same thing as discounting future dollars because of the value of time. Furthermore, we must remain painfully aware of the fact that future costs can be underestimated as well as overestimated. As often as not, such cost estimates should be increased rather than reduced.[30]

## Choosing a Discount Rate

Returning now to the difficult problem of choosing a reasonable rate for

---

[29] If a decisionmaker wants to expand the concept of "cost" beyond that which we have presented, if he wants to incorporate into his concept of "cost" the problems associated with allocating the real burdens of a government program, then (1) there will be no way of identifying the cost of a program short of estimating its impact on the *total* fiscal program of the government (that is, the cost will inevitably depend upon a precise specification of two or more *complete* alternative fiscal programs) and (2) there will be no very meaningful way of adding up the real burdens of a program into a single number (that is, the real burdens imposed upon a number of different individuals will have as many different dimensions as there are people).

[30] The absence of reliable estimates of costs or benefits increases the *value of flexibility* rather than the *value of time*, although the two often appear identical. One way to preserve flexibility, for example, is to postpone decisions or expenditures as long as possible. Consequently, we often modify a program to postpone expenditures, even though the resultant costs might be slightly higher, since this gives us the flexibility of canceling the program should our cost or benefit estimates prove to be in error. On the other hand, prudence often requires us to speed up a program because of uncertainties.

discounting future dollars, we should first take note of a common and very inappropriate method of discounting. Too often we attempt to compare alternatives simply by adding up undiscounted dollar expenditures for a 5- or 10-year period, and then neglect all subsequent expenditures. In doing this we are choosing two discount rates, neither of them defensible. We are choosing a discount rate of zero for the next 5 or 10 years, and a very high (actually infinite) rate for every subsequent year. Finding a completely satisfactory method of discounting might be very difficult, but improving on this very common procedure would be easy.

The proper choice of a discount rate depends, just as cost depends, upon *alternatives*. Alternatives, in turn, depend upon the decisionmaker's authority and interests. These basic facts should sound very familiar to the reader by now. It remains only to apply them to the problem of choosing a discount rate.

Suppose the Army receives a bid for the production of rifles, and that the bid happens to offer the Army the choice of either reimbursing the manufacturer on the final delivery date in the amount of $1,000,000 or providing the manufacturer with progress payments in amounts totaling $900,000. Which choice should the Army make? *A rational choice cannot be made until it is known what other, similar options are available throughout the total procurement and operation program.* A multitude of opportunities can be found in the total Army program for trading off higher expenditures at a later date for lower expenditures today. It can postpone replacement of old equipment, for example, but incur the penalty of higher operating costs over the next few years. It can postpone needed repairs or maintenance servicing, but suffer higher repair costs next year. It can replenish stocks of consumable supplies in small amounts only as needed, but forgo the cost savings that might be obtained by ordering in large, bulk quantities. It can adopt construction methods or building designs that reduce current outlays but lead to earlier obsolescence or added maintenance expenditures. In a multitude of such ways, the Army is continuously comparing the value of a dollar this year with the value of a dollar next year. The Army is continuously trading off this year's dollars for next year's, and vice versa.

Now, to answer the question about whether to pay $1,000,000 upon final delivery of the rifles or $900,000 in progress payments. If the Army has other opportunities to use $900,000 in ways that will save much more than $1,000,000 a year from now, then the best choice is to postpone payment for the rifles. The availability of these other alternatives means that $900,000 today has a value to the Army, and a cost to the Army, that exceeds $1,000,000 next year. *The appropriate discount rate for use in comparing future dollars with today's dollars depends upon the alternative opportunities available for exchanging one for the other.*

Since the Army has a host of alternative exchange opportunities, each yielding a different exchange rate, which of these rates is the relevant one to use for discounting? The relevant exchange opportunity is the best discoverable unexploited opportunity available to the decisionmaker. In other words, as with the problem of measuring cost generally, the best actual alternative is the relevant measure – indeed, it is the meaning – of cost.

Several comments are in order at this point. First, there is no reason to presume that we should use a constant interest rate as we look forward from year to year. A dollar in 1970 may be worth as much to the Army as $1.10 in 1971, but a dollar in 1971 could be worth as much as $1.50 in 1972. The relevant exchange rates will depend upon many things: the budgetary generosity of Congress in various years, the specific operational missions of the Army in these years, new technological developments, the changing international scene, and so on.

Second, although we can estimate appropriate discount rates to apply today (for both short and long time periods) by looking at currently available exchange opportunities, we can only make informed guesses about the appropriate discount rates to be used next year. That will depend on various unpredictable things, notably the size of next year's budget, the state of the world next year, and revised expectations about the future.

Third, if the Army – to return to our example – is not permitted by Congress to shift money freely from one budget category to another, it may be that the relevant discount rate will vary from one category to another. Because of limitations in procurement funds, the Army may be unable to exploit opportunities to save 2 dollars next year for each procurement dollar spent this year, while in some other budget category it may be able to spend a dollar to save only a dollar and a half next year.

Fourth, if the Army is not doing a good job of comparing alternative exchange opportunities, it may be that several different and inconsistent exchange rates can be determined within a given budget category. The Army might be neglecting some opportunities to exchange 80 cents today for a dollar next year while, simultaneously, it may be exploiting opportunities to spend 95 cents this year to save a dollar next year. What exchange rate should a cost analyst use then? There is no obvious answer to this question, but the analyst can at least identify an obvious need for the Army to review its program. As a matter of fact, unless the Army knows what its actual discount rates are in various categories, it is extremely likely that inconsistent rates will be found in its total program and that, consequently, it will not be getting maximum effectiveness for each dollar spent. That is precisely why discount rates, and cost analysis generally, deserve more attention than they are receiving.

### Equalizing Discount Rates

We have just noted that we might find unequal, or inconsistent, discount rates effective within the total Army program and that this inevitably implies inefficiency. Similarly, it is very likely that effective discount rates, or marginal exchange opportunities between current dollars and future dollars, are different for the Army than for the Navy, or the Air Force, or the Department of Transportation, or General Motors. These differences not only pose a problem for the cost analyst, but they also suggest a need for review of budget allocations and of expenditure patterns.

The decisionmaker who does not equalize marginal exchange opportunities within his realm of authority can fairly be said to be guilty of mismanagement. He should not be postponing expenditures at an ultimate cost penalty of 20 percent per year while simultaneously spending money to avoid a cost penalty of only 10 percent per year. This means that the head of every government unit should have some notion of his marginal exchange opportunities between current and future dollars, and he should be sure that all of his "spending" and "postponing" decisions are consistent with that marginal rate.

It is important to realize, however, that executives on subordinate levels cannot properly be blamed for inconsistencies between their own discount rate and the discount rate of other organizations on the same level. The Strategic Air Command cannot be expected to shift some of its budget to the Air Training Command simply because the Air Training Command has marginal opportunities to "invest" money at a greater rate of return. The Strategic Air Command is vitally interested in maximizing total military preparedness, of course, but it is much more aware of its own needs, and its own contributions to defense, than those of other military Commands. The only decisionmakers that can properly be blamed for inconsistent discount rates between two government units are those with authority and responsibility to allocate budgets between the two.

The task of determining the effective exchange ratio between current and future dollars, or the appropriate discount rate, is one of the challenges of any cost analysis. Sometimes, however, the task can be made relatively easy. For example, suppose that, because of very efficient budget allocations at the top level in the DOD, there is widespread consistency in the effective discount rates throughout the military services. Then a cost analyst for any decisionmaker within these services can properly use the same discount rate. In fact, the Office of the Secretary of Defense might specify a common discount rate and direct its use as a way of establishing this consistency. But now suppose that this discount rate is different from, say, the rates used by the Department of Transportation or General Motors. Is it possible to specify some single, universally appropriate, discount rate that should be used for all government decisionmakers, and perhaps all private decisionmakers as well?[31]

As we have suggested earlier, ambitions on the part of the cost analyst to represent the ultimate level of authority and wisdom are seldom realistic. He must choose some manageable level of "sub-optimization" and estimate the appropriate discount rate accordingly. Several obstacles prevent him from discovering and representing the "ultimate" level of optimization: the diffusion of authority within our society, the lack of common agreement among these decisionmakers about the appropriate balance between current and future needs, the absence of a perfectly functioning market mechanism at work that might allow these different governmental and private decisionmakers to make mutually convenient loans to each other and hence bring their varied choices and opportunities into balance.

As a result, there are different effective exchange rates between present and future dollars, rather than a single pervasive rate. No Congressman, no decisionmaker, no cost analyst is compelled by any economic logic to believe that any specific one of the multitude of current interest rates, explicit and implicit, within the public or the private sectors of our economy represents either the best interests or the revealed preferences of our society. [32]

This is not to deny, however, that it would be well to have a single,

---

[31] For a good discussion of the consistency problem, see the statement by Elmer B. Staats, Comptroller General of the United States, before the Subcommittee on Economy in the Government. *Congressional Record – Senate*, January 30, 1968, pp. S-632 to S-634.

[32] Since this statement may seem contrary to common assumption, perhaps we need to stress the point. For many government operations we do not even know what the effective discount rates *are*, let alone what they should be. We are often unable to predict or measure in a satisfactory way the actual consequences of many government programs and, worse, in many cases we cannot even distinguish "investment" from "consumption" or "costs" from "benefits." It follows that we do not know the actual marginal rates of return on government investments. Furthermore, the proper overall balances between investment and consumption, and between public and private expenditures, and between short-run and long-run interests, and between the desires of this generation and future generations are, and will remain, controversial political issues. All of these unsettled issues, plus questions of monetary policy generally, affect the exchange ratios between current and future dollars. The cost analyst must determine the relevant discount rate for his decisionmaker, rather than presume to know the ultimately proper rate.

consistent discount rate effective in our economy. We are only pointing out that such a discount rate is a laudable ambition, not an accomplished fact. If we want to bring more consistency, and hence more allocative efficiency, into the realm of government expenditure, we will first need to begin estimating the actual exchange rates between current and future dollars in the various government departments and programs. We will also need to distinguish the *investment* budgets from the *operating* budgets for these various departments and programs.[33] Neither task will be easy, and the cost analyst cannot afford to wait until these ambitions are achieved. In other words, the cost analyst is certain to be frustrated if he seeks a unique, universally applicable, and indisputably proper discount rate. The task of the cost analyst is to reveal relevant alternatives to the decision-maker. For this purpose, he needs to know who the decisionmaker is, and what options and authorities he possesses. His task is to discover the exchange opportunities within the decisionmaker's realm of influence. As always, costs are to be found in these alternatives. Costs *are* alternatives.

Two techniques often used in handling the problem of time in cost analysis are the computation of "balancing discount rates" and the estimation of "residual value." Suppose that the cost analyst is called upon to compare the costs of two clearly defined alternative methods of accomplishing identical ends. If he is unsure of the relevant discount rate to use in making the comparison, he may simply calculate the constant discount rate that would equate the present value of the costs of the two alternatives. This is sometimes referred to as "break-even" analysis. The decisionmaker can then decide whether he feels that the appropriate discount rate is higher or lower than the "balancing discount rate," and accordingly decide which of the two has the lower real cost.

A very different problem is dealt with by the "residual value" technique. Frequently the cost analyst attempts to estimate the "residual value" of all the resources of a program at the end of, say, a 5- or 10-year period. He does this because it is usually impractical to attempt to trace out the costs or benefits of a program year-by-year until the end of its existence or even for any extended period into the future. Instead, he attempts to make reasonably precise monthly or annual cost estimates for a limited number of years and then to summarize the status of the program at the end of this period. In comparing alternative programs, we want to make note of the

---

[33] The Department of Defense's Planning-Programming-Budgeting System (PPBS) attempts to make such a distinction. Since 1965, attempts have also been made in other parts of the Federal Government, although progress has been extremely slow and the quality of the results has varied widely.

possibility that the resources of one may have greater "residual value" at the end of our arbitrary planning and analysis period than the other.

We need to make only a few brief comments about this procedure. First, as a practical matter, adoption of some such procedure is inescapable. Second, because of the value of time and the discount rate, the costs and benefits of a program 15 or 20 years hence are, dollar for dollar, much less important than those of the next 5 or 10 years. Additionally, because of the flexibility available to us with the passage of time, the actual consequences of current program decisions tend to diminish with the passage of time. Third, we should note that an estimation of "residual value" is not really a way of escaping the task of looking into the long-run future, because there is no way of estimating this value at the end of 10 years except by looking further into the future. Fourth, we should note that "residual value" is not necessarily equivalent to "scrap value." It may be that an aircraft carrier is worth nothing more at the end of 10 years than its value to a scrap-iron dealer, but hopefully it will be worth far more. Scrap value is, at best, a minimum limit of residual value. Fifth, "residual value" is not necessarily equivalent to "replacement costs." The carrier could be worth less. At best, if we assume reasonable planning foresight, replacement costs would represent a maximum limit of residual value. It may be that the best a cost analyst can do with respect to "residual value" is to estimate a minimum and a maximum value. Sixth and last, we should take advantage of this one last opportunity to note the close relationship of cost analysis and benefit analysis. The estimated residual value of an item at the end of a given planning period is often treated as a credit against its *cost* (although, as we will indicate in Chapter 8, this is usually not a preferred treatment), and the estimated residual value of the item in its most likely use at the end of the period will be the cost of assigning it to any other possible use at that time.

### "Macro-Cost Analysis" and "Micro-Cost Analysis"

Before concluding this chapter, it may be helpful to the reader to note some of the differences in the nature of the problems confronting the cost analyst depending upon whether he is analyzing exceptionally broad program choices or relatively small choices. Much current cost analysis lies in an intermediate range between what might be called "macro-cost analysis" and "micro-cost analysis." We will indicate the nature of the distinction between the two, contrasting each of them with more typical cost analysis efforts and suggesting the different analytic problems and procedures associated with them. Actually, the distinctions are matters of degree rather than differences in kind.

Macro-cost analysis concerns alternative *total programs* at, say, the Department level or at the level of the Federal Government. The cost analysis problems involved are likely to be different from those in the more typical "systems" cost analyses in several ways. Macro-cost analyses will also differ from *budget* analyses for various important reasons that have already been discussed.

The first, most obvious way in which macro-cost analysis differs from the typical cost analysis is that reliance upon marginal cost estimates becomes less and less permissible as we deal with larger and larger programs. *Market* prices are *marginal* prices. These prices indicate the value of the alternatives available, assuming relatively small shifts in the allocation of resources. Large government programs, however, may require such large amounts of various specific resources that their current market price, or marginal price, is a poor estimator to use in assessing total program costs. In order to develop better cost estimates, the macro-cost analyst will need to concern himself not simply with current market prices but with supply and demand schedules as well. These schedules, of course, are not readily available. Determining the acceptability of marginal prices as cost estimators, and adjusting them if they are not acceptable, is one of the challenges facing macro-cost analysis.

A second way in which macro-cost analysis differs from the typical cost analysis is in the nature of the relevant alternatives, and hence in the source of meaningful cost estimates. Most of the prices we use in cost analysis are indicators of the value of resources to some employer other than the one for whom we are estimating costs. That is to say, we are usually estimating the price that a particular employer must pay in order to outbid other possible employers, and we use this price as our cost estimate. We usually look for, and measure, alternatives outside of the province of the particular agency for whom we are estimating costs. This procedure is reasonable if our employer is only one of many comparable employers, such as a single manufacturing company or a single weapons system manager in the Defense Department, or a single transportation company, or a single hospital. When the size of a program is very large, however, the relevant alternative uses of resources are very likely to be found inside, not outside, the province of the agencies involved with the program.

As an illustration of this problem, consider estimating the cost of a DOD program that would preempt the majority of our naval architects or our aeronautical engineers over the next 5 or 10 years. We will not get a valid estimate of the cost of this program simply by estimating the salaries that these people could earn in other active programs. The relevant costs are likely to be hidden. That is, they will probably lie in alternative programs that are inactive or nonexistent – alternative DOD programs cancelled or never initiated because the needed funds or personnel were otherwise committed. As the cost analyst moves further in the direction of macro-cost analysis, he will increasingly face the difficult challenge posed by the fact that relevant costs will lie not in "active" alternatives clearly signalled by market bids for resources, but in "dormant" alternatives being neglected.

To present this second characteristic of macro-cost analysis another way, we could simply note that, while typical cost analyses are often concerned with finding the least-cost way to accomplish a given mission, macro-cost analysis must often be concerned with identifying the alternative missions that can be accomplished with given resources. In an ultimate sense, of course, these two tasks are not really as different as they may appear to be. The difference is that in typical analyses, we usually presume that the marketplace has already identified and evaluated the best alternative uses or missions. In macro-cost analyses, this assumption will often be unrealistic.

For these reasons, macro-cost analysis represents a real challenge to the analyst. He will need to discern and outline alternatives to total programs, or at least alternative uses for their critical resources, for this will often be the only way to discover and present a meaningful picture of costs.

Micro-cost analysis is concerned not with estimating the total cost of some system or program or policy, but with discerning cost interrelations between specific elements of systems, programs, or policies. For example, the amount of weight or space allocated to a sub-component of an aerospace system affects the amounts of weight and space available for all other subsystems. Cost analysis in terms of weight or space, in such instances, could be essential for understanding the real cost implications of many specific decisions.

A great deal more "costing" or "pricing" needs to be done at the "micro" level if the multitude of small, day-to-day decisions being made are to be rationally guided by cost considerations. The challenge to the micro-cost analyst is to determine trade-off ratios between two or more different cost dimensions. Although this is occasionally easy, it is often very difficult, and the trade-off ratios are likely to be transitory, changing continuously with any alterations in program decisions, system configurations, external circumstances, and so on. As an example of the trade-off ratios needed, we may need to know how much of a sacrifice in pounds is acceptable in order to reduce space requirements by one cubic foot, or to increase reliability by one-tenth of a percent, or to reduce maintenance manhours by one hour, or to save one dollar of production costs.

Micro-cost analysis, like macro-cost analysis, can be viewed simply as a difference in degree from the conventional "system" cost analysis, which steers its course between the two. Yet even differences in degree can be important, and considerable special attention is warranted to refine and extend cost analysis techniques based on simple trade-off ratios when dealing with micro-cost analysis problems.

## Summary

Cost is the value of benefits lost. Costs, like benefits, are the consequences of decisions; and costs, or consequences, can only be identified by clearly specifying the decision and comparing it with some alternative. The cost analyst seeks to identify and, wherever feasible, to measure and then evaluate the benefits forgone by choosing one course of action, one policy or program, rather than another. An indication of costs can be provided to the decisionmaker by enumerating required resources, or by determining alternative uses of these resources, or by estimating the value of these alternative uses. When we use dollars to estimate costs we are attempting to accomplish all three of these steps simultaneously. But only rarely will dollar expenditures be a full and completely valid measure of total costs. Although dollars are an especially useful measure of costs, often other measures can be simpler and more useful.

No responsible decisionmaker can afford to ignore costs, for to do so is to ignore benefits. Getting the greatest benefit for a given cost and minimizing cost for a given level of achievement are converse sides of a coin. Cost analysts, like decisionmakers, occasionally ignore costs – for example, by restricting their attention to costs that are easy to measure in dollars and then representing these partial costs as the "total cost."

Relevant costs depend upon the sphere of influence and the breadth of interest of the decisionmaking agency. The cost analyst must always keep in mind who his customer is, and must be clear about the options and constraints available. Relevant costs are those costs that depend upon the choice made, given the choices available. Elements of the world that are common to all relevant alternatives are "given" or "cost-free."

Time is valuable, and the cost analyst cannot treat dollar receipts or expenditures as if they were equal no matter when they occur. Future dollars must be discounted at a rate that reflects the decisionmaker's options.

**Suggested Supplementary Readings**
1. Paul A. Samuelson, *Economics: An Introductory Analysis*, 7th ed. (New York: McGraw-Hill Book Company, 1967), Chap. 3, "Price Functioning of a 'Mixed'

Capitalistic Enterprise System," and Chap. 24, "Analysis of Costs." (A most lucid, but nonmathematical, treatment of these subjects.)
2. Paul A. Samuelson, *Foundations of Economic Analysis* (Cambridge: Harvard University Press, 1948), Chap. IV, "A Comprehensive Restatement of the Theory of Cost and Production." (Although over 20 years old, this still remains one of the best treatments of the theory of cost and production. A mathematical treatment.)
3. James M. Henderson and Richard E. Quandt, *Microeconomic Theory – A Mathematical Approach* (New York: McGraw-Hill Book Company, Inc., 1958), Chap. 3, "The Theory of the Firm" and Chap. 8, "Optimization Over Time." (Excellent treatments of both these subjects.)
4. James M. Buchanan, *Cost and Choice* (Chicago: Markham Publishing Company, 1969).

# Chapter 4

# INTRODUCTION TO
# MILITARY COST ANALYSIS

The necessary background for the remainder of this book is now essentially complete. Chapter 2 defined our interests: resource allocation decision problems concerning military systems and forces some years hence, and the relationship of systems analysis to that decision process. Chapter 3 provided a compass for achieving our interests: various concepts from economic theory that are basic to the foundations of military cost analysis.

We now need a map, so that we can move into the field of military cost analysis *per se*. The purpose of the present chapter is to provide such a map. Because the main emphasis will fall on basic ideas and concepts, not on the specifics of methods and procedures, the remainder of the book may be viewed as an elaboration upon many of the points to be made in this chapter.

**The Central Problem**

The main problem facing the military cost analyst is to develop and apply concepts and techniques for assessing the economic cost of proposed alternative future actions under conditions of uncertainty.

In national security problems, such alternative actions usually take the form of some combination of the following:

1. Proposed *new* capabilities for the future – for example, new weapon or support systems[1] or something similar thereto.
2. Proposed *modifications* of existing or presently programmed capabilities.
3. Proposed *deletions* from the presently planned force.
4. Proposed *combinations* or *packages* of (1) through (3) – that is, total force structures or major subsets of total force structures for the future.

This statement of the problem implies a set of characteristics describing the conceptual framework within which military cost analysis must be performed.[2] These characteristics are so fundamental that we shall spend

---

[1] These terms will be made explicit later in this chapter.
[2] Of course, many of these characteristics apply equally to nonmilitary contexts.

a considerable amount of time discussing them. The reader will note that in one way or another they all relate back to the concepts set forth in Chapters 2 and 3. Also, it should be remembered that our context is *long-range* planning. In other contexts the set would vary considerably from those presented here.

## Major Characteristics of Cost Analysis

Except for the first item, the distinguishing features of the conceptual framework for military cost analysis that are outlined and discussed in the following paragraphs are not ordered in terms of importance. They are all important, and most of them are interrelated.

### Emphasis on Output-Oriented Packages of Capability

Assessments of the economic cost of alternatives must be developed and presented in a form useful to systems analysts and decisionmakers. This may seem obvious, but examples abound to suggest that it is frequently forgotten or ignored. But unless this requirement is fulfilled, all the rest can be for naught. It thus belongs at the head of any list of characteristics essential to cost analysis.

What is meant by an "output" orientation? The phrase draws its meaning from systems theory, in which the key analytic problem is to discern how a system – military or nonmilitary – acts upon what it is given (the "inputs") to produce what results (the "output"). The outputs are most fruitfully discerned, of course, in reference to the objectives they have presumably been designed to achieve, and, indeed, it is only on this basis that they can be evaluated fairly. Thus, the worth of a system – or the relative merits of it and its competitors – depends essentially upon the link between outputs and objectives. Ultimately, rational choice among competing alternatives in a universe of scarce resources rests upon this fact. Since the business of cost analysis is to help inform such choices, it necessarily focuses on that linkage and defines its problems accordingly. Hence the phrase "output orientation."

In the current jargon, output-oriented packages of military capability are called "weapon and/or support systems" or "program elements."[3] Aggregations of the packages are called "force structures" or "major programs." The key point is that military cost analysis concepts, methods, and techniques must be geared to deal with these packages or aggregations

---

[3] In many cases, "program elements" are based on organizational units: Army divisions, Navy task forces, and so on. Where "weapon system" is used in a general context in this book, the term should be interpreted to include these kinds of program elements.

of packages because they are the focal point of interest to the decision-makers.

All of this sounds commonsensical enough. But the next question is: What are these packages, and what should be included in them? Here we have one of the fundamental problems in systems analysis and hence cost analysis; and the reader will have to be patient because there is no quick answer. Most of the characteristics discussed below relate to it, and indeed much of the rest of this book is concerned directly or indirectly with this problem. As we shall see, the specific content of any one of these "planning packages" is *context dependent*. It cannot be defined once and for all, except at very high levels of abstraction.

At this point let us merely try to get some feeling for the nature of the problem by using a hypothetical example. Suppose that the planners are considering alternative ways of defending the continental United States against a future intercontinental ballistic missile attack. One of the alternatives is a proposed ground-based interceptor missile system. In addition to various measures of the possible effectiveness of this proposed system, the planners must also know what the economic cost is likely to be – the incremental cost to *develop*, *procure*, and *operate* the new capability over a period of years. This is often referred to as the "cost of the system." What does this mean? What is to be included? In general terms it means the cost of everything required to generate the desired new capability: hardware, manpower, new facilities, supplies, and so on. In other words, the "cost of the system" includes the cost of everything *directly related to the decision* to achieve this proposed new capability; it excludes the cost of items not so related, such as the costs of administrative and support activities that would go on regardless of the decision under consideration.

### Additional Parts of the Framework of Analysis

The output-oriented packages of military capability just introduced represent the most important part of the framework for military cost analysis. However, two other parts are necessary. One has already been alluded to indirectly: the "life cycle" identification. This means that for a proposed new weapon system or program element, provision should be made for segregating the costs of the proposal into three cost categories:

1. *Research and development costs* – that is, the resources required to develop the new capability to the point where it can be introduced into the operational inventory at some desired level of reliability.
2. *Investment costs* – that is, the one-time outlays required to introduce the capability into the operational inventory.

3. *Operating costs* – that is, the recurring outlays required year by year to operate and maintain the capability in service over a period of years.

An illustration of the relationship of these costs in the life of a system is presented in Fig. 4.1.

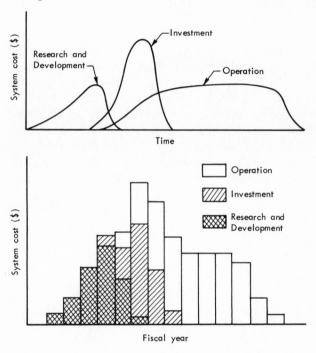

Fig. 4.1 – Examples of weapon system life cycle cost profiles

The life cycle identification is important for several reasons. One is that it helps insure that the total resource impact of a proposal will be identified. Oftentimes decisionmakers may become preoccupied with investment costs, to the relative neglect of the fact that a stream of operating cost over a period of years is an inevitable consequence of their decision. Life cycle costing helps to avoid such a pitfall. Again, we are brought back to the fundamental point of attempting to identify the *full economic cost* of a proposed future course of action.

Another reason why the life cycle identification is important is that it facilitates the analytical process. Usually systems analysts and long-range planners want to vary force sizes, the number of years various capabilities are assumed to be in the operational inventory, and the like. The life cycle identification is essential for this kind of "parametric" examination. Research and development costs, for example, are largely independent of operational force size and the number of years a capability is assumed to be in the operating inventory. Investment costs are related to force size, but are essentially independent of the number of years of operation. Operating costs are a function of both force size and number of years of operation.

So far the output side has been stressed. But in order to generate costs of alternatives in the appropriate output-oriented packages, the analyst has to start on the *input* side. Therefore, an input structure must be provided. This means that we must set up *resource* categories (for equipment, facilities, manpower, and so on) and *functional* categories (for maintenance, training, and so on). These categories must be meaningful and useful from several points of view: in easing the problem of data collection; in permitting computational convenience; in helping to indicate significant areas of critical resource impact – special equipment or facilities requirements, special manpower skills, and so on; and in helping to insure completeness in identifying all resources required to obtain a proposed military capability. An example of input-oriented categories that satisfy these conditions for some systems is presented in Table 4.1.[4]

TABLE 4.1

**Example of an Input-Oriented Structure**

|  | Cost of Proposed Alternative | |
|---|---|---|
|  | System A | System B |
| *Research and Development* | | |
| Preliminary design and engineering .. | | |
| Fabrication of test equipment .. .. | | |
| Test operations .. .. .. .. | | |
| Miscellaneous .. .. .. .. | | |
| Total R & D .. .. .. .. | | |
| | | |
| *Investment* | | |
| Facilities .. .. .. .. .. | | |
| Major equipment .. .. .. .. | | |
| Initial inventories .. .. .. .. | | |
| Initial training .. .. .. .. | | |
| Miscellaneous .. .. .. .. | | |
| Total investment .. .. .. | | |

---

[4] This is an aggregated example. Input structures are discussed in more detail in Chapter 5.

*Operating Cost*
   Equipment and facilities replacement  ..
   Maintenance    ..    ..    ..    ..
   Personnel pay and allowances  ..    ..
   Replacement training    ..    ..    ..
   Fuels, lubricants, and propellants    ..
   Miscellaneous    ..    ..    ..    ..

      Total operating (1 year)    ..    ..

*Total System Cost*
   R & D + Investment + 5-Year Operating

   R & D + Investment + 10-Year Operating

Regardless of what particular set of input categories is established, it is vitally important to define carefully what is included in each category. This is a fundamental prerequisite to the development of estimating relationships (to be discussed later in Chapter 6) and to working out consistent estimates of the cost implications of alternative proposals for future military capabilities. It should be noted here that in a given case not all the categories will be assigned numbers. The discussion of incremental costs in Chapter 3 makes it clear that a proposed system for the future may, for example, be able to utilize facilities made available from the phase-out of an existing system. In this case, the investment-in-facilities category for the new system would be zero, or close to it, unless there were competing uses for the facilities in question.

While on the subject of input structures, one additional point should be made pertaining to the appropriate level of detail. In long-range planning, trying to structure problems in great detail is usually not rewarding;[5] indeed, in most cases it is impossible. However, it is important to have input structures that are specific enough to determine those aspects of a proposal which are really new and those which are not – for example, in the case of proposed new equipments, aspects related to manufacturing state of the art. Even the most advanced system proposals contain many elements which are not significantly new. These should be separated from those which *are* new, so that the analytical effort can be concentrated on the latter. In the hardware area this usually means going down at least to the subsystem level, and very often even lower.[6]

---

[5] As we shall see later, the attempt to increase the amount of detail will not necessarily increase the accuracy of the estimate.

[6] When we speak of hardware, the term "system" refers to the whole hardware item in

**The Requirement to Estimate Economic Cost**

One of the main themes established in Chapters 2 and 3 is that the costs that are relevant in making resource allocation decisions for the future are economic costs: the estimated economic implications of the decision under consideration. This has direct and very significant implications for the characteristics of a military cost analysis capability.

First and foremost, it means that military cost analysis concepts and techniques must be designed to deal with *alternatives*. Without alternatives there can be no costs from the point of view of resource allocation decisions.

To illustrate, consider the following hypothetical example: Suppose that we take the decisions *made to date* regarding the future strategic offensive and defensive forces. Suppose further that on the assumption of no new decisions, the implications of the decisions to date are permitted to unfold over a future time horizon. Under these conditions the cost implications will in effect be a "spendout" of the actions implied by the fixed set of decisions. As research and development and initial investment are completed, the spendout cost curve will gradually decline over time and approach the operating cost level of the planned strategic forces in the future. (See curve AB in Fig. 4.2.) In analytical studies the spendout of past decisions is often called the "base case." The main characteristic of

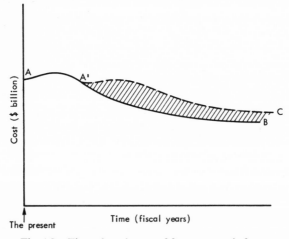

Fig. 4.2 – Time-phased costs of future strategic forces

question. "Subsystem" refers to the broadest categories for grouping together all the components of the item. For example, in the case of a ballistic missile, or similar aerospace vehicle, the subsystems are airframe, power plant, guidance, and payload.

the base case is that it, taken alone, implies no substantive problem for a decisionmaker to consider.

Now suppose that the decisionmakers begin to consider changes (alternatives) to the base case. If one of the changes under consideration is a net addition to the currently planned future force, the cost profile will look something like the shaded area in Fig. 4.2 (the difference between the area under curve AA'C and the area under curve AB). From an analytical point of view, it is these types of costs that are most relevant in assisting decisionmakers in grappling with resource allocation problems. The cost implications of *changes* (increments or decrements) to some established position are central to the decisionmaking process.

As an example of another type of output that a military cost analysis capability must be capable of generating, let us consider the Fig. 4.3. Here

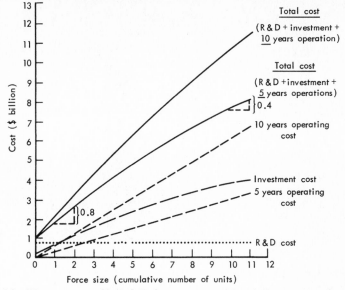

Fig. 4.3 – Weapon system X: R & D, investment, and 5 and 10 years operating cost

we have the estimated costs of a proposed future military capability called Weapon System X. The costs are generated in terms of research and development, investment, and annual operating cost (5 or 10 years), and are expressed as a function of force size (cumulative number of operational units). This type of output is useful analytically because it permits consideration of either the incremental cost of a block of units beyond a given cumulative unit number, or the cost of the last unit (marginal cost) at some point.

Consider the total cost curve labeled "R & D + Investment + 5 Years Operation" in Fig. 4.3. Since the slope of this curve is declining as force size increases, the marginal costs are declining.[7] For example, the marginal cost of the second unit is $0.8 billion; the marginal cost of the eleventh unit is $0.4 billion. The marginal cost curve is plotted in Fig. 4.4.

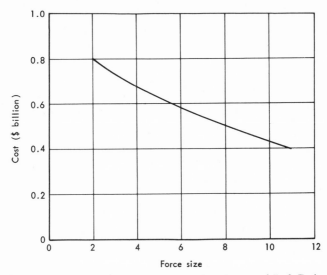

Fig. 4.4 – Weapon system X: Marginal cost curve (based on total R & D, investment, and 5-year operation curve contained in Fig. 4.3)

Another problem area that a military cost analysis capability must be able to handle is joint costs. Economic theory tells us that if costs are in fact joint, then by definition they cannot be separated into meaningful portions and assigned to the various activities which collectively generate them.[8] Yet joint cost considerations arise in many contexts in military cost analysis studies – for example, in assigning the costs of support activities to output-oriented elements of combat capability such as weapon systems. As always, the basic objective is to determine the economic cost consequences of proposed alternatives. This means that arbitrary accounting-type allocations of support costs to combat program elements are ruled

---

[7] If the total cost curve were linear, marginal costs would be constant; for example, Total cost curve: $C = \alpha + \beta X$, Marginal cost: $\frac{dC}{dX} = \beta$ (a constant).

[8] Arbitrary accounting-type allocations can be made, but these serve no useful purpose in resource allocation decisionmaking.

out. To cite a specific instance in the case of the Air Force: The operating costs of Headquarters, United States Air Force; the Air Force Academy; the Air Force Accounting and Finance Center; Headquarters, Air Force Systems Command; and the like, usually should *not* be allocated to Air Force weapon systems. These support activities are essentially independent of the Air Force's combat force mix. On the other hand, the costs of certain depot maintenance activities in the Air Force Logistics Command and of certain courses in the Air Training Command may be, and often are, appropriately identified as part of the incremental cost of a proposed weapon system.[9]

One final topic under the heading of "economic costs" should be mentioned briefly: time phasing. The matter of time phasing is very much related to many of the subjects discussed previously. However, it is singled out here because of its importance in the cost analysis process.

In many long-range planning contexts, especially force structure analyses, explicit time phasing of resource requirements is a prime consideration. Even in narrower contexts where individual proposals for new capabilities (for example, weapon systems) are being compared using "static" costs,[10] it is often desirable to generate time-phased basic cost estimates. For one thing, this is likely to permit a better assessment of incremental costs, since the availability of inherited assets is a function of time. For another thing, it provides a good basis for an explicit treatment of the time preference problem. With time-phased cost streams available as a base case, it is a matter of simple calculation to discount these streams in any way (or ways) that the analyst, or his critics, deem appropriate in the context of the problem at hand.

### Explicit Treatment of Uncertainty

We have already emphasized the fact that in most long-range planning decision problems, uncertainties are usually prevalent, and that systems analysts must do everything possible to identify major areas of uncertainty and to show clearly their implications for the various alternatives under consideration. Uncertainty must be treated explicitly, not swept under the rug. Conceptually this means that *measures of dispersion*, in addition to

---

[9] This is an example of one of the most important points made in Chapter 3: relevant costs are those, and only those, that are a consequence of the particular decision at hand.

[10] By "static" costs we mean the sum of the costs of research and development + investment + operation over a fixed period of years. (For example, see the total cost curves in Fig. 4.3.)

expected values, must be taken into account.[11] While variances in a precise statistical sense usually cannot be calculated in most systems analysis problems, ranges of values (to serve as measures of dispersion) can be computed to reflect the implications of various assumptions about the state of the world in the future (the threat, for example).

What is the impact of this on cost analysis? The subject of uncertainty will be discussed in one way or another throughout the remainder of this book. At this point we want merely to sketch out some of the major points. Above all else is the requirement that cost analysis techniques be designed to permit parametric types of analyses. That is, the cost analysis models and the estimating relationships contained in these models must be "open ended" with respect to key cost-generating variables, so that ranges of values of these variables can be fed into the analysis to see what effect they have on the cost of final outcomes. Through such a procedure, cost sensitivities can be explored and this, in turn, can shed light on the problem of uncertainty.

As an illustration, consider the following: Suppose that in a given analytical study the analyst is very uncertain about a key parameter (call it $P$) in one of the alternatives being considered (call it Weapon System Y). Suppose further that the current "conventional wisdom" says that $P^*$ is the most likely value of $P$. The analyst, however, decides to go beyond merely using $P^*$ as an input into his cost model, and proceeds to let $P$ vary over its relevant range ($P_1$ to $P_2$) to see what the impact on total system cost might be. As suggested in Fig. 4.5, the results of this sensitivity analysis might take one of several forms.

---

[11] To illustrate this point, consider two equal cost alternatives ($X_1$ and $X_2$) with the following probability distributions of their respective benefits:

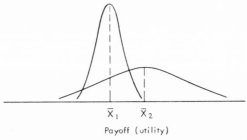

Payoff (utility)

If the decisionmaker is given only the expected (mean) values, he would no doubt choose $X_2$ (the highest expected payoff). On the other hand if measures of dispersion are also made available to him, he might well decide to choose $X_1$ with a lower expected value than $X_2$ but at the same time having a much lower degree of uncertainty of outcome (a smaller spread in the probability distribution).

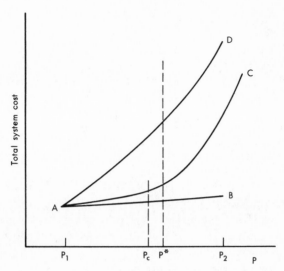

Fig. 4.5 – Examination of the sensitivity of weapon system Y cost to variations in the value of parameter $P$

If the result is a curve like AB, then uncertainties about $P$ do not matter very much, at least as far as system cost is concerned. System cost is not very sensitive to variations in $P$. Curve AC portrays a different situation. Here system cost is essentially insensitive to $P$ up to a critical point $P_c$, where it then begins to explode. The decisionmakers would certainly want to know about this state of affairs; but they would not have this knowledge if the analyst computed only one case – a "point estimate" – based on the conventional wisdom ($P^*$). Finally, AD illustrates the case where system cost is markedly sensitive to variations in $P$ over the entire relevant range of values for $P$. Again, the decisionmakers would want to know about this kind of sensitivity, and as a result of this knowledge they might want to explore ways of hedging against uncertainties in $P$.

As another illustration, let us consider the case of a proposed Army hard point defense system as part of a study of alternative ways to defend the continental United States against ballistic missile attack. Because of uncertainties about the threat, and for other possible reasons, there will be uncertainties about the physical characteristics and operational concepts of the proposed system: force size, specific characteristics of the hardware, specifics of deployment, degree of hardness (p.s.i. overpressure) of the system, and the like.

Now if the cost analyst is to do his job properly in support of the systems analysis process, he will not prepare a single estimate of the cost of the proposed system based on a set of expected values for variables like those listed above. Rather he will prepare a series of analyses of the cost of the system, with alternative assumptions about key variables in the problem; and he will explore the sensitivity of total system cost to changes in these variables. This, of course, involves much more work than merely generating expected value ("point estimate") cases; but it is the heart of a meaningful cost analysis effort. Development of cost models which are in part computerized can help a great deal in doing these parametric types of analyses. (We shall discuss such models in Chapter 7.)

### Accuracy Requirements and Possibilities

Closely related to the subject of uncertainty is the matter of accuracy in military cost analysis studies. Two frequently heard statements are:

1. We must always strive for a high degree of accuracy in an *absolute* sense.
2. A higher degree of accuracy can be attained by going into a greater amount of detail.

The first statement needs clarification on at least two counts: the need for accuracy and the possibility of achieving it in problems of long-range planning.

As indicated previously, long-range planning is characterized by major uncertainties, a wide range of alternatives that must be considered, a paucity of detailed information and data, and the like. This means, for the most part, that highly accurate cost estimates are most unlikely in an absolute sense. Furthermore, requirements for a high degree of accuracy in absolute terms are not paramount either, since most long-range planning studies focus on the *relative* comparisons of alternative courses of action.

These considerations have a marked impact on how cost analysis activities in support of systems analysis should be carried out. Once we recognize, for example, that the concepts and methods of cost analysis should be directed more toward comparative or relative accuracy, we immediately have a requirement to develop and use analytical techniques that will permit us to treat alternatives consistently. It is important to understand these points because in the long-range planning context the analyst can in effect waste much time and effort if he tries to pursue an objective as elusive (and perhaps as irrelevant) as a high degree of accuracy in an absolute sense.

Let us turn now to the second statement: A high degree of accuracy can be attained by going into a greater amount of detail. That such a statement cannot be true in general should be obvious; nevertheless, a significant body of opinion seems to believe that it is true. It is especially likely to be false in a long-range planning context, where typically there are considerable gaps in our knowledge about many of the alternatives being considered, where quantitative information and a data base are limited, and where other uncertainties abound. Under these circumstances, it is not at all clear that a higher degree of accuracy can be attained by trying to force the analysis into a finer and finer grain of detail. With a limited data base, the analyst can rapidly find himself using essentially fictitious numbers to fill in the overly detailed categories, with the result that the output of the analysis is no better than that obtained by working at higher levels of aggregation. In such instances, concentrating the analytical effort at an appropriate (relatively high) level of aggregation and using carefully derived statistical estimating relationships are the most likely means of producing fruitful results.

For example, we often find that useful long-range planning relationships between cost and gross measures of system characteristics may be discovered at relatively high levels of aggregation, whereas similar relations cannot be determined at the "nuts and bolts" level. A related point is the following: Even if the data base permits the derivation of detailed relationships, they may not be useful in long-range planning because the explanatory variables (for example, system performance and physical characteristics) may be specified in a degree of detail that is simply not available in proposals for alternative military capabilities 10 or more years into the future.

### The Requirement for Systematic Collection of Data and Information, and the Derivation of Estimating Relationships

To say that the results of a military cost analysis are no better than the information and data that go into the analytical effort may seem tautological. Yet this *is* a very important point, and it must be faced explicitly. A really effective cost analysis capability cannot exist without systematic collection and storage of comparable data on past, current, and near future programs. Even this is not enough. The data must be processed and analyzed with a view to the development of estimating relationships which may be used as a basis for determining the cost impact of future proposals. In the case of output-oriented packages of future military capability, these relationships should relate various categories of cost impact to physical, performance, and operational characteristics. Without an extensive and continuously updated inventory of estimating relationships, cost analysis as viewed in this book is impossible. Such an inventory is particularly a prerequisite to a "sensitivity analysis" approach to the cost analysis problem.

The part of the task that is concerned with derivation of estimating relationships is not easy, but it is not as demanding as the one involved in continuously collecting and storing a consistent body of basic data and information to serve as the foundation for developing useful estimating relationships. In some instances there are wide gaps in the existing data base. In other instances – which are most prevalent – data and information exist; but they are partially or completely in the wrong format, they are generated in terms of categories that are defined differently from one location to another, they are in such a form that cost data cannot be related explicitly to the relevant quantity or physical characteristics information, or they are inconsistent or incomparable in some other fashion. The Department of Defense, the aerospace industry, and other organizations have been working hard for years to improve this situation, and much progress has been made.[12] Much more remains to be done, however, which means that cost analysts will still have to devote a major effort to attempting to adjust basic data and information for inconsistencies and other deficiencies.

### How Cost Enters into the Systems Analysis Process
Given a cost analysis capability having characteristics like those described in the preceding paragraphs, how is the output of such a capability introduced into the systems analysis process?

Recall that two basic conceptual approaches for making comparisons in systems analysis studies were mentioned in Chapter 2: (1) the fixed budget approach and (2) the fixed effectiveness approach. Let us discuss each of these briefly from the standpoint of how cost considerations fit into the total analytical effort.

#### Fixed Budget Approach
In the fixed budget case, the alternatives being considered are compared on the basis of effectiveness likely to be attainable for the specified budget level. Here, the cost analysis work is one of the first things that must be done, because the effectiveness calculations cannot be completed until the cost analysts have determined the quantity of each alternative (or combination of alternatives) that can be obtained for the given cost level.

Figure 4.6 provides a highly simplified example to illustrate the role of

---

[12] In the hardware area the Department of Defense's Cost Information Report (the CIR System) represents an example of a significant step toward developing a consistent data base for use in deriving equipment cost-estimating relationships.

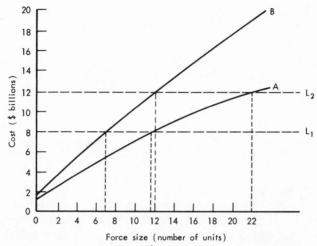

Fig. 4.6 – System cost versus force size for alternatives A and B

cost analysis in the fixed budget framework for comparing alternatives.[13] Only two alternatives are involved:[14] proposed new military capabilities A and B. The results of the cost analysis are shown in terms of total system cost as a function of force size for each alternative (curves A and B in Fig. 4.6).

If the specified cost level to be used in the comparative analysis is $8 billion, 11.5 units of alternative A or 7 units of alternative B are obtainable. This is an important output of the cost analysis,. which then becomes the key input to the effectiveness analysis.[15]

Notice that in this illustration the results do not scale linearly with respect to changes in the stipulated cost level. For example, if $L_1$ is increased by 50 per cent to $L_2 = \$12$ billion, the outcome is 22 units of A or 12 units of

[13] In order to keep the example simple and to concentrate on the problem at hand, we shall deliberately set aside many considerations that are very important in a real cost analysis situation: the explicit treatment of uncertainty, problems associated with time, and so on.

[14] As indicated in Chapter 2, *many* alternatives usually have to be examined – particularly in the early stages of a systems analysis study.

[15] Here we have one example of why cost functions relating cost to the scale of proposed future programs are useful in systems analysis work.

Many of the cost functions emphasized in conventional economic theory relate cost to rate of output. Rate-of-output cost functions are also useful in certain types of problems in systems analysis. For example, in studying military aircraft systems the analyst often examines how system cost (for a fixed force size) changes as the activity rate (for example, flying hours per aircraft per month) is varied over a certain range.

B. The increase in the number of units is greater than the increase in $L_2$ over $L_1$:

$$L_2/L_1 = 12/8 \quad = 150\%$$
$$A_2/A_1 = 22/11.5 = 191\%$$
$$B_2/B_1 = 12/7 \quad = 171\%$$

In a simple way this demonstrates that in the context of the fixed budget approach, nonlinearities may imply the desirability of conducting the comparisons for more than one cost level; for example, three cases might be examined: high, medium, and low.

### Fixed Effectiveness Approach

In the fixed effectiveness approach for comparing alternatives, the analysis attempts to determine that alternative (or feasible combination of alternatives) which is likely to achieve some specified level of effectiveness at the lowest economic cost. Here, the cost analysis is important in making final comparisons, given that the effectiveness analysis has estimated the quantity of each alternative that is required to attain the stipulated level of capability.

As one simple illustration of this approach, suppose that two alternatives C and D are under consideration, and that the results of the effectiveness analysis indicate the following ranges of quantities (number of units) of C or D required to attain some specified level of effectiveness $E_0$:

|                | C  | D  |
|----------------|----|----|
| Low            | 20 | 4  |
| Expected value | 22 | 6  |
| High           | 24 | 12 |

Notice that in this case the range for D is considerably greater than for C because of uncertainty.

Suppose now that the estimated total system costs as a function of force size for C and D are as shown in Fig. 4.7 (curves C and D). Taking the expected value outputs from the effectiveness analysis, we see from Fig. 4.7 that D is the least cost alternative for attaining effectiveness level $E_0$: $7.5 billion for D vs. $15.3 billion for C, or a factor-of-2 difference in favor of D. If the uncertainties in the effectiveness analysis are taken into account, alternative D still holds up well, even in the situation where the worst case (highest cost) for D and the best case (lowest cost) for C are paired up. Thus, if all the uncertainties have been taken into account, alternative D appears to be a dominant solution – something which the systems analyst is always seeking, but rarely finds.

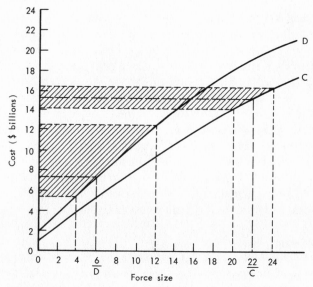

Fig. 4.7 – System cost versus force size for alternatives C and D
(fixed effectiveness = $E_0$)

**A Word of Caution**

As a final comment on the discussion in this section, it should be repeated that these examples have been highly simplified in the interest of clarifying main points of principle. Otherwise, the reader may be led to believe that systems analysis in real life is a simple mechanistic process. Nothing could be farther from the truth. Discussion in later chapters will help to convey the complexity that is typical of systems analysis problems and the cost analysis part of the total analytical process.

One important point should be made now, however. The systems analysis process is typically a complex endeavor requiring continuous interaction among the contributing disciplines, of which cost analysis is only one. It also requires continuous re-cycling or iteration as the analysis unfolds and attempts to weed out the less interesting alternatives. Thus, the total analytical process involves examination and comparison of numerous sets of alternatives – not just "A vs. B" as shown in our simple examples.

In the early stages of a study the analysts frequently use a quick and convenient cost and effectiveness model in order to consider and reject most of the alternatives in a given set. Subsequently, a more refined and analytically demanding cost and effectiveness model is used to help determine choices among the few remaining alternatives.

**Some Examples of the Outputs of Cost Analysis Studies**

It may be helpful to close this chapter with a few brief examples of some of the outputs of cost analyses which are useful in the systems analysis process. Our objective is to give the reader a bit more of the flavor of what military cost analysis is all about, in light of the conceptual framework presented in this and previous chapters. We will save for later discussion the problem of how the outputs were obtained.

For these illustrations we shall assume that the "output-oriented package of military capability" is a weapon system, or its equivalent, and that force structures are made up of combinations of these packages. In this discussion four types of contexts of military cost analysis will be considered: *intra*system comparisons, *inter*system comparisons, force-mix comparisons, and total force structure cost analyses.

### Intrasystem Comparisons

In the case of intrasystem comparisons, the primary emphasis is on explorations of how system cost varies as the configuration of the proposed system is changed.

Total system cost as a function of force size for varying numbers of years of operation represents one form of intrasystem cost analysis. One type of output of such a study was illustrated previously in Fig. 4.3. Another way of displaying the output is given in Fig. 4.8.

A very important class of intrasystem cost analysis comparisons is that pertaining to the examination of variations in total system cost as the physical characteristics and the operational concept of the system are varied, assuming a fixed number of years of operation. Here, we shall in effect be applying some of the ideas set forth in Chapter 3 – for example, the concepts of total cost and marginal cost (the rate of change of total cost with respect to some key variable). System designers and decision-makers are interested in such explorations because the resulting trade-off information can be very useful in reaching judgments about the optimum configuration of the system.

As an illustration of this type of analysis, consider the case of a future aircraft system where the mission requires that a fleet of aircraft be continuously airborne on a series of stations which cover a large geographical area. A Navy antisubmarine warfare (ASW) mission in the future is a possible example.

Continuously airborne alert aircraft systems typically involve a host of significant variables: endurance hours of the aircraft to be employed in the system, extent of the area coverage, nature of the payload requirements, aircraft maintenance policy (one, two, or three shifts), and the like. Intra-

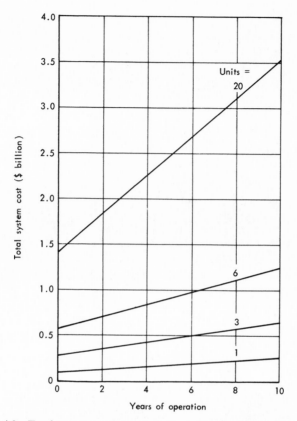

Fig. 4.8 – Total system cost for weapon Z as a function of force size and number of years operation

system cost analyses must usually explore the consequences of variations in these variables.

Figure 4.9 shows an example for a future ASW system to patrol and destroy ballistic missile-carrying enemy submarines, where aircraft endurance hours and area coverage (nautical miles out to sea from U.S. coastlines) are varied. Here total system cost is defined to be the costs of research and development + investment + 5 years of operation. Notice that as the area coverage is extended, the requirement for longer endurance becomes increasingly more severe.

Figure 4.10 contains another ASW system cost example. Here total system cost (defined as in Fig. 4.9) for each pound of payload (electronics, ASW missiles, and so on) on station is expressed as a function of the pounds

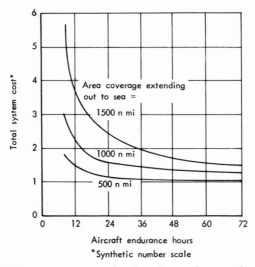

Fig. 4.9 – ASW system cost versus aircraft endurance for several area coverages

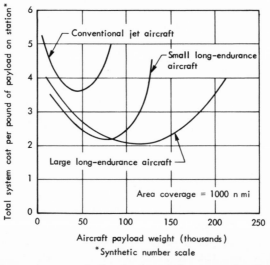

Fig. 4.10 – System cost per pound of payload on station versus aircraft payload weight

of payload carried per aircraft.[16] Curves are shown for three types of aircraft that might be candidates for use in the proposed ASW system.

---

[16] Area coverage is fixed at 1,000 nautical miles.

Notice that the use of conventional jets in this mission application results in a considerably higher minimum cost point than for long-endurance aircraft, and that system cost per pound of payload on station is very sensitive to individual aircraft payload weight. Note also that as we move to the large, long-endurance aircraft, the costs become much less sensitive to a particular loading or payload weight. This might suggest that if the size of the payload to perform the future mission is clouded by uncertainties, then flexibility may be achieved by choosing the large, long-endurance aircraft.

### Intersystem Comparisons

Intersystem comparisons were illustrated briefly earlier in this chapter (see Fig. 4.7, for example). We shall now present two additional cases to illustrate somewhat different aspects of cost analysis in support of the systems analysis process.

For the first example, consider proposed systems G and H as alternatives for doing some particular national security task in the future. The estimated total system costs (research and development + investment + a fixed number of years of operation) of G and H are as portrayed in Fig. 4.11.

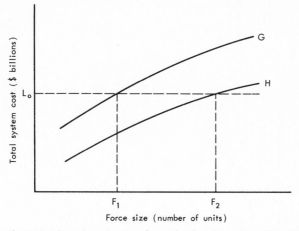

Fig. 4.11 – System cost versus force size for alternatives G and H

Suppose that certain key effectiveness measures that can be quantified explicitly are comparable for G and H, but that H has less qualitative post-attack performance capability (QPAPC) than G. The difference in the system cost curves for G and H in Fig. 4.11, then, essentially represents the costs that must be incurred to get more QPAPC. But there are other ways to view the problem. Suppose, for example, that the force planners have a given budget (represented by $L_0$ in Fig. 4.11) to spend to supplement the already planned forces in the mission area under consideration. For $L_0$, they can get a force size of $F_1$ for alternative G or a much larger force $(F_2)$ of system H. The planners may judge that the larger force of H may more than compensate for its lower QPAPC. Or they may decide that $F_2$ of H is roughly equivalent to $F_1$ of G and decide to select H for other qualitative reasons, such as political considerations.

As a second example of intersystem comparisons, consider the following: Suppose there are two new proposed alternatives, systems J and K, which are estimated to be capable of doing the same national security task in the future with essentially the same degree of effectiveness for the time period of interest. Suppose further that the time-phased total system costs (in constant dollars) over a 15-year period in the future are as portrayed in Fig. 4.12. Here, the time preference assumption is a *zero* discount rate

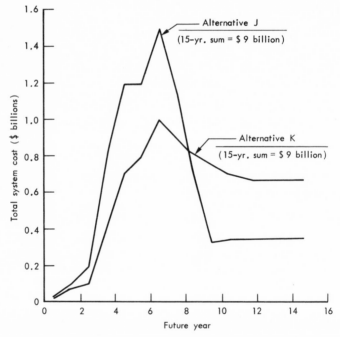

Fig. 4.12 – Time-phased system costs for systems J and K, discounted for time preference at 0.0% for the first 15 years, ∞ thereafter

for the first 15 years and an infinite rate thereafter. Notice that in each case when the yearly costs are summed over the 15-year period, the totals are the same ($9 billion each for J and K).

On the basis of the data presented so far, we have an equal-effectiveness, equal-cost situation; so presumably the decisionmakers would be indifferent regarding the choice of J or K – at least on the basis of the quantitative information available at this point.

Notice, however, that the time impacts of the costs for J and K are considerably different. The basic reason for the difference is that alternative J requires higher cost outlays (relative to K) early in the period because of greater research and development and investment costs. Apparently these outlays pay off in terms of an efficient operational system having relatively low operating costs later in the period.[17] Alternative K, on the other hand, has lower research and development and investment costs than J. Let us assume that this implies a less efficient operational system than J, with the result that larger operating costs are required to accomplish the specified task with the same degree of effectiveness as J. Indeed, the costs for K during the latter years of the 15-year period are about twice those of J.

In view of these differences in the time impact of the costs of J and K, the question arises as to whether the planners would still be indifferent regarding the choice of J or K if the time preference assumptions were varied. Suppose the base case (Fig. 4.12) were modified to reflect the following range of time preference specifications:

(1)  4.75% for 15 years; ∞ rate thereafter
(2)     6% for 15 years; ∞ rate thereafter
(3)   10% for 15 years; ∞ rate thereafter
(4)   15% for 15 years; ∞ rate thereafter.

The results, expressed in terms of present value costs in billions of constant dollars, would be as follows:[18]

| Case | System J | System K | Difference |
|------|----------|----------|------------|
| Base | $9.0 | $9.0 | $ 0 |
| (1) | 6.3 | 5.9 | 0.4 |
| (2) | 5.8 | 5.3 | 0.5 |
| (3) | 4.5 | 3.9 | 0.6 |
| (4) | 3.3 | 2.7 | 0.6 |

Here we see that the absolute cost differences between alternatives J and K increase slightly as the discount rate becomes larger.[19] Depending upon

---

[17] This need not always be the case, however.

[18] The time-phased cost profiles for modifications (2) and (3) are portrayed in Figs. 4.13 and 4.14.

[19] The *relative* differences, however, increase much more markedly; for example:

Modification (1): 0.4/6.3 = 6%
Modification (4): 0.6/3.3 = 18%.

the details of the context for the particular decision at issue, the decision-makers may no longer be indifferent regarding the choice of J or K. If absolute cost differences are important, the planners are not likely to ignore a difference of some $500 million.

In any event, the cost analysts should calculate and present the implica-

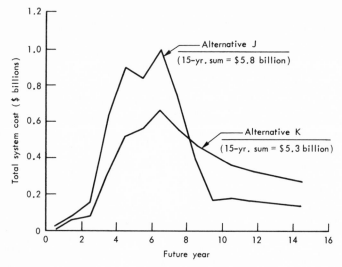

Fig. 4.13 – Time-phased system costs for systems J and K, discounted for time preference at 6% for the first 15 years, ∞ thereafter

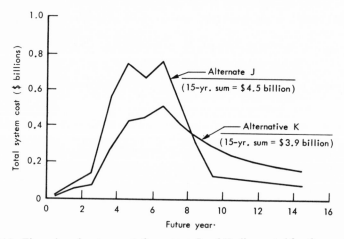

Fig. 4.14 – Time-phased system costs for systems J and K, discounted for time preference at 10% for the first 15 years, ∞ thereafter

tions of alternative assumptions about the rate of discount.[20] The decision-makers will then have a better basis for taking time preference considerations into account.

### Cost Analyses of Force Mixes

Comparisons of alternative force mixes[21] in some future mission area comprise an important subset of the total spectrum of problem areas dealt with in systems analysis studies. Numerous examples of past applications could be cited, among them studies of alternative future mixes of:

1. Airlift, sealift, and prepositioning.
2. Regular and reserve forces in a given mission area.
3. Land-based and sea-based tactical airpower.
4. Land-based (fixed or mobile) strategic missile systems and water-based strategic missile systems.

In all these instances, significant complementarities exist among the alternative modes being considered. Complementarity is the key factor leading to force-mix studies.[22]

The fixed budget approach is very common in dealing with force-mix problems. A particular form of this approach that is often used is one in which the presently planned force mix (and its implied cost level) is taken as the base case or point of departure for the analysis. Within the cost level of the base case, numerous variations in the various modes being considered are postulated and the effectiveness of the resulting total force mixes is evaluated quantitatively and qualitatively.

If the modes being examined are land-based and sea-based tactical

---

[20] As pointed out in Chapter 3, the discount rate need not be held constant over the planning period of interest; it may be assumed to increase as a function of time. For example, if we assume 5 per cent for the first 5 years, 10 per cent for the next 5, and 15 per cent for the last 5 years of the planning period, the result is as follows:

| Alternative | Present Value ($ Billions) |
|---|---|
| J | $5.5 |
| K | 4.7 |
| Difference | $0.8 |

[21] A force mix consists of a combination of various types of program elements – for example, weapon and/or support systems.

[22] However, the reader should not gain the impression that complementarities exist *only* in force-mix contexts. Practically all resource allocation problems contain elements of *both* substitutability and complementarity. For an excellent discussion of this in the context of the economic theory of consumer behavior, see J. R. Hicks, *Value and Capital*, 2nd ed. (Oxford: The Clarendon Press, 1950), Chapter III, "Complementarity".

airpower, for example, a postulated increase in the currently planned force of sea-based tactical air would have to be obtained by reducing the planned force of land-based tactical air. In all analyses of this type, the cost analysis study is a key input to the systems analysis, and it must be done first in order to generate the force mixes to be evaluated in the effectiveness analysis.

Let us consider an illustrative example of the cost portion of such an analysis. For simplicity, we shall assume that only two modes, X and Y, are being examined;[23] and that the currently planned future total force level of X plus Y is $P_x + P_y = P$, implying a total cost of $C_p$. This is the base case.

Now assume that three changes in the number of organizational units of mode X in the base case are postulated: $P_x - 1$, $P_x + 2$, and $P_x + 5$. The question then becomes: What does this imply in the form of incremental changes to the planned forces of mode Y, and what are the resulting *total* force mixes of X and Y?

The cost analysts have to start out by estimating the incremental cost implications of $P_x - 1$, $P_x + 2$, and $P_x + 5$: that is, $-\Delta C_{-1}$, $\Delta C_2$, and $\Delta C_5$.[24] Since the total cost level of both modes must always be $C_p$ (the cost level of the base case), these incremental costs of the postulated force changes in mode X will *change sign* when applied to mode Y. The problem then becomes one of taking $+\Delta C_{-1}$, $-\Delta C_2$, and $-\Delta C_5$, and through a cost analysis of force elements in mode Y, generating the implied incremental force changes in mode Y. (Call these $P_y + \Delta Y_{-1}$, $P_y - \Delta Y_2$, and $P_y - \Delta Y_5$.) This is one of the key outputs of the cost analysis effort.

The results of the above, in terms of organizational units of X and Y, may be summarized as follows:

| Case | Mode X | Mode Y |
|------|--------|--------|
| Base Case | $P_x$ | $P_y$ |
| I | $P_x - 1$ | $P_y + \Delta Y_{-1}$ |
| II | $P_x + 2$ | $P_y - \Delta Y_2$ |
| III | $P_x + 5$ | $P_y - \Delta Y_5$ |

Suppose that the cost analysts have completed their work and that the results are as portrayed in Fig. 4.15. Here, the *total* force mixes (mode X

---

[23] In an actual systems analysis problem these modes could be any one of a number of possibilities: for example, land-basing vs. sea-basing for a certain type of military capability. Within each mode there would normally be several program elements (e.g., weapon and/or support systems).

[24] In this example, the "deltas" denote increments (positive or negative, depending upon the prefacing sign).

plus mode Y) are plotted as a function of the number of organizational units of *mode X*.[25] Notice that in each case the total force is expressed in terms of the total number of combat-ready major equipments available from the number of organizational units in mode X and mode Y. This is the key output of the cost analysis, which, in turn, is one of the main inputs to the effectiveness analysis.

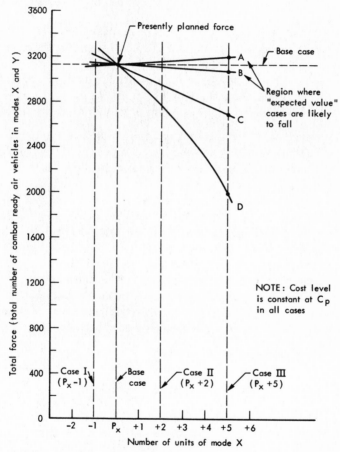

Fig. 4.15 – Total number of combat-ready air vehicles (mode X + mode Y) as a function of force size of mode X

Notice also that the cost analysts calculated a range of estimates for each case. The curves A and B bracket the region where the "expected value" cases are likely to fall. On the basis of A and B alone, the conclusion

[25] Recall that in all instances the total cost level is constant at $C_p$.

is that there is essentially a one-to-one cost trade-off between units of mode X and mode Y as incremental changes are made to the planned force over the range postulated in the study for the stipulated total force cost level $C_p$.

This, however, may not be the whole story, since major uncertainties are usually present in a force-mix analysis like the one we are considering. Examples are:

1. Uncertainties about how support activities (and hence support costs) change as incremental changes are made to the currently planned number of combat units.
2. Uncertainties about the cost of new major equipments in the future.
3. Uncertainties about what should be assumed regarding the useful life of the combat weapon systems in the total force mixes.

While uncertainties like these taken one at a time may not have a significant impact on the outcome of the cost analysis,[26] they may be of considerable importance when taken in various combinations. In any event, cost analysts should explore such possibilities through sensitivity analyses.

Suppose that in our hypothetical illustration the cost analysts did their job properly and that examples of the results are as portrayed by curves C and D. Suppose further that these situations are well within the realm of possibility. While curve C may or may not have a significant impact on the effectiveness analysis, curve D is very likely to. The analysts responsible for the effectiveness analysis would certainly want to know about such possibilities and the details of the specific assumptions that produce them. Again, this is an example of how cost analysts try to face up to uncertainty explicitly and to not be satisfied by merely calculating expected value cases.

### Total Force Structure Cost Analysis

Systems analyses involving comparisons among individual systems and among force mixes of subsets of total forces represent the heart of an analytical effort in support of the long-range planning process. Ultimately, however, the long-range planners must put all the pieces together in the form of projected total force structures. As in the case of examining pieces of the total force, they will want to investigate alternatives.

While no one has yet been able to devise ways of quantitatively assessing the effectiveness of total force structures, something can nevertheless be done regarding the *cost* aspects of total force planning.[27] A well-rounded

---

[26] That is, the total number of combat-ready major equipments in mode X plus mode Y.
[27] In many instances, however, effectiveness measures can be derived for *increments* to a total force – a most important consideration in force planning deliberations. Incremental costs must, of course, be related to the increments in effectiveness.

military cost analysis capability must therefore include the ability to investigate the cost implications of alternative future total force proposals. This must be done not only in terms of dollar measures like total obligational authority (TOA),[28] but also in terms of various physical units of measure, like manpower.

The output of a total force structure cost analysis typically has many dimensions, and the information can be summarized and presented in a variety of possible formats and in various levels of aggregation. One possibility is illustrated in Table 4.2. While this particular format provides for conveying a good deal of information, it is still at a very high level of aggregation with respect to both program element detail and cost category detail. One form of breakdown of the research and development, investment, and operating cost categories that is often used is the Department of Defense's conventional budget structure: construction, procurement, operations and maintenance, military personnel, and RDT&E (research, development, test, and evaluation).

To be of real use to long-range force planning decisionmakers, a cost analysis capability for investigating total force structures must be able to assess rapidly the resource impact of alternative proposals. Since total force cost analysis typically involves thousands of calculations, this requirement cannot be met unless the methods used are automated in part.[29]

The heart of total force structure comparisons centers around the examination of alternatives to some base case. As pointed out previously, this base case usually takes the form of the projected force structure implications of major program decisions made to date. Then the long-range planning activities focus primarily on examining proposed alternatives to the base case.

As we said earlier, the base case represents a "spendout" of the major program decisions made as of some point in time, assuming no new research and development, investment or operational concept decisions beyond that point. The result is a declining total force cost curve as a function of future time out to the point where the total becomes essentially the operating cost of the projected total force (see Fig. 4.16).[30]

---

[28] TOA is a technical term which we shall define explicitly in a later discussion. Broadly speaking, it means the gross funding requirements, year-by-year, that are necessary to support a given projected force. Particularly for investment items (for example, equipments and facilities), a given TOA in year $N$ usually results in expenditures in years $N, N+1, N+2$, or even later.

[29] Total force structure cost models are discussed in some detail in Chapter 7.

[30] Oftentimes because of particularly heavy investment commitments contained in decisions "made to date," the spendout total cost curve goes up before it starts its decline.

TABLE 4.2

**Illustrative Format for Presenting Summary of Total Force Structure Cost Analysis**

| Force Structure | | Manpower Requirements (Thousands of People) | |
|---|---|---|---|
| Major Program and Program Element | No. of Units (End of FY) | Military | Civilian |
| | '68 '69 '70 '71 '72 ... '78 | '68 '69 '70 '71 '72 ... '78 | '68 '69 '70 '71 '72 ... '78 |
| **STRATEGIC OFFENSIVE AND DEFENSIVE FORCES** | | | |
| *Offense* <br> B-52 Manned Bomber System <br> Minuteman ICBM System <br> Fleet Ballistic Missile System <br> ... <br> etc. | | | |
| Total Offense | | | |
| *Continental Defense* <br> F-106 Manned Interceptor System <br> NIKE Missile Interceptor System <br> Ballistic Missile Defense System <br> ... <br> etc. | | | |
| Total Defense | | | |
| TOTAL STRATEGIC OFF. AND DEF. FORCES | | | |
| **GENERAL PURPOSE FORCES** | | | |
| Infantry Divisions <br> Armored Divisions <br><br> Navy Attack Carriers (CVAs) <br> F-111 Land-Based Tactical Air System <br> ... <br> etc. | | | |
| TOTAL GENERAL PURPOSE FORCES | | | |
| **AIRLIFT AND SEALIFT FORCES** | | | |
| Navy Transport Ships <br> Navy Forward Floating Depots (FDLs) <br> C-141 Strategic Airlift System <br> C-5A Strategic Airlift System <br> ... <br> etc. | | | |
| TOTAL AIRLIFT AND SEALIFT FORCES | | | |
| **OTHER MAJOR PROGRAM AREAS** | | | |
| (Listed by Major Program and Program Elements in each, as above) <br> ... | | | |
| GRAND TOTAL | | | |

| Expenditures (or "Total Obligational Authority") in Millions of 1968 Dollars | | | |
|---|---|---|---|
| Research and Development | Investment | Operation | Total Expenditure |
| '68 '69 '70 '71 '72 ... '78 | '68 '69 '70 '71 '72 ... '78 | '68 '69 '70 '71 '72 ... '78 | '68 '69 '70 '71 '72 ... '78 |

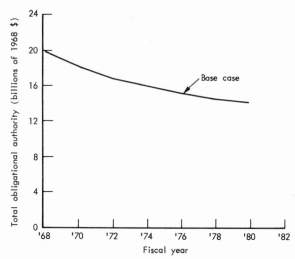

Fig. 4.16 – Illustration of a "spendout" (base case) calculation of total force cost

Suppose now that the planners want to consider certain phase-outs of the projected forces in the base case and at the same time to consider substantial phase-ins of new capabilities in several mission areas. What is the net result on the total obligational authority (TOA) level for the total force? The outcome may look something like that for "force variation No. 1" portrayed in Fig. 4.17.

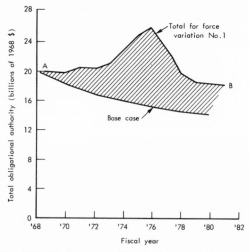

Fig. 4.17 – Net impact on TOA of force variation No. 1

Here the base case is the same as in Fig. 4.16, and the curve AB represents the total for force variation No. 1. The shaded area indicates the net increment of TOA estimated to be required if the postulated variation should be adopted. Notice that in the later time periods the curve AB represents, in a sense, a "second generation spendout" of research and development, investment, and operational concept decisions implied by force variation No. 1.

Upon examining these results the force planners may judge that for political or other reasons the peak TOA requirements in the mid-1970s for force variation No. 1 are too high. They therefore engage in an exercise to see if another alternative can be postulated which will cut down the TOA peak considerably and at the same time not result in an unacceptable degradation in the effectiveness of the total force. Suppose that they come up with force variation No. 2, which has the estimated TOA curve shown in Fig. 4.18 (curve AC).

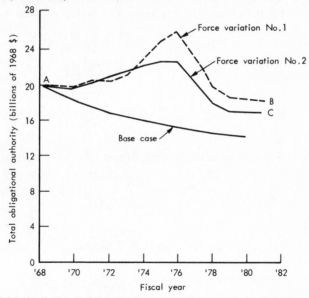

Fig. 4.18 – TOA levels implied by the base case, force variation No. 1, and force variation No. 2

Further examination of these results might indicate that force variation No. 2 is not acceptable either, and that therefore another iteration in the planning process should be initiated. This process could continue through a number of re-cyclings.

In sum, long-range total force structure planning is typically an iterative, experimental process; and if a military cost analysis capability is to be useful in serving that process, it must be set up to provide the kinds of information needed by the force planning decisionmakers. A fundamental requirement is to be able to assess rapidly the future resource implications of *numerous* proposed alternatives to the currently projected total force.

## Summary
The main points contained in this chapter may be summarized as follows:

1. The central problem facing military cost analysts is to develop concepts and procedures for assessing the economic cost implications of proposed alternative future courses of action under conditions of uncertainty.

2. Some of the more important distinguishing features of the conceptual framework for military cost analysis are:

   a. An output-oriented analytical capability for developing and presenting results in terms of program elements (e.g., weapon and/or support systems) of interest to the long-range planning decisionmakers.

   b. Provision for life cycle identification (research and development, investment, and operating costs) and for an appropriate input structure.

   c. Emphasis on generating the *economic* costs of alternatives: for example, incremental or marginal costs, explicit treament of time preference, and so on.

   d. Provision for explicit treatment of uncertainty.

   e. Emphasis on accuracy in a relative or comparative sense.

   f. A recognition that the backbone of a cost analysis capability is the systematic collection of data and information, and the derivation of estimating relationships.

3. The specifics of how the cost analysis activity feeds the systems analysis process are somewhat different, depending upon whether a fixed budget or fixed effectiveness approach is used in the analysis.

4. The four general types of contexts for military cost analysis are:

   a. Intrasystem comparisons.

   b. Intersystem comparisons.

   c. Force-mix comparisons.

   d. Total force structure comparisons.

**Suggested Supplementary Readings**
1. Norman V. Breckner and Joseph W. Noah, "Costing of Systems," Chap. 3 in Stephen Enke (ed.), *Defense Management* (Englewood Cliffs, N.J., Prentice-Hall, Inc., 1967).

2. G. H. Fisher, "Resource Analysis," Chap. 7 in E. S. Quade and W. I. Boucher (eds.), *Systems Analysis and Policy Planning: Applications in Defense* (New York: American Elsevier Publishing Co., Inc., 1968).
3. William H. Sutherland, *A Primer of Cost Effectiveness* (McLean, Va.: Research Analysis Corporation, 1967), Chap. 3, "Costing Procedures."
4. J. Morley English, "Concepts of System Resource Requirements," Chap. 5 in J. Morley English (ed.), *Cost-Effectiveness* (New York: John Wiley & Sons, Inc., 1968).
5. Bernard H. Rudwick, *Systems Analysis for Effective Planning* (New York: John Wiley & Sons, Inc., 1969), Chap. 9, "Resource Analysis."

Chapter 5

# THE INPUT SIDE

## Inputs in Cost Analysis

So far in this book our orientation has been primarily toward output-oriented packages of military capability, such as weapon systems, which are in some way related to the attainment of national security objectives. This focus is necessary, of course, since the output dimension is of the first importance to long-range planning decisionmakers, and hence to systems analysts. The problems and the results of cost analyses must be structured in terms of programs and program elements that the planners are considering in their deliberations.

While this is the prime requirement for the major product of the military cost analysis effort, it bears repeating that the basic work of cost analysis must be conducted in terms of a different dimension. The cost analyst simply cannot estimate the cost of an output-oriented package of military capability *per se*. Such packages must be broken up into their basic resource components (manpower, equipments, facilities, and the like) and functional categories made up of combinations of these resource components (maintenance, training, and so on).[1] We shall refer to sets of these resource and functional categories as "input structures." These constitute one of the major components of the so-called input side of military cost analysis.

Another major part of the input side is what may be called the "descriptive information" input to the cost analysis process. By this we simply mean the set of specifications describing the proposed new output-oriented package under consideration. If the package happens to be a weapon system, the set of descriptive information will include such data as major equipment specifications (performance characteristics, physical characteristics, and so on) and key specifications regarding the operational concept (deployment scheme, activity rates, dispersal scheme, and so on). Some subset of these system specifications will feed into the estimating procedure established for each one of the categories (or subcategories) in the input structure.

---

[1] The basic resource inputs can, in effect, be aggregated into various kinds of input packages. That is, we can pick up the inputs at various levels of aggregation from the disaggregated array of resources, at the one extreme, to the aggregate of the dollar costs of these resources, at the other. The task is to identify levels of aggregation, or input packages, that can be related to outputs and that are helpful in the estimation process.

100

Suppose, for example, that one of the categories in the input structure for future Weapon System X is called "maintenance of major equipment." Suppose also that an analysis of historical maintenance data for major equipments somewhat similar to that proposed for use in System X yields a statistical estimating relationship which says that maintenance cost ($C$) can be estimated as a function of equipment weight ($W$), equipment speed ($S$), and expected activity rate ($A$).[2] We have, therefore:

$$C = f(W, S, A). \tag{1}$$

Now from the system description information for System X, suppose that the values for the maintenance cost generating variables are $\hat{W}$, $\hat{S}$, and $\hat{A}$. Substituting these in equation (1) we obtain the estimated major equipment maintenance cost for System X:

$$\hat{C} = f(\hat{W}, \hat{S}, \hat{A}). \tag{2}$$

Estimates of cost for other categories in the input structure are obtained in a similar fashion, although in some cases the route is less direct. For example, some of the input structure categories may have estimating relationships containing "number of personnel" as an explanatory (cost-generating) variable. Here, an intermediate step is required. Using certain of the input data in the system description, and possibly other information as well, a manpower estimating subroutine or submodel is used to estimate the personnel requirements (number of officers, enlisted men, and civilians) for manning of the proposed new system. These manpower requirements estimates are then fed into the estimating procedures for those categories in the input structure requiring "number of personnel" as an input.[3]

In summary, for a particular output-oriented package of military capability under consideration, the "input side" of cost analysis consists of four interrelated major components:

1. A set of descriptive information setting forth major equipment performance or physical characteristics, key specifications of operational concept, and the like.
2. An input structure containing well-defined resource and functional categories.
3. Estimating procedures (for example, estimating relationships) for each category or subcategory in the input structure.

---

[2] If the system is an aircraft system, activity rate may be flying hours per year, for example.

[3] For example, the estimating equation for "personnel facilities" may well contain "number of officers" and "number of enlisted men" as cost-generating variables.

4. Submodels or subroutines for making certain intermediate calculations (of manpower requirements, for example) which may
be used in several categories in the input structure.

## An Example

Perhaps it would be helpful to present an example to demonstrate how
all of these pieces fit together in the cost analysis process. To do this we
shall not go into detail for all categories in the input structure. Rather, a
few will be singled out to illustrate some of the main points to be emphasized in this chapter.

Let us assume that a systems analysis is being conducted to examine
alternative ways of meeting national security objectives in the strategic
offensive mission area some 10 to 15 years from now. One of the proposed
alternatives is a new strategic manned bomber aircraft called the B-x. The
cost analysts are called upon to estimate the total system cost[4] for the proposed output-oriented package of military capability labeled the "B-x
System." That is to say, what would be the dollar expenditure implications
of a decision to add a certain force size of B-x's to the future strategic
forces, assuming a concomitant phase-out of existing B-52 units?[5]

TABLE 5.1

**B-x Aircraft Characteristics**

| | |
|---|---|
| Gross takeoff weight .. .. | 350,000 lb |
| Empty weight .. .. .. | 133,910 lb |
| AMPR weight .. .. .. | 102,700 lb |
| Wingspan .. .. .. .. | Variable: 77 ft (swept) |
| | 145 ft (extended) |
| Length .. .. .. .. | 182 ft |
| Height .. .. .. .. | 31.7 ft |
| Engines .. .. .. .. | 4 |
| Thrust per engine, dry .. | 16,650 lb |
| Thrust per engine, augmented .. | 25,800 lb |
| Maximum speed at altitude .. | Mach 2.2 (1,260 K) |
| Fuel capacity .. .. .. | 201,450 lb |
| Range .. .. .. .. | 6,300 n mi |
| Crew size and composition .. | 3 (2 pilots, 1 navigator-bombardier) |
| Runway requirement .. .. | 5,000 ft to clear 50 ft |
| Armament .. .. .. | Same as B-52 |

---

[4] Research and development, investment, plus a number of years operating cost.
[5] The discussion to follow is based on the analysis of the B-x by W. E. Mooz, which is
presented in full in Chapter 9 of E. S. Quade and W. I. Boucher (eds.), *Systems Analysis
and Policy Planning: Applications in Defense* (New York: American Elsevier Publishing
Co., Inc., 1968).

*The descriptive information* for the B-x system includes aircraft characteristics like those presented in Table 5.1. It also includes data on the B-x operational concept like the following:

1. The organizational unit is assumed to be similar to the present B-52 system – a wing-type organization with 15 aircraft per wing, with an additional 10 percent in command support (maintenance pipeline).
2. Phasing assumption: As B-52 wings are phased out of the operational force in the future, they are replaced wing-by-wing by the B-x.
3. Deployment and basing: Each B-x wing will operate from a base within the continental United States that it has inherited from the B-52.
4. Force size: 10 wings assumed for the base case.
5. Number of years of operation: 5 years assumed for the base case.
6. Maintenance guidelines: Similar to current Strategic Air Command practice for the B-52.
7. Alert concept: Seven B-x aircraft in each wing are to be on continuous ground alert.
8. B-x crew schedule (hours per month):

   | | |
   |---|---|
   | Ground alert duty ... ... ... ... | 130 |
   | Flying time (B-x) ... ... ... ... | 22 |
   | Flying time (training and mission support aircraft ... ... ... ... ... | 8 |
   | Nonflying duty ... ... ... ... | 40 |
   | Total ... ... ... ... ... | 200 |

9. Number of aircraft assumed to be required for the research and development program: 10 vehicles.

The *input structure* to be used in building up total system cost estimates for the B-x is portrayed in Table 5.2. This is presented only as an example of one of several possibilities, not as the "preferred" input structure. The important point, whatever input structure is chosen, is that the various categories be carefully defined. For example, does the category "Primary Mission Equipment Maintenance" include both base level and depot level maintenance? (In our example, it does.) Does depot maintenance include a pro rata share of the headquarters administrative costs of the Air Force Logistics Command depot where the maintenance is assumed to be per-

TABLE 5.2

**Example of an Input Structure**

| Research and Development | Investment Costs | Operating Costs |
|---|---|---|
| Design and Development | Facilities | Facilities Replacement and Maintenance |
|   Airframe | Primary Mission Equipment (PME) | PME Replacement |
|     Initial Engineering |   Airframe |   Airframe |
|     Development Support |     Manufacturing Labor |     Manufacturing Labor |
|     Initial Tooling |     Manufacturing Materials |     Manufacturing Materials |
|   Engines |     Sustaining and Rate Tooling |     Sustaining and Rate Tooling |
|   Avionics |     Sustaining Engineering |     Sustaining Engineering |
| System Test |     Other |     Other |
| Flight Test Vehicle Production |   Engines |   Engines |
|   Airframe |   Avionics |   Avionics |
|     Manufacturing Labor | Unit Support | PME Maintenance |
|     Manufacturing Materials | Aerospace Ground Equipment (AGE) | PME Fuels, Oils, & Lubricants (FOL) |
|     Sustaining and Rate Tooling | Other Equipment | Unit Support Aircraft Maintenance |
|     Sustaining Engineering | Initial Inventories of Supplies |     and FOL |
|     Other |     (Excluding Spares) | AGE Replacement and Maintenance |
|   Engines | Initial Inventories of Equipment | Personnel Pay and Allowances |
|   Avionics |     Spares and Spare Parts | Personnel Replacement Training |
| Flight Test Operations | Personnel Training (Initial) | Annual Travel |
| Flight Test Support | Initial Travel | Annual Transportation |
| | Initial Transportation | Annual Services |

formed? (In our example, the answer is "no," since these costs are essentially insensitive to the decision to have or not to have the B-x.)

At this point we have two of the four basic ingredients of the cost analysis process: the system description information for the B-x, and the input structure. For simplicity in this illustration we shall assume the following for the remaining two ingredients:

- The existence of a cost analysis procedure (for example, a set of estimating relationships) for each of the categories and subcategories in the input structure.
- The existence of the necessary submodels or procedures to feed inputs to various categories in the input structure.[6]

Our task is now to show briefly how the four pieces fit together. Since the objective here is to illustrate basic principles, it is not necessary to discuss in detail the data base and the estimating procedures for each category in the input structure. Rather, we shall select a few cases to serve as examples: facilities investment, investment in primary mission equipment, and primary mission equipment maintenance.[7]

**Facilities Investment**
From the B-x System descriptive information it is apparent that the facilities investment cost for the B-x will not be very great, because the B-x is assumed to inherit facilities from the phase-out of the B-52s. Here the main task of the cost analyst is to compare the estimated facilities requirements for the B-x with those of the existing B-52s and see if there are any significant deficiencies. Suppose that this is done, and that only a few instances are found where deficiencies are likely to exist, one of them being fuel storage facilities:

|                         |                  |
| ----------------------- | ---------------- |
| B-x estimated requirement | 4.49 million gal |
| Typical B-52 base        | 2.54 million gal |
| Deficiency              | 1.95 million gal |

Suppose now that an analysis of underground fuel storage costs produces

---

[6] For example, in the *manpower* area we would take various data from the system description information (such as the organizational unit concept, the alert concept, or the crew activity rate schedule) and various bits of information from other sources (such as Unit Manning Documents for present strategic bomber systems), and then, using the manpower submodel, we would derive estimates of the number of officers, airmen, and civilians required to man the B-x System.

[7] The numbers used in the illustrations to follow are hypothetical.

the relationship shown in Fig. 5.1. On the basis of this estimating relationship it would appear that a construction cost of about $0.65 per gallon

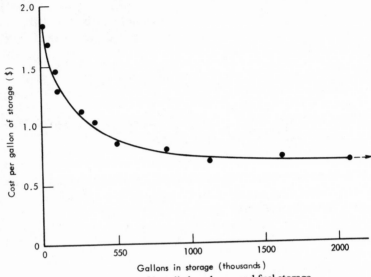

Fig. 5.1 – Cost of installed underground fuel storage

would be appropriate for the problem at hand. Therefore, the estimated
incremental cost per base for the B-x is:

$$(1.95 \text{ million gal}) (\$0.65) = \$1.3 \text{ million.}$$

Using similar methods, assume that we find that the B-x requires an
additional $1 million per base for other incremental facilities, such as
specialized maintenance facilities. The total incremental cost for all
facilities, then, becomes $2.3 million per base, or $23.0 million for the
total B-x System (the 10-wing base case).[8]

### Investment in Primary Mission Equipment
The problem here is to estimate the investment cost of the initial inventory of operational B-x aircraft. Cost analysis of proposed future major
equipments is typically a rather complicated process. However, for the
purposes of the present discussion, it is not necessary to treat the subject
in great detail.

Generally speaking, the costs of proposed future manned aircraft are

---

[8] As we shall see later, this is a very small fraction of the total B-x System cost. In other
cases, facilities cost can be a major item in total system cost.

estimated by using statistically derived estimating relationships which express cost per aircraft as a function of variables expressing performance or physical characteristics, and cumulative production quantity. The quantity variable need not necessarily be part of the basic estimating equation. For example, it is fairly typical to have the following:

$$C_b^q = f(x_1, x_2, \ldots, x_n; \ y_1, y_2, \ldots, y_m), \tag{3}$$

where $C_b^q$ = production unit cost of aircraft type $b$ (in our case manned bombers) for "normalized" cumulative quantity $q$ (for example, cumulative number of aircraft produced = 100 is often used in practice[9])

$x$'s = set of bomber aircraft performance characteristics (speed, range, and so on)

$y$'s = set of bomber aircraft physical characteristics (weight, wingspan, and so on),

and

$$C_b = g(Q \,|\, C_b^q), \tag{4}$$

where

$C_b$ = cost of varying quantities of aircraft type $b$, given $C_b^q$

$Q$ = cumulative production quantity.

Thus, (3) is the basic equation which expresses cost per aircraft as a function of performance and physical characteristics at some point on a cost-quantity curve (say, at cumulative output quantity 100). Then an appropriate cost-quantity function is fitted through this point to express aircraft cost as a function of cumulative quantity.[10]

From this general description the reader will no doubt get the impression that the cost of the total aircraft is estimated as an entity. This is usually not the case. Generally speaking, the total aircraft is broken down into its major subsystems: airframe, engines, avionics. Then each of these may be broken down further. For example, airframe may be segregated into functional categories like manufacturing labor cost, manufacturing materials cost, tooling, engineering, and so on. In sum, the cost analysis task is disaggregated into numerous components, and appropriate estimating relationships are developed for each. Then these relationships

---

[9] Selection of a number for $q$ is, of course, somewhat arbitrary. However, it should be (1) large enough to avoid the abnormalities and irregularities characteristic of units fabricated early in the production run, and (2) not so large as to rule out inclusion of relevant historical cases in the data base used to derive the basic estimating equation.

[10] This is one of the simplest procedures. Other methods are more complex, but this need not concern us here.

are combined to get a cost-quantity estimating equation for the total aircraft (total flyaway production cost).

Suppose that this has been done for our B-x example, and that the end
result of the estimating relationship work is the cost-quantity curve shown
in Fig. 5.2.[11] (Line AB is the cost-quantity relationship for the total B-x
aircraft.) Let us now use this relationship to develop the estimate of
production cost for B-x aircraft for the category "Investment in Primary
Mission Equipment."

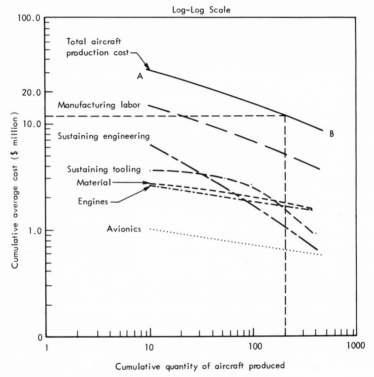

Fig. 5.2 – Cost-quantity relationship for the B-x

Aircraft cost is, of course, a function of total quantity produced. How
many will be needed, in total, for our B-x base case? From the B-x System
description information,[12] we know that the first 10 aircraft are required

---

[11] Here we are using a cumulative average cost-quantity curve. This means that the
point on the curve for cumulative output 100, for example, represents the total production cost for 100 units divided by 100. (Cost-quantity relationships are discussed in
some detail in the next chapter.)

[12] See items (1), (4), (5), and (9), p. 103.

for the development program, 150 aircraft (15 per wing for a 10-wing force) are required for the basic unit equipping (U.E.) of the B-x wings, 15 aircraft are needed for command support (10 percent of basic U.E.), and a certain number of vehicles must be procured as replacement aircraft for the expected peacetime attrition over a 5-year period. We must make an estimate of this last quantity.

Suppose that the cost analysts have examined the attrition rate history of a number of past and current bomber aircraft, and that the result is the estimating relationship portrayed in Fig. 5.3. Here, aircraft lost because of peacetime attrition is plotted as a function of total system flying hours. From the data contained in the B-x system description information, we can calculate the total system flying hours for the base case: 515,000.[13] Using

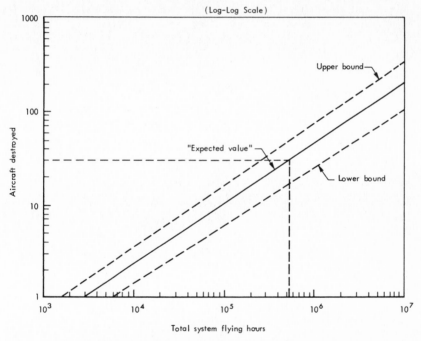

Fig. 5.3 – Bomber aircraft attrition vs. flying hours

---

[13] The B-x operational concept calls for 7 aircraft in each wing to be on *continuous* ground alert. The ground alert duty for each crew is assumed to be 130 hours per month, and the flying time in the B-x for each crew is specified to be 22 hours per month.

The amount of aircraft time that must be spent on ground alert duty is:

$$\frac{24 \text{ hr} \times 365 \text{ days} \times 7 \text{ aircraft}}{12 \text{ mo}} = 5,110 \text{ hr/mo}$$

the "expected value" curve in Fig. 5.3,[14] the estimated number of B-x aircraft to be procured for attrition is about 32.

We can now add up the number of B-x aircraft required for the total system:

| | |
|---|---|
| 1. R & D aircraft | 10 |
| 2. U.E. aircraft (15 × 10 wings) | 150 |
| 3. Command support (10% of U.E.) | 15 |
| 4. Replacement (5-year operation) | 32 |
| Total | 207 |

The 165 aircraft shown as items (2) and (3) are the ones pertaining to the category in the input structure that we are interested in here – the investment in primary mission equipment for the initial operational inventory. However, we have to consider items (1) and (4) in order to achieve the desired result.[15] Here is an example of a case where several categories in the input structure have to be considered simultaneously.

Returning now to curve AB in Fig. 5.2, we see that:

(1) Cumulative average cost through unit 207 = $11.3 million.
(2) Cumulative average cost through unit 10 = $30.7 million.
(3) Total cost of 207 units is 207 × $11.3 million = $2339.1 million.
(4) Total cost of the first 10 units is 10 × $30.7 = $307.0 million.

The difference between (3) and (4) gives us the total cost of units 11 through 207: $2032.1 million. Thus, the average cost of these 197 aircraft (that is, the 165 we are interested in plus the 32 aircraft estimated for replacement) is:

$$\frac{\$2032.1 \text{ million}}{197 \text{ aircraft}} = \$10.3 \text{ million per aircraft.}$$

---

for each wing of B-x's. Dividing this figure by the 130 hours per month that each crew is assumed to spend on ground alert gives us the number of crews per wing: 5,110/130 = 39 (rounded). Since each crew is assumed to fly 22 hours per month in the B-x, the flying schedule for each wing is:

22 hr/mo × 39 crews = 858 hr/mo.

The total of flying hours for the 10-wing B-x force for 5 years, then, is:

858 hr/mo × 60 mo × 10 wings = 515,000 (rounded).

[14] In order to keep this illustration simple, we shall use "expected value" numbers throughout the example.

[15] The 10 R & D aircraft pertain to the category in the input structure called "Flight Test Vehicle Production." The 32 replacement aircraft pertain to "PME Replacement" under operating costs. (See Table 5.2.)

Finally, then, the investment cost of the B-x aircraft procured for the initial inventory of primary mission equipment for a 10-wing force is:

$$(150 + 15 \text{ aircraft})(\$10.3 \text{ million}) = \$1699.5 \text{ million}.$$

### Primary Mission Equipment Maintenance

As a final example, let us consider a category under the operating cost heading: "Primary Mission Equipment Maintenance."

One way to estimate the maintenance cost for proposed future manned aircraft systems is to use generalized estimating relationships. These may be derived from an analysis of historical data and information on equipments similar to the ones being considered for the future. The objective is to try to develop relationships which express maintenance cost as a function of cost-generating variables such as equipment physical or performance characteristics, activity rate, and the like.

Suppose that in the case of the B-x example the cost analysts have made a careful examination of base and depot maintenance data for past and current bomber aircraft systems and that the following relationship is deemed appropriate for use in estimating maintenance cost for the B-x:[16]

$$C_m = 46.34 + 0.0556X_1 + 0.0824X_2,$$

where

$C_m$ = maintenance (base + depot) cost per flying hour (in dollars)
$X_1$ = level-off production cost of the aircraft in thousands of dollars[17]
$X_2$ = bomber aircraft maximum speed (at altitude) in knots.

To determine the value of $X_1$ to use for the B-x, we take the cumulative average production cost curve AB in Fig. 5.2 and plot it on an arithmetic grid. The result is portrayed in Fig. 5.4. From this it would appear that cumulative output 1,000 is a reasonably good point to pick for the "level-off" cost. We therefore shall use \$6.3 million for the value of $X_1$ for the B-x.

From the B-x system description (see Table 5.1), the maximum speed at altitude for the B-x is 1,260 knots. This is the value of $X_2$.

---

[16] Here we shall not discuss the mechanics of deriving estimating relationships. This subject is taken up in the next chapter.
[17] "Level-off cost" is defined in this case as the point on the cumulative average cost quantity curve (plotted on arithmetic grids) where aircraft cost becomes essentially horizontal to the quantity axis.

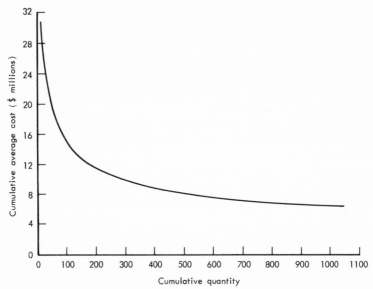

Fig. 5.4 – Cost-quantity relationship for the B-x plotted on arithmetic grid

Substituting $X_1 = \$6,300$ and $X_2 = 1,260$ in the maintenance cost estimating relationship, we have:

$$C_m = 46.34 + 0.0556(6300) + 0.0824(1260)$$
$$= 46.34 + 350.28 + 103.82$$
$$= 500.44.$$

Thus, we have an estimate of about $500 per flying hour for the maintenance cost of the B-x. The total B-x system flying hours for a 5-year period were computed previously as 515,000 (see footnote 13, page 109). The maintenance cost for the total system can therefore be estimated to be:

($500 per flying hr)(515,000 hr) = $257.5 million.

### Total System Cost for the B-x

We have presented simplified illustrations of how costs might be estimated for three categories in the input structure for the B-x. Costs for other categories would be generated in a similar manner.

Suppose that the cost analysts have done this and that the results for the base case are as shown in Table 5.3. Undoubtedly these results would not be very useful to the systems analysts. The base case (10-wing force) is a "benchmark" point estimate; as such, it is merely the beginning of the cost analysis effort.

TABLE 5.3

**Summary of costs for the B-x System**

(Base Case)

|  | Percent of Total | Cost (In $ Millions) | Percent of Grand Total |
|---|---|---|---|
| *Research and Development* | | | |
| Design and Development .. .. | 60.7 | 824.0 | |
| System Test .. .. .. .. | 39.3 | 534.0 | |
| Total .. .. .. .. | 100.0 | 1358.0 | 24.4 |
| *Initial Investment (10 Wings)* | | | |
| Facilities .. .. .. .. | 1.1 | 23.0 | |
| Primary Mission Equipment (PME) | 77.5 | 1699.5 | |
| Unit Support Aircraft .. .. | — | 0.0 | |
| Aerospace Ground Equipment (AGE) .. .. .. .. | 5.4 | 119.0 | |
| Other Equipment .. .. .. | — | 0.0 | |
| Stocks .. .. .. .. | 0.1 | 2.0 | |
| Spares .. .. .. .. | 15.5 | 339.9 | |
| Personnel Training .. .. | 0.1 | 1.2 | |
| Initial Travel .. .. .. | — | 0.1 | |
| Initial Transportation .. .. | 0.3 | 6.9 | |
| Total .. .. .. .. | 100.0 | 2191.6 | 39.3 |
| *Operation (10 Wings, 5 Years)* | | | |
| Facilities Replacement and Maintenance .. .. .. | 12.4 | 250.5 | |
| PME Replacement .. .. .. | 16.3 | 329.6 | |
| PME Maintenance .. .. .. | 12.7 | 257.5 | |
| PME Fuel, Oil, and Lubricants (FOL) .. .. .. .. | 6.7 | 136.5 | |
| Unit Support Aircraft Maintenance and FOL .. .. .. .. | 0.6 | 13.1 | |
| AGE R & M .. .. .. | 5.6 | 112.5 | |
| Personnel Pay and Allowances .. | 37.3 | 755.0 | |
| Personnel Replacement Training .. | 5.4 | 110.0 | |
| Annual Travel .. .. .. | 0.1 | 2.9 | |
| Annual Transportation .. .. | 0.1 | 2.2 | |
| Annual Services .. .. .. | 2.8 | 56.0 | |
| Total .. .. .. .. | 100.0 | 2025.8 | 36.3 |
| Grand Total .. .. .. | | 5575.4 | 100.0 |

The next step is very likely to be to calculate the system costs for several force sizes, so that a plot like that shown in Fig. 5.5 may be developed. Notice that in Fig. 5.5 total system cost is increasing at a decreasing rate as the force size expands; that is, marginal cost with respect to number of wings is declining.

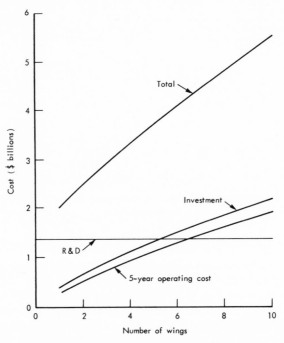

Fig. 5.5 – B-x system cost as function of force size

Another thing that might be done is to examine the sensitivity of total B-x system cost to possible errors in the input data. Suppose, for example, that there are significant uncertainties about some of the estimating relationships used to derive estimates of the primary mission equipment (PME) costs for the B-x system. What would be the impact on total system cost if the estimating error were 25 per cent? Or 50 per cent? The results of the sensitivity analysis portrayed in Fig. 5.6 indicate that a 25 percent error in PME cost would change total system cost by about 7.5 percent, while a 50 percent error would result in a change of 15 percent in system cost.

Many other types of analyses may be done, depending upon the nature of the systems analysis study that the cost analysis effort is supporting.

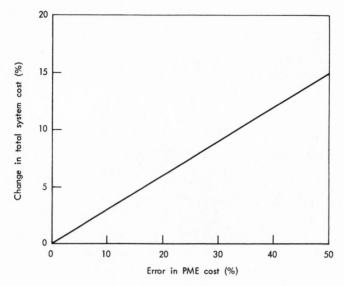

Fig. 5.6 – Effect on total system cost of estimating errors in B-x primary mission equipment cost

Major equipment characteristics, system operational concepts, and so on, can be varied to evaluate their system cost implications.

An example of a cost sensitivity analysis pertaining to operational concepts is given in Fig. 5.7. Here, the limits of operation of the B-x system are defined in terms of ground alert and flying time, along with the system operating cost per wing for various operating configurations. Notice that the operating costs turn out to be heavily dependent upon the flying schedule, and that they are affected to only a small degree by the addition of ground alert duty.

The line AB represents the boundary for "minimum system operations," where the only flying done is for minimum crew training. The line BC represents the boundary for "maximum use" situations, where the total available aircraft time is completely consumed by flying duty, ground alert, and maintenance. Between the upper and lower boundaries lie other possible operational configurations. Costs for any of these may be found from the plot within the shaded area.

**Further Comments on Input Structures**
In the B-x example the use of one form of input structure was illustrated (see Tables 5.2 and 5.3). This represents a specific application of a more

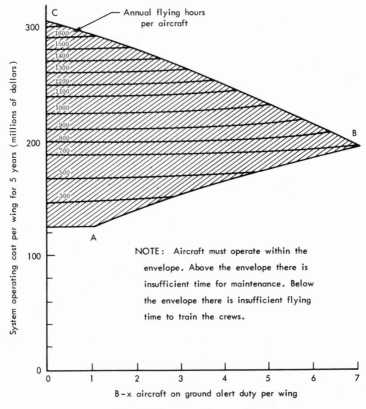

Fig. 5.7 – B-x operating envelope

general format (see Table 5.4) which is applicable to a wide variety of output-oriented entities of military capability, including ground forces and Navy task forces.[18]

Alternative forms of input structure might be used, depending upon the specific requirements of the analytical problem at hand and the preferences of the decisionmakers for whom the work is being done. For example, in some cases the Department of Defense's conventional budget categories (or some variant thereof) are used as a basis for the input structure. One such possibility is illustrated in Table 5.5.

Nothing very definitive can be said regarding what the specific detail of

[18] See Norman V. Breckner and Joseph W. Noah, "Costing of Systems," Chapter 3 in Stephen Enke (ed.), *Defense Management* (Englewood Cliffs, N.J.: Prentice-Hall, Inc., 1967), pp. 48–50.

TABLE 5.4

**Example of One Form of Generalized Input Structure**

*Research and Development*
Preliminary design and engineering
Fabrication of test equipment
Test operations
Miscellaneous

*Investment*
Facilities (installations)
Equipment:
  Primary mission
  Support
  Other
Stocks:
  Initial inventories of supplies (e.g., fuels)
  Initial inventories of equipment spares and spare parts
  Initial training
Miscellaneous:
  Initial transportation
  Initial travel
  Intermediate and support major command investment[a]
  Other

*Operating Cost*
Equipment and facilities replacement:
  Primary mission equipment
  Support equipment
  Other equipment
  Facilities
Maintenance:
  Primary mission equipment
  Support equipment
  Other equipment
  Facilities
Personnel pay and allowances
Replacement training
Fuels, lubricants, and propellants
  Primary mission equipment
  Other
Miscellaneous:
  Transportation
  Travel
  Intermediate and support major command operating costs[a]
  Other

[a] These categories usually cannot be assigned values in the case of individual systems.

the input structure should be. It is difficult, for example, to argue which of the two structures shown in Tables 5.4 and 5.5 is to be preferred. The

TABLE 5.5

**Example of an Input Structure Based on
Department of Defense Conventional Budget Categories**[a]

*Research and Development*
  Military construction
  Research, development, test, and evaluation (RDT & E)

*Investment*
  Military construction
  Procurement
  Military personnel[b]
  Operations and maintenance[b]
  Other

*Operating Cost*
  Procurement[c]
  Military personnel
  Operations and maintenance
  Other

[a] Shown here at the highest level of aggregation. Each category has a substructure beneath it.
[b] These items are primarily operating cost categories. However, certain personnel and operations and maintenance costs show up under investment when they are incurred in the process of building up *initial* capabilities, and hence may be thought of as being "capitalized" operating costs. Initial training is an example of an activity where this occurs.
[c] Includes replacement-type procurements only.

answer depends significantly on the nature of the analytical problem in any particular case. The level of specific detail may not be so important, provided that the resulting input structure is complete, contains categories that have been carefully defined, and is related in some fashion to the format in which basic data (past, current, and near future) are available.[19]

These requirements of a useful input structure are important, since they must be reasonably well fulfilled in order to facilitate the development of estimating relationships for the various categories or subcategories in the structure.

Estimating relationships form the heart of a military cost analysis capability. They are essentially "input-output" devices relating various categories of cost to key cost-generating variables such as performance characteristics of major equipment. This is such an important subject that we shall devote the next chapter to it.

[19] The relationship between data formats and input structures need not necessarily be direct in all cases; in fact, it usually cannot be.

## Summary

The main points contained in this chapter may be summarized as follows:

1. While the results of military cost analyses must be focused on output-oriented packages of military capabilities (for example, weapon systems), the cost analyst must concentrate on the input side in order to obtain final results.

2. Several major elements have to be present on the input side:
   a. A well-defined input structure.
   b. A list containing system description information and data – major equipment characteristics, facts about the operational concept, and so on.
   c. An estimating procedure (including, for example, estimating relationships) for each category and subcategory in the input structure.
   d. A set of subprocedures or submodels (a manpower requirements model, for example) which generate inputs for use in the estimating relationships for many of the categories in the input structure.

3. While the specific detail of the input structure can vary considerably, three major characteristics are important:

   a. The categories must be exhaustive and mutually exclusive.
   b. The categories in the structure must be carefully defined.
   c. The categories must relate in some fashion to the format of existing data and information systems.

### Suggested Supplementary Readings

1. Department of Defense, *Cost Information Reports* (*CIR*) *for Aircraft, Missile, and Space Systems*, Budget Bureau No. 22–R260, April 21, 1966.
2. W. E. Mooz, "The B-x: A Hypothetical Bomber Cost Study," Chap. 9 in E. S. Quade and W. I. Boucher (eds.), *Systems Analysis and Policy Planning: Applications in Defense* (New York: American Elsevier Publishing Co., Inc., 1968).

# Chapter 6

# ESTIMATING RELATIONSHIPS

## Introduction

Estimating relationships are a vital part of the cost analyst's kit of tools. The discussion of the "input side" in Chapter 5 indicated their key role in the estimating procedures for each category and subcategory in the input structure, and illustrated their use in examples for three input categories. In effect, estimating relationships are "transformation devices" which permit cost analysts to go from basic inputs (for example, descriptive information for some future weapon system or other type of program element) to estimates of the cost of output-oriented packages of military capability.

In discussing the very important subject of estimating relationships, it is imperative that certain fundamental points about their derivation and use be clearly explained. The main purpose of this chapter is to deal with these points in some depth. Perhaps the groundwork for such a discussion can best be established by using a simple illustration from the realm of nonmilitary affairs.

Suppose that Mr. A runs a small plant which manufactures a simple piece of equipment (call it X). Suppose further that for some time he has been building X in three sizes: small, medium, and large, with gross weights of 2, 4, and 8 pounds, respectively. Since the beginning, the plant has been essentially constant in size, and has been operated at about the same rate of output.

Until now Mr. A has not paid very close attention to his formal cost accounting records; but from casual observation and from "experience" it has seemed to him that the manufacturing cost (in dollars) of producing X has tended to be about twice the weight (in pounds) of X. He therefore has thought that a reasonably good "rule-of-thumb" estimating relationship is about $2 per pound.

Subsequently, inquiries from several of Mr. A's customers seemed to indicate that a demand was developing for a scaled-up version of product X which might weigh as much as 18 or 20 pounds. He began to consider seriously the possibility of altering his plant to meet this potential demand. Several questions came to mind. Would the manufacturing cost of the scaled-up version of X be $2 per pound? Would the fact that he might have to increase the size of his plant and operate at a different rate of output change costs significantly? As a starting point, he decided to do a much more careful analysis of his past and present production costs than had ever been done before.

Mr. A went to his historical cost accounting records and began to take samples of the past manufacturing costs of the 2, 4, and 8 pound versions of product X. He soon discovered, however, that at certain times in the past there had been changes in raw material prices and changes in certain of the pay rates for his employees. Some changes had also been made in the accounting system which resulted in redefinition of the content of some of the accounts used to accumulate manufacturing costs. To ensure consistency and comparability in the data base to be used in his analysis, Mr. A decided to normalize the data with respect to price level changes,[1] and to make certain adjustments to correct for the differences in account definition.

Having satisfied himself that he had a reasonably consistent set of basic data from the historical records, he then made the plot shown in Fig. 6.1.

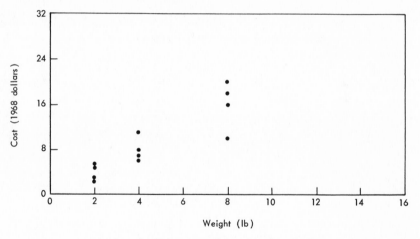

Fig. 6.1 – Cost of product X as a function of weight

This shows that the manufacturing cost of product X is in fact a function of weight, but with considerable variability. What is the average relationship? Mr. A took the mean value for each of his three cases and connected

---

[1] To do this he used an appropriate price index to "deflate" the historical data and to express them in terms of constant 1968 dollars. [For a discussion of price deflation, see William A. Spurr and Charles P. Bonini, *Statistical Analysis for Business Decisions* (Homewood, Ill.: Richard D. Irwin, Inc., 1967), pp. 471–473.]

these points with a line as shown in Fig. 6.2. This seems to indicate that, on the average, over the weight range 2 to 8 pounds, Mr. A's original rule-of-thumb relationship of $2 per pound is about right.

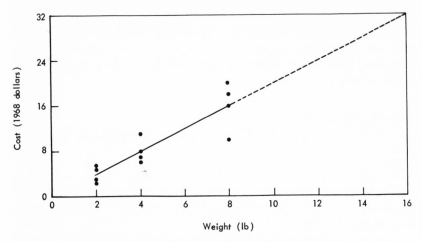

Fig. 6.2 – Cost of product X as a function of weight

But what about projecting considerably beyond the experience base – out to weights of 16 or 18 pounds, for example? Could we expect that the $2 per pound relationship would hold reasonably well? As Mr. A pondered this question, these considerations went through his mind:

1. He recalled that a friend, who is a cost engineer for an aircraft company, had said that usually the cost per pound of airframe weight for large aircraft tends to be lower than for smaller aircraft. Could there be a similar "scaling" relationship involved in the production of product X, particularly in going to weights in the neighborhood of 20 pounds?

2. From a course in the principles of economics taken a number of years ago, Mr. A remembered that a firm's unit costs can vary considerably as the rate of output changes or the scale of the plant is altered. Since both of these things might happen in the future for Mr. A's plant, he wondered whether the $2 per pound relationship portrayed in Fig. 6.2, in which both rate of output and plant size are held essentially constant, would continue to hold.

3. Examining Fig. 6.2 again, Mr. A was impressed with the variability of the costs around the average relationship. Since he was very careful in assembling his data base and in making the appropriate adjustments to ensure consistency, he thought it unlikely that much of the variability

could be accounted for by gross errors in the basic data. He concluded that an explanatory variable (or variables) in addition to weight was having some influence on cost.

For these three reasons, and others, Mr. A concluded that while his rule-of-thumb of $2 per pound might be appropriate for *some* purposes over the 2 to 8 pound weight range, it certainly could not be assumed to hold for much higher weight ranges or for different rate-of-output or plant-size situations. He therefore decided he would have to explore the problem further.

### Some Fundamental Points

At this point we can leave our example, for it has already served the purpose of providing a basis for outlining the fundamental points about estimating relationships that we wish to make in this chapter:

1. Estimating relationships are analytic devices which relate various categories of cost (either in dollars or physical units) to cost-generating or explanatory variables.

2. They may take numerous forms, ranging from informal rules of thumb or simple analogies to formal mathematical functions derived from statistical analyses of empirical data.

3. A most important step in the derivation of estimating relationships is to assemble and refine the data that constitute the empirical basis of the relationship to be developed. Typically, the raw data are at least partially in the wrong format for analytical purposes, have various irregularities and inconsistencies, and the like. Adjustments, therefore, almost always have to be made to ensure a reasonably consistent and comparable data base. No degree of sophistication in the use of advanced mathematical statistics can compensate very much for a seriously deficient data base.

4. Given the data base, any of a wide variety of techniques may be used to derive appropriate estimating relationships. The range extends all the way from unaided judgment and simple graphical procedures through complex statistical techniques. Here, considerable judgment must be exercised. The particular method used is strongly related to the nature of the problem, and particularly to the nature of the data base. For example, it usually does not make sense to try to fit a complicated multivariate function to a data base having a very small sample size, since it is easy to run out of degrees of freedom in such cases.[2] Even with a relatively large

---

[2] In a statistical sense, the term "degrees of freedom" may be taken to mean the sample size minus the number of coefficients (parameters) in the estimating equation.

data base, one must avoid mechanically running large numbers of correlation analyses on the computer to determine that combination of explanatory variables which maximizes the correlation coefficient.[3] As we shall see later, high correlation coefficients, in and of themselves, do not necessarily ensure statistically significant relationships.

5. Care must also be exercised in the *use* of estimating relationships. The user must have a good understanding of the data base and the procedures used in deriving the estimating relationship.[4] Above all, he must exercise care in extrapolating beyond the range of experience (the sample) underlying the relationship. Scaling factors, for example, may have to be taken into account, especially when – as happens very often – we are estimating the costs of future equipments or activities which are different from those of the past, present, and near future.

## Types of Estimating Relationships

Estimating relationships can take on a wide range of possible forms. They may be classified in numerous ways: for example, informal vs. formal, continuous vs. discontinuous, mathematical vs. nonmathematical, linear vs. nonlinear, statistically derived vs. nonstatistically derived, and so on.

There seems to be no "best" (or even singularly "good") way of classifying the various types. This need not bother us here, however, since our objective is merely to point out to the reader that estimating relationships exist in many forms and that numerous possible types may be useful in practice.

In the following paragraphs we shall list and illustrate briefly several kinds of estimating relationships. The list is not complete, but it is fairly representative of the total spectrum of types.

### Simple Linear Forms

Estimating relationships do not have to be expressed in terms of complicated mathematical functions to be useful. In fact, a considerable number of relationships used in military cost analysis are of the form

$$C = \alpha \quad \text{(a constant)}, \tag{1}$$

or

$$C = \beta X \quad \text{(a linear homogeneous function).[5]} \tag{2}$$

---

[3] The correlation coefficient is a measure of the degree of relationship between the dependent variable and the explanatory variables. It ranges from zero (no correlation) to plus or minus unity (perfect correlation).

[4] This is particularly important when the user himself has not derived the relationship.

[5] Equation (2) is a special case of the linear form $C = \alpha + \beta X$, with $\alpha = 0$. When a linear function passes through the origin, it is said to be homogeneous.

The use of (2) is particularly prevalent. The numerical value of $\beta$ may be determined in a number of ways: by a simple averaging process, by using formal statistical regression analysis,[6] by policy considerations,[7] and the like.

Examples of cases where linear homogeneous estimating relationships have been used in the past are:

1. Personnel pay and allowances cost as a function of number of personnel.
2. Construction costs for a given type structure as a function of square feet.
3. Facilities maintenance cost as a function of facilities initial investment cost.

We should also point out that most rule-of-thumb estimating relationships are in effect linear homogeneous functions. In the example at the beginning of this chapter we presented an illustration of such a case. On the basis of experience, Mr. A felt that the manufacturing cost of fabricating product X was about $2 per pound, at least over the range of 2 to 8 pounds.

This rule-of-thumb statement may be formalized in the form of a linear homogeneous function. We can write, for example:

$$C = 2W, \tag{3}$$

where

$C$ = manufacturing cost of product X in 1968 dollars,
$W$ = weight of product X in pounds over the range $W = 2$ to 8.

While equation (3) is a formal statement, it is not an estimating relationship derived on the basis of a very formal analytical procedure – like a statistical least-squares curve-fitting method, for example.[8] However, an

[6] Regression analysis refers to the statistical measurement of the relationship between the dependent variable and explanatory variables, and to the determination of quantitative measures of the reliability of that relationship. (For example, see Spurr and Bonini, *op. cit.*, pp. 554, 563.)
[7] For example, a provisioning policy decision may be in effect which says that initial inventories of major equipment spares and spare parts are to be 20 percent of major equipment investment cost. If it is felt that this policy will hold for future equipments, then the estimating relationship for initial spares is $C_s = .2I_e$, where $C_s$ = cost of major equipment initial spares and spare parts and $I_e$ = initial investment cost of major equipment.
[8] For a discussion of the method of least squares, see Spurr and Bonini, *op. cit.*, pp. 558–561. In the case of a linear relationship between two variables, the least-squares method results in a "best fit" to the data in the sense that the sum of the squared deviations from the relationship is smaller than it would be for any other line.

estimating relationship need not necessarily be derived on the basis of formal statistical analysis to be useful, at least for some purposes.

Rules of thumb obtained from an expert's opinion may be useful provided that the expert has the necessary experience and judgment.[9] Similarly, the opinions of several experts may be sought, and the results averaged together to form a "collective opinion," rule-of-thumb relationship. Several promising experiments are now under way to test this procedure.[10]

Another frequently used simple linear form is the two-variate case in which the location coefficient is not equal to zero:

$$C = \alpha + \beta X. \tag{4}$$

We shall discuss this functional form in the context of a scatter diagram.

In two-dimensional cases, the use of scatter diagrams can be very useful in deriving estimating relationships. An example is portrayed in Fig. 6.3,

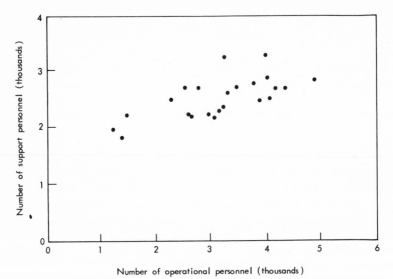

Number of operational personnel (thousands)

Fig. 6.3 – Support personnel versus operational personnel for weapon systems of type A

---

[9] The use of rules-of-thumb relationships obtained from expert opinion may be particularly useful in cases where the cost analyst does not have sufficient time to conduct a formal empirical investigation, or where expert opinion in certain technical areas is needed to help formulate initial hypotheses to be tested in subsequent formal statistical analyses.

[10] Most notably, the work of N. C. Dalkey and others at Rand on the Delphi technique. [See N. C. Dalkey, *Delphi*, Paper P-3704 (Santa Monica, Calif.: The Rand Corporation, October 1967).]

where number of support personnel is plotted as a function of number of operational personnel for a certain class of weapon systems. Visual inspection suggests that support personnel might well be estimated as a linear function of operational personnel. If we draw in a free-hand curve, the result may be something like that shown in Fig. 6.4.

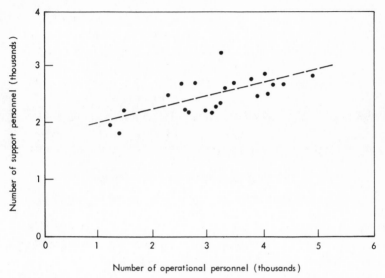

Number of operational personnel (thousands)

Fig. 6.4 – Support personnel versus operational personnel

More formal methods may, of course, be used; for example, mechanical curve-fitting techniques (like least squares) or normal linear regression analysis.[11] If the latter were applied to our sample contained in Fig. 6.3, the results would be like those portrayed in Fig. 6.5. Here, in addition to the regression equation $S_p = 1,793 + 0.25\ O_p$, certain statistical measures of uncertainty have been computed and taken into account. These help the user in forming judgments about the reliability of the estimating relationship.

### Step Functions
The types of estimating relationships discussed so far imply a continuous relationship between cost and the explanatory variable. This, however, need not be the case. Cost can be at a constant level over a certain range of

---

[11] See Spurr and Bonini, *op. cit.*, pp. 563–571. In a normal linear regression analysis, the distribution of the points above and below the regression line is assumed to follow a normal curve.

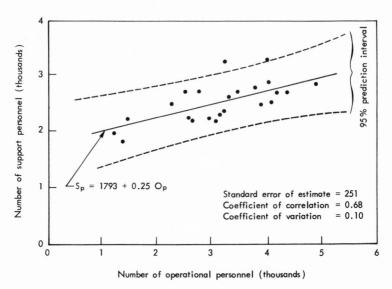

Fig. 6.5 – Support personnel ($S_p$) versus operational personnel ($O_p$)

the explanatory variable, then suddenly jump to a higher level at some point and remain constant for a time, then jump to another level, and so on. This kind of relationship is known as a "step function."

Step functions may be presented either in tabular form or in terms of a

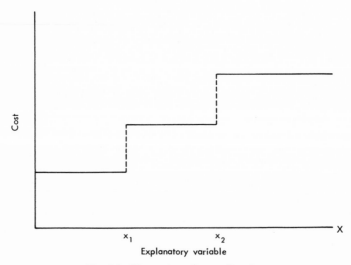

Fig. 6.6 – Illustration of a step function

graphical display. The latter is illustrated in Fig. 6.6. These types of functions can be especially useful in portraying the cost behavior of support activities which come into existence in "chunks" as, for example, the size of a combat force is increased.

### Multivariate Functions

Cost cannot always be explained adequately in terms of one explanatory variable. Very often, therefore, estimating relationships will take the form of multivariate functions (that is, estimating equations having more than one explanatory variable).

Examples of areas where multivariate estimating relationships have been developed in the past are:

1. Navy ship investment cost as a function of full load displacement, speed, and unit quantity of ships produced.
2. Navy ship maintenance cost as a function of full load displacement and type of power plant.
3. Army helicopter airframe cost as a function of helicopter speed and airframe unit weight (for a standardized quantity).
4. Phased array radar investment cost as a function of number of transmitting elements, average radiated power output (watts), number of receiving elements, number of dummy elements, and number of targets tracked.
5. Aircraft maintenance cost as a function of aircraft gross weight, speed, and activity rate (flying hours).

Some multivariate estimating relationships are linear in the explanatory variables. An example is the following:

$$C_a = 16 + 0.050X_1 + 0.082X_2, \tag{5}$$

where

$C_a =$ depot maintenance cost per flying hour (in 1968 dollars)[12] for aircraft of type $a$,

$X_1 =$ aircraft level-off production cost (in thousands of 1968 dollars),

$X_2 =$ aircraft combat speed (in knots).

In many instances, however, linear functions are not appropriate.[13] One nonlinear form that is often used is the exponential function:

---

[12] This means that the data base underlying the estimating relationship is to be "normalized" for price level changes, with 1968 taken as the base year.

[13] Linear functions may also be inappropriate for the two-dimensional case discussed previously. Examples of nonlinear forms involving one explanatory variable are: $Y = \alpha X^\beta$, and $Y = \alpha + \beta_1 X + \beta_2 X^2$.

$$Y = \alpha X_1^{\beta_1} X_2^{\beta_2} \ldots X_n^{\beta_n}. {}^{14} \tag{6}$$

This form is particularly useful in estimating the cost of major equipment. A specific example is the following:

$$T = 0.123(W^{0.84})(S^{1.07})(R^{0.40}), \tag{7}$$

where

$T$ = number of hours required to provide tooling for a production rate of $R$ aircraft airframes per month,
$W$ = aircraft gross takeoff weight in pounds,
$S$ = aircraft maximum speed in knots,
$R$ = production rate in airframes per month.

## The Data Problem

As indicated in the introduction to this chapter, one of the most vitally important steps in the derivation of estimating relationships is to assemble an appropriate data base. No amount of sophisticated statistical analysis can compensate much for gross inadequacies in the data base.

Since the data problem is fundamental, military cost analysts typically devote a considerable amount of their time to collecting data, to making adjustments in the raw data to help ensure consistency and comparability, and to providing for proper storage of information so that it may be retrieved rapidly when it is needed. In fact, of the total time involved in the process of developing estimating relationships, more effort is typically devoted to the assembly of a consistent data base than to anything else. With the appropriate information at hand, the analytical task of deriving estimating equations is often relatively easy, given the kit of analytical tools and powerful computational devices now available.

### Why Is There a Data Problem?

The reader may well wonder why the data problem is so severe. After all, the Department of Defense has been developing information systems and collecting a huge volume of data in numerous areas for many years. And contractors in the aerospace industry have been doing the same thing. How could there be a data problem?

---

[14] The parameters ($\alpha$ and the $\beta$'s) may be estimated by performing a logarithmic transformation on equation (6) and thus converting the problem to one of normal linear regression. Or, by using special techniques, the parameters in (6) may be estimated directly. See C. A. Graver and H. E. Boren, Jr., *Multivariate Logarithmic and Exponential Regression Models*, RM-4879-PR (Santa Monica, Calif.: The Rand Corporation, July 1967).

This is a legitimate question, which has several answers. Here, we shall try to select a few of the more important ones.

*Information in the Wrong Format.* Information systems in the Department of Defense and the aerospace industry have indeed generated a tremendous amount of data. In many instances, however, these data are not in an appropriate format to be very useful in a military cost analysis activity serving the long-range planning process.

The main reason for this is that these information systems were established primarily to serve the needs of managers of functional areas of operational activity (such as maintenance or supply), of managers responsible for fiscal integrity or fiduciary accounting requirements ("keeping hands out of the till"), of managers concerned with critical resource items across the board (for example, personnel), of budgeteers concerned with the conventional budget, and the like. In short, the orientation of a large number of past and existing information systems is toward the input side *per se*, with little or no provision for making meaningful translations reflecting impacts on what we have called output-oriented packages of military capability.[15]

*The "Matching Up" or Integration Problem.* Particularly when the objective is to derive estimating relationships, the analyst must not only collect historical *cost* data in the right format. He must also obtain information on quantities, physical and performance characteristics, activity rates, and other types of cost-generating variables – all of which must be matched specifically to the cost data points.

Sometimes this is difficult because information on the cost-generating variables must be extracted from different sets of records than those containing the cost data. And differing sets of records are often compiled on different principles involving lot size, time period covered, or the like.

*Differences in Definitions of Categories.* A different, though equally common, kind of "matching up" problem occurs when the definition of the content of categories in the input structures set up for the cost analysis fails to correspond to the definition of analogous categories in the existing data and information collection systems.

As we pointed out in Chapter 5 in discussing input structures, it is not possible to set up an input structure that will simultaneously meet the requirements of cost analyses in support of long-range planning and be in

[15] The suggestion is often made that the analyst who probes the data base at successively greater levels of detail will eventually find the kinds of identifications he needs. Sometimes this is true. On the other hand, he is likely to find that if an information system is structured in terms of, say, "object classes," then going into more detail simply yields greater amounts of information in the same terms (object classes).

complete harmony with existing data systems at any point in time. Differences in definition of certain categories in the input structure and their counterparts in the existing data base are therefore bound to be present and to produce difficulties for the cost analyst. He will often have to adjust the raw data to correct for these differences in definition.

*The Influence of Temporal Factors.* Historical data are, of course, generated over time. This means that numerous dynamic factors will influence the information being collected in a certain area. First of all, the information collection systems themselves have a habit of changing over time – for example, the appropriate definition of the content of various categories being used to accumulate the historical data may change as the system evolves. Similarly, in the case of financial data, price level changes will occur and be reflected in the information being collected over time.

In addition to these types of temporal considerations is the important fact that, for the most part, the Department of Defense deals with a rapidly changing environment, both in hardware and in organizational and operational concepts. Almost by definition this means that even with a near-perfect information collection system, only a relatively small sample of data can be generated for a given era or class of technology. In the equipment area, for example, the analyst is lucky if he can obtain 15 or 20 good data points for a certain class of hardware. He is more likely to have less than half that number.

By the nature of things, therefore, the analyst is all too often in the world of extremely small samples. As all good statisticians know, this poses real problems in our attempts to develop statistically sound relationships which will permit us to project forward to military capabilities in the distant future.

*Comparability Problems.* Implied in much of the previous discussion is the need for comparability among various case histories in a given data base. Comparability problems abound – some of them not yet mentioned. For example, the effort to collect data on a certain class of equipments from more than one Service typically gives rise to what might be called the "interservice comparability" problem. While several attempts at standardization have been made in recent years,[16] there are still significant differences (definitional and otherwise) in the systems used to collect information in the Army, Navy, and Air Force, or indeed even within a given Service. Moreover, we have differences in the accounting systems

---

[16] In the equipment area, the Department of Defense's new *Cost Information Reports (CIR) for Aircraft, Missile, and Space Systems* represents a serious attempt to deal with the comparability problem. It also attempts to correct other deficiencies: for example, the "matching up" problem referred to previously.

among the contractors serving the Department of Defense. All of this means that more often than not the cost analyst will find himself in a position of having to make adjustments to correct for noncomparabilities in the data base.

### Dealing with the Data Problem

Although the discussion of problems concerning the data base is by no means complete, it should convince the reader that there is such a thing as a data problem. The question now is: What can be done about it?

At first thought, one might be tempted to say: "If there is a data problem, let's solve it once and for all by establishing *the* information collection system to meet all our needs." Is such a thing feasible?

We think not, for several reasons. Some of the more important are the following:

1. Cost analysis problems in support of systems analyses typically vary considerably from one study to another. The requirements for estimating relationships – and hence data and information requirements – are not constant over time, or even for a given small interval of time. In short, the cost analyst who is working in support of the long-range planning process cannot specify his information needs "once and for all." Hence the impossibility of establishing a universal, all-purpose information system.

2. Even if something approaching such a system could be created, we would still have to worry about economics. Large information systems – especially those designed for complete enumerations – are very expensive. This poses a systems analysis problem in itself. Would the large incremental cost of a new "complete" information system be justified in terms of the benefits to be derived – particularly in the long-range planning context, where high precision in an absolute sense is usually not a prime requirement? The answer is probably "no."[17]

3. In addition, there is the problem of small samples, which arises from the fact that the Department of Defense has to deal with a rapidly changing technology. As indicated previously, this means that in many instances only a relatively small number of observations will be available for a certain era or class of technology. Here, even a near-perfect information system cannot increase the sample size.

Where does all this leave us? On the one hand, a strong argument has been advanced for the importance of an appropriate data base. On the other hand, trying to solve the problem once and for all does not seem feasible, at least in a general sense. Fortunately, however, there are many

---

[17] As will be pointed out later, there are alternatives to complete enumerations on a recurring basis.

reasonable alternatives to establishing fully comprehensive information systems. Let us consider some of them.

*Use of Ad Hoc Sample Surveys.* One possibility that could be given more attention than it has received in the past is sampling, or something akin to sampling. This can be an inexpensive way of obtaining information that may be very useful in deriving estimating relationships for use in long-range planning studies.

Suppose, for example, that the cost analyst is faced with the problem of developing output-oriented estimating relationships for some functional area like maintenance or supply. Suppose further that the existing cost accounting systems accumulate historical cost data in categories such as labor, material, and overhead, and that no provision is made for identifying these costs with end-product packages of military capability (for example, weapon systems). Conceivably one solution would be to overhaul the entire formal accounting system to accumulate historical cost data in the desired form. This, however, could be very expensive, and considerable time would have to elapse to permit design, test, and implementation of the new accounting system.

An alternative would be to select a few representative cost categories in the current format and to establish for perhaps a month or two a "ticketing" system to accumulate costs in terms of weapon systems. (Such an arrangement would be supplementary to – and hence would not disturb – the existing formal accounting system.) This approach has been used on numerous occasions in the past, and the results have been good – at least for the purpose of deriving estimating relationships for long-range planning.[18] In any event, sampling procedures seem worthy of consideration as an alternative to establishing new complete enumeration systems across the board.

*Techniques for Assisting in Handling the Small Sample Problem.* We have indicated that the military cost analyst very often finds himself confronted with small samples. Can anything be done to help ease the problems that attend this fact? Let us consider two possibilities.

---

[18] The author has conducted simple tests in several instances where complete enumerations were available. The procedure was as follows: Take the complete enumeration as a data base and, using regression analysis, derive an estimating relationship – say $C = \hat{\alpha} + \hat{\beta}X$. Then take random samples of 15 or 20 observations from the complete enumeration and derive similar relationships on the basis of these sample data bases. Then test the resulting estimates of $\alpha$ and $\beta$ against the values obtained from the complete enumeration to see if there is a significant difference. In about 90 percent of the cases examined, no significant difference existed (at the 0.05 level) between estimates of the regression coefficients obtained from the small samples and those obtained by using the complete enumeration as a data base.

The first is extremely simple, but it can help a great deal. Particularly in deriving estimating relationships for use in long-range planning studies, the cost analyst should not necessarily restrict himself to the *historical* record in assembling his data base. In many cases he should seriously consider increasing the number of observations by including appropriate data points based on estimates made by experts for the very near-term future, or by taking advantage of certain kinds of qualitative information.

Suppose, for example, that we have only four data points available from the historical record. (See Fig. 6.7.) Suppose further that the analyst must

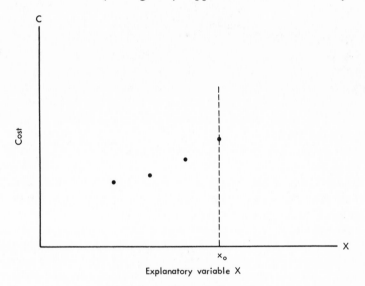

Fig. 6.7 – Small sample illustration

derive an estimating relationship which will help him project beyond the range of the historical sample (beyond the value $X_0$ of the explanatory variable). On the basis of the four data points alone, it is not very clear what kind of relationship between $C$ and $X$ should be postulated. For example, the curves AB and CD in Fig. 6.8 would seem about equally plausible. Here is a case where the cost analyst should probe further and attempt to get some sort of additional information (either quantitative or qualitative) to help him make an informed judgment. After further exploration, for example, he might be able to find two more data points in the form of *estimates* for the near future made by reputable experts in the field under consideration. If the methods used to make these estimates seemed trustworthy, the cost analyst might decide to use them to supple-

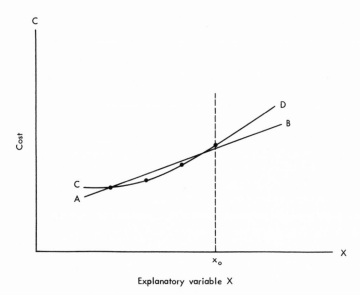

Fig. 6.8 – Small sample illustration: Some plausible estimating relationships

ment his historical data base, with results like those shown in Fig. 6.9, which suggests the appropriateness of a linear hypothesis as a basis for projecting out to the vicinity of $x_1$.

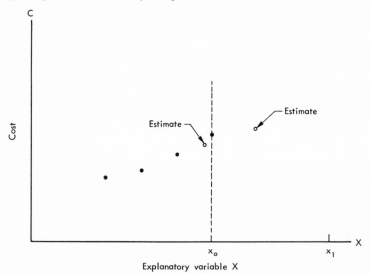

Fig. 6.9 – Supplementing the historical data base

Let us assume, however, that our cost analyst wants still further substantiation – if possible. Recalling that in his initial search for an appropriate explanatory variable he had talked to engineers who were experts in designing the type of system he is investigating, he decides to consult with them again in the hope of obtaining some other evidence to help him establish the linear hypothesis. This discussion – though largely qualitative – is persuasive; he thus obtains further reason to believe that projections for large values of the explanatory variable $X$ should be made on the basis of a linear relationship between $C$ and $X$.

This simple example illustrates two points about how one can deal with very small samples: (1) Under certain conditions the size of the sample can be increased by judiciously using estimates for the near future to supplement the historical data base; (2) It may be possible to use qualitative information to assist in deciding what kind of estimating relationship is most appropriate.

As another example, let us consider a case where the sample is very small and we seek to gain additional information by lowering the level of aggregation one notch.

In analyzing the cost of major equipment, cost-quantity relationships are very important. As the cumulative number of units increases, unit cost usually declines.[19] Suppose that we are interested in a certain type of airframe (call it X) and that we have only three data points. (The log-log plot of the data base is shown in Fig. 6.10.) No other points are available

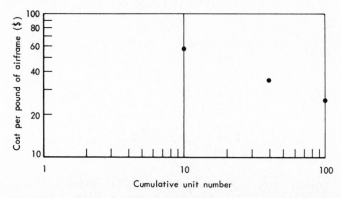

Fig. 6.10 – Airframe $X$: dollars per pound vs. cumulative unit number

[19] For a thorough treatment of cost-quantity relationships, see Harold Asher, *Cost-Quantity Relationships in the Airframe Industry*, R-291 (Santa Monica, Calif.: The Rand Corporation, 1956).

for this airframe, not even through the rather primitive techniques we have just described. But assume that the cost analysis is part of a systems analysis study in which large numbers of airframe X – 1,000 or more – are being considered. Should the analyst simply assume a log-linear relationship, connect his three data points, and extend the line out to cumulative outputs of 1,000 or more? Most probably not. An experienced analyst knows all too well the dangers of mechanical extrapolation, for reasons involving scaling factors and other considerations as well.

Since the sample size cannot be increased, what can be done? One possibility is to see if additional information can be obtained by dis-aggregating. Suppose that our cost analyst goes back to the original data source and finds that additional detail is in fact available – perhaps a

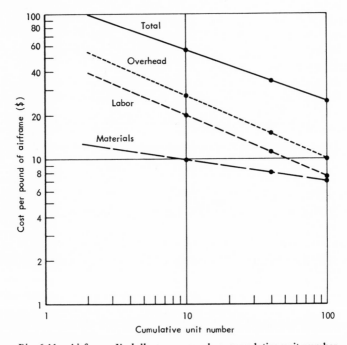

Fig. 6.11 – Airframe $X$: dollars per pound vs. cumulative unit number

breakdown of the total airframe in terms of labor, materials and overhead. A plot of such data is shown in Fig. 6.11. This slight addition to the data base immediately provides useful insights into the projection problem. If we assume log-linear relationships for the components (labor, material, and overhead),[20] it is obvious that on the basis of the available information the total curve cannot be log-linear when projected out to large cumulative unit numbers because the materials curve has a significantly different slope than the labor and overhead curves.[21]

If the curves in Fig. 6.11 are extrapolated out to cumulative unit number 1,000, as in Fig. 6.12, and their influence is taken into account, the total

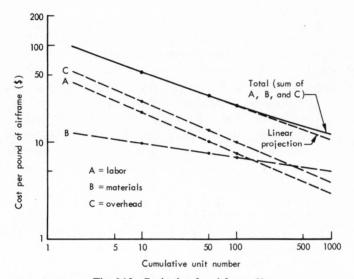

Fig. 6.12 – Projection for airframe $X$

cost curve assumes the shape indicated. Here it is clear that the cost analyst has benefited from the information obtained by disaggregating one level in the data base. Merely extrapolating out to cumulative output 1,000 on the basis of the three original data points no longer seems appropriate. The difference between the two curves increases still further for cumulative unit numbers beyond 1,000.[22]

Although going into slightly more detail can thus help in cases involving

---

[20] In general this is not necessarily a good assumption; but we shall use it here to keep the example simple. The argument is even stronger if the component curves are assumed to be convex on logarithmic grids.

[21] If the component curves are linear but nonparallel, the total curve (sum of the components) must be convex on logarithmic grids and must approach as a limit the flattest of the component curves. (See Asher, *op. cit.*, pp. 70–72.)

[22] In the study that provides the basis for this example, the difference was only about $1.50 per pound at cumulative unit number 1,000. At cumulative output 5,000, however, the difference between the linear projection and the nonlinear total curve was about $3 per pound.

very small samples, it would be a mistake to generalize from our example and conclude that in all (or even most) instances the assembly of a more and more detailed data base will, in itself, make for better understanding of the problem.

*The Use of Experiments to Broaden the Data Base.* Sometimes the cost analyst finds that there is simply a void in the existing data base. This is likely to be the case when the planners are considering new proposals for distant future military capabilities that require major equipments or operational concepts markedly different from those of the past and the present.

In some instances existing estimating relationships can be used to conduct simulations which will furnish a first approximation to the cost of such capabilities. In other instances, however, the cost analyst cannot assume that the structural parameters in the existing set of estimating relationships are appropriate for the new military systems being considered. He must therefore develop new relationships, or devise techniques for adjusting the present ones. But how does he do this if the necessary data base does not yet exist? One possibility is to see if any relevant experiments are being conducted pertaining to the subject at hand, and if not, to try to initiate such an experiment. Let us consider two examples.

A number of years ago, military cost analysts were confronted with the task of estimating the cost of the first generation of proposed stainless-steel airframes for the mid-1960s. These proposals usually required rather extensive use of stainless-steel honeycomb paneling, the production of which would involve a significant advance in the manufacturing state of the art. The historical data base at that time was, of course, confined almost entirely to the experience accumulated in producing aluminum airframes, and little was known about the fabrication costs of stainless-steel honeycomb panels – particularly, large panels.

In talking to the aerospace contractors who were wanting to build stainless-steel airframe structures, the cost analysts found that one of them was conducting a rather elaborate experiment. A special shop had been set up to explore a variety of manufacturing operations on aluminum, stainless-steel, and titanium structures. Taking aluminum as the base case, the objective of the experiment was to determine the probable incremental labor costs involved in working the other two materials for a representative sample of various types of manufacturing operations. Armed with data from the experiment, the cost analysts were then in a position to devise techniques for adjusting the historical data base (aluminum experience) so that it would be more appropriate for dealing with the stainless-steel airframe problem.

In visits to still other contractors' plants, the cost analysts found that several were experimenting with the construction of stainless-steel honey-comb paneling. In sessions with the people conducting these operations the analysts obtained a wealth of information (both quantitative and qualitative) about how honeycomb cost might vary with the size and shape of the core cell, the shape and size of the panel, the number of panel inserts, and the like. As a result, they were able to improve considerably their ability to estimate the cost of stainless-steel airframes. The expenditure of time and travel budget on field work paid off well.

As another example, let us consider a problem in estimating the cost of an operational concept – specifically, the cost of alert capabilities for weapon systems in peacetime. Several years ago, force planners were considering the possibility of placing certain future weapon systems on much higher degrees of peacetime alert than was then the case in the operational forces. Naturally they wanted the cost analysts to estimate the incremental costs associated with varying levels of alert posture. They soon found that the existing formal data base did not contain much information that would be very helpful in devising estimating relationships for this problem.

The analysts decided to do some survey and field work. They found that one of the military services was about to launch a field exercise (experimental test) involving an existing weapon system to see what levels of alert might be feasible in an operational sense. At that time there was no plan to observe and record systematically what the incremental resource requirements were for the various degrees of alert called for in the test. The cost analysts suggested to the exercise director that this might be a good idea. He agreed and told the cost analysts to design and conduct that part of the experiment. They did so, and as a result obtained a wealth of quantitative and qualitative data that helped a great deal in solving their problem. Again, the investment in field work paid off. The then existing historical data base was supplemented substantially.

*Making Adjustments to the Raw Data Base.* To be usable to the cost analyst, data must be consistent and comparable. Yet often they are neither. Hence, before estimating relationships can be derived, the raw data have to be adjusted for such things as price level changes, definitional differences, production quantity differences, and the like.

This book is not the appropriate place for a detailed discussion of techniques used in making adjustments to the data base. However, we do want to make a few remarks about the problem, and at the same time to stress the fundamental importance of developing a reasonably consistent data base as the necessary first step in the derivation of estimating relationships.

Usually, in dealing with the data adjustment problem no deep conceptual issues are involved, and the procedures used are fairly straightforward, though often time-consuming. For example, in normalizing the data base for price level changes, the analyst must seek out (or construct) the appropriate price indexes,[23] adjust them to the desired base year, and then "deflate" the observations in the data base.[24] The result is that the data points are expressed in terms of base year "constant" dollars.

Similarly, adjustments for definitional differences are usually simple in principle, although somewhat tedious in practice. The following is an illustration of what might be expected: a cost analyst may be examining data in the hardware area from a sample of some 15 or 20 observations and discover that the cost element "quality control" is missing for some of the earlier case histories. He may conclude that no quality control was exercised back in the 1950s, or that this function is included in some other cost element. The latter is correct, of course. Traditionally, quality control was carried in the burden account, and it was only in the late 1950s that it began to appear (at the request of the Department of Defense) as a separate element. Hence to use historical cost data on equipments built prior to the change, some portion of overhead cost has to be converted to quality control in order to have a consistent and comparable data base for the development of estimating relationships.

Making such an adjustment is seldom easy, but the return can be substantial. One way to view the payoff is in terms of the benefits derived from increasing the size of the data base (the sample size). Without the adjustments, the data points in question could probably not be included in the data base because of noncomparabilities, inconsistencies, and the like. By putting forth the effort to make appropriate adjustments, the analyst in effect increases his sample size. And in a world of very small samples, increasing the data base by even a few observations can have a high payoff in terms of increasing the reliability of estimating relationships.

**Summary Comment**

Rather typically, cost analysts working as an integral part of a systems analysis activity spend at least half their time struggling with the data problem. In this section we have tried to convey some flavor of the total

---

[23] Sometimes this can be quite difficult, even when various data sources for the purpose are available, such as *Employment and Earnings* and *Wholesale Prices and Price Indexes*, both published by the U.S. Bureau of Labor Statistics.

[24] Index number theory and the process of statistical deflation are discussed in most standard texts on statistical analysis. For example, see William A. Spurr and Charles P. Bonini, *Statistical Analysis for Business Decisions* (Homewood, Ill.: Richard D. Irwin, Inc., 1967), Chap. 18 and pp. 471–73, 496.

problem and some notion of the types of techniques that may be employed to solve it. Basically, however, what is required is ingenuity, persistence, and just plain hard work.

**Derivation of Estimating Relationships**
As this discussion has suggested, estimating relationships may be derived in various ways, using a wide range of analytical techniques. The derivation process itself may be described from a number of points of view, no one of which can be labeled as "best" for all circumstances.

From a conceptual standpoint the derivation of estimating relationships may perhaps best be viewed as a process involving the testing of hypotheses. This implies that the cost analyst should start out by developing a theory about the possible generators of cost for the particular activities, equipments, or facilities under consideration. Then certain hypothesis can be formulated and tested in light of the available data base. Usually, numerous iterations are required in the testing process before the preferred relationships are determined.

This approach is in marked contrast to one which is all too common today: the purely empirical approach. By "pure empiricism" we mean the following. The cost analyst rather arbitrarily assembles all the data he can find which have anything whatever to do with the problem. He then feeds these data into a computerized correlation program and determines that statistical relationship which has the highest correlation coefficient. If he is lucky, he may wind up with a statistically sound estimating relationship, but the chances are against such an outcome. It is much more likely that he will come up with a nonsensical result. For example, he may derive a multivariate estimating equation having a coefficient of multiple correlation equal to 0.99, but at the same time having certain regression coefficients which are of the wrong sign or not significantly greater than zero.

In arguing against "pure empiricism" we are not arguing against the *appropriate* use of quantitative methods in the process of deriving estimating relationships. The point is rather that statistical methods should not be applied mechanically, and not without having first done the necessary homework to be able to structure the problem and to formulate hypotheses to be tested. This homework may take many forms, depending upon the problem. It may, for example, involve trips to the field or to manufacturing plants to observe certain types of operations; it may involve discussions with design engineers, engineers concerned with the state of the art in manufacturing, and with persons in charge of running certain types of field activities; it may involve reading the technical literature in certain hardware areas. Without engaging in this type of preliminary work, the cost analyst is not likely to be in a very good position to derive meaningful estimating relationships.

### A Simple Example

Let us consider a simple example to illustrate some of the main characteristics of the "testing of hypotheses" approach to the derivation of estimating relationships.

Suppose that Mr. A, a cost analyst, has the problem of developing a generalized estimating relationship for the maintenance cost of a certain class of major equipments to be produced in the future. Not being very familiar with these equipments, he reads the limited amount of literature that is readily available and talks to some of his colleagues about the problem.

On the basis of this brief preliminary investigation, Mr. A begins to feel intuitively that a certain explanatory variable (call it $x$)[25] might appropriately be included in the required maintenance cost estimating relationship. Somewhat against his better judgment, Mr. A decides to forgo any further background research and to go ahead and attempt to derive an estimating relationship for maintenance cost ($c$) as a function of explanatory variable $x$.

From his knowledge of the subject so far, Mr. A sees no reason why he cannot postulate a linear relationship between $c$ and $x$. His preliminary hypothesis is, therefore:

$$c = \alpha + \beta x.$$

Mr. A now proceeds to collect historical data on $c$ and $x$ from past and current operations involving maintenance on major equipments which are analogous to those being postulated for the future.[26] He then makes the necessary adjustments to the raw data (for example, price level adjustments) and winds up with a reasonably homogeneous data base consisting of 15 observations.

Before attempting any statistical curve fitting, Mr. A decides to make a simple plot of the data in the form of a scatter diagram. The results are portrayed in Fig. 6.13. Since the available data base does not seem to indicate any systematic relation between $c$ and $x$, Mr. A begins to doubt his original hypothesis. He decides to reject it, to go back to the beginning, and to do a considerable amount of additional background research.

---

[25] This might be, for example, a performance or physical characteristic.
[26] As implied by our discussion of the data problem in the preceding section of this chapter, assembling the data base can be a laborious undertaking.

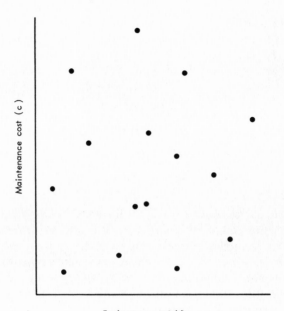

Fig. 6.13 – Maintenance cost versus explanatory variable, $x$

After further reading of the literature, Mr. A visits several installations currently performing maintenance on equipments analogous to those being projected for the future. He observes these operations, talks at length to the people in charge, and examines some of the data made available to him at each installation.

It soon becomes apparent that variable $x$ is indeed not likely to be a very significant determinant of maintenance cost. Furthermore, in view of the opinions expressed by the maintenance supervisors, and other information as well, it becomes evident that variables $w$ and $y$ should be very good candidates for inclusion in a generalized maintenance cost estimating relationship, and that variable $z$ might be a possibility.

Mr. A decides to test these hypotheses. He therefore arranges with the people at the several maintenance installations to help him with the data collection problem. They make their records available and suggest contacts at other installations. They also provide information which will be helpful in making adjustments for inconsistencies and noncomparabilities in the raw data.[27] The end result is that after a considerable amount of work, Mr.

---

[27] We must warn the reader that things do not often go as smoothly as this in the real world!

A is able to assemble a reasonably consistent data base containing 20 observations for the variables $c$, $w$, $y$, and $z$. He is now ready for the next round in his hypothesis testing exercise.

At this point Mr. A has several hypothesis to be examined:

$$H_1 : c = f(w, y, z)$$
$$H_2 : c = g(w, y)$$
$$H_3 : c = h(w, z)$$
$$H_4 : c = i(y, z).$$

He realizes, of course, that a two-variate function – for example, $c = j(w)$ – might turn out to explain variations in $c$ just as well as the functions listed above.[28] This possibility, therefore, is to be left open, even though the background research at the field installations suggests that an appropriate estimating equation should contain $w$ and $y$, and possibly $z$. Similarly, $H_3$ and $H_4$ are to be tested, although the *a priori* evidence implies that they are likely to be weaker than $H_1$ and $H_2$.

Mr. A decides not to specify the functional form just yet. His observations and discussions with maintenance experts at the field installations suggest to him that a linear hypothesis might be as appropriate as anything else, but he prefers to decide this later.

As a first pass at the problem, Mr. A constructs several scatter diagrams plotting $c$ vs. $w$, $c$ vs. $y$, and $c$ vs. $z$. (See Figs. 6.14 to 6.16.) The impressions formed as a result of the visits to maintenance activities in the field tend to be substantiated by these plots. Explanatory variables $w$ and $y$ appear promising, $z$ seems doubtful, and a linear hypothesis looks about as good as any alternative.

Since he has a fairly good data base consisting of 20 observations,[29] Mr. A decides to proceed with a formal regression analysis.[30] The specific

---

[28] Here we are using "explained variation" in a statistical sense.

[29] In many areas of application, 20 observations would be regarded as a small sample. In military cost analysis for long-range planning, however, it is relatively large.

[30] In the discussion to follow, it is necessary to use statistical concepts and to refer to statistical techniques. Since this book is not a text on statistics, we cannot get into detail regarding statistical methods. We shall, however, refer repeatedly to specific works in the literature, so that readers interested in statistical matters may pursue a particular subject in depth.

A good treatment of statistical regression analysis is contained in William A. Spurr, and Charles P. Bonini, *Statistical Analysis for Business Decisions* (Homewood, Ill.: Richard D. Irwin, Inc., 1967), Chaps. 22, 23.

hypotheses to be examined are:

$$H_1 : c = \alpha + \beta_1 w + \beta_2 y + \beta_3 z$$

$$H_2 : c = \alpha + \beta_1 w + \beta_2 y$$

$$H_3 : c = \alpha + \beta_1 w + \beta_3 z$$

$$H_4 : c = \alpha + \beta_2 y + \beta_3 z$$

$$H_5 : c = \alpha + \beta_1 w$$

$$H_6 : c = \alpha + \beta_2 y$$

$$H_7 : c = \alpha + \beta_3 z \,[31]$$

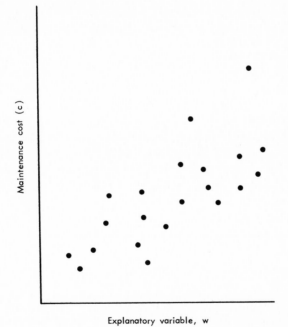

Explanatory variable, $w$

Fig. 6.14 – Maintenance cost versus explanatory variable, $w$

[31] This notational scheme does not assume that the coefficients are the same under all hypotheses; for example, $\beta_3$, under $H_1 \neq \beta_3$ under $H_4$.

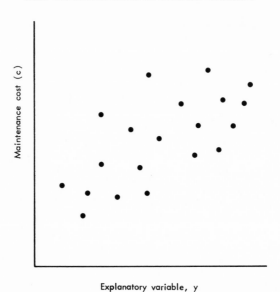

Explanatory variable, y

Fig. 6.15 – Maintenance cost versus explanatory variable, *y*

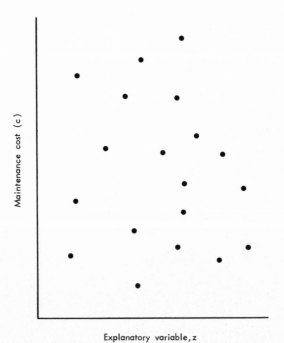

Explanatory variable, z

Fig. 6.16 – Maintenance cost versus explanatory variable, *z*

Since a number of cases have to be computed, Mr. A decides to use a computer program[32] to derive estimates of the coefficients in the several regression equations and to obtain various statistical measures – for example, standard errors of estimate, standard errors of regression coefficients, and the like.[33] Although the computer program automatically calculates correlation coefficients, Mr. A, being a good statistician, is not preoccupied with them. He places particular emphasis on the standard error measures and their use in conducting various statistical significance tests.

For example, in looking over the standard errors of the regression coefficients, he finds that in all cases the standard error for $\beta_3$ is several times the estimated value of $\beta_3$ itself. This raises some question about whether the variable $z$ should be included in the desired estimating relationship. To check the matter further, Mr. A conducts a statistical test (a "t" test) on $\beta_3$ in all regression equations containing $z$ as an explanatory variable.[34] In all cases the tests indicate that the value of $\beta_3$ is not significantly greater than zero at the 0.05 level of significance.[35]

Mr. A now decides to discard $z$ as an explanatory variable, because:

1. The *a priori* information obtained during the visits to maintenance installations in the field indicated that $z$ was only a possible (but not very likely) candidate,
2. The statistical tests corroborated the *a priori* notions.

As a result, hypotheses $H_1$, $H_3$, $H_4$, and $H_7$ are rejected. This leaves $H_2$, $H_5$, and $H_6$.

Recall that the *a priori* information suggests rather strongly that both $w$ and $y$ should be included in the desired estimating equation. This implies that $H_2$ should be accepted and $H_5$ and $H_6$ rejected. Mr. A decides to try to find statistical corroboration.

First of all he notes that the *relative* standard errors of estimate[36] for the regression equations in $H_5$ and $H_6$ are in both instances considerably greater than that for the regression equation in $H_2$. Also, in the case of the

---

[32] One such program is the so-called BMD computer program. See *ibid.*, pp. 603–608.

[33] For a description and discussion of these measures, see *ibid.*, pp. 561–563, 566–568, 573–574, 599–603.

[34] For a description of this testing procedure, see *ibid.*, pp. 566–567, 602.

[35] The significance level of the test is the probability of making a Type I error – rejecting a null hypothesis when it is in fact true. (See *ibid.*, pp. 281–282.) In the example in the text above, the null hypothesis is that $\beta_3$ (in the "population") = 0. The alternative hypothesis is $\beta_3$ (in the population) > 0.

[36] This is sometimes called the coefficient of variation. It is defined as the standard error of estimate divided by the sample mean of the dependent variable.

multiple regression equation for $H_2$, an analysis of variance indicates that the incremental increase in explained variance attributable to the addition of explanatory variable $y$ is statistically significant at the 0.01 level of significance.[37]

As a result of these statistical corroborations of the *a priori* information, Mr. A decides to reject $H_5$ and $H_6$ and to accept $H_2$ tentatively. His estimating relationship, therefore, is

$$c = \hat{\alpha} + \hat{\beta}_1 w + \hat{\beta}_2 y. \text{ [38]}$$

Final acceptance, however, depends on further statistical testing. The purpose of these additional tests is primarily to see whether the assumptions of the regression model are reasonably well fulfilled in the problem at hand.

Among the more important of these assumptions are:[39]

1. The residuals[40] are independent,
2. The residuals are normally distributed,[41]
3. The data points have a uniform dispersion about the regression plane,
4. The explanatory variables are independent.[42]

Mr. A decides to check his regression equation to see if the four assumptions are met reasonably well. He makes the following analyses:

1. The observed residuals (the differences between the observed values of $c$ and the values of $c$ computed from the regression equation for

---

[37] This requires the use of a statistical testing procedure employing the F ratio. See Taro Yamane, *Statistics: An Introductory Analysis*, 2nd ed. (New York, Evanston, and London: Harper & Row, 1967), pp. 806–808. When F is significantly large, it can be shown that the F-testing procedure is equivalent to a "t" test for the significance of the regression coefficient of the explanatory variable in question ($\beta_2$ in our example above). See *ibid.*, p. 808.

[38] Here, $\hat{\alpha}$, $\hat{\beta}_1$, and $\hat{\beta}_2$ are the numerical estimates of the coefficients in the regression equation.

[39] See Spurr and Bonini, *op. cit.*, pp. 601, 610.

[40] The residuals are the deviations of the actual values of the dependent variable from the true regression plane.

[41] The normality assumption is not necessary if one wishes only to estimate the values of the regression coefficients. However, the assumption *is* necessary for making valid significance tests – for example, "t" tests on the regression coefficients. It is also necessary if one is to use the standard error measures to make valid statements about the reliability of the regression equation. See *ibid.*, p. 565.

[42] This is the "collinearity" problem. The net regression coefficients may be unreliable if the explanatory variables are highly correlated. (For a good demonstration of why this is so, see *ibid.*, p. 610.) However, while collinearity affects the reliability of individual components of the regression equation, it may not significantly reduce the predictive capability of the *total* regression equation. (See *loc. cit.*)

the observed values of $w$ and $y$) are determined, and a statistical test for independence is made.[43] At the 0.05 significance level, the hypothesis of no correlation among the residuals is accepted.

2. The observed residuals are plotted graphically and Mr. A concludes that they approximate a normal distribution.

3. A "three-dimensional" plot of the regression plane and the data points is made,[44] and he concludes that the observations scatter above and below the plane in a reasonably uniform dispersion pattern.

4. A correlation of explanatory variables $w$ and $y$ is computed, and the correlation coefficient is found to be not significantly greater than zero.[45] Mr. A thus also confirms the final assumption.

On the basis of these results, he concludes that the main assumptions of the regression model are acceptably fulfilled. He decides, however, to make one more check: a rough test of the estimating equation's predictive capability.

Somewhat by accident Mr. A happened to find two additional historical cases. How well might his estimating equation do in "predicting" these data points, which are not a part of his sample data base? He computes estimates of maintenance cost ($c$) for these two cases and finds the results to be very close to the actual $c$'s. (The actual $c$'s are well within plus and minus one standard error of estimate from the regression plane.) Since the values of the explanatory variables $w$ and $y$ for the two extraneous cases are within the ranges of $w$ and $y$ in the sample, this check is not a very powerful one from the standpoint of predicting *beyond* the range of the sample. It does, however, reinforce confidence that the estimating equation is consistent with the existing body of information. Being able to test predictive power beyond the range of the sample is something that the analyst is rarely able to do. This is one of the reasons why extrapolating beyond present experience requires caution. (We shall return to this point later.)

Mr. A is now ready for the last step in the process of deriving an estimating relationship: documentation of his work and storing it in the estimating relationship data bank. Since others will be using his estimating equation, it is very important that documentation be complete.

---

[43] One such procedure is the Durbin-Watson test. See Yamane, *op. cit.*, pp. 809–813.

[44] For an example of such a plot, see Spurr and Bonini, *op. cit.*, p. 592.

[45] For a discussion of significance tests on the correlation coefficient, see Yamane, *op. cit.*, pp. 462–467.

Mr. A prepares a report containing the following types of information:

1. A summary of his background research, including information about his trips to field installations and his initial impressions about hypotheses to be tested.
2. A complete presentation and description of the raw data base and the adjustments made to it.
3. A description of the hypotheses that seemed worthy of serious examination ($H_1, \ldots, H_7$).
4. A description of the testing process itself, indicating the tests used and the reasoning leading to the acceptance of $H_2$ and the rejection of the alternatives.
5. A presentation of the complete set of statistical measures pertaining to the accepted regression equation (all adjusted for degrees of freedom[46]). For example:

   a. Standard error of estimate.
   b. Relative standard error of estimate (coefficient of variation).
   c. Standard errors of the regression coefficients.
   d. The Beta coefficients[47].
   e. The equation for the standard error of forecast.[48]
   f. The coefficient of multiple determination and the coefficient of multiple correlation.[49]

6. A listing of special caveats or restrictions that should be observed by users of the regression equation.

### Comments on the Example

In our hypothetical illustration things went fairly smoothly for Mr. A, at least after his initial false start. For example, in his background research

---

[46] The term "degrees of freedom" refers to the difference between sample size and the number of constants in the regression equation. (See Yamane, op. cit., pp. 391, 505–506.) In our hypothetical example, d.f. $= (20-3) = 17$.

[47] The Beta coefficients measure the relative importance of each explanatory variable in influencing the dependent variable. (See Spurr and Bonini, op. cit., p. 603.)

[48] The standard error of forecast (sometimes referred to as the "prediction interval") represents a measure of the *total* sampling error for any new observation. It is made up of the standard error of estimate and the standard error of the regression plane. This measure may be used to set up "confidence limits" about the regression plane. These limits are nonlinear in that they get progressively wider as we move away from the point on the regression plane determined by the sample means of the explanatory variables. (See *ibid.*, pp. 568–571, 602, 629–630.)

[49] The coefficient of multiple determination is the ratio of explained variance to total variance. The coefficient of multiple correlation is the square root of the coefficient of multiple determination. (See *ibid.*, pp. 600–601.)

efforts he was quite successful in obtaining useful information which enabled him to set up meaningful hypotheses to be tested. Also, he was fortunate to get an acceptable solution to the data problem: a reasonably consistent sample containing 20 observations. Finally, the end results were fairly clear cut. The *a priori* information was corroborated by the statistical analysis in such a way that it was possible to accept one hypothesis ($H_2$) and reject the others.

The reader should not gain the impression that things are always this tidy in real life. They are not. However, the illustration was made "optimistic" deliberately, in order to concentrate on several basic points regarding the derivation of estimating relationships. The most fundamental of these is simply this: The analyst should engage in the necessary background research to enable him to set up meaningful hypotheses to be tested. The choice of an estimating relationship should be based on a *combination* of (1) the *a priori* information, (2) the results of the statistical analyses, and (3) the exercising of good judgment in interpreting (1) and (2). Derivation of estimating relationships should not be based on mechanical statistical manipulations alone.

Other major points illustrated by the example are:

1. Once again, the importance of getting a reasonably good solution to the data problem.
2. Explicit consideration of the assumptions underlying the statistical model and the testing of these assumptions.
3. The desirability of attempting to check the estimating relationship for cases outside the sample data base.
4. The importance of documentation.
5. Recognition that several types of analytical techniques may be useful.

This last point deserves some emphasis. In the example, Mr. A used methods from both ends of the complexity spectrum: simple scatter diagrams and other graphical techniques on the one hand, formal regression analysis on the other. There are many possibilities in between. Although it would be inappropriate to attempt to describe them in any detail in this book, we might simply list a few of them to indicate that the analyst does not have to attempt formal regression in all instances. (For example, in cases of very small samples, formal regression analysis usually makes little sense. Degrees of freedom could be very small, zero, or even negative.) In addition to the graphical methods and formal regression analysis used in our example, the list of other techniques available for describing relationships among variables in a given set of data points includes many mechanical curve-fitting methods. Some of the more important of these are the following:

1. Least squares. A variety of types of mathematical functions can be fitted by using least-squares procedures.[50] Some examples are:

$$Y = a + bX$$

$$Y = a + bX + cX^2$$

$$Y = a + bX_1 + cX_2 + dX_3$$

$$Y = a + bX_1 + cX_1^2 + dX_2 + eX_2^2$$

$$1/Y = a + bX$$

$$\log Y = \log a + b \log X$$

2. Simple methods for two-variate linear equations. Possibilities here include:

   a. The method of selected points.[51]
   b. The method of averages.[52]
   c. Freehand graphic methods.[53]

3. Special graphic and algebraic methods for multivariate functions. The principal types of procedures under this heading are:

   a. The method of successive elimination.[54]
   b. The method of successive approximations for curvilinear multivariate functions.[55]
   c. Nomographic methods.[56]

---

[50] See Spurr and Bonini, *op. cit.*, pp. 558–561, 597–599, 635–637; and Mordecai Ezekiel and Karl A. Fox, *Methods of Correlation and Regression Analysis* (New York: John Wiley and Sons, Inc., 1959), pp. 61–63, 83–90, 96–98, 170–187, 206–208.

In many cases computer programs are available which may be used to assist the analyst in his curve-fitting explorations. For example, see W. J. Dixon (ed.), *BMD Biomedical Computer Programs* (Los Angeles: Health Sciences Computing Facility, University of California, Los Angeles, January 1, 1964).

[51] See Dale S. Davis, *Nomography and Empirical Equations* (New York: Reinhold Publishing Corp., 1955), pp. 4–6.

[52] See *ibid.*, pp. 6–8.

[53] See Spurr and Bonini, *op. cit.*, pp. 556–558.

[54] An example for a 3-variate linear function is presented in *ibid.*, pp. 594–597.

[55] For example, see Ezekiel and Fox, *op. cit.*, pp. 210–245.

[56] For example, see Davis, *op. cit.*, Chap. 8.

4. Special methods for fitting a variety of nonlinear forms – for example, alterations of fundamental forms, trigonometric functions, hyperbolic functions, Gompertz equations, and so on.[57]

Finally, to help round out our listing of alternative statistical methods, we must briefly mention statistical procedures which are much more complex than those discussed so far: the method of maximum likelihood for estimating the parameters in a system of simultaneous equations, and a variation of it called the method of reduced forms ("limited information, maximum likelihood" method).[58] While these methods were developed by econometricians for use in handling problems in the field of economics, they may be applied in other disciplines as well. The military cost analyst should at least know about them, even though in most instances he will not be concerned with problems requiring their use.

The basic reason why these methods were developed can be illustrated briefly by the following model from macroeconomics:[59]

$$C_t = \alpha + \beta Y_t + u \tag{8}$$

$$Y_t = C_t + I_t \tag{9}$$

$$I_t = \text{exogenous,} \tag{10}$$

where

$C_t$ = aggregate consumption expenditures in year $t$
$Y_t$ = national income in year $t$
$I_t$ = aggregate gross investment in year $t$ (assumed to be exogenous to the system)
$u$ = a random disturbance with $E(u) = 0$,

$$E(uu_{-r}) = 0 \quad \text{for all} \quad r > 0, \quad E(u^2) = \sigma_u^2 \text{ [60]}$$

$\alpha$ and $\beta$ = p arameters, where $\beta$ is the marginal propensity to consume.

[57] *Ibid.*, Chap. 3.
[58] Substantive discussion of these methods is beyond the scope of this book. Interested readers should refer to the econometrics literature. For example, Lawrence R. Klein, *A Textbook of Econometrics* (Evanston, Ill., and White Plains, N.Y.: Row, Peterson and Company, 1953), Chaps. III and IV.
[59] See Lawrence R. Klein, *Economic Fluctuations in the United States* (New York: John Wiley and Sons, Inc., 1950), pp. 7–8. This simple model is purely illustrative. The reader should not form the impression that econometricians use models like this for anything other than pedagogical purposes. For a recent example of a substantive macroeconometric model, see James S. Duesenberry, Gary Fromm, Lawrence R. Klein, Edwin Kuh (eds.) *The Brookings Quarterly Econometric Model of the United States* (Chicago: Rand McNally and Company, 1965).
[60] $E$ denotes the operation of mathematical expectation, and $\sigma_u^2$ is the variance of the disturbance.

Assume that we are interested in estimating the parameters $\alpha$ and $\beta$ from a body of historical data. Can equation (8) be estimated by classical regression methods in isolation from the rest of the system? The answer is "no," because $Y_t$ is not an independent variable. $Y_t$ influences $C_t$ and $C_t$ influences $Y_t$.[61] Equation (8) does not reflect a one-way causal relation, since $Y_t$ and $C_t$ are both endogenous to the system. Hence the need for "simultaneous" methods for estimating $\alpha$ and $\beta$ in the context of the total system of relationships. The method of maximum likelihood for estimating the parameters in a system of simultaneous equations is designed for dealing with this type of problem, such that consistent estimates of the parameters may be obtained.[62]

In our example, the same result may be obtained by converting the system to its "reduced form": that is, by solving for the endogenous variables in terms of the exogenous variable $I_t$:

$$Y_t = \frac{\alpha}{1-\beta} + \frac{1}{1-\beta} I_t + \frac{u}{1-\beta} \tag{11}$$

$$C_t = \frac{\alpha}{1-\beta} + \frac{\beta}{1-\beta} I_t + \frac{u}{1-\beta}. \tag{12}$$

Here, we may estimate equations (11) and (12) by classical regression methods, since $Y_t$ and $C_t$ are both expressed as functions of the variable $I_t$, which is "independent" (exogenous to the system). When this is done, the result is an estimate of $1/(1-\beta)$ and $\alpha/(1-\beta)$. Having an estimate of $1/(1-\beta)$, we can derive an estimate of $\beta$, the marginal propensity to consume; and having also an estimate of $\alpha/(1-\beta)$, we can then compute an estimate of the location parameter $\alpha$. These will be consistent estimates of the structural parameters $\alpha$ and $\beta$. In our example, the direct application of the full maximum likelihood method would produce the same results as use of the reduced-form procedure.[63]

In summary, the main point is that in cases where an estimating relationship cannot be regarded as "standing alone," we cannot proceed directly with classical regression methods of estimation if we hope to obtain consistent estimates of the parameters. More specifically, unless we can

---

[61] If equation (8) were of the form $C_t = \alpha + \beta Y_{t-1} + u$, then we could proceed directly by using classical regression procedures. In this case $Y_{t-1}$ is exogenous and hence an independent variable for purposes of statistical estimation of $\alpha$ and $\beta$.

[62] An estimator $\hat{\theta}$ for a parameter $\theta$ has the property of *consistency* if $P(\hat{\theta} \to \theta) \to 1$ as the sample size approaches $\infty$. That is to say, the estimate moves near the true parameter value with probability approaching unity as the size of the sample increases without limit.

[63] Klein, *op. cit.*, p. 8.

logically postulate a "one-way" causal relation from explanatory variables to the dependent variable, we should specify additional structural equations or identities and then proceed with "simultaneous" methods of estimation – either the full maximum likelihood procedure or the reduced-form method.

## Use of Estimating Relationships

When a good analyst talks about the use of generalized estimating relationships, his main theme is invariably: "Be careful – use good judgment!" In developing estimating relationships for use as part of a systems analysis in support of long-range military planning, this is particularly true.

Generalized estimating relationships are basically devices for synthesizing our knowledge about past, present, and near-future military capabilities by relating resource requirements to key structural characteristics of these capabilities. The main purpose of having such synthesized descriptions is to help us in assessing resource impacts of proposed *new* military systems and forces for the distant future. While generalized estimating relationships form the very heart of the cost analyst's body of tools, they are by no means self-sufficient, and many problems arise in using them in the cost analysis process.

Some of these problems are more or less mechanical in nature. For example, in cases where the analyst takes an "off-the-shelf" estimating relationship from the data bank, he must check to make sure that the definition of the categories of resource items built into the relationship is the same as that required in the problem at hand. Similarly, if the estimating relationship furnishes estimates of dollar cost, the analyst must check to see what kind of dollars are provided – 1965, 1967, or what? If the base year built into the relationship is different from that required in the current study, an adjustment must be made.

A host of problems like these confront the cost analyst when he uses estimating relationships. While they are important and oftentimes troublesome, the analyst can usually solve them through persistence and a reasonable amount of ingenuity. There are other problems, however, which are much more fundamental and much less easily handled. Let us examine a few of them briefly, and in so doing indicate rather pointedly why care and good judgment are necessary when using generalized estimating relationships.

### Examples of Some Major Problems

As indicated in Chapter 2, uncertainty is one of the most troublesome factors in conducting systems analyses of problems involving distant future planning. Uncertainty is also the major source of difficulty in using estimating relationships in the cost analysis process supporting such studies. Two major types of uncertainty are:[64]

1. Statistical uncertainty: chance elements in the real world.
2. Uncertainty about the "state of the world" in the future: techno-logical, strategic, political, and so on.

Let us use this categorization of uncertainties as a context for discussing some of the major problems involved in using generalized estimating relationships.

As a first step, consider a case where there are no state-of-the-world uncertainties, and assume that we have an estimating relationship for $C$ (cost) as a function of explanatory variable $X$, as shown in Fig. 6.17.

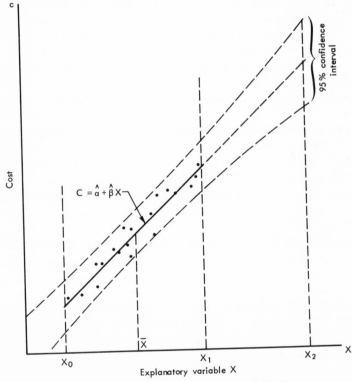

Fig. 6.17 – Cost versus explanatory variable $X$

---

[64] Refer back to Chapter 2, pp. 11–13.

Suppose now that we want to use $C = \hat{\alpha} + \hat{\beta}X$ to estimate $C$ for a specified value of $X$, say $X_2$, beyond the range of $X$ in the sample ($X_0$ through $X_1$). If state-of-the-world uncertainties are zero, then the following will hold true:

1. The value of $X_2$ is known without error.
2. The "universe" beyond the range of the sample ($X_0$ through $X_1$) is exactly the same as that within the sample.

Even under these conditions – which are exceedingly rare in the realm of military cost analysis for long-range planning – the analyst is still confronted with statistical uncertainty. In our example this is reflected by the 95 percent confidence interval for an individual forecast presented in Fig. 6.17.[65] Notice that the bounds for this interval are nonlinear, and that they get continuously farther apart as the value of $X$ departs from the mean value in the sample ($\overline{X}$). For example, at $X_2$ the confidence interval is about twice as wide as it is at $\overline{X}$. This illustrates rather dramatically why one has to be careful about projecting beyond the range of the sample, *even when state-of-the-world uncertainties are zero*.

But the "statistical uncertainties only" case is not the usual one. Other uncertainties are likely to be present. For example, the analyst may not always know the values of the explanatory variables with precision. Even more troublesome is the likelihood that the universe toward which the analyst is projecting will differ widely in some respects from the universe reflected in the sample data base. Such factors as manufacturing state-of-the-art, materials technology, system operational concepts and efficiencies, and the like may be different in the future than for the past and the present. All of these considerations are supplementary to statistical uncertainty *per se*, and they usually cannot be treated by methods based on present statistical theory.

It is not enough, of course, to argue that the cost analyst should be careful in using generalized estimating relationships. The question is, what can be done to help ensure prudence?

**Some Examples of "Being Careful"**

No one has yet devised a "standard procedure" that will guarantee caution in the application of generalized estimating relationships. Basically what is required is informed judgment on the part of the cost analyst, and this is

---

[65] A 70 percent confidence band would be narrower and a 99 percent band would be wider than the 95 percent interval shown in Fig. 6.17. For a discussion of confidence intervals in regression analysis, see Spurr and Bonini, *op. cit.*, pp. 567–571.

something that cannot be reduced to a mechanical process. However, a number of steps may be taken to facilitate proper use of estimating relationships in long-range planning studies. We shall discuss a few representative examples briefly in the following paragraphs.

In cases where generalized estimating relationships have been derived by formal statistical methods, the cost analyst may turn to the relative standard error of estimate (coefficient of variation), the confidence interval for an individual forecast, or some other measure, and use these statistics to help decide what should be done about statistical uncertainty. If, for example, the relative standard error of estimate is about 5 percent, the analyst may feel comfortable in taking an expected value estimate as provided by the regression equation and using it without further question. On the other hand, if the relative standard error of estimate is 30 or 40 percent, he may want to do some sensitivity testing. Here the objective would be to explore the impact on final results (for example, total system cost) of possible estimating errors for the particular input category under consideration.[66]

With respect to uncertainties about the values of explanatory variables, several precautionary steps may be taken. As an illustration, let us consider the major equipment area. Here, costs of future equipment proposals are often estimated from relationships having equipment performance or physical characteristics as explanatory variables. Where the analyst is uncertain as to what values of these variables should be inserted into the estimating equation, the first thing he should do is be skeptical about the numbers presented by *advocates* of the proposed new equipment. We know from past experience that participants in the advocacy process often tend to overstate performance characteristics or to understate certain physical characteristics – like weight, for example. Under these conditions the cost analyst should consult with design engineers who are neutral, and seek their advice regarding appropriate values of equipment characteristics to be used as explanatory variables.

The analyst can also make a few simple sensitivity calculations to help him decide how much he should worry about uncertainty about the explanatory variables. For example, suppose we have the following equipment estimating equation:

$$C = 80 + 2.5X_1 + 0.04X_2;$$

and that the "expected values" of the explanatory variables for some future

---

[66] For an illustration of this kind of analysis, refer back to the B-x example in Chapter 5, pp. 114–115.

situation are $X_1 = 38$ and $X_2 = 650$. The "base case," therefore, is:

$$C = 80 + 2.5(38) + 0.04(650)$$

$$= 80 + 95 + 26$$

$$= 201.$$

What happens if we are relatively certain about $X_1$, but uncertain about $X_2$? Assuming a 50 percent change in $X_2$ ($X_2 = 650 + 325$  1,000) and assuming $X_1 = 38$, we have:

$$C = 80 + 2.5(38) + 0.04(1000) = 215,$$

or a 7 percent change relative to the base case. Here, the analyst would probably not be too concerned about uncertainties in $X_2$.

Other cases might be (1) a 50 percent increase in $X_1$, with $X_2 = 650$ and (2) a 50 percent increase in both $X_1$ and $X_2$. The results are:

| | Value of C | Percent Change[67] |
|---|---|---|
| (1) | 249 | +24 |
| (2) | 263 | +31 |

In both of these cases the analyst might not be indifferent to uncertainties in the explanatory variables, and he might choose to do further sensitivity testing to explore the impact of these uncertainties on final results (e.g., total system or program cost).[68]

Let us now turn to a situation that requires the greatest possible care: the common situation in which the cost analyst has to project to the distant future and he has good reason to doubt that the characteristics of that future "universe" are the same as those reflected in the data base underlying his estimating relationships. Here, mechanical application of generalized estimating relationships can be especially dangerous. What usually happens in such instances is that the relationships are used primarily as a reproducible *point of departure* in the estimating process. Something else – usually involving a considerable effort – has to be done before the final estimates are obtained.

The problem discussed earlier, of analyzing the costs of stainless-steel airframes, is a good case in point. Recall that in this instance military cost analysts in the mid-1950s faced the problem of estimating these costs for systems that would not be operational until the mid-1960s. The then existing airframe cost-estimating relationships, expressing cost as a

---

[67] Relative to the base case (201).
[68] See the B-x example in Chapter 5.

function of aircraft performance and physical characteristics and production quantity, contained estimates of structural parameters reflecting a materials technology and a manufacturing state-of-the-art which were different from the stainless-steel environment projected for the future. As a result, the cost analysts were confronted with major "state-of-the-world" uncertainties in addition to the usual statistical uncertainties which are always present.

Were the existing estimating relationships – derived primarily from experience with aluminum airframes – of any use in projecting to the future stainless-steel universe? The answer is a qualified "yes." Let us illustrate the point in a simplified example.

Suppose that the existing estimating equation for the direct labor hours part of total airframe was as follows (for normalized cumulative unit number 100):

$$H = \hat{\alpha}(W^{\beta_1})(S^{\beta_2})u, \text{ [69]}$$

where

$H$ = direct labor hours for cumulative unit number 100,
$W$ = airframe weight in thousands of pounds,
$S$ = aircraft maximum speed in knots,
$u$ = a random disturbance.

We would not expect this relationship to hold in a direct fashion for stainless-steel airframes. However, the cost analysts might use it as a documentable point of departure or "base case" in the process of moving to the "universe" of stainless-steel airframes. Suppose that this was done in our example and that the values $W_0$ and $S_0$ were substituted in the estimating equation, resulting in a "point of departure" estimate for direct labor hours (at cumulative unit number 100) of $H_0$.

Suppose further that the cost analysts were able to obtain information from the experiments in stainless-steel fabrication referred to earlier.[70] Let us assume, for example, that data from those experiments (reflecting *then current* manufacturing methods and tooling) indicated that for the first generation of stainless-steel airframes, direct labor hours might be 3 to 5 times the hours experienced on conventional aluminum airframes.[71] On the basis of these data, then, the point-of-departure estimate would be modified as follows:

---

[69] $\alpha$, $\beta_1$, and $\beta_2$ represent estimated values for the parameters $\alpha$, $\beta_1$, and $\beta_2$.
[70] See p. 140.
[71] These numbers are illustrative only.

Upper bound estimate $= 5H_0$
Lower bound estimate $= 3H_0$

These are the results of the first iteration. Suppose now that the cost analysts, in talking to knowledgeable engineers from the industry, found that some possibility existed for advances being made in fabrication methods which would reduce the labor hour differentials (stainless vs. aluminum), even for the first generation of stainless-steel airframes. The engineers felt that, if these improvements were to materialize, the 3 to 5 factors obtained from the experiments might be reduced by about 25 percent. On the basis of this information the results of the first iteration would be modified as follows:

Upper bound case:        $5H_0$
Mid-range cases:    $(.75)(5)H_0 = 3.75H_0$
                         $3H_0$
Lower bound case:    $(.75)(3)H_0 = 2.25H_0$

Subsequent iterations might take place if other relevant supplementary information could be brought to bear on the problem. However, we shall terminate our example at this juncture, since we have gone far enough to illustrate our main points.

Let us summarize these briefly:

1. The analyst must be particularly careful in using generalized estimating relationships when the characteristics of the future universe are, or are likely to be, different from those reflected in the estimating relationships to be used for projection.

2. In such instances generalized estimating relationships are usually used as a starting point in the estimating process. This is vitally important, since without such a documentable point of departure the main alternatives are: (a) to try to build an estimate in detail from the "ground up" (often not feasible in systems analyses of distant future equipments and activities); or (b) to use guesswork and subjective analogies to present experience (an alternative generally to be avoided if possible).

3. The point-of-departure estimate must then be modified in light of supplementary information, both quantitative and qualitative. This may involve several iterations before the final estimate, or range of estimates, is determined. The modifications to the point-of-departure estimate should be documented as explicitly as possible.

## Summary

The main points contained in this chapter may be summarized as follows:

1. Estimating relationships are devices which relate various categories of cost (either in dollars or physical units) to cost-generating or explanatory variables. Very often these explanatory variables represent characteristics of system performance, physical characteristics, specifications in the operational concept, and the like.

2. Estimating relationships may take numerous forms, ranging from informal rules of thumb or simple analogies to formal mathematical functions derived from statistical analyses of empirical data.

3. One of the most important steps in the derivation of estimating relationships is the assembly of the appropriate information and data base to serve as the basis for determining form and content.

4. More often than not, the existing data base is deficient in one way or another; for example,

   a. Information may be in the wrong format for analytical purposes.
   b. Various irregularities, inconsistencies, and noncomparabilities may be present.
   c. Gaps in information may exist at various critical points.
   d. Only a small number of relevant cases from the historical record may be available – the "small sample" problem.

5. Solution to parts of the data problem may be through major overhaul of present information systems and through the establishment of new, complete systems. Neither, however, appears feasible as a general solution – at least in the near future. Short of such major efforts are numerous alternatives. Some examples are:

   a. Use of sampling techniques on an *ad hoc* basis.
   b. Supplementing the existing historical data base by including estimated data points for the near future.
   c. Statistical adjustment and manipulation of the existing data base.
   d. Obtaining additional information by conducting experiments.

6. The process of deriving estimating relationships may be characterized in various ways. Conceptually, it may be viewed in terms of the testing of hypotheses. This implies that the cost analyst should start out by developing some kind of "theory" about the possible generators of cost for the particular class of activities, equipments, facilities, or whatever under consideration. Then certain hypotheses can be set up and tested in light of the available data base. Techniques used in the testing process may

range all the way from simple graphics to complex mathematical statistical procedures.

7. Care must be exercised in the use of estimating relationships, particularly in extrapolating beyond the range of experience (the sample). When "state-of-the-world" uncertainties are present – very often the case – the initial estimate derived from an estimating relationship must frequently be modified in light of supplemental information (both quantitative and qualitative).

### Suggested Supplementary Readings

1. Dale S. Davis, *Nomography and Empirical Equations* (New York: Reinhold Publishing Corporation, 1955). (A good reference text for mechanical curve-fitting techniques.)
2. J. Johnston, *Statistical Cost Analysis* (New York: McGraw-Hill Book Company, Inc., 1960). (Contains interesting examples of subjecting certain economic hypotheses about cost-output relationships to empirical testing.)
3. William A. Spurr and Charles P. Bonini, *Statistical Analysis for Business Decisions* (Homewood, Ill.: Richard D. Irwin, Inc., 1967). (Chapters 22–24 contain excellent discussions of statistical regression analysis.)
4. Carl F. Christ, *Econometric Models and Methods* (New York: John Wiley & Sons, Inc., 1966). (An excellent book on econometric theory and methods of analysis.)

# Chapter 7

# COST MODELS

## Introduction

Chapters 5 and 6 stressed an input orientation. We now want to change direction and steer around toward the output side. In so doing, however, we must carry with us an understanding of the input problem, so that we will be able, ultimately, to relate inputs and outputs to each other. Put another way, one of the main objectives of the present chapter is to narrow the gap that exists at this point between Chapters 5 and 6 on the one hand and Chapter 4 (Introduction to Military Cost Analysis) on the other.

For this purpose we focus intentionally on the subject of cost models. The term "cost model" has a wide variety of meanings, of course, depending upon the context, but it does have one rather general connotation: that of an integrating device designed to facilitate the analytical process. At once we are at the center of the matter, for "integration" in this context refers to the bringing together of the various factors on the input side and relating them to some specific type of output-oriented military capability in the future.

Our aim here is restricted, however. It is to discuss cost models in such a way that the reader will gain insights into what they are like, and, more importantly, how they help the cost analyst in his job of serving the systems analysis process. The objective is not to present a "cookbook" treatment of how to build a cost model.

Cost models may be classified in any of several ways. One possible basis for categorizing them is in terms of the extent to which the model manipulates the inputs. Here, the very simplest cost model only summarizes the facts provided by the analyst; it might consist merely of rules for sub-totaling and totaling the information supplied as inputs. Although such models may be run on a computer, they are actually performing the routine functions of adding machines and typewriters. A slightly more complex model may require a minor amount of multiplication in order to turn out a few intermediate outputs to be summarized and displayed. Somewhat more complex models may provide for making choices of estimating techniques depending upon specific inputs. The most complex may involve the use of fairly sophisticated analytical techniques such as nonlinear programming or probabilistic iterations.

Cost models can be categorized according to the function they serve. Some models are designed to assist long-range planners. Others are for use in programming, where this term implies a more detailed level of planning and application in the near future. Still others are designed for use in preparing next fiscal year's conventional budget. Function is worth noting, since it influences the design of the model in many ways. The level of detail to be represented is one of the most obvious. For example, a model designed for use in near future budgeting would not usually be useful for long-range planning, because it would require (as inputs) unavailable detail. It might also utilize categories and identifications in forms which are not of interest to long-range planners.

Cost models can be categorized according to the likelihood of repetitive use. Some are "one-shot" devices. The input data and the model itself may require considerable preparation, but they are nevertheless designed for a single specific application. Once the need has been met the model is a thing of the past, although it may still exist in files, and it may be used later in designing another model. Other models, of course, are designed to be used many times, providing many sets of cost estimates. This second type may require more care in its design because of the likelihood that it will be used when the designer is not available.

Cost models can also be classified in terms of the subject matter they are intended to represent. Some models deal with relatively minor parts of the total subject being considered by a decisionmaker, while others attempt to represent almost the entire structure of the problem. One categorization on this principle is as follows:

1. Resource requirements submodels.
2. Individual system cost models.[1]
3. Mission area force-mix cost models.
4. Total force cost models.

This particular classification scheme will be used as a basis for the remainder of the chapter. But rather than discuss each category in detail, we shall limit our attention primarily to one of the most widely used model types – individual system cost models – and consider a specific example as fully as space permits. In presenting and discussing the example, special emphasis will be placed on the *analytical use* of the model in the systems analysis process. After considering the example in some depth, we shall then return to our classification of models and discuss each one briefly.

---

[1] Here, the word "system" is used in a broad sense to include numerous types of output-oriented packages of military capability – for example, Navy task forces, Army division "slices," and so on.

To focus attention on the basic concepts, principles, and techniques used in developing a cost model, we have made many simplifying assumptions in the following example, and we have used extremely simple estimating relationships. Although the resulting model thus fails to reflect the richness of detail and complexity involved in models used in actual practice, it will be adequate for our purpose, which is simply to launch the discussion of cost models. The reader, therefore, should concentrate on the fundamentals that are illustrated and not worry about the specific numbers and estimating relationships used in the example.

### Hard Point Defense Systems: An Example of a System Cost Model

Suppose that we are participating in a systems analysis effort concerned with the question of defense against intercontinental ballistic missiles in a distant future time period. The problem of ballistic missile defense is complicated, and there are numerous alternative ways (for example, weapon system proposals) to accomplish the mission.

An important part of the problem involves hard point defense (HPD); that is, active defenses for further protecting hardened military installations against enemy intercontinental ballistic missiles (ICBMs).[2] One type of HPD system includes hardened radars, a hardened control center, and ground-launched interceptor missiles housed in hardened underground silos deployed about the defended site – for example, one of our own ICBM sites. The interceptors are thought of as very high speed, high acceleration, guided missiles which fly for short periods of time and intercept enemy reentry vehicles at relatively low altitudes. There are of course many possible configurations of HPD systems.

Proposals for future HPD systems must be evaluated in relation to other ways of reducing vulnerability. The systems analysts would have to explore, for example, whether a desired level of survivability of our own ICBM forces could be attained more cheaply by employing HPD, by buying more offensive ICBMs, by employing a mobile operational concept for the ICBMs, by some combination of these measures, or by some other means. In any event, it is clear that the cost of future HPD systems is a very important aspect of the problem.

Suppose the systems analysts have decided to conduct just such an evaluation of alternatives. We shall be called upon to furnish estimates of the resource impact of several configurations of a proposed HPD system.

---

[2] A "hardened" installation is one designed to withstand the overpressure and other effects of a nearby nuclear burst. Hardening, therefore, is one measure that might be taken to reduce vulnerability (increase survival) to an enemy ICBM attack. Dispersal is another measure; mobility is still another.

COST MODELS                                                          169

From the design of the systems analysis study, it is clear to us that we shall
have to treat the cost analysis problem in a "parametric" fashion, because
the systems analysts want to examine numerous force sizes (numbers of
force units) of HPD systems, varying numbers of interceptor missiles per
force unit, several types of missiles with different performance levels, and
so on.

Given a tentative description of the problem, we set out to assemble the
necessary inputs and to organize them in a rather formal way in the context
of HPD. In other words, the task is to put together an individual HPD
system cost model. A description of the simplified version of the model is
presented in the following paragraphs.

To help keep the example simple we shall use a limited number of cost
categories. These are listed in Table 7.1. Notice that total HPD system cost

TABLE 7.1

Cost Categories for the HPD Example[a]

$R$ = Research and Development
$I$ = Investment:
    $I_1$ = Facilities (missile silos, control centers, personnel quarters, and so on)
    $I_2$ = Interceptor missiles
    $I_3$ = Ground environment equipment (radars, computers, launchers, launch
        control center equipment, checkout equipment, maintenance equipment,
        and training equipment)
    $I_4$ = Initial inventories of spares and spare parts for $I_2$ and $I_3$
    $I_5$ = Initial training costs
    $I_6$ = Miscellaneous investment (initial transportation and travel, site activation
        cost, and so on)
$A$ = Annual Operating Cost:
    $A_1$ = Equipment maintenance
    $A_2$ = Personnel pay and allowances
    $A_3$ = Miscellaneous operating cost (including recurring travel and transportation,
        replacement training, and so on)
$TSC$ = Total System Cost = $R+I+AY$, where
    $Y$ = number of years of system operation

[a] All categories are to be expressed in terms of millions of constant (e.g., 1969) dollars.

is defined as research and development + investment + $Y$ years operating
cost.[3]

_____

[3] In this example we ignore time phasing, time preference, and related matters.

TABLE 7.2

**Key Variables used in the HPD Model**

---

$N$ = Number of force units (batteries or battalions if an Army operated system; squadrons if Air Force operated).

$M_u$ = Number of unit equipment (U.E.) interceptor missiles per force unit.[a] ($M_u$ = 10, ..., 50)

$M_f$ = Number of training missiles fired per force unit per year for $Y$ years.

$M_p$ = Number of missiles per force unit for depot maintenance pipeline.

$M$ = Total number of missiles to be procured for the operational inventory[b] for the entire system = $N(M_u + M_f + M_p)$.

$H$ = Index of hardness of the interceptor missile sites. ($H$ = 3, ..., 20)

$P_{o,m}$ = Number of operations and maintenance personnel per force unit.

$P_{a,s}$ = Number of administrative and support personnel per force unit.

$P$ = Total number of personnel per force unit = $P_{o,m} + P_{a,s}$.

$Y$ = Number of years of system operation

---
a

[a] The term "unit equipment" refers to the authorized quantity of major equipment for the direct accomplishment of the primary mission.

[b] Missiles procured for the research and development test program are excluded from $M$.

The key variables in the model are listed in Table 7.2. (Notice that some of these are defined only over a specified interval.) In addition to these variables we shall consider three types of interceptor missiles:

1. Missile A, having performance index = $p_a$
2. Missile B, having performance index = $p_b$      $(p_b > p_a)$
3. Missile C, having performance index = $p_c$      $(p_c < p_a)$

**Cost Categories in the Model**

We are now ready to describe the basic structure of the model. Let us do this by taking up each of the HPD system cost categories in turn:

1. *Research and Development* $(R)$. Here, we shall assume the existence of a set of relationships (a submodel) which estimates system research and development (R & D) cost primarily as a function of the performance characteristics of the interceptor missile and of the main components of the ground environment equipment, especially the radars. Suppose that this submodel yields the following set of HPD system R & D costs:[4]

$R = 500$, if a system using missile A (performance index = $p_a$) is assumed,

$R = 700$, if a system using missile B (performance index = $p_b$) is assumed,

$R = 400$, if a system using missile C (performance index = $p_c$) is assumed.

---

[4] All dollar costs are expressed in terms of millions of constant dollars.

2. *Facilities Investment Cost* $(I_1)$. An analysis of HPD facilities require-ments and costs indicates that facilities cost per force unit (for a given level of hardness, say $H = 3$) may be split into two parts: that which is essentially constant, and that which varies approximately as a function of the number of U.E. interceptor missiles per force unit $(M_u)$. (The second part is conditioned heavily by the construction costs of the missile silos.) Further analysis shows that this basic estimating relationship may be adjusted for hardness level by a function $F(H)$ which is equal to unity for $H = 3$, and which increases at a decreasing rate over the range $H = 3$, ..., 20.[5] Let us assume that in our example all of these considerations lead to the following equation for HPD system facilities investment cost:

$$I_1 = N(1.9 + 0.085M_u)[F(H)],$$

where

$$F(H) = 0.50 + 0.18H - 0.0044H^2$$

$$H = 3, \ldots, 20.$$

3. *Interceptor Missile Investment Cost* $(I_2)$. The investment cost of the operational missile inventory for the total HPD system may be calculated as follows:

$$I_2 = M[F(M)],$$

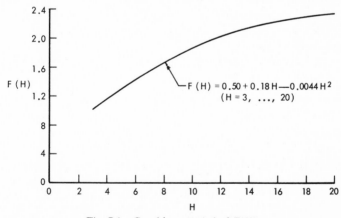

Fig. 7.1 – Graphic portrayal of $F(H)$

[5] $F(H)$ is portrayed graphically in Fig. 7.1.

where $F(M)$ is the cumulative average interceptor missile cost function defined as:[6]

$$F(M) = \alpha M^{-0.234},$$
$\alpha = 1.4$ if missile performance is $p_a$ (missile A),
$\alpha = 2.3$ if missile performance is $p_b$ (missile B),
$\alpha = 0.9$ if missile performance is $p_c$ (missile C).

Here, we assume that the values of $\alpha$ were obtained from analyses of the outputs from a submodel which estimates the level of the cost-quantity relationship (at some normalized quantity) as a function of the proposed missile performance characteristics. The exponent $-0.234$ is the slope of the cost-quantity relationship. In this case we have assumed an "85 percent" log-linear, cumulative-average curve, which implies that each time the total quantity of units produced is doubled, average production cost declines to 85 percent of the average cost prevailing before the doubling

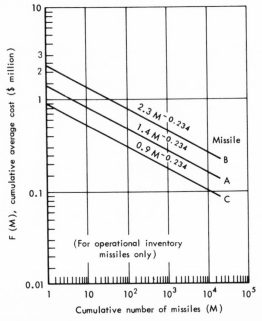

Fig. 7.2 – Cost-quantity relationships for missiles A, B, and C

---

[6] If $M = 100$, then $F(100)$ gives the cumulative average cost of missiles 1 through 100 produced for the operational inventory. Missiles produced for the R & D test program are exluded from $F(M)$ and included in system R & D cost. Therefore, $F(M)$ is defined for *operational inventory missiles* only, beginning with production unit number one.

of output.[7] The function $F(M)$ is shown graphically in Fig. 7.2 for the three values of $\alpha$.[8]

Let us now make a slight simplification in the equation for $M$. In Table 7.2, $M$ is defined as follows:

$$M = N(M_u + M_f + M_p).$$

We shall assume that the number of training firings per force unit per year is 4, and that the number of maintenance pipeline missiles may be estimated at 10 percent of the force unit's U.E. missiles $(M_u)$. Therefore,

$$M_f = 4Y$$

and

$$M_p = 0.1M_u.$$

Substituting these quantities into the equation for $M$, we obtain $M$ as a function of $N$, $M_u$, and $Y$:

$$M = N(M_u + 4Y + 0.1M_u)$$
$$= N(1.1M_u + 4Y).$$

4. *Ground Environment Equipment* $(I_3)$. This category is made up of several types of equipment,[9] some of which are quite complex. In a real life cost analysis, the requirements and costs for each type of equipment must be estimated by using separate subroutines or submodels. But to avoid complicating our model unduly, we shall assume that the estimating procedure for $I_3$ may be approximated simply as a function of force size and the number of U.E. interceptor missiles per force unit $(M_u)$, with an allowance for the fact that the investment cost of ground equipment per U.E. missile declines as $M_u$ varies from 10 to 50.[10] The result is:

$$I_3 = NM_u[F(M_u)], \qquad (M_u = 10, \ldots, 50)$$

where

$$F(M_u) = 6M_u^{-0.69}.$$

---

[7] See Harold Asher, *Cost-Quantity Relationships in the Airframe Industry*, R-291 (Santa Monica, California: The Rand Corporation, July 1, 1956), Chapter 2. Also see Herbert R. Kroeker and Robert E. Peterson, *A Handbook of Learning Curve Techniques* (Columbus, Ohio: The Ohio State University Research Foundation, 1961), Chapter 2.

[8] We have assumed a log-linear, cost-quantity relationship in order to help keep the HPD model simple. In reality one usually finds that major equipment cost-quantity relationships plotted on log-log paper tend to "flatten out" (become convex) as cumulative output increases. See Asher, *op. cit.*, Chapter 4.

[9] See the definition of $I_3$ in Table 7.1.

[10] This decline occurs because some parts of the ground environment do not change as $M_u$ increases. On the other hand, launching equipment, for example, does increase as $M_u$ increases.

The function $F(M_u)$ is portrayed graphically in Fig. 7.3.

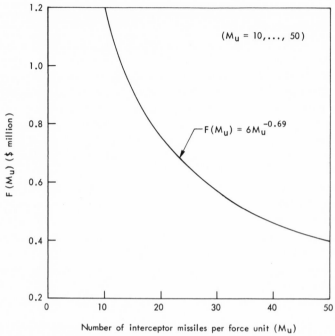

Fig. 7.3 – Graphic portrayal of $F(M_u)$

5. *Initial Spares and Spare Parts* $(I_4)$. Here, we shall assume that analyses of equipment spares and spare parts requirements and costs indicate that $I_4$ may be approximated by taking about 15 percent of the investment cost of the total interceptor missile inventory and about 25 percent of the investment cost of the ground environment equipment. This gives:

$$I_4 = 0.15 I_2 + 0.25 I_3$$
$$= 0.15 M[F(M)] + 0.25 N M_u[F(M_u)].$$

6. *Initial Training of Personnel* $(I_5)$. Suppose that analyses of initial training costs for defense missile systems suggest that a weighted average cost per man tends to be about \$4,000 if personnel are trained "from scratch" and about \$2,000 if most of the key personnel are inherited from the phase-out of other weapon systems. If this is so, initial training cost for the total system may be estimated as

$$I_5 = \beta N P$$

where

$$\beta = 0.004 \text{ (complete training case)}$$
$$\beta = 0.002 \text{ (transition training case).}$$

At this point we shall have to introduce the manpower requirements submodel. In actual practice, manpower submodels are often quite complex. They must, for example, distinguish between officers, enlisted men, and civilians; and more often than not, such models will provide for further classification within these three main categories. They also often provide for estimating requirements for operations and maintenance personnel as functions of the major equipment characteristics, system operational concepts, and the like. Determination of administrative and support personnel requirements may involve somewhat detailed estimating procedures, or it may involve the use of a simple aggregative estimating equation. In any event, the manpower requirements subroutine can be a substantial model in itself; and in many cases the personnel calculation is very important because total system cost is often very much a function of the numbers and types of manpower required to man the system.

Obviously we cannot get into this degree of detail in our example. We shall therefore have to make drastic simplifications. In order to include some semblance of a manpower requirements submodel in the example, let us postulate the following: Operations and maintenance personnel may be estimated as a function of the number of U.E. missiles per force unit, and incremental administrative and support personnel can be estimated as a function of the number of operations and maintenance personnel.[11] No distinction will be made between officers and enlisted men. The results are as follows:

$$P_{o,m} = 50 + 2M_u \ (M_u = 10, \ldots, 50)$$

$$P_{a,s} = 0.4P_{o,m}$$

$$P = P_{o,m} + P_{a,s} = 50 + 2M_u + 0.4(50 + 2M_u)$$

$$= 70 + 2.8M_u.$$

Substituting this value of $P$ in the training cost equation, we obtain:

$$I_5 = \beta NP = \beta N(70 + 2.8M_u).$$

---

[11] Administrative and support personnel requirements are "incremental" because it is assumed that the HPD force unit gets a certain amount of support from the installation it is assigned to defend.

7. *Miscellaneous Investment Cost* $(I_6)$. It will be assumed that miscellaneous investment cost can be estimated as a simple linear function of the number of force units:

$$I_6 = 2.5N.$$

8. *Total Investment Cost* $(I)$. Total investment cost for a proposed HPD system is:

$$I = \sum_{i=1}^{6} I_i.$$

9. *Equipment Maintenance Cost* $(A_1)$. Suppose that analyses of equipment maintenance activities suggest that annual missile maintenance cost may be estimated at about 10 percent of the investment cost of the U.E. inventory, and that the annual maintenance cost of ground environment equipment tends to average about 20 percent of initial investment cost. On the basis of these data, the equipment maintenance cost equation may be written as

$$A_1 = 0.1NM_u[F(M)] + 0.2NM_u[F(M_u)].$$

10. *Personnel Pay and Allowances* $(A_2)$. We shall assume that $A_2$ may be approximated by taking a weighted average pay and allowances cost factor and applying it to the total number of personnel in the HPD system:

$$A_2 = 0.006NP = 0.006N(70 + 2.8M_u)$$

$$= 0.42N + 0.0168NM_u.$$

11. *Miscellaneous Annual Operating Cost* $(A_3)$. It is assumed that miscellaneous operating cost can be estimated as a simple linear function of the total number of personnel in the system:

$$A_3 = 0.003NP = 0.003N(70 + 2.8M_u)$$

$$= 0.21N + 0.0084NM_u.$$

12. *Total Annual Operating Cost* $(A)$. Total annual operating cost is the sum of the individual operating cost categories:

$$A = \sum_{i=1}^{3} A_i.$$

13. *Total System Cost* $(TSC)$. Total HPD system cost is defined as follows:

$$TSC = R + I + YA.$$

**Use of the Model**

With the model completely described, let us now attempt to suggest a few of the ways the cost model of an individual system can be used in the analytical process.

One of the first questions that might be asked is: What "drives" the model? What are the key variables that matter the most? In many of the models used in real life analytical work the answer to this question is not immediately obvious. In our case, however, the model is so simple that the answer is readily apparent. Total force size ($N$) and number of U.E. missiles per force unit ($M_u$) appear in almost every component of the model. Therefore, these two variables must play a key role in determining the output of the model. The assumed number of years of system operation ($Y$) could also be important. So might the performance characteristics of the interceptor missile, but this is less obvious.

All of this can be seen more clearly if we assemble the model in more compact form. If the categories are added up and certain terms combined, the results are as follows:[12]

1. *Research and Development* cost is a function of missile performance:

$$R = \begin{cases} 500 \text{ if missile performance is } p_a \text{ (missile A)} \\ 700 \text{ if missile performance is } p_b \text{ (missile B)} \\ 400 \text{ if missile performance is } p_c \text{ (missile C).} \end{cases}$$

2. *Investment* cost is primarily a function of force size, hardness level, number of U.E. missiles per force unit, and missile performance:

$$I = 1.9N[F(H)] + 0.085NM_u[F(H)] + 1.15M[F(M)] + 1.25NM_u[F(M_u)]$$
$$+ \beta N(70 + 2.8M_u) + 2.5N,$$

where

   a.  $F(H) = 0.50 + 0.18H - 0.0044H^2$         $(H = 3, \ldots, 20)$
   b.    $M = 1.1NM_u + 4NY$              $(M_u = 10, \ldots, 50)$
   c.  $F(M) = \alpha M^{-0.234}$
            $\alpha = 1.4$ for missile A (performance $= p_a$)
            $\alpha = 2.3$ for missile B (performance $= p_b$)
            $\alpha = 0.9$ for missile C (performance $= p_c$)
   d.  $F(M_u) = 6M_u^{-0.69}$
   e.    $\beta = \begin{cases} .004 \text{ for complete training case} \\ .002 \text{ for transition training case.} \end{cases}$

---

[12] In subsequent discussion, we shall refer to this as the *basic HPD cost model*.

3. *Annual Operating* cost is mainly a function of force size and number of U.E. missiles per force unit:

$$A = 0.1NM_u[F(M)] + 0.2NM_u[F(M_u)] + 0.0252NM_u + 0.63N.$$

4. *Total System Cost* is influenced by all of the above and the number of years of system operation $(Y)$:

$$TSC = R + I + AY.$$

Let us now demonstrate the use of the model. Hopefully, in exercising the model we can show how it serves as a useful integrating device between inputs and outputs in the cost analysis process.

Very often one of the first things systems analysts want to know is how total system cost $(TSC)$ varies with force size – usually for some "base case" system configuration that they have in mind. Suppose that in our example the systems analysts do have a base case, and that its configuration results in the following values for the key variables in the HPD cost model (call this *Case 1*):

1. Missile performance index $= p_a$. Therefore, missile A is to be the interceptor in the basic system, which means:

$$R = 500$$

$$F(M) = 1.4M^{-0.234}.$$

2. Hardness level is 3. Hence $F(H) = 1.$[13]
3. Number of U.E. interceptor missiles per force unit $(M_u) = 10$, which means that $F(M_u) = 1.2.$[14]
4. Assume all system personnel are initially trained from scratch. Thus, $\beta = 0.004$.
5. Assume number of years of system operation $(Y) = 10$.
6. Given that $M_u = 10$ and $Y = 10$, the total stock of interceptor missiles becomes purely a function of force size; that is, $M = (1.1)(10)N + (4)(10)N = 51N$.

Given (1) through (6) above, the cost model reduces to a relatively simple function of $N$:

$$TSC = 500 + 53.462N + 68.65N[1.4(51N)^{-0.234}].[15]$$

---

[13] See Fig. 7.1.
[14] See Fig. 7.3.
[15] The value of the quantity inside the brackets can be readily approximated from Fig. 7.2. For example, for $N = 100$, the cumulative average cost of 5100 missiles is \$0.19 million (read from the missile A curve).

If this function is plotted over the range of force units 50 through 250, the result is the total system cost ($TSC$) curve shown in Fig. 7.4.[16] The $TSC$ vs.

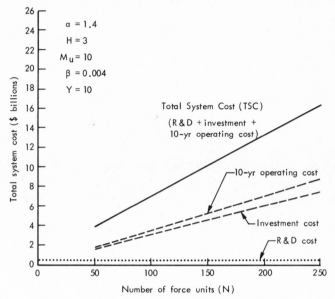

Fig. 7.4 – HPD system cost versus force size (Case 1)

force size cost function gives an explicit statement of how total system cost changes as the force size is varied for a specified set of system characteristics – the Case 1 set in this instance. In Fig. 7.4 we see that total cost is essentially linear over the range of interest ($N = 50$ to $N = 250$) and that therefore marginal cost is constant.[17]

As pointed out in Chapter 4, the $TSC$ vs. force size function is a fundamentally important part of the cost model. It enables the cost analyst to answer readily a very relevant class of questions which typically arises

---

[16] The compenent curves (R & D, investment, and 10-year operating cost) were computed from the basic HPD cost model (see pp. 177–178).

[17] Using the formula for the slope of a line through two given points, the $TSC$ curve in Fig. 7.4 can be approximated by:

$$TSC = 0.8 + 0.064N.$$

Marginal cost, therefore, is:

$$\frac{d(TSC)}{dN} = 0.064.$$

in the systems analysis process.[18] In the context of our illustration, for example, the systems analysts might want to know how much HPD could probably be attained at a stipulated cost level – say $10 billion. For the Case 1 HPD configuration, the answer (from Fig. 7.4) is about 150 force units or 1,500 U.E. interceptor missiles for a 10-year operational period. The possible effectiveness of this HPD force must then be calculated and compared with the estimated increases in offensive missile force survivability which might be achieved through *alternative* survivability measures obtainable from the $10 billion.

Or, alternatively, the systems analysts might specify a desired level of survivability and determine the configurations and quantities of various alternative measures that might be used to attain it. With corresponding sets of *TSC* vs. force size functions available, the costs of the various alternatives may be easily determined. For example, if one of the alternatives is 200 force units of Case 1 HPD, the estimated total system cost (see Fig. 7.4) would be about $14 billion.

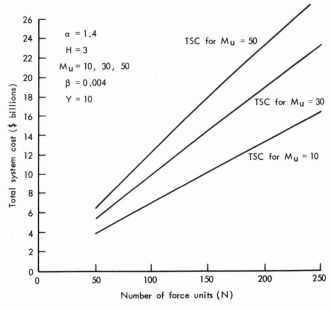

Fig. 7.5 – HPD system cost versus force size for $M_u = 10$, 30, 50 (Case 2)

---

[18] Perhaps it should be pointed out that we have come "full circle" since Chapter 4. There, *TSC* vs. force size costs functions were presented as examples of one type of output from the cost analysis process, with no indication as to how that output might be obtained. Now, with the benefit of the input-oriented Chapters 5 and 6, and with the aid of our illustrative cost model, we begin to see the relationships among inputs and outputs.

Let us now return to the basic HPD cost model and consider examples of other forms of output that may be obtained from it. As suggested previously, from the structure of the model it would seem that HPD total system cost might be quite sensitive to the number of U.E. interceptor missiles per force unit ($M_u$). Obviously this is an important variable, since the systems analysts would no doubt want to consider force units with varying complements of U.E. interceptor missiles.

To illustrate the sensitivity of $TSC$ to $M_u$, let us keep the same specifications as those for Case 1, except that $M_u$ will be computed for three values: 10, 30, and 50. We shall call this exploration Case 2. The results of exercising the basic HPD model are portrayed in Fig. 7.5. Here it is apparent that HPD $TSC$ is indeed very sensitive to $M_u$, but that it becomes somewhat less so as $M_u$ is increased. That is, the first partial derivative of the $TSC$ function with respect to $M_u$ is apparently increasing at a decreasing rate.[19] This can be seen more clearly by computing Case 3, which has the same specifications as Case 2 except that force size ($N$) is held constant at 150 and $M_u$ is varied over its entire range (10 through 50). The outcome is shown in Fig. 7.6 (Case 3).

Why do we get these results? We would expect $TSC$ to increase at a decreasing rate for several reasons. One, for example, is the influence of the negatively sloped missile cost function $F(M)$. More important is the fact that all components of facilities and the ground environment do not

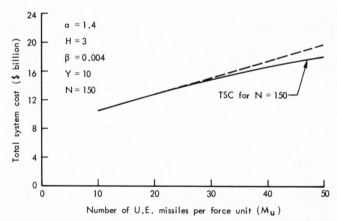

Fig. 7.6 – Total system cost versus number of missiles per force unit (Case 3)

---

[19] That is, for $M_u = 10, \ldots, 50$:

$$\frac{\partial(TSC)}{\partial M_u} > 0; \frac{\partial^2(TSC)}{\partial M_u^2} < 0.$$

increase in proportion to increases in $M_u$, and some components do not change at all. Thus, total costs as shown by the curve in Fig. 7.6 increase at a decreasing rate as $M_u$ increases.

At this point the reader may be beginning to wonder about a side issue which in many instances can be important: the matter of computational burden. Let us digress briefly to offer a few comments about the computational problem.

Even in the case of an extremely simple model – like our HPD example – the computational burden can be rather heavy, particularly if numerous sensitivity analyses are to be made. Can anything be done to facilitate the process? The answer is "yes"; a great deal can be done in many instances. This is especially true for models like our HPD example which lend themselves naturally to programming on an on-line, time-sharing computer system like JOSS.[20] This was done for the basic HPD cost model,[21] with the result that the analyst can readily explore variations in combinations of the following: $\alpha$, $H$, $M_u$, $\beta$, $Y$, and $N$.[22]

Let us now return to our basic HPD model and illustrate a few more of the types of information that a cost model can provide the analyst.

Systems analysts often worry about what should be assumed about the number of years new capabilities might be in the operational force. Does it make any difference in the relative comparisons among alternatives? In order to help explore this question, the cost analyst must be readily able to furnish total system costs for varying assumptions about years of operation. Our basic HPD model is "open" with respect to number of years of operation $(Y)$, so that it is relatively easy to examine the impact on total system cost $(TSC)$ of various assumptions about $Y$. As an illustration, let us go back to Case 1 and keep all specifications the same except for $Y$. What happens if $Y = 5, 10$, and $15$? (Call this Case 4.)

---

[20] JOSS is a trademark and service mark of The Rand Corporation for its computer program and services using that program.
[21] The author is indebted to H. E. Boren of The Rand Corporation research staff, who programmed the model on Rand's JOSS system. Programming time was about 20 minutes – eloquent testimony to the value of such a system to an experienced professional.
[22] Here, we must insert a note of caution. First of all, most real life models are much more complicated than our HPD example, and hence are more difficult to automate. In any event, it is important to emphasize the point that the analyst must not be over-enamored with computerization. Above all, a model must be constructed with a view to building a reasonably good representation of reality – not primarily with a view toward automation. Giving computerization first priority puts the cart before the horse. Only when the analyst is satisfied that he *does* have a reasonably good representation for purposes of the problem at hand does it become important to explore the possibilities of appropriate automation – even if only parts of the model can be so treated. This can greatly facilitate sensitivity analyses, which are so vital to the analytical process.

The results are graphed in Figs. 7.7A and 7.7B. As might be expected,

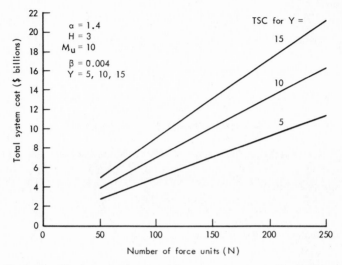

Fig. 7.7A – Total system cost versus force size for $Y = 5, 10, 15$ (Case 4)

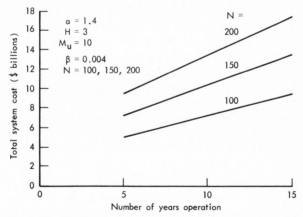

Fig. 7.7B – Total system cost versus number of years operation

HPD $TSC$ is quite sensitive to variations in $Y$. However, two other things are apparent: The $TSC$ curves remain essentially linear throughout the range $Y = 5$ to $15$,[23] and the slopes of the $TSC$ curves in Fig. 7.7A

---

[23] This is not always the case. Oftentimes the negatively sloped equipment cost-quantity curve makes the system investment cost curve ($I$ as a function of force size) increase at a decreasing rate. This can sometimes cause the total system cost curve ($TSC$ as a function of force size) to increase at a decreasing rate, particularly for lower values of $Y$.

(marginal costs with respect to force size) increase as $Y$ is increased. For example:

| Value of $Y$ | Marginal Cost |
|---|---|
| 5 | ~0.04 |
| 10 | ~0.06 |
| 15 | ~0.08 |

These variations might be important in the overall analysis.

Is the model correct when it shows increases of marginal cost (with respect to force size) as $Y$ is increased? If it did not, then something would be wrong. This is obvious from the following: Research and development cost is independent of $Y$. Investment cost is largely independent of $Y$, except for the increase in the stock of missiles for training firings each year. Total system operating cost, however, is very much a function of $Y$ in the following way. In most instances, including our HPD example, annual operating cost *per force unit* is essentially constant for a given set of system characteristics. The equation for total system annual operating cost can therefore be written as a linear homogeneous function of force size $(N)$:

$$A = \Phi N \qquad (\Phi = \text{a constant}).$$

Then for $Y$ years the total system operating cost is $\Phi YN$. Thus, the slope of the operating cost curve becomes steeper as $Y$ increases. This in turn increases the slope of the total system cost curve $(R+I+AY)$ as $Y$ increases. Hence the reason for the behavior of the $TSC$ curves in Fig. 7.7A.

So far we have not varied the primary mission equipment (interceptor missile) characteristics. Cases 1 through 4 have utilized missile A with performance index $p_a$, which implies $\alpha = 1.4$. Certainly the systems analysts will want to examine the consequences of different hardware characteristics in terms of both system cost and effectiveness. From the viewpoint of the cost side of the problem, what are the implications for $TSC$ if the higher performance interceptor (missile B) – which costs almost 65 percent more per copy than missile A – is assumed? What if missile C is assumed? *A priori* it is not clear from the basic HPD cost model what the answer is, although it would seem that $TSC$ might be fairly sensitive to variations in missile specification because the missile cost function, $F(M)$, shows up quite prominently in both investment and operating cost.[24]

To examine this question, let us take the Case 1 specifications and use

---

[24] Refer back to the basic HPD cost model, pp. 177–178.

the model to test two variations: $\alpha = 2.3$ (representing missile B) and $\alpha = 0.9$ (representing missile C). (Call this Case 5.) The results, shown in Fig. 7.8, do not suggest that *TSC* is dramatically sensitive to variations

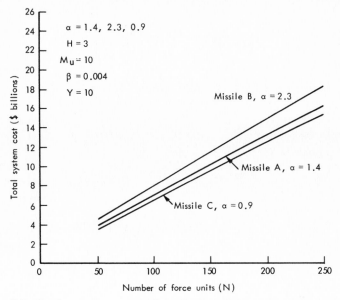

Fig. 7.8 – Total system cost versus force size for Missiles A, B, and C (Case 5)

in $\alpha$. But here, the number of U.E. missiles per force unit $(M_u)$ is held constant at 10. Would the results be similar for higher values of $M_u$? Suppose we modify Case 5 and explore this possibility: Let $M_u$ vary over its entire range for two force sizes $N = 150$ and $N = 250$. (Call this Case 6.) The results are presented in Fig. 7.9. It would seem that the differences in total system cost attributable to the type of interceptor missile used in the system tend to increase as $M_u$ increases. These differences also tend to be greater as force size $(N)$ increases. These influences are portrayed in a different way in Fig. 7.10, where total system cost is plotted as a function of missile type (represented by $\alpha$) for $M_u = 10$, 30, 50 and for two force sizes $N = 150$ and $N = 250$.

In the cases examined so far, total system cost is either moderately sensitive or very sensitive to key system parameters that we have chosen to vary. Is it possible to offer examples of *in*sensitivity?

In Cases 1 through 6 the hardness level index $(H)$ has been held constant at $H = 3$, for which value $F(H) = 1$. What if higher values of $H$ are specified? Would the impact on *TSC* be very great? *A priori*, we would think

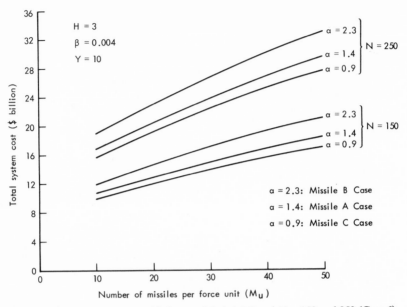

Fig. 7.9 – Total system cost versus $M_u$ for $\alpha = 0.9, 1.4, 2.3$ and $N = 150$ and 250 (Case 6)

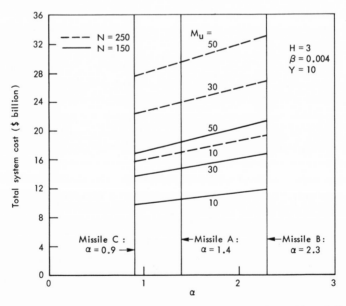

Fig. 7.10 – Total system cost versus type of missile: for $M = 10, 30, 50,$ and $N = 150$ and 250

not; but let us exercise the model and find out. Suppose the specifications for Case 1 are used, except that $H$ is permitted to vary over its entire range ($H = 3, \ldots, 20$) for three levels of total force size, $N = 100, 150, 200$. The results are portrayed in Fig. 7.11. Here it is evident that HPD *TSC*

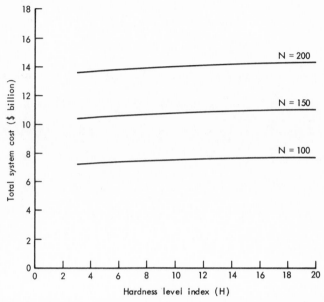

Fig. 7.11 – Total system cost versus hardness index for 3 levels of force size

is not very sensitive to variations in $H$,[25] and that this conclusion is independent of force size. Again, this is something that the systems analysts would want to know. For one thing, if we are uncertain about what degree of hardness might be required in the future, the lack of *TSC* sensitivity to variations in $H$ means that we need not worry very much about the implications of such uncertainty as far as the *cost* considerations are concerned – at least over the range of $H$ considered in the analysis. The implications for system effectiveness, however, could be more important.

As a final example, let us use the model to calculate two extreme cases: one representing the set of most expensive HPD configurations and one representing the class of least expensive system configurations. To do this we shall specify the following sets of inputs to the basic HPD cost model:

---

[25] That is to say: $\dfrac{\partial(TSC)}{\partial H} \cong 0.$

| Input Item | High Value | Low Value |
|---|---|---|
| α | 2.3 | 0.9 |
| H | 20 | 3 |
| $M_u$ | 50 | 10 |
| β | 0.004 | 0.002 |
| Y | 15 | 5 |
| N | 50–250 | 50–250 |

The results of the "high-low" calculation are shown in Fig. 7.12. The

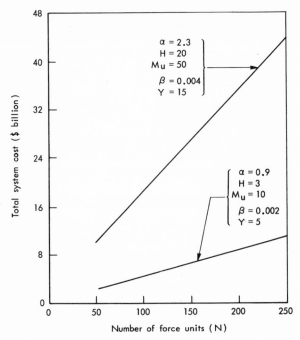

Fig. 7.12 – Total system cost versus force size: High-Low cases

reader may be somewhat surprised at the size of the region between the
high and low curves. While our example is hypothetical, the results
portrayed in Fig. 7.12 are not atypical of those obtained from real life
cost models used to support the long-range planning process.

The reasons for such large *TSC* regions are many and varied; but one
of the main ones is that when the time horizon extends 5, 10, or more years
into the future a wide range of options is open for consideration. In the
HPD example this means a broad range of possible system configurations

(including number of years of operation), which in turn happens to have widely varying impacts on *TSC*.

Another way to view the matter is in terms of uncertainty. For the distant future, major "state-of-the-world" uncertainties abound. These uncertainties imply a variety of possible system configurations, each set of which relates to a different part of the total state-of-the-world spectrum in the future. In a sense, then, the range between high and low cases, like that portrayed in Fig. 7.12, reflects the extent of major uncertainties existing in the area of national security being studied.

**Lessons from This Example**

Let us conclude our illustration at this point and sum up. While the simple model used in the example is only moderately representative of reality, it hopefully served as a pedagogical vehicle for helping to make several main points about cost models.

These are:

1. A cost model may be viewed as an integrating device for systematically bringing together the various factors on the input side (cost categories, system configuration specifications, estimating relationships, and so on) and relating them to some specific type of output-oriented military capability in the future (hardpoint defense in our example).

2. The use of such an integrating device can facilitate the analytical process by:
   a. Helping the cost analysts gain insights into the problem at hand:
   b. Helping the cost analysts to serve better the systems analysts in the sense of having the capability to provide readily estimates of resource impact associated with a wide range of questions that good systems analysts typically must explore;
   c. Helping to organize an efficient computational procedure, whether automated or not, so that a range of relevant cases can be properly examined and various sensitivities explored.

3. Cost models and computer programs (automation) should not be viewed as being synonymous. Building a representation of reality (the model) appropriate to the class of problems under consideration is the primary objective. Automation is secondary. However, when automation (in full or in part) can be accomplished without significant sacrifices in the representation of reality, it usually should be attempted. Even partial automation can often greatly facilitate the capability to do sensitivity analysis.

## Types of Cost Models

Let us now return to the categories of cost models outlined in the introduction to this chapter:

1. Resource requirements submodels.
2. Individual system cost models.
3. Mission area force-mix cost models.
4. Total force cost models.

Each of these is discussed briefly in the following subsections.

### Resource Requirements Submodels

As pointed out earlier, resource requirements submodels are usually a part of a model in some broader context. Indeed, they may be developed for almost any category in the overall input structure. However, the more formal types of submodels are usually constructed for those cases where the resource impact is likely to be relatively large, where analytical problems have to be explored in some depth in their own right, or where the computational burden is significant. Examples of areas where such models have been used include major equipment requirements and costs, manpower requirements, personnel training requirements and costs, and facilities requirements and costs.

Let us take the major equipment area and discuss it in more detail. Consider, for example, the case of a fleet of future manned aircraft designed for continuous airborne duty on a series of stations covering a large geographical area.[26] In instances like this, total system cost is highly sensitive to the total number of aircraft required to perform the mission. The total number of aircraft required in the system is, in turn, very much a function of such variables as aircraft performance characteristics (especially endurance), fly-out distance from base to station, number of stations, aircraft maintenance policy (one, two, or three shifts), and the like. Thus, the task of computing and analyzing total system aircraft requirements for a range of hardware and operational concept characteristics can be substantial. Here is an example of a case where the effort involved in constructing a rather formal aircraft requirements submodel is likely to pay off in terms of greatly facilitating the cost analyst's understanding of the problem and hence his ability to support the systems analysis process.[27] In addition to dealing with aircraft requirements, such

---

[26] A case in point is the antisubmarine warfare (ASW) mission example presented in Chapter 4, pp. 82–85.

[27] Such models have been developed and used in practice. For example, see R. L. Petruschell, *Project Cost Estimating*, P-3687 (Santa Monica, Calif.: The Rand Corporation, September 1967).

a model could also be designed to draw upon a data bank of relevant aircraft cost functions (including cost-quantity relationships), so that once aircraft requirements are computed, the dollar cost impact can also be determined.[28]

### Individual System Cost Models

Our hardpoint defense illustration is an example of one type of individual system cost model.[29] It is a rather specialized model in that it pertains only to the HPD part of ballistic missile defense. The model is also "static" in the sense that no provision is made for explicit treatment of time-phasing of resource impact by fiscal year over a period of years. The output is in effect an *index* of cost consisting of the sum of costs for research and development, investment, and a stipulated number of years of operating.

Other individual system cost models can be somewhat different, of course, from that used in our example. For one thing, they might be much more general. They could, for example, pertain to a range of types of missile systems – not just to HPD. (If this were true, the input side of the model would have to be more "open-ended" than the HPD case.)

And, indeed, some of these models are structured quite generally, with a view to automation (at least in part), and with provision for storing a sizable data bank of estimating relationships covering a wide range of hardware and operational concept configurations within the relevant class of weapon systems. Here, the inputs to the model would be primarily sets of system description information, and the computer program would automatically select the appropriate combination of estimating relationships for use in any given case.

Individual system cost models may also be structured in terms of the form of output that is desired. For example, if time-phased cost estimates are required, then explicit provision must be made for inputting major equipment delivery schedules, force unit activation schedules, or some other form of timetable of projected military capabilities. The model must

---

[28] For example, see H. E. Boren, Jr., *DAPCA: A Computer Program for Determining Aircraft Development and Production Cost*, RM-5521-PR (Santa Monica, Calif.: The Rand Corporation, February 1967).

[29] For examples of other types see:

(1) T. Arthur Smith, "Army Force Cost Models – An Example," in T. Arthur Smith (ed.), *Economic Analysis and Military Resource Allocation* (Washington, D.C.: Office, Comptroller of the Army, 1968), pp. 65–78. (An Army division cost model.)

(2) Report No. NADC-AW-6734, *System Cost and Operational Resource Evaluator (SCORE) Executive Routine*, published by the Naval Air Development Center, Warminster, Pennsylvania. (A general-purpose computerized model for estimating weapon system cost.)

then contain a procedure for tying the cost estimates to the specified timetable and for generating alternative patterns of timing of the cost impacts.

A frequently used approach is to make the basic calculations on the basis of deliveries or force unit activations, and then to use a series of lead and lag factors to convert the basic calculations into time-phased estimates of total obligational authority, expenditures, or some other alternative form of time-phased output. Finally, a procedure may be included in the model for handling alternative assumptions about time preference – that is, assumptions about alternative discount rates. The final output will therefore be in a form similar to that discussed in Chapter 4 and illustrated in Figs. 4.12, 4.13, and 4.14.

Provision can also be made in the cost model of an individual system for computing total system costs in specific relation to various measures of system output or effectiveness, such as cost per pound of payload in orbit, cost per sortie, cost per target killed, and the like. The example concerning antisubmarine warfare presented in Chapter 4 is a case in point, since the cost model calculated total system cost per pound of payload on station as a function of aircraft payload weight for several types of aircraft. (See Fig. 4.10 in Chapter 4.)

### Mission Area Force-Mix Cost Models

In Chapters 2 and 4 we referred to systems analyses of alternative force mixes in some mission area:

1. Mixes of land-based and sea-based tactical airpower.
2. Mixes of airlift, sealift, and prepositioning.
3. Mixes of strategic offensive and defensive forces.

Studies involving comparisons of alternative force mixes have become increasingly important in recent years. Systems analysts have come more and more to realize that in many cases simple intersystem comparisons are too narrow to produce meaningful results. In principle the solution is to examine total forces, the limiting case being the total Department of Defense force structure. In practice, however, total force contexts are likely to be too broad, especially with respect to effectiveness considerations.

A reasonably workable middle ground is the study of a mission area force mix, which is, in effect, a major subset of the total force. Here, enough of the total problem is included to permit taking into account most of the relevant interactions among weapon and support systems and other types of activities. At the same time the context is limited sufficiently to permit a considerable amount of useful analytical work.

A salient feature of mission area force-mix comparisons is that more often than not they cut across agency lines: that is, they involve projected military capabilities for some combination of the Army, Navy, and Air Force. Obviously, we could not very well do a force-mix study of the strategic offensive and defensive forces without considering the Navy's fleet ballistic missile systems and the Army's ballistic missile defense system in addition to the Air Force's projected systems. Nor could we study tactical airpower for the future without considering proposed capabilities for the Navy's sea-based systems in addition to the Air Force's land-based systems.

Let us now turn to force-mix *cost* considerations – cost models in particular. We shall not discuss mission area force-mix cost models in great detail here, because an example of one is presented and discussed in some depth in Chapter 9.[30]

The reader may well question why we have included mission area force-mix cost models in our categorization of cost models. If we have a reasonably complete inventory of individual system cost models, why cannot these be used in dealing with a force-mix problem? Are not the outputs of the individual models simply additive, so that the cost of a proposed force-mix alternative could be easily obtained from the components? On the other hand, if we have a total force structure cost model, why cannot it be used to estimate the cost implications of alternative proposals for a mission area subset of the total force? These are reasonable questions. We shall have to try to answer them.

Now it may be true that for some problems the analysts could essentially take estimates derived from individual system cost models and merely add them up. However, this is not true in general. One reason is that there may be significant interactions among the components of the force mix that should be taken into account. The proposed phase-out of systems in one part of the mix might free resources (such as base facilities and personnel) that could be used by systems postulated for concomitant phase-in in another part of the force mix. If the objective is to estimate the incremental cost of the stipulated mission area force mix, then these interactions should be taken into account. Simple addition of cost estimates obtained from individual models in isolation from one another might well produce the wrong result.

Moreover, other costs, which are usually excluded from individual weapon system models, may have to be taken into account. For example, the costs of command and administrative activities – which are primarily

---

[30] Moreover, some of the points made regarding total force structure cost models in the following section apply to mission area force-mix models as well.

a function of mission area force size rather than mix – would have to be included in the estimated costs of proposed force mixes which are significantly larger than those currently planned.

Similar problems arise if we attempt to use a total force structure cost model to deal with mission area force-mix problems. In principle, this should be possible. However, there is a difference here between principle and practice, primarily because most total force models are "total" for only one service: the Army, the Navy, or the Air Force. Since most relevant mission area force-mix problems are interservice in nature, the typical solution to this problem has been simply to develop a more or less specialized force-mix cost model tailored just to the requirements of the problem at hand,[31] drawing of course on individual system cost models wherever possible.

There are other difficulties as well in using total force structure models. For example, it is not always clear that the structure and estimating procedures of the separate models are reasonably consistent with one another. And, unfortunately, it is rare that a given group of cost analysts has access to more than one of these models.

Thus, as systems analysts increasingly focus their attention on studies of mission area force mixes, the cost analysts must continue to build models of this type.

### Total Force Cost Models

Total force cost models, as we have just seen, are designed to span a broad context – presently the boundaries of an individual service. To the knowledge of the author, no Department of Defense-wide *analytical* cost model exists today;[32] nor is one likely to be developed in the near future.

To put the matter very simply, the main purpose of a total force cost model is to estimate the resource impact of proposed alternative total force structures for a given military service. A force structure is a time-phased specification of numbers of force units (such as divisions, carrier task forces, or squadrons) by fiscal year over a period of future years for a selected complete set of weapon and support systems.[33] A postulated force structure is the primary, though by no means the only, input to a total

---

[31] An example for strategic offensive and defensive forces is presented in Chapter 9.

[32] That is, "analytical" in the sense that we are viewing cost models in this chapter. In principle, a consistent Department of Defense-wide total force model could be developed. But it would be a tremendous task – one that is probably not feasible in the near future.

[33] Here again we are using the word "systems" in a broad sense. In addition to military capabilities traditionally referred to as systems (the Minuteman weapon system, the Polaris weapon system, the Nike weapon system, and the like), we use the term to include Army divisions, Navy task forces, and so on.

force cost model. The main outputs are estimates of time-phased manpower requirements and of time-phased dollar costs (total obligational authority or expenditures). These outputs are typically identified from any of several points of view:

1. Major program area (strategic offensive and defensive forces, general purpose forces, transport forces, and so on).
2. Program elements (such as weapon and support systems) within each major program area.
3. Major cost category (research and development, investment, and operating cost).
4. Summary resource and functional categories (for example, procurement, construction, operations and maintenance, and military personnel).[34]

Total force cost models must of necessity be at least partially automated, since determining the time-phased cost impact of even a *single* 10-year plan for one of the military services typically involves several hundred thousand calculations. To carry out such an exercise entirely by hand computation would require an unacceptably long time. In most service force planning deliberations the planners typically examine not just one plan (total force structure) but many alternatives – sometimes as many as 50 – and the resource impact of all the alternatives must be estimated within a reasonable period of time. Planners cannot wait several months for the results. Because a total force cost model must thus have a relatively short "turnaround" time, it must be automated wherever it is possible to do so without seriously compromising the basic estimating procedures used in the model.[35]

Another motive for automation is related to one of the distinguishing features of a properly structured total force model: the capability to take into account certain interactions among program elements in the force in

---

[34] For an example of a cost format structured in these terms, see Table 4.2 in Chapter 4.
[35] Turnaround time is typically very much a function of the particular force structure being examined. If it is similar in content to a case calculated previously, it can essentially be treated as an iteration of the previously run case. Here, turnaround time can be very short – perhaps a matter of several hours. At the other extreme, if a postulated force structure contains new weapon systems for which key estimating relationships are not contained in the data bank, the turnaround time can be long – sometimes several weeks or longer. In such cases a research effort is required to assemble and develop the necessary input data.
In general, short turnaround time requires the availability of a well-stocked cost data bank of estimating relationships and other key input data, and a well-trained staff of cost analysts. No amount of automation can significantly make up for serious deficiencies in either.

a way that is not possible in smaller models. We have already referred to this point briefly in the discussion of mission area force-mix cost models.

To assess properly the *incremental* cost impact of proposed force structures, the model must be able to estimate *net* resource requirements in several areas, especially facilities, personnel training, fuel stocks, and general purpose equipment. Systems and activities proposed for phase-out in one part of a projected force structure may free resources (such as trained personnel) that may be used by new systems postulated for phase-in in another part of the force.

This so-called "inherited assets" problem can best be dealt with in the context of a projected total force for the particular service under consideration.[36] Thus, a properly structured total force model should contain automated subroutines which will "search" a projected total force structure, pick up surpluses of assets made available by phase-outs, and redistribute these assets to new systems or to existing systems projected to remain in the force. For example, a cost subroutine for personnel training would search a proposed total force structure for numbers and types of personnel made surplus by phase-outs, and "assign" these personnel to new systems or activities. The initial training costs associated with this inherited manpower would be either zero or the cost of transition training. In cases where no personnel resources were inherited, gross requirements for new systems and for replacement personnel for activities remaining in the force would be equal to net requirements,[37] and initial training costs would be computed on a full cost basis – that is, personnel would be assumed to be trained from scratch.

We should emphasize that the automated subroutines designed to deal with the inherited assets problem need not (indeed, cannot) use refined estimating methods. This is so because in long-range planning "first approximation" estimates of cost are usually all that is required, and in most cases all that is attainable. The output of the types of subroutines referred to here is in keeping with the accuracy requirements of long-range planning. Use of these devices in the programming of near-future activities would not be appropriate.

So far, two distinguishing characteristics of total force cost models have been mentioned: their broad scope and their consequent ability to take into account more completely certain interactions among the program elements in a total force. One other characteristic is worthy of mention.

---

[36] In principle the problem should be handled Department of Defense-wide. As mentioned earlier, however, such broad contexts, while correct in principle, cannot be dealt with in practice at present.

[37] Gross requirements minus inherited assets equal net requirements.

Since the objective of a total force model is to estimate the total cost of a projected total plan to a service, specific provision must be made for procedures to determine the estimated costs of numerous service-wide support activities. These costs are not (and should not be) included in intersystem and mission area force-mix cost studies.

Examples of service-wide support activities are: basic research and exploratory (nonsystem) development, the service academies, support for major command headquarters and the service's headquarters in the Pentagon, service-wide supply system operations, service finance center operations, service-wide communications networks, and so on. Since the nature of these activities is not primarily a function of the combat force mix, their costs are not allocated to combat program elements, or even to primary mission areas (such as strategic operations or continental defense).[38] Typically, these general support costs account for a major fraction of the total cost of a service's long-range plan – sometimes as much as a third or more.

Present total force cost models usually deal with the general support area in highly aggregative terms. Basically, the idea is to try to distinguish among (1) those service-wide support costs which are essentially independent of the size of the combat force structure and which may be projected more or less on a "level of effort" basis; (2) those support costs which may be appropriately projected as a function of the total combat force size; and (3) those which must be given special treatment (usually calculated by hand outside the model).

So much for our brief description of total force cost models. Let us now consider their uses.

In view of what was said in the discussion of mission area force-mix cost models, the reader may well question the utility of total force cost models. If systems analysts do not have analytical techniques to evaluate total force structures (especially those required to estimate effectiveness), why should cost analysts expend the considerable effort required to build total force cost models, to operate them, and to keep them updated? Part of the answer has already been given: such models allow us to take into account certain interactions among program elements within and across various mission areas. But other reasons might be mentioned.

---

[38] Similarly, general support costs in a given mission area are not allocated to the end-product program elements in that mission area – for example, a pro-rata share of the operating costs of Headquarters, Strategic Air Command is not identified with the Minuteman weapon system. This goes back to a basic principle set forth in Chapter 4: arbitrary, accounting-type cost allocations are inappropriate in cost analyses done in support of the systems analysis process.

In the first place, the fact that systems analysts do not as yet have methods for quantitatively analyzing the effectiveness of total force structures does not in itself imply that total force cost models cannot be useful in the long-range planning process. For one thing, such models can be used to calculate a set of relevant equal-cost total force structure alternatives. With the cost aspects of the problem "normalized," so to speak, the decisionmakers can then better concentrate their attention on the utility considerations, with the aid of whatever partial effectiveness measures the systems analysts can provide. This is a significant point, because it is very difficult, if not impossible, to make effective comparisons if the costs and the effectiveness of alternatives are both varying at the same time. Since the determination of equal-cost alternatives over a number of years in the future is a difficult, iterative process, especially for total force structures, total force cost models of the type we have been discussing are almost indispensable in making the process feasible.

Moreover, these models have an important role in another process. Each of the military services must periodically prepare an official description of its total force structure plan for the distant future. These plans, which are submitted to the Joint Chiefs of Staff and to the Office of the Secretary of Defense, provide the point of departure for the annual planning, programming, and budgeting cycle for the Department of Defense.

In the more distant past, these plans were developed for the most part on a "pure requirements" basis. That is to say, the plans represented the total force size and mix that the services wished to have, assuming essentially no resource constraints. The results were exceedingly visionary, and – predicatably enough – had little or no impact on what actually was approved in the real planning process.[39]

In recent years, however, the services have been required to develop their long-range force structure plans with resource constraints taken into account explicitly. This has meant that cost considerations have had to enter the planning process at the outset.

At the present time, force planners typically go through an iterative process of "cutting and piecing," "putting and taking," and exercising many alternatives. Most of these alternatives have to be "costed out" in a proximate fashion to see whether they generate unacceptable levels of cost in the future or infeasible peaks in certain years. Here we have an excellent example of a situation where a total force cost model can be extremely

---

[39] It was not uncommon for the services to develop projected force structures which implied future cost levels twice as high as those programmed for the near future (in terms of constant dollars).

useful. Indeed, it is difficult to imagine how the planning process could be carried out without such models. The services do in fact use them.

Finally, let us consider still another use of total force cost models. In many instances cost analysts have found that developing, operating, and updating these models provides insights and knowledge about the institutional and structural "ecology" of a given service that is otherwise difficult to obtain. This, in turn, has facilitated doing a better job in cost analyses of narrower problems – such as intersystem comparisons and mission area force-mix comparisons. It has also helped in better organizing the cost analysis activity's own research program concerned with developing new concepts and analytical tools.

A related point concerns the usefulness of the output of total force cost models to systems analysts – not in a technical analytical sense, but rather in orienting them to appreciate the full scope of their concern. In carrying out an intensive study of a relatively small subset of a total force, systems analysts can become overly parochial. Experience has shown, however, that this parochialism can be tempered somewhat by exposure to total force structures and their estimated resource impacts. Oftentimes the result is a more enlightened and useful analysis of the smaller problem itself.

In summary, total force structure cost models, in spite of institutional and practical constraints on their development and use, can be very helpful in grappling with certain kinds of long-range planning problems. Rather than emphasize their current limitations in use, we would instead stress their potential for the future.

In this spirit, and in terms of technical improvements, presently used total force cost models need bolstering in several areas. One, for example, concerns the development of better subroutines or submodels for dealing with the interaction problem. Also, improved methods and techniques are needed for estimating the cost of service-wide support activities. In sum, much remains to be done in this important area of cost models.

## Summary

The subject of cost models is very broad, and a single chapter can hardly do it justice. Our aim has simply been to give the reader a general idea of what cost models are like, and, more important, the role they play in helping the cost analyst in his job of serving the systems analysis process.

A cost model may be viewed as an integrating device designed to facilitate the analytical process by bringing together the various factors on the input side and relating them to some type of output-oriented military capability in the future.

We attempted to illustrate this through the use of a highly simplified cost model: an individual system cost model concerned with hard point defense. The structure of the model was described, and then the model was "exercised" to show various outputs and their relation to specifications from the input side. The objective here was to indicate briefly how the model might be used to help gain insights into certain types of questions – from the standpoint of both the cost analyst and the systems analyst. Considerable emphasis was placed on sensitivity analysis.

Cost models may be categorized and discussed in many different ways. Several of these were pointed out, and the following classification – based on the size of the domain being modeled – was discussed at length:

1. Resource requirements submodels.
2. Individual system cost models.
3. Mission area force-mix cost models.
4. Total force cost models.

All of these models are important, and military cost analysis depends on all of them. However, we did stress the growing importance of mission area force-mix cost models at the present time. Systems analysts have come more and more to see mission area force-mix comparisons as feasible and meaningful analytical work. Such work is not unduly narrow, yet it is not so broad as to preclude substantive analysis. Cost analysts have therefore had to devote increasing attention to cost models designed to serve this important area. In the more distant future, however, some form of total force structure cost model may gradually begin to replace mission area models.

The chapter also emphasized that cost models and computer programs (automation) are not synonymous. Building a representation of reality (the model) appropriate to the class of problems under consideration is the primary objective. Automation is secondary. However, when automation (in full or in part) can be accomplished without significant sacrifices in the quality of the model, it usually should be attempted. Even partial automation can often greatly facilitate the capability to do sensitivity analysis.

**Suggested Supplementary Readings**
1. R. L. Petruschell, *Project Cost Estimating*, P-3687 (Santa Monica, Calif.: The Rand Corporation, Sept. 1967). (Contains a good example of a requirements sub-model.)
2. R. D. Specht, "The Nature of Models," Chapter 10 in E. S. Quade and W. I. Boucher (eds.), *Systems Analysis and Policy Planning: Applications in Defense* (New York: American Elsevier Publishing Co., Inc., 1968). (A good general discussion of models and model building.)
3. T. Arthur Smith, "Army Force Cost Models – An Example," published in T. Arthur Smith (ed.), *Economic Analysis and Military Resource Allocation* (Washington, D.C.: Office, Comptroller of the Army, 1968), pp. 65–78.

Chapter 8

# SPECIAL TOPICS

## Introduction

We have now come full circle, beginning with our early emphasis on the nature and importance of an output orientation, following that with a detailed examination of inputs, and concluding – in the last chapter – with a discussion of cost models, which returns us to the matter of outputs. We could, therefore, proceed directly to examples of systems analyses and show how the cost considerations are handled in each case. But before turning to these topics, it would be worthwhile to pause briefly to consider certain special subjects that deserve particular emphasis. The first two have already been mentioned in previous chapters; the third has not. Each is central to an understanding of military cost analysis:

1. The treatment of uncertainty.
2. The treatment of problems associated with time.
3. The role of wartime costs: are they relevant or not in systems analyses of long-range planning problems?

Let us consider these topics in turn.

## Treatment of Uncertainty

Practically all aspects of life in the real world are in one way or another subjected to risks or uncertainties. Even in so seemingly simple a task as laying bricks, uncertainty is apt to be present in a very real way:

> Ponder for a moment the experience of the Barbados bricklayer who wrote the following letter requesting sick leave of his employer:
>
> "Respected sir, when I got to the building, I found that the hurricane had knocked some bricks off the top. So I rigged up a beam with a pulley at the top of the building and hoisted up a couple of barrels full of bricks. When I had fixed the building, there was a lot of bricks left over.
>
> "I hoisted the barrel back up again and secured the line at the bottom, and then went up and filled the barrel with extra bricks. Then I went to the bottom and cast off the line.
>
> "Unfortunately, the barrel of bricks was heavier than I was and before I knew what was happening the barrel started down, jerking me off the ground. I decided to hang on and halfway up I met the barrel coming down and received a severe blow on the shoulder.

"I then continued to the top, banging my head against the beam and getting my finger jammed in the pulley. When the barrel hit the ground it bursted its bottom, allowing all the bricks to spill out.

"I was heavier than the barrel and so started down again at high speed. Halfway down, I met the barrel coming up and received severe injuries to my shins. When I hit the ground I landed on the bricks, getting several painful cuts from the sharp edges.

"At this point I must have lost my presence of mind, because I let go to the line. The barrel then came down giving me another heavy blow on the head and putting me in the hospital.

"I respectfully request sick leave."[1]

As indicated numerous times in this book, uncertainty is a key characteristic of the types of long-range planning problems typically addressed in systems analysis studies. Uncertainty, perhaps more than anything else, tends to compound the severity of the analytical problems faced by systems analysts. So much so, that we may be tempted at times to "simplify the situation" by conducting the analysis in terms of "certainty equivalents" (using, say, "expected values"). While this may be permissible in special cases, it is not to be recommended as appropriate general practice, since it can often result in furnishing the decisionmakers with misleading information.

The point, in its most general terms, is that analysts must face up to uncertainty explicitly and use the concepts and techniques appropriate to the problem at hand. The purpose of the discussion in the following paragraphs is to indicate how the cost analyst can do so.

### Background Discussion

Let us begin by considering the difference between *risk* and *uncertainty*. This is in part a question of semantics, and for some purposes the distinction between the two terms is not important. In this context, however, it seems desirable to make a technical separation.[2]

A *risky* situation is one in which the outcome is subject to an uncontrollable random event stemming from a *known* probability distribution. The toss of a true coin, for example, involves a risk, with the probability of a head turning up being 0.5. An *uncertain* situation, on the other hand, is characterized by the fact that the probability distribution of the uncontrollable random event is *unknown*.

---

[1] C. J. Hitch, *Uncertainties in Operations Research*, P-1959 (Santa Monica, Calif.: The Rand Corporation, April 1960), pp. 6–7.
[2] We shall use the same distinction as that made by Albert Madansky in Chapter 5, "Uncertainty," contained in E. S. Quade and W. I. Boucher, (eds.) *Systems Analysis and Policy Planning: Applications in Defense* (New York: American Elsevier Publishing Co., Inc., 1968).

Oftentimes probability distributions are assigned to uncertain situations, but these are of necessity subjective in nature. That is, they are based on the personal judgment and experience of the analyst, the decisionmaker, or someone else regarding the relative "likelihood" of unknown events. They are not based on incontrovertible empirical or theoretical derivations.[3]

We now see why the title of this subsection is "treatment of *uncertainty*." Rarely in systems analysis studies, and in cost analyses in support of such studies, are objective probabilities available. For the most part the types of problems treated involve situations of uncertainty rather than of risk.

Let us turn now to a discussion of uncertainty in the context of cost analysis *per se*. Although here the prime concern is with cost analysis, we must keep the *total* problem in mind. Cost analysis does not exist in a vacuum. Cost analyses of future proposals are made for a purpose; and in terms of long-range planning that purpose is usually to provide inputs to a total systems analysis or decisionmaking activity involving many considerations other than cost. It should be emphasized that these "other considerations" (involving utility or "effectiveness") are also plagued by uncertainties – often greater than those facing the cost analyst.

Can we gain any significant insights into the uncertainty problem facing military cost analysts by examining the historical record? Suppose, for example, we were to attempt to compare cost estimates of proposed new military capabilities (such as weapon systems) made during the conceptual phase of development with estimates (or even actual cost information) obtained during a much later stage in the program – say at the time of phase-in to the operational force. Call the early estimate $C_e$ and the late estimate (or actual) $C_a$. Is the ratio $C_a/C_e$ typically different from unity, and if so, by how much?

Several empirical studies of this type have been made, using data from the 1950s and early 1960s. Most of them pertain to the hardware portion of total packages of military capabilities.[4] A few (all unpublished) pertain to total weapon systems. The results are similar in both cases.

These studies indicate that the ratio $C_a/C_e$ is typically substantially greater than unity, even after adjusting for price level increases during the

---

[3] If the latter were the case, we would be dealing with a risky situation and the distribution would be called an *objective* probability distribution.

[4] For example, see Merton J. Peck and Frederic M. Scherer, *The Weapons Acquisition Process: An Economic Analysis* (Boston: Division of Research, Graduate School of Business Administration, Harvard University, 1962), pp. 21–23; and Robert Summers, *Cost Estimates as Predictors of Actual Weapon Costs: A Study of Major Hardware Articles*, RM-3061-PR (abridged) (Santa Monica, Calif.: The Rand Corporation, March 1965).

time interval examined, and after adjusting for differences in quantity. The adjusted or "normalized" ratios tend to average about 2 to 3.[5] These numbers may be viewed as one crude measure of uncertainty in cost analyses made in the past.[6] It is doubtful that future environments will be any less uncertain.

The question arises as to why early estimates of the costs of future military capabilities tend to be lower than actual totals or estimates made later in the system acquisition cycle.[7] Is it because of inherent deficiencies or "errors" in the cost analysts' tools (such as estimating relationships)? Or is it because mission requirements change over time, with the result that weapon system configurations must be changed (often with attending cost increases) to meet the more demanding requirements?

The historical record seems to indicate that both of these factors play a role. Which is the more significant? Unfortunately, the form of the data in the historical record available to researchers does not permit determination of a defensible quantitative answer. Yet the case histories (which are mostly qualitative in nature) suggest that the primary source of differences between early and late estimates is traceable to the second factor – "requirements uncertainty." The first factor, which may be called "cost-estimating uncertainty *per se*," seems to be relatively less important. The conclusion of one of the evaluations of the historical record in the major equipment area is as follows:

> ... In principle it would be possible to factor into two parts the total error in cost estimates as they are prepared: (1) the part due to errors in the costing of the configuration supplied to the cost estimator (i.e., the intrinsic error in cost estimating) and (2) the part due to changes in the configuration as development progresses.

---

[5] Usually we find considerable variability around these averages, with the frequency distribution of the ratios skewed to the right. Only a few of the ratios are less than unity, while a number of them "tail off" to the right beyond the mean. In one study of the hardware area, the ratios ranged from 0.7 to 7.0. (See Peck and Scherer, *op. cit.*, p. 22.)

[6] At this point the reader may wonder whether these ratios reflect uncertainty or bias. We cannot answer this question with high confidence. However, examination of the underlying details of the information and data base used to derive the ratios suggests that uncertainty is probably the main factor.

The 1950s and early 1960s – the period considered in these studies – were a time of marked reassessments regarding state-of-the-world uncertainties (the threat, future technological possibilities, and so on). For the most part, these reassessments led to increased mission requirements and hence more stringent weapon system specifications. We should not conclude from this particular period of history, however, that there is a general "systematic upward bias" that can be predicted for the future. In short, it would seem more appropriate to interpret the data in terms of uncertainties rather than in terms of biases.

[7] Recall that we have "normalized out" price level changes and effects attributable to variations in quantity.

In practice it has not been possible to carry out this separation. However, it is our belief that the intrinsic errors in costing a fixed configuration tend to be small relative to the other source of error in the costing of most major items of military equipment.[8]

Numerous reasons may be given for changes in configuration of proposed new military capabilities as they proceed through the acquisition cycle. The reasons for these changes are in turn the main sources of what we are calling requirements uncertainty. Some examples are the following:

1. With respect to the system's hardware, the original design may fail to meet the desired performance characteristics, and as a result the hardware configuration has to be changed. Or sometimes performance characteristics themselves may be changed in response to a change in the projected threat, with a resultant change in hardware specifications and hence cost. Another possibility is that an attempt may be made to obtain the system sooner than was originally intended by substituting resources for time.

2. A change in system specifications may be induced purely by errors of omission in establishing requirements initially for some part of the system. For example, early in the intercontinental ballistic missile program, this happened with respect to the ground support equipment (GSE). Correction of the error led to rather marked changes in system GSE requirements, and hence to an increase in GSE cost.

3. Such change may have an indirect effect on other parts of the system. Personnel requirements, for example, may be changed – and a change of that sort is often very sensitive to changes in the operational concept of the system (for example, the degree of system dispersal or alert capability).

4. The strategic situation may change. This may lead to a respecification of hardware performance characteristics. Or, even if the hardware is not affected, the method of deploying and employing the system may have to be changed. For example, to reduce vulnerability of the system to surprise attack, a higher degree of dispersal, hardness, or alert capability may be required to meet the

---

[8] A. W. Marshall and W. H. Meckling, *Predictability of the Costs, Time and Success of Development*, P-1821 (Santa Monica, Calif.: The Rand Corporation, December 1959), p. 9. Similar conclusions hold for total weapon systems and forces.

The present author has also attempted to quantify the relative importance of cost estimating and requirements uncertainty, but without substantive success. On the basis of this work, however, it appears that requirements uncertainty is typically 5 to 10 times more important than cost-estimating uncertainty in cost analyses of proposed future military capabilities.

new strategic situation. The impact of such changes on system installations and personnel requirements, to cite two examples, is obvious. A reevaluation of the strategic situation may produce changes in system force size (number of units to be procured for the operational force) or in the number of years the system is planned to be kept in the operating inventory. Both of these may be regarded as a form of requirements uncertainty, resulting in a substantial impact on total system cost.

These are only examples of a few of the many reasons why the configuration of a proposed new system may change. But the key point is that requirements uncertainty can lead to wide variations in total system cost, even in the complete absence of cost-estimating uncertainty (if this were possible).

Let us now turn to *cost-estimating uncertainty*. Why do we find variations in estimates of the costs of proposed future military capabilities, even if requirements uncertainty is zero? The following are a few of the reasons:

1. Estimating relationships used in cost analyses of future military capabilities cannot be assumed to hold exactly. This simply means that in estimating a certain cost component as a function of some explanatory variable (or variables), we usually cannot assume that these variables will predict the particular cost exactly, even if the values of the explanatory variables are known with certainty. For example, if a certain cost $(C)$ is to be estimated as a linear function of explanatory variables $X_1$ and $X_2$, the estimating relationship may be written as

$$C = \hat{\alpha} + \hat{\beta}_1 X_1 + \hat{\beta}_2 X_2 + \mu,$$

where $\mu$ must be introduced as a random variable to take account of the fact that $X_1$ and $X_2$ do not explain completely the variations in $C$.[9]

2. Another source of cost-estimating uncertainty arises from the fact that data used as a basis for cost analyses are themselves subject to error. Putting it another way, the observations used in deriving

---

[9] If we assume a *normal* linear regression model, the following specifications are placed on $\mu$: (a) $\mu$ is distributed normally with mean zero and variance $\sigma^2$, (b) Successive values of $\mu$ are mutually independent, (c) $\mu$ is independent of $X_1$ and $X_2$.

Under these conditions, normal regression theory permits derivation of estimates of the parameters $\alpha$, $\beta_1$, and $\beta_2$ having desirable statistical qualities, and also permits the calculation of a prediction interval for a value of $C$ estimated on the basis of specified values of $X_1$ and $X_2$. The prediction interval is a measure of the uncertainty of the estimating relationship.

cost-estimating relationships invariably contain errors – even if these data come from carefully kept historical records. Statisticians call these "errors of measurement" or "errors in the observations." An illustration is provided by the following simple linear regression model:

$$x = \eta + d$$
$$y = \theta + e$$
$$\theta = \alpha + \beta\eta,$$

where the observed variables $x$ and $y$ are assumed to deviate from true values $\eta$ and $\theta$ by the amounts of the random errors $d$ and $e$.[10]

3. In cost analyses of advanced military systems and forces, the cost analyst very often uses estimating relationships derived from past or current experience. Here, one cannot always be very confident that a relationship that holds reasonably well now will continue to hold satisfactorily for the advanced system being considered. Oftentimes the analyst must of necessity extrapolate beyond the range of the sample or data base from which the estimating relationship was derived. As pointed out in Chapter 6 in the discussion of estimating relationships, our confidence decreases (uncertainty increases) as we project beyond the region of central tendency in the data base, even when "requirements uncertainty" is zero.[11] Prediction intervals become wider and wider. (See Fig. 8.1.) This illustrates how additional cost-estimating uncertainty arises when we are forced to extrapolate beyond the data base.

Let us now summarize this background material: Cost analyses of future military capabilities are usually subject to many uncertainties. Although these uncertainties may be categorized in numerous ways, we have chosen to separate them into two main types:

1. Requirements uncertainty (analagous to "state-of-the-world uncertainties" discussed in Chapter 2).[12]
2. Cost-estimating uncertainty (analagous to "statistical uncertainties" discussed in Chapter 2).[12]

[10] The equation $\theta = \alpha + \beta\eta$ is assumed to hold exactly. It is also assumed that $E(x) = \eta$, $E(y) = 0$, $E(d) = 0$, and $E(e) = 0$. (The operator $E$ denotes mathematical expectation.) For a detailed discussion of this type of "errors in the variables" model, see L. R. Klein, *A Textbook of Econometrics* (Evanston, Ill. and White Plains, N.Y.: Row, Peterson and Co., 1953), Chapter VII; and Albert Madansky, "The Fitting of Straight Lines When Both Variables Are Subject to Error," *Journal of the American Statistical Association*, March 1959, pp. 173–205.
[11] See pp. 158–159.           [12] See pp. 12–13.

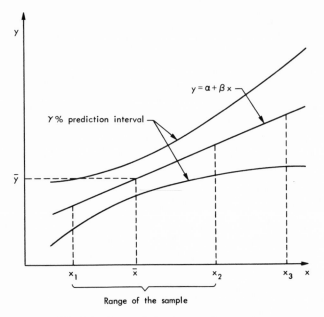

Fig. 8.1 – Extrapolating beyond the sample

While the nature of the historical record does not permit a precise, quantitative determination of the relative importance of the two types of uncertainty, it is clear that requirements uncertainty is by far the most important in most cases.

### Some Approaches to the Problem of Uncertainty

Given the nature of the problem, let us now consider some approaches to the treatment of uncertainty in cost analysis studies. Before turning to specifics, one very important general point should be emphasized: What the cost analysts do in any particular case is very much a function of the design of the systems analysis study of which the cost analysis is a part. This, however, is, or should be, a two-way street. Cost analysts have a responsibility to assist in the study design process. In addition to making suggestions initially regarding how the cost considerations should be handled, they also have a responsibility to help steer the project leader back on course if during the conduct of the study the wrong costing concepts are being used, the inputs provided by the cost analysts are being misused, and the like.

How *uncertainty* is to be treated in the overall study is usually a very important consideration.[13] But how the cost analyst can help in dealing with this problem is difficult to say, since what should be done in any particular case is likely to be very context dependent. However, the following three examples are illustrative of the types of considerations involved:

Can *cost-estimating* uncertainties properly be ignored? Very often they can be – especially in long-range planning studies involving broad, relative comparisons of numerous alternatives. It is up to the cost analysts to provide information and analytical argument to help the project leader resolve this issue. If cost-estimating uncertainties can safely be ignored, the overall analysis can be structured in a more straightforward way than would otherwise be the case.[14]

Another important consideration concerns the use of *a fortiori* argument in the overall analysis.[15] Good systems analysts are always seeking possibilities for making a cutting *a fortiori* argument. The cost analysts must be in a similar frame of mind, with a view to presenting cost considerations concerning the alternatives under investigation which may have implications for constructing *a fortiori* arguments. Sometimes cost sensitivity analyses can uncover such possibilities or provide clues which suggest new hypotheses to be tested. Clearly, the best cost analysts are those who are well-grounded in overall systems analysis concepts and techniques, and such a background is particularly important in dealing with the problem of uncertainty.

One final example of how cost analysts may contribute to the overall analysis on matters regarding uncertainty: Oftentimes the study comparisons indicate that none of the alternatives being considered for the future hold up very well in view of the uncertainties involved. This will induce a good project leader to start asking questions like the following: Can we think of a *new* alternative (hopefully not extremely expensive) which will hold up better than those we have considered so far? Can we think of some ingenious, low-cost ways of *hedging* against the postulated uncertainties? Are there some reasonable-cost exploratory development

---

[13] That is, it *should* be an important consideration. However, all too often in many past studies the matter of uncertainty has been given inadequate treatment. This is understandable (though not excusable) because facing up to uncertainty explicitly usually complicates the analysis. "Sweeping uncertainty under the rug" may make life much simpler, but the study results may be misleading because of it.

[14] We hasten to add that while cost-estimating uncertainties can sometimes be safely suppressed, *requirements* uncertainties rarely can be so treated.

[15] Recall that in Chapter 2 we pointed out that use of *a fortiori* argument is one of the methods that may be employed to deal with "state-of-the-world" uncertainties. (See Chapter 2, p. 13.

programs in key subsystem areas which should be initiated now to obtain more information regarding technological uncertainties? And so on. In dealing with questions of this type, the role of the cost analyst is obvious. Here again a really good cost analyst will participate actively in the process of exploring new strategies for meeting the uncertainties which are central to the problem under investigation.

So much for general comments. Let us now turn to some of the specifics of approaches that may be taken to the problem of uncertainty. We shall start with *cost-estimating* uncertainty.

As suggested a moment ago, one of the first things the cost analyst should do in considering the problem of cost-estimating uncertainty is to try to ascertain whether in a given study this kind of uncertainty can appropriately be suppressed. If so, the analysis can be structured more simply, since "expected value" or "most likely" cost estimates may be computed for use in the systems analysis.

Obviously, systems analysts prefer using this approach wherever possible. The cost analysts, however, must take steps to ensure that it may be employed safely. Here, a number of things may be done, all of which utilize essentially the same basic information: input structures[16] and the estimating relationships or procedures for each category in such structures. If estimating relationships have been derived statistically, measures such as standard errors, prediction intervals, and so on, will usually be available. These may be used to help the cost analysts form judgments regarding cost-estimating uncertainty for each cost category in the input structure used to analyze total system (or force) cost for the alternatives under consideration. Given such judgments, several approaches may then be considered.

One of the simplest is to single out those cost categories which are deemed to be subject to the greatest cost-estimating uncertainty. Questions like the following may then be posed: Supposing that our "expected value" estimates for these selected categories are in error by 25 to 30 percent, what is the impact on total system (or force) cost? If the resulting ranges of total system cost are small, the conclusion might well be to ignore variances attributable to cost-estimating uncertainty.

Another approach would be to take the judgments about cost-estimating uncertainty for each of the cost categories; to convert these judgments into high, medium, and low estimates for each category; and finally to combine these to obtain high, medium, and low cost cases for total system (or force) costs for all the alternatives being considered. Again, if these

---

[16] For example, see Tables 5.4 and 5.5 in Chapter 5.

ranges are fairly narrow relative to other uncertainties in the total problem, the project leader may decide to use the "medium cases" in making his comparisons among alternatives. If the ranges are rather wide, he may decide to use medium and high cases, low and high cases, or whatever combination seems appropriate.

As a final example, we have an approach that is essentially a more formal case of the preceding alternative. Here the cost analysts are required to formalize their subjective judgments about cost-estimating uncertainty for each cost category in the input structure. They are required to specify a subjective probability distribution[17] for each cost category, and then a Monte Carlo technique is used to combine these component distributions to arrive at a distribution of total system (or force) cost.[18] (This is shown schematically in Fig. 8.2.) Oftentimes these distribu-

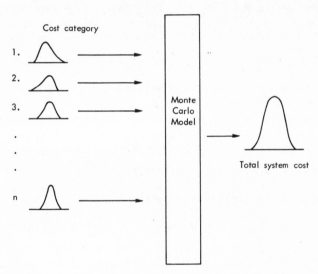

Fig. 8.2 – Use of Monte Carlo method to obtain distribution of total system cost

---

[17] A beta function is often used.
[18] Basically, Monte Carlo is a method for approximating the answer to a problem by means of an analytical experiment with random numbers. For a good brief discussion of the technique, see E. S. Quade (ed.), *Analysis for Military Decision* (Chicago: Rand McNally & Co., 1964), pp. 240–243.

For a detailed example of the use of Monte Carlo in treating uncertainty in weapon system cost analysis problems, see Paul F. Dienemann, *Estimating Cost Uncertainty Using Monte Carlo Techniques*, RM-4854-PR (Santa Monica, Calif.: The Rand Corporation, January 1966).

tions of total system cost have relatively narrow spreads,[19] in which case point estimates (such as mean values) would probably be used in the systems analysis comparisons. In other instances variances may have to be taken into account. If so, the project leader has a compact description of cost-estimating uncertainty in the form of the distribution of total system (force) cost.

At this point, however, a word of caution is in order. Since cost-estimating (statistical) uncertainties are typically swamped by requirements (state-of-the-world) uncertainties in systems analysis studies, we must be careful not to go overboard in our efforts to treat cost-estimating uncertainties. As Charles Hitch has pointed out, this can easily be "expensive window dressing."[20] In many cases a limited amount of simple sensitivity testing can help a great deal in determining whether or not to ignore cost-estimating uncertainties. And such simplifications should be made whenever it is reasonable to do so. This enables the analyst better to concentrate his efforts on requirements uncertainties. Let us now turn to this subject.

To set the stage, brief reference to the discussion of state-of-the-world uncertainties in systems analysis in Chapter 2 seems appropriate. Recall that we outlined several techniques which are most often used in dealing with state-of-the-world uncertainties: sensitivity analysis, contingency analysis, *a fortiori* analysis, and creation of new alternatives.[21] All of these techniques are focused to a considerable extent on helping the systems analysts in their continuous search for dominances among the alternatives being examined. In the limit, an alternative is a dominant solution if in the comparative analyses it shows up better than all other alternatives, no matter how the state-of-the-world uncertainties are assumed to be resolved. This, of course, almost never happens in practice, although such solutions must always be sought.

What is more likely, but still rare, is that a certain alternative will be a "dominant solution" in the sense of holding up well no matter how several (or even just a few) of the *most important* state-of-the-world uncertainties are assumed to be resolved. If such an alternative can be found, the systems analysis study uncovering it must be regarded as an outstanding success in terms of its contribution to the decisionmaking process. However, the most likely situation is where none of the alternatives stand up very well over

[19] A ratio of the standard deviation to the mean equal to about 5 percent seems fairly typical. (*Ibid.*, p. 22.)
[20] C. J. Hitch, *An Appreciation of Systems Analysis*, P-699 (Santa Monica, Calif.: The Rand Corporation, August 1955), p. 7.
[21] See Chapter 2, pp. 12–13.

more than a small range of the state-of-the-world uncertainty spectrum. In this case the systems analysts try to seek new alternatives or to improve the alternatives already examined.

Such considerations help to shape the role of the cost analysts in assisting the systems analysis process with respect to state-of-the-world uncertainties – what we have been calling "requirements uncertainties" in cost analysis studies. What can the cost analysts do to help deal with requirements uncertainty?

Several approaches to the problem have been used in practice or proposed. Examples are the following:

1. Supplemental discounting,
2. Adjustment factors,
3. Special studies,
4. Cost sensitivity analysis.

Let us discuss each of these briefly.

*Supplemental Discounting.* We have already referred to the process of discounting future costs to equalize them with respect to time preference.[22] Advocates of supplemental discounting procedures suggest that an additional rate be applied to allow for uncertainties about future technology, the enemy threat, and the like. Thus, if in a given study the decisionmakers wish to use a 5 percent rate to equalize for time preference and a supplemental rate of 10 percent to reflect their general feelings about requirements uncertainties, the total rate applied to the costs of all the various alternatives being considered would be 15 percent.

While this procedure has been used in a few systems analysis studies in the past, most analysts today prefer to distinguish between discounting for time preference and for uncertainty. The general, though not unanimous, opinion is that requirements uncertainty is best treated as an explicit problem in the systems analysis process, and is not one that should be handled in a general way through the use of an aggregate supplemental discount factor.[23] This may be done through the use of techniques referred to previously, such as contingency analysis, or *a fortiori* analysis. The cost analysts can make major contributions to this type of activity by conducting cost sensitivity analyses – a subject we will return to later.

*Use of Adjustment Factors.* The use of adjustment factors to allow for requirements uncertainty has been advocated primarily for application in

---

[22] For example, see Chapter 4, pp. 86–89.

[23] For example, see Harry P. Hatry, "The Use of Cost Estimates," Chapter 4 of Thomas A. Goldman (ed.), *Cost-Effectiveness Analysis* (New York: Frederick A. Praeger, Publishers, 1967), p. 65.

cost analyses of future major equipment proposals. The argument runs somewhat as follows: For reasons indicated earlier, estimates of the cost of new major equipment proposals made during the conceptual phase of the hardware development cycle tend to be less than the actual (or near actual) costs at the time equipments are procured for the operational inventory. In cases where these "average factor increases" $(F$'s$)$[24] can be derived statistically from historical records, it has been suggested that they be applied to cost estimates of future hardware proposals made for use in long-range planning studies.

The simplest of the proposed applications suggests that if for a certain class of major equipment the historical record indicates an average $F = 2$, then cost estimates of future equipments of this general type made during the conceptual phase of development should be multiplied by 2. A more sophisticated proposal suggests that instead of using an $F$ derived by a simple averaging process, a functional form should be developed which expresses $F$ as a function of several explanatory variables. For aircraft and missile systems the proposed function is:[25]

$$F = f(t, A, L, T, u),$$

where

$t =$ the timing within the development program, expressed as the fraction of the program that has already elapsed when the estimate is made;

$A =$ the measure of the technological advance required by the development program, expressed in terms of a numerical scale ranging from about 5 to 16 for the chronologies studied;

$L =$ the length of the development program, expressed in months;

$T =$ the calendar year in which the estimate is made;

$u =$ a random variable.

Apparently, the use of such gross adjustment factors has been rare in systems analysis planning studies. The precise reasons are not clear, but we may speculate somewhat as follows:

1. Many analysts feel uneasy about using gross adjustment factors as a means for dealing with requirements uncertainty. Instead, they prefer to single out special problem areas – technological uncertainties, manufacturing state-of-the-art uncertainties, and the like – and treat them explicitly in the cost analysis process.

---

[24] That is, $F =$ actual (or near actual) cost divided by estimated cost made early in the development cycle.
[25] See Summers, *op. cit.*, pp. 32–33.

2. Use of gross adjustment factors was advocated most fervently at a time when cost analysts were somewhat more prone to develop "point estimates" than is the case today. Present-day concepts and methods tend to stress ranges of estimates and the use of parametric analyses to explore the possible consequences of various types of uncertainties.

*Special Studies.* As pointed out previously, very often in systems analysis studies the ranking of the alternatives being compared is very sensitive to ways in which major requirements uncertainties are assumed to be resolved in the future. That is, no significant dominances of any kind can be discovered. This may lead systems analysts to ask questions like the following: Can we think of ways the decisionmakers can appropriately buy time or additional information? Are there ways for hedging against some of the more important requirements uncertainties?[26] In questions like these, cost is a most important consideration. Decisionmakers usually like to take such measures, provided they do not cost too much.

Here, the cost analysts can make valuable contributions to the decision-making process by conducting special analyses. Some examples:

1. How much might it cost to initiate exploratory development efforts in critical, long lead-time subsystem or component areas, with a view to helping preserve a wide range of options for the future?
2. What would be the cost of conducting experiments in a certain critical technical area aimed toward obtaining additional information and thereby reducing technological uncertainties?
3. What would be the cost of conducting field exercises designed to help resolve uncertainties about novel operational concepts being proposed for future military systems?

*Cost Sensitivity Analysis.* We have stressed repeatedly that *good* systems analysts are very ingenious at designing and structuring analyses which will in some way take into account major uncertainties. Directly or indirectly this usually involves a considerable amount of sensitivity analysis designed to explore systematically the implications of varying assumptions about the distant future environment. In fact, a number of the most useful systems analyses in the past have not come up with a specific set of preferred courses of action at all. For the most part they have been extensive, carefully done sensitivity analyses which clearly point out to the decisionmakers what is important and what is not, and which systematically explore the ways in which the ranking of various alternatives

---

[26] See Madansky, *op. cit.*, p. 95.

changes as the assumptions about resolutions of major uncertainties are varied. Cost considerations are, of course, a key part of such investigations.

In examining alternative future military capabilities under conditions of uncertainty, the types of questions cost analysts must be prepared to deal with in support of the systems analysis process are many and varied. A few examples are:

1. In studying alternative mixes of General Purpose forces for the future, it is found that the response time requirements of these forces are usually sensitive to assumptions made about the threat. How do force-mix costs change as response time requirements are varied? Over what range can significant improvements in response time be obtained for modest increases in cost? At what point do the costs begin to increase at a very rapid rate?

2. Related to (1) is the question of the preferred mix of future Regular and Reserve Forces in some mission area. Usually the preferred mix is sensitive to response time to peak capability requirements – which are in turn dependent upon how uncertainties about the threat are assumed to be resolved – and to peacetime operating cost differentials existing between similar type Regular and Reserve Forces units. How significant are these cost differentials? How do they vary with state-of-readiness capability? How do total force-mix costs change as the fraction of Regular to Reserve Forces is varied?

3. In cases where the effectiveness of proposed alternatives for the future depends heavily on technological advances to be attained, what are the consequences if these advances are only partially met? For example, will force sizes have to be increased to compensate for degraded effectiveness? To what extent? What are the costs of these incremental force requirements?

4. The potential penetration capability of alternative mixes of strategic retaliatory forces for the future is very much a function of the types and levels of enemy defenses. How do strategic force-mix costs vary with alternative technical penetration options? Is there a set of penetration aids which will cover a range of possible enemy defenses at modest incremental force-mix cost? At what level of enemy defenses does our offensive force-mix cost reach infeasible proportions? Are there penetration aid options that should be preserved by means of subsystem development programs? What are these hedges against uncertainties about enemy defenses likely to cost?

A common thread runs through all of these examples: If the cost analysts are to facilitate significantly the systems analysis process in dealing with requirements (state-of-the-world) uncertainties, they must be in a position to carry out a wide range of *cost-sensitivity analyses*. A necessary condition for doing extensive sensitivity testing is that cost analysis methods and models must be parametric in nature. That is, they must be "open-ended" with respect to key cost-generating explanatory variables such as major equipment performance characteristics, operational concepts, force size, number of years a particular military capability is assumed to be in the operational inventory, and the like.[27] The values of these variables will typically change as alternative assumptions are made regarding the nature of requirements uncertainties in the distant future. As values of these explanatory variables change, the related costs will also change, therby permitting exploration of the sensitivity of costs to differing assumptions about requirements uncertainty.

In summary, if cost analysis concepts and methods are established along the lines suggested in Chapters 5–7, the cost analysts will be in a good position to assist the systems analysis process in dealing with requirements uncertainty. Resourceful sensitivity testing on the part of cost analysts can be invaluable to the systems analysts in their unending search for dominances and ingenious ways for hedging against major uncertainties pertaining to the distant future.

## Problems Associated with Time

There are many problems associated with time, and only the most important of them can be considered here. We should begin by emphasizing that our aim in this discussion is primarily to clarify the issues – something that very much needs to be done at the present time – and to outline alternative ways of resolving some of these issues. In this, as in other topics of cost analysis, there is little agreement as to which methods should be preferred, and there is considerable agreement that no method is likely to perform well in all cases.

### Background Discussion

In dealing with problems associated with time, much depends upon the design of the systems analysis study of which the cost analysis is a part. In many instances the comparisons among alternatives made in systems analyses are conducted in essentially a static framework. Effectiveness

---

[27] Our illustration of a hard point defense cost model presented in Chapter 7 is an example of this.

measures are calculated for some future point in time, and the costs used in the comparisons are expressed in terms of static indexes – that is, single numbers obtained by summing the costs of research and development, investment, and a specified number of years of operation.

Timing considerations are, of course, taken into account to some extent in the work leading up to the static comparisons. For example, estimates of operational capability dates have to be examined to help ensure that the proposed future capabilities being compared are really relevant alternatives in terms of the time period of interest. Similarly, time-phasing matters have to be given some attention in assessing the incremental costs of the postulated alternatives. In many cases incremental costs are in part a function of inherited assets ("sunk" costs) and are therefore time-context dependent. Finally, the use of cost indexes made up of the sum of the costs for research and development, investment, and a specified number of years operation implies an assumption about time preference. Very often the implicit assumption is a zero rate of discount for the postulated "life cycle" time period for a proposed new capability, and an infinite rate thereafter.[28]

If a given systems analysis is essentially static, does this imply that it is a "bad" analysis? Not necessarily.[29] Static analyses may be quite appropriate for dealing with certain types of issues up for decision. For example, if the purpose of the study is to help in making system development choices, the chances are that explicit treatment of time-phasing throughout the analysis may not be necessary. On the other hand, if the purpose is to assist in the force structure planning process, time-phasing of the alternatives being considered is very important. Even here, however, explicit treatment of time may not be necessary during the early stages of the analysis, where the main problem is to screen a very large number of alternatives with a view to ferreting out the most interesting cases. Further and more complete analyses can then be done on this selected set, and time-phasing considerations can be studied explicitly.

Sometimes it is useful to compute the *costs* on an explicitly time-phased basis, even though it is not feasible (or deemed necessary) to compute the corresponding estimates of system *effectiveness* year by year over a period

---

[28] If, for example, a proposed new capability has a 10-year development and procurement lead time and a 10-year operational life is assumed, a zero rate of discount would apply to the first 20 years and an infinite rate thereafter.

[29] In the present author's experience, whether an analysis is "good" or "bad" usually depends upon much more fundamental issues than whether it is "dynamic" or "static." For example, many analyses are bad simply because they are addressed to the wrong issues or they sweep major uncertainties under the rug. Here, no amount of introduction of time dynamics can remedy the situation.

of years. The following are examples of the possible advantages of such a procedure:

1. The costs are likely to be of higher quality for reasons pointed out previously – for example, explicit time-phasing usually permits a better assessment of incremental costs.
2. Implications for funding can be examined.[30] Alternatives which generate huge funding (obligational authority) requirements in any one or two fiscal years may just not be feasible from a fiscal management point of view. Estimates of the year-by-year funding requirements for the alternatives under examination will provide a basis for checking for unacceptable bulges.
3. Implications for possible impact on the economy may be portrayed. This may be done by taking the time-phased funding requirements estimates referred to in (2) and converting them to expenditures or some other measure of impact on the economy.[31]
4. Time preference considerations regarding the cost part of the analysis can be decided upon explicitly.

We can now readily crystallize the main points here. In most military planning problem areas the sequence of events is important – sometimes critically so – and systems analysis must provide for explicit treatment of problems associated with time. Our models must be "dynamic"; the key parameters in them must bear dates.

No one would argue about this in principle. However, when it comes to systems analysis in practice, the hard realities are that introducing time explicitly into all phases of the analysis is neither easy nor painless.[32] In many instances it is just not feasible, particularly with regard to assessments of effectiveness.

In any event, the important consideration is to determine where in the study time can appropriately be either suppressed or treated implicitly rather than explicitly. In such areas the use of static measures of total system cost may be perfectly adequate. In the remainder, however, time must be treated explicitly. Here, the cost analysts must be prepared to generate time-phased cost estimates (obligational authority or expenditures) year by year over a period of years. They must also be prepared to

---

[30] This is particularly important when total force structures are being investigated.

[31] In the case of facilities, major equipments, and other capital items, the expenditure stream will typically follow a distributed time-lag pattern over two to four years after the fiscal year in which the funding requirements (obligational authority) are granted.

[32] For example, it can complicate the computational process enormously. It can also complicate the selection of criteria for evaluation of alternatives.

deal with a variety of assumptions regarding time preference and other subjects as well.

Let us now turn to specific topics regarding treatment of timing problems.

### Time Preference

For a number of years a considerable effort has been devoted to the treatment of time preference in systems analysis studies.[33] Papers have been written, chapters in books have been devoted to the subject, Congressional committees have conducted special hearings on discounting and related matters, seminars have been held on what discount rate should be used, and the like. Yet, in spite of all this activity a considerable lack of agreement exists among professional practitioners regarding the specifics of how time preference should be treated – for example, with respect to what discount rate should be used. Also, somewhat surprisingly, there is often a lack of clarity in stating and discussing some of the key issues.

In the discussion to follow we shall not attempt to resolve all of the controversies. We would hope, however, to help clarify some of the relevant issues, to outline reasonable alternatives for dealing with certain types of problems, and to suggest that in many instances the subjects of present disagreements may not, in practice, be so important in systems analyses of defense planning problems.

Let us begin by raising four issues:

1. Can time preference considerations be treated in military systems analysis studies in the same way as in other problem areas – for example, in cost-benefit analyses of proposed water resources projects?
2. Is there such a thing as "undiscounted" costs?
3. Should the discount rate include a supplemental rate for uncertainty?
4. What discount rate should be used for time preference in systems analysis studies?

We shall discuss each of these in turn.

---

[33] In a strict technical sense the term "time preference" as used in economic theory refers to the psychological considerations of individual consumers. It determines how much of his income an individual will consume now and how much he will reserve in some form of command over *future* consumption. For example, see John Maynard Keynes, *The General Theory of Employment, Interest and Money* (New York: Harcourt, Brace and Co., 1936), p. 166.

In this book the term is used in a more general sense. By "time preference" we simply mean that decisionmakers usually do not regard a dollar today as being equivalent to a dollar (with price levels constant) at some future time. If the pure rate of interest, for example, is 5 percent, then $1.00 today would be equivalent to $1.05 a year from now (prices constant).

*Are Problems in the Military Context the Same as in Other Realms?* The main answer to this question has to be "no," although oftentimes in general discussions of the treatment of time preference the distinction between military and other problem areas tends to be blurred.

In nonmilitary areas – like water resources, for example – the usual procedure is somewhat as follows:[34] Take the proposals for various future projects to be considered; estimate their time-phased future benefits (in dollars) and the corresponding future costs (in dollars); and then, using an appropriate rate of discount, calculate the "present worth" of each project (present value of outputs minus present value of costs). Presumably those projects having significantly positive present values are candidates for "go ahead."

At this point, however, another problem may arise: given a specified budget to be devoted to projects, the total of all proposals having positive present worths may not be attainable from the stipulated budget level. Thus, some ranking of the project proposals must be attempted. Numerous methods have been devised for doing this.[35] One scheme, for example, is to rank the projects on the basis of internal rate of return: that is, that rate of discount which reduces present worth to zero.[36]

The main point of this discussion is that in at least *some* significant nondefense problem areas, benefits and costs can be expressed reasonably well in terms of the same unit (such as dollars or dollar proxies).[37] In these instances, the time preference problem can be solved relatively easily by discounting the time-phased benefit and cost estimates for proposed government projects at an appropriate rate – presumably at a rate that reflects the percentage rate of return that the resources needed by a pro- posed project would otherwise provide in the private sector.[38]

---

[34] See Roland N. McKean, *Efficiency in Government Through Systems Analysis, with Emphasis on Water Resources Development* (New York: John Wiley & Sons, Inc., 1958). Part 2 has a good discussion of some of the general problems of analysis. Parts 3 and 4 deal specifically with water-resource projects.

[35] See *ibid.*, Chap. 5.

[36] *Ibid.*, pp. 89–92, 122–123.

[37] Some practitioners might quarrel a bit with this statement. They perhaps would prefer to say something like the following: "In theory it can be done, but in practice it is exceedingly difficult to find commensurables between costs and effectiveness measures."

[38] That is to say, "the correct discount rate is the opportunity cost potential rate of return on the resources that would be utilized by the project." See William J. Baumol, "On the Appropriate Discount Rate for Evaluation of Public Projects," contained in *The Planning-Programming-Budgeting System: Progress and Potentials, Hearing Before the Subcommittee on Economy in Government of the Joint Economic Committee, Congress of the United States*, 90th Cong., 1st Sess. (Washington, D.C.: U.S. Government Printing Office, 1967), p. 153.

In the realm of national security planning, things are different. In practically all cases the benefits and costs of proposals for future military capabilities cannot be measured in the same unit. While for most long-range planning studies costs can appropriately be measured in dollars, benefits cannot. In fact, benefits *per se* are usually not measured directly at all. Rather, sets of various effectiveness measures[39] are calculated which are assumed to be positively correlated with the possible military worths (utilities) of alternative future systems and forces. Furthermore, the "time preference" of desired military capabilities and of the levels of effectiveness they are supposed to attain are very much a function of our time-phased estimates of the enemy threat and of enemy reactions to our proposed responses to his threat. In a competitive environment involving action, reaction, counteraction, and so on, we would hardly want to handle time preference by a simple "discounting" of future capabilities. Hitch and McKean put the matter this way:

> ... it may appear to be more straightforward and appropriate in many problems to stipulate a desired capability over future time than to do any discounting of capabilities. Indeed in many instances it may appear to be the only feasible method of handling time paths for gains or capabilities. If the enemy threat were an increasing one, so usually would be our desired capability to counter it. The stipulated capability would presumably avoid "soft spots" if our intentions were defensive; it might point toward a maximum at some particular point of time if our intentions were to take the initiative. The general considerations which cause us to discount the future might be taken into account partly by attaching little or no weight to capabilities after some arbitrary cut-off point or horizon. Also, of course, the cost streams would still be discounted to seek the lowest-cost means of achieving the stipulated capability.[40]

All of this is related to a more general problem: the seemingly built-in tendency of governments to undervalue future outputs.[41] Given this tendency, one has to be very careful about considering "discounting" estimates of future effectiveness, especially in the national security realm. Discounting future amounts simply means that command over general resources now is worth more than command over the same amount of

---

[39] Estimated numbers of enemy targets destroyed, numbers of enemy casualties, rate of movement of the FEBA (forward edge of the battle area), fraction of U.S. population surviving a postulated enemy first strike, and so on.

[40] Charles J. Hitch and Roland N. McKean. *Economics of Defense in the Nuclear Age* (Cambridge: Harvard University Press, 1960), p. 215. In the context of nonmilitary problems, McKean reaches the same conclusion: "If gains and costs cannot be expressed in the same unit, the best that can be done usually is to specify the time path of the task as a 'requirement' and to discount the cost stream." (*Efficiency in Government Through Systems Analysis, op. cit.*, p. 99.)

[41] For a good discussion of this, see Hitch and McKean, *op. cit.*, pp. 217–218.

resources next year. *It does not mean that specific outputs are valued more now than in the future.*[42]

In view of all these considerations, the best way to handle time-phased comparisons of proposed future military capabilities is as follows:

1. Specify a desired schedule of effectiveness over the time period of interest,
2. Seek that alternative (for example, a specific force mix) which minimizes the cost to attain the stipulated time-phased effectiveness schedule. In this seeking process the time-phased cost streams may be discounted for time preference using an appropriate range of discount rates.[43]

*Is There Such a Thing as Undiscounted Costs?* Somewhat surprisingly, this is an issue that needs clarification. We can do so rather quickly, however, since once the question is posed properly there is likely to be little argument about the correct answer.

Let us consider the case of a hypothetical new Weapon System X, the total cost of which is estimated to be as follows:

| | |
|---|---|
| Development (*D*) | $ 965 million |
| Investment (*I*) | 5875 million |
| Operating Cost (*A*)[44] | 2505 million |
| | |
| Total System Cost | $9345 million |

---

[42] *Ibid.*, p. 212. Hitch and McKean present a good example of this in the context of planning decisions in the 1950s: "Suppose that an enemy is expected to have no ballistic missile capability in the early 1960's, a gradually increasing but less than decisive capability until 1965, and, after 1965, the ability to annihilate us if we have no defense. In these circumstances, anti-missile capabilities are clearly worth more to us in 1965 than in 1960. In fact, the appropriate value in the current year is zero – if the enemy cannot attack with missiles and if there are no by-products from an immediate capability like effective training for next year. On the other hand, some anti-missile capability in 1965 and later would be, on this supposition, of enormous value." (*Loc. cit.*)

[43] As we shall indicate later, one of these should be a "base case," where the discount rate is zero for the time period of interest and infinity thereafter. In many instances decisionmakers like to see this base case expressed in terms of obligational authority, because of its relevance to deliberations about funding feasibilities. Also, they may wish the base case to be calculated in terms of expenditures, which for some purposes are a rough measure of resource impact on the economy.

[44] Including the build-up of operating costs during the time of phase-in of the system into the operational inventory and 5 years of operation thereafter. (See the "A" column in Table 8.1.)

The total system cost of $9345 million is often referred to as an "un-discounted cost." Is this so? The answer is clearly "no." There is some *implied* assumption about time preference here. Let us explore some possibilities.

Suppose that we take the "static" cost estimates above and work out their time-phased patterns over a period of future years. The results are portrayed in Table 8.1. Here, one interpretation is that the time-preference

TABLE 8.1

**Time-Phased Cost Streams for Weapon System "X" (In $ Millions)**

| Future Year | D | I | A | D+I+A |
|---|---|---|---|---|
| 1 | 30 | | | 30 |
| 2 | 100 | | | 100 |
| 3 | 250 | | | 250 |
| 4 | 325 | 400 | | 725 |
| 5 | 200 | 1100 | 10 | 1310 |
| 6 | 50 | 1300 | 40 | 1390 |
| 7 | 10 | 1500 | 80 | 1590 |
| 8 | | 900 | 150 | 1050 |
| 9 | | 600 | 200 | 800 |
| 10 | | 75 | 275 | 350 |
| 11 | | | 350 | 350 |
| 12 | | | 350 | 350 |
| a ⟨ 13 | | | 350 | 350 |
| 14 | | | 350 | 350 |
| 15 | | | 350 | 350 |
| Total | 965 | 5875 | 2505 | 9345 |

[a] The assumed 5-year period for which the system has its full operational capability.

assumption is a zero rate of discount for 15 years and an infinite rate thereafter. But things can get rather tricky at this point. For example, is there an implicit assumption about the expected useful life of the system? One would think so. It is either 5 years or more than 5 years, but the analyst does not know this or else chooses to ignore the matter. What might be the implications of its being greater than 5 years?

Let us calculate a case where the expected operational life of Weapon System X is assumed to be 15 years (instead of 5), and where the cost analyst ignores this information and chooses to use $D + I + 5A = \$9345$ million as the estimated cost of the system. But if the expected life of the system is 15 years, one might expect that the total system cost would be the original $9345 million plus an increment of 10 years operating cost, as follows:

| | | |
|---|---|---|
| System cost for first 15 years | = | $ 9345 million |
| Operating cost for next 8 years | | |
| (8 × $350 million) | = | 2800 million |
| Operating cost for 24th year | = | 200 million[45] |
| Operating cost for 25th year | = | 100 million[45] |
| | | |
| Total system cost[46] | = | $12,445 million |

Notice that we have not used a positive discount rate in any of these calculations. But there is an *implied* positive discount rate if the cost analyst uses "5-year system cost" ($D + I + 5A$ = $9345 million) when the system is assumed to have an expected life of 15 years in the operational force. One way to demonstrate this is to take the time-phased cost stream for Weapon System X for 25 years and ask what rate of discount would be required to make the present value of the 25-year cost stream equal to $9345 million (that is, the present value of the costs for the first 15 years discounted at a zero rate). Solving the following equation:

$$9345 = \frac{30}{(1+r)} + \frac{100}{(1+r)^2} + \frac{250}{(1+r)^3} + \cdots + \frac{100}{(1+r)^{25}},$$

we have the discount rate, $r \cong 0.03$.[47] Thus, given this particular formulation of the problem, there is an implied discount rate of 3 percent even though the cost analyst may think he is dealing with an "undiscounted" situation.

---

[45] Annual operating cost declines as the system is phased out.

[46] That is, $D + I + 15A$ = $12,445 million.

[47] The basic equation is the formula for computing the present value of a time-phased stream of future amounts:

$$P = \sum_{i=1}^{n} \frac{A_i}{(1+r)^i},$$

where $P$ = present value, $A_i$ = the amount of the cost (or gain) in the $i$th year (or period), $r$ = the discount rate (in this case assumed to be the same for all years), $n$ = the total number of years (or periods).

The stream of costs in the numerators of the fractions on the right side of the equation in the text above is obtained from the $D + I + A$ column in Table 8.1, plus 10 additional years as follows: $350 million per year for years 16 through 23, $200 million for the 24th year, and $100 million for the 25th year. The equation can be solved for $r$ rather easily by use of an iterative process – particularly if an on-line, time-sharing computer system is available.

Another way to formulate the problem is as follows. Suppose that the assumptions are the same as in the previous case, except that the decision-makers want to use an explicit discount rate for time preference of 5 percent in considering system costs defined as $D + I + 5A$. We may now ask what rate of discount would be required to make the present value of the 25-year cost stream equal to $6497 million (that is, the present value of the costs for the first 15 years discounted at a 5 percent rate). Here, we must solve for $r$ in the following equation:

$$6497 = \frac{30}{(1+r)} + \frac{100}{(1+r)^2} + \frac{250}{(1+r)^3} + \dots + \frac{100}{(1+r)^{25}}.$$

The result is $r \cong 0.07$. Thus, in the second formulation of the problem the implied discount rate is 7 percent, even though the analysts may think that only a 5 percent rate is being used.

In summary, the preceding examples demonstrate the following points:

1. There is no such thing as an "undiscounted" situation.
2. The use of static indexes of cost (such as a sum of the costs of development + investment + a number of years operation) implies some sort of assumption about time preference, and very often this assumption may not be immediately obvious.
3. The main issue, therefore, is not whether a given case is "undiscounted," but rather whether the time preference assumptions have been made clear. Here, the analyst can be of considerable help to the decisionmakers by treating time preference considerations explicitly and by exploring the implications of alternative assumptions in the context of the particular decision at issue.

*Use of a Supplemental Discount Rate.* Supplemental discounting is a subject that we discussed earlier when considering the treatment of uncertainty. Our conclusion there was that, particularly in military systems analysis studies, the use of supplemental discounting as a way of allowing for uncertainty should be discouraged. Discounting should be for time preference only.

We bring the matter up again here because very often in discussions of problems associated with time the subject of discounting is remarkably unclear.[48] In particular it is often impossible to tell whether the discount rates being talked about are for time preference only, for time preference plus a premium for risk, for time preference plus a supplemental rate for uncertainty, or what.

---

[48] There are exceptions, of course; for example, see Baumol, *op. cit.*, and the discussion following presentation of his paper.

Because these questions are elementary, and current discussions leave much to be desired, we should spend a moment with them here. Let us now turn to specifics.

*What Discount Rates Should Be Used*? A survey of the literature indicates that a great deal of effort has been devoted to the question regarding what rate of discount should be used in long-range planning studies in the Federal Government generally and in the Department of Defense particularly. In spite of the considerable amount of discussion of the subject, however, a substantial degree of difference of opinion *seems to exist* among the experts. We underline the phrase "seems to exist," because in many of the discussions it is not always clear whether the rate of discount being considered is confined to time preference only, or to time preference plus a supplemental rate for risk or uncertainty.

In any event, the following is representative of the range of opinion contained in the literature to date:

1. In a recent survey of practices in 23 Federal agencies (conducted by the General Accounting Office), the rates ranged from about 3 to 12 percent for those agencies currently using positive rates of discount in their planning studies.[49]

2. ". . . there is no justification for the use in present circumstances [September 1967] of any discount figure significantly lower than 4.75 percent. . . . The reason is straightforward. We have seen that 4.75 percent is the lowest opportunity cost rate for any group from whom resources might be transferred to a government project.[50]

3. "An interest rate of around 15 percent, I believe, is appropriate for military and other government planning, as this rate is approximately equal to the marginal rate of return before taxes on capital in the private sector. . . . "[51]

4. "The specific discount rate appropriate to Department of Defense studies is still being debated, with values from 5 percent to 15 percent typically being suggested."[52]

---

[49] *Interest Rate Guidelines for Federal Decisionmaking, Hearings Before the Subcommittee on Economy in Government of the Joint Economic Committee, Congress of the United States,* 90th Cong., 2d Sess. (Washington, D.C.: U.S. Government Printing Office, 1968), p. 4.
[50] Baumol, *op. cit.,* p. 158.
[51] William A. Niskanen, Jr., *The Role of Costs in Military Decision Making,* an address before the Joint Conference of the Canadian Operations Research Society and the Operations Research Society of America, Montreal, Canada, May 28, 1964, p. 5.
[52] Hatry, *op. cit.,* p. 66.

5. "The best estimate may simply be a rough average rate of return in the private economy...."[53]

6. The discount rate that the government should use in making its investment decisions is "a rate that is consistent with itself through the rate of growth of national product and the rate of decline in the marginal utility of national product that it implies."[54]

Where do these opinions leave us? What rate of discount *should* be used in systems analyses of long-range military planning problems? As a practical matter, perhaps too much effort has already been expended in attempting to obtain a precise answer to this question. There are many other facets of military systems analysis, as practiced presently, which need sharpening up before more attention is devoted to the discount rate question. Hitch and McKean have reached a similar conclusion:

> Because of uncertainties about future costs and capabilities, it is not worthwhile to devote an inordinate amount of time to refining one's estimate of "the" proper discount rate. Historical studies show that projections of cost and performance of weapon systems, particularly those made at early stages of development, have often been wide of the mark. For systems analysts to put great effort into determining "the" discount rate would probably be less productive than other uses of their time.[55]

Moreover, analysts should not worry too much about the discount rate because in most long-range planning studies in the *military* realm the ranking of the alternatives is likely to be insensitive to the time preference discount rate over a relevant range of rate assumptions. This is especially likely to be the case when time-phasing considerations are treated explicitly and the systems analysis comparisons are made in the proper analytical framework. As pointed out previously, when time-phasing is done explicitly, the correct framework for comparing alternatives is to stipulate a desired schedule of effectiveness over the future time period of interest and then seek that alternative which minimizes cost. Under these conditions, where all alternatives have to meet the time-phased requirements of the specified effectiveness schedule, it is not likely that the time-impact patterns of the cost streams for the various alternatives will be significantly different – that is, different enough that varying the assumptions about time preference over a reasonable range will alter the ranking of the alternatives.

However, there are instances where the comparisons might be sensitive to time preference assumptions. One possibility arises if the relationship

---

[53] Hitch and McKean, *op. cit.*, p. 214.

[54] E. B. Berman, *The Normative Interest Rate*, P-1796 (Santa Monica, Calif.: The Rand Corporation, September 15, 1959), pp. 1, 30–31.

[55] Hitch and McKean, *op. cit.*, p. 213.

between acquisition costs (development plus investment) and operating cost is markedly different for the alternatives being considered.[56] A rather extreme case is shown in Fig. 8.3. Here, future alternatives A and B are

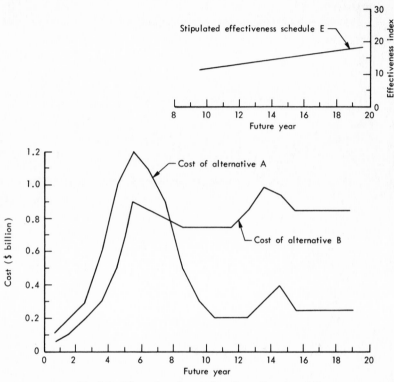

Fig. 8.3 – Time-phased costs for alternatives A and B

required to satisfy the specified effectiveness schedule E over a period of years beginning about 10 years from the present. Because of development and production lead times, both alternatives have substantial costs (mostly development and investment) occurring during future years 1 through 10 before operational capabilities become effective. Notice, however, that the two alternatives have markedly different levels of operating cost, and that both A and B have to incur modifications in years 12–15 to enable them to meet the requirements of the increasing effectiveness schedule over time.

The time preference assumption in Fig. 8.3 is a zero discount rate for 20 years and an infinite rate thereafter. On the basis of these assumptions

[56] See Hitch and McKean, *op. cit.*, p. 215.

the total system costs for A and B are $9 and $14 billion respectively. Here, alternative A is the least-cost choice to meet effectiveness schedule E over a period of distant future years. Is the choice sensitive to the discount rate for time preference?

Let us explore the consequences of assuming Baumol's minimum rate of 4.75 percent, and of two higher rates: 7 and 10 percent.[57] The results are as follows:

|  | *Present Value (in Billions)* | |
| --- | --- | --- |
| *Discount Rate* | *Alt. A* | *Alt. B* |
| 0 | $9 | $14 |
| 0.0475 | 6 | 8 |
| 0.07 | 5 | 6 |
| 0.10 | 4 | 5 |

Thus, over a wide range of assumptions about time preference the ranking of the alternatives does not change, even in this rather extreme case involving marked differences in the ratios of acquisition and operating costs for the two alternatives. However, for the higher rates of discount the differences in total system cost become less significant – so much so that the decisionmakers would probably be indifferent in choosing between A and B on the basis of the data presented above.

Another extreme case arises when the cost stream for one alternative has a large peak early in the planning period being considered and another alternative has a cost stream with a big hump late in the period. Here variations in the time preference assumptions might well make a difference in the choice. This case is very unlikely to arise in practice, however, because alternatives having such extremely different time-impact patterns would probably not be geared to the same stipulated effectiveness schedule. Therefore, they would not be relevant alternatives to be considered in a systems analysis study of capabilities for some defined future time period.

The upshot of our discussion about the discount rate would seem to be the following:

1. In long-range military planning studies involving relative comparisons among alternatives, the question of precisely what discount rate to use may not be as important as some writers have suggested. What *is* important is to make the time preference assumptions *explicit* and to test for the consequences of alternative assumptions. This is particularly important when "static" indexes of total system cost (development + investment + a period of years operation) are used.

---

[57] In all cases we assume the rate to be infinite after 20 years.

2. When time-phasing is introduced explicitly, the best way to compare alternatives is to specify a desired pattern of effectiveness or capability over the period of interest and to seek that alternative which meets the stipulated capability at least cost.

3. In doing (2) the "base case" time preference assumption should be a zero rate of discount for the period under examination in the systems analysis study. (Cost streams calculated on this basis are of interest to decisionmakers because of their relevance to deliberations about funding and other considerations.) In addition, the cost analysts should do a sensitivity analysis to explore the implications of a range of discount rates – for example, from 4 to 10 percent. Here, the objective is to determine whether the ranking of the alternatives is sensitive to the discount rate. Very often it will not be.[58]

4. In those cases where the discount rate is likely to make a difference to the decision, we have to face up to the question of an appropriate rate for the particular decision context at hand. Such a rate depends primarily upon the exchange opportunities available to the decisionmakers within their framework of authority and responsibility. (See the discussion on "Choosing a Discount Rate" in Chapter 3.)

**The Problem of Residual Value**
Another topic related to problems associated with time is the matter of "residual value." It arises primarily because long-range planners cannot look extremely far into the future. Because possible enemy threats, technological factors, and other considerations for the very distant future cannot be known, planners typically restrict their projections to some limited period – say 10, 15, or 20 years.

Limiting the time horizon gives rise to the problem of residual value in cases where it is felt that proposed alternatives might have military worth beyond the planning period being considered. To see this more clearly, let us present an example. Suppose that the planners are comparing two alternative new military capabilities (weapon systems A and B). Both have development and procurement lead times of about 10 years, and both must meet a specified effectiveness schedule (E–E') for a 10-year period as shown in Fig. 8.4. The cost profiles for A and B over the assumed 20-year planning period are about the same (the solid line cost stream in Fig. 8.4). On the basis of this information, and assuming a "cut-off" of all costs and benefits

---

[58] A related technique is called "break-even analysis." This procedure determines a "break-even rate of discount" – that is, that rate of discount which makes the two leading alternatives equal in terms of present value system cost for the specified schedule of effectiveness.

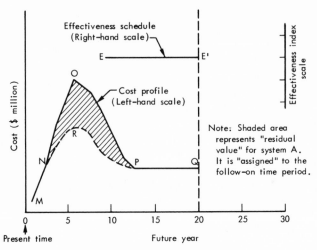

Fig. 8.4–"Residual value" example

after the 20th year, the decisionmakers would presumably be indifferent about a choice between A and B.

Suppose, however, that someone comes forward with an argument asserting that a part of system A (for example, its major equipment) is likely to have some kind of military worth after year 20; and that if this is the case, a portion of the *investment costs* of system A should be subtracted from the initial 20-year time horizon and "assigned" to a follow-on period (say, years 21 through 30).[59] In practice this "assignment" has usually been done on the basis of some kind of judgment about the "useful life" of the major equipment in question.

A very crude calculation might be done as follows: For the general type of major equipment being considered, useful life in past history has been about 20 years. Therefore, for the proposed equipment, half of its investment costs should be "charged" to the initial planning period and half to the years 21 through 30. More "sophisticated" procedures might charge relatively less to years 21 through 30 to allow for the greater uncertainty about "useful life" in the more distant time period.

Suppose that something like this is done in our example, and that as a result a "residual value" (shaded area in Fig. 8.4) is calculated for alternative A and assigned to the time period 21–30 years. The cost profile for

---

[59] Such assignment of costs to a subsequent planning period is often proposed in the case of new Navy ships – especially aircraft carriers. It should be pointed out that "residual value" does not refer to scrap value, but rather to some kind of "military worth" (usually unspecified).

A now drops considerably (from MNOPQ to MNRPQ) for the planning period being considered; and unless someone can come forward with a similar "residual value" argument for system B (whose costs are still MNOPQ), alternative A will be preferred over alternative B. Thus, in this case the introduction of someone's speculation about the "useful life" ("military worth"?) of the major equipment in alternative A some 20 to 30 years in the future changes what is equal choice between A and B into an easy choice of A over B.

Let us now offer a few comments on the example:

1. Judgments about "useful life" or "military worth" beyond the initial planning period would seem to pertain to effectiveness or benefit considerations. This being the case, it seems somewhat strange to deal with possible supplemental benefits by arbitrarily taking *costs* out of one period and putting them into another (the follow-on period).

2. Subtracting costs from the initial planning period and assigning them to the follow-on period may deprive the decisionmakers of information they usually want to have. For example, they want to know the timing of the economic impact of alternatives being proposed for the future. They also want to know approximately when the obligational authority required to finance such alternatives would have to be obtained from the Congress. Exclusive use of "residual value costing" tends to confuse these issues.

3. Making *meaningful* assessments of possible military worth of major equipments (or other major assets) for periods 20 to 30 years in the future is most difficult. That is the main reason why long-range planners set up a limited time horizon in the first place. Beyond that time period it is probably impossible to consider the relevant issues in a useful way. If on certain occasions the planners find that something definitive can be said about possible follow-on military usefulness of future equipments or other assets, the matter should be dealt with explicitly. This may be done, for example, by extending the initial time horizon or by considering two sequential planning periods. Such a treatment would eliminate the need to consider "residual value costing."

Thus, we might draw the following conclusions:

1. The residual value costing idea as practiced in some systems analysis studies is not to be recommended as a general procedure. It is likely to confuse more issues than it clarifies.
2. If for some reason residual value costing is used, the "full cost" case should also be presented to the decisionmakers. This will enable them to get a proper picture of the time impact of obligational

authority or expenditure requirements during the planning period being considered.

3. The residual value problem should be considered primarily as an effectiveness or benefit issue. If in a particular case definitive issues exist regarding the possible military value of future assets in the follow-on period, this information should be presented to the decisionmakers explicitly – not in terms of arbitrary transfers of cost from the initial planning period to the follow-on period.

## Wartime Costs

So far in this book the subject of "wartime costs" has not been addressed – at least not explicitly. In the context of comparisons among possible alternative capabilities for the distant future, the main emphasis has been on the resource impact of peacetime activities to acquire and sustain future postures for deterring war and for fighting a war for a limited period of time should deterrence fail.[60] Hitch and McKean took a similar view in *The Economics of Defense in the Nuclear Age*:

> Our major emphasis in this volume is on peacetime preparations for war and on deterring war. This means that we are interested *mainly* in peacetime, not wartime costs. We are trying to make the most of the resources available for national security in peacetime. In principle, the wartime costs are relevant. In practice, we can frequently ignore them. For in the case of general nuclear war, we expect the war to be fought with the forces in being at its outbreak. The major economic problem is to maximize the capability of these forces by using resources efficiently before the war starts – so efficiently that we hope an enemy will never dare start it. In the case of limited war there may well be significant production of weapons and expenditure of resources after the limited war begins (as in the case of Korea), but occasional wars for limited objectives will cost little compared with the year-in year-out costs of peacetime preparedness. It is estimated that the "cost of United States forces in Korea over and above the normal cost of such forces if no action was taking place" was approximately five billion dollars in the fiscal year 1951/52, about 11 percent of total United States expenditures for major national security programs that year.[61]

In years past, few analysts seemed to question the appropriateness of using so-called "peacetime costs" in comparative analyses of long-range

---

[60] "Limited period of time" usually means a time interval sufficient to permit the economy to gear up for production to replace resources consumed during the initial phases of the war and to sustain the effort thereafter. This applies to essentially the entire range of the spectrum of warfare except the two extremes: (1) the all-out thermonuclear exchange and (2) the *very* small, short-term limited war.

[61] Hitch and McKean, *op. cit.*, pp. 169–170.

planning problems.[62] Perhaps the thinking then was conditioned by general nuclear war scenarios, in which "wartime costs" were rather academic. The situation in limited non-nuclear wars and controlled-response nuclear war, however, could be quite different. Particularly since the Vietnam experience, questions have been raised concerning possible biases arising in comparisons among alternatives when "wartime costs" are not fully taken into account in long-range planning studies. Our task here is to explore this question and to try to clarify some of the issues.

If the issue is put: "Are wartime costs relevant in systems analyses of long-range planning problems?" – the answer in principle would seem to be "yes," as Hitch and McKean have pointed out.[63] In practice, however, in making relative comparisons among proposals for distant future military capabilities, there will no doubt be cases where a substantial portion of wartime costs may appropriately be ignored.[64] In other instances this may not be so, and some attempt, however crude, will have to be made to reflect the more important wartime costs.

At this point let us explore briefly the meaning of "peacetime costs," as currently used in many systems analysis studies. For some new proposed capability for the distant future, these costs consist of research and development, investment, and operation over a period of time (say 5 or 10 years). Do these so-called "peacetime costs" contain any elements of "wartime costs"? Indeed they do. Some are obvious; for example:

1. The cost of inventories of wartime readiness reserve stocks of ammunition, spares and spare parts, and other consumable supply items. In principle these items are stocked on the basis of estimates of possible wartime consumption rates for appropriate periods of

---

[62] We continue to put peacetime costs in quotation marks, because, as will be indicated later, the concept as used in practice contains a rather complex mixture of "peacetime" and "wartime" costs. In fact, it would seem that there is no such thing as *pure* "peacetime costs." For, after all, were it not for the contingency of war, there would presumably be no peacetime military activities and hence no associated costs. One definition of "peacetime costs," therefore, might be: "costs incurred or sustained for military and related activities during peacetime *in anticipation of war.*" "Wartime costs" would then be defined in incremental terms as "those military and related costs incurred during actual conflict situations."

[63] Some practitioners argue that estimates of wartime *dollar* costs are irrelevant in systems analysis studies. For example, see J. G. Abert, *Some Problems in Cost Analysis*, Research Paper P-186 (Arlington, Virginia: Institute for Defense Analyses, June 1965), Chap. V, "The Irrelevancy of Wartime Costs."

[64] We stress that the context of this book is long-range planning with emphasis upon relative comparisons among alternatives, particularly to serve as a guide to research and development decisions. In other contexts – planning for current operations in an existing or likely wartime situation – explicit consideration of wartime costs cannot appropriately be ignored.

time (say 30 to 120 days), so that the system can function in a postulated wartime environment until production can be geared up to meet wartime requirements.[65] The costs of such inventories in no way reflect the wartime costs of long-duration campaigns. They do, however, reflect an important *portion* of the costs of short-duration campaigns and of the initial period of long-duration wars.[66] In any event these are "wartime costs" which are incurred in peacetime.

2. The personnel costs associated with manning levels which are considerably higher than those required for a standby peacetime operation: major equipment crew manning requirements stemming from estimated wartime crew ratios, the manning of maintenance activities, and the like. Tactical airpower systems, for example, are typically manned in peacetime for a potential wartime sortie-generation capability which is considerably higher than that required for peacetime readiness postures. Again certain elements of "wartime cost" are reflected in the estimates of "peacetime cost."

Other ways in which certain "wartime costs" are reflected in "peacetime costs" are somewhat more subtle. To see this clearly, let us consider the following example. Suppose that the long-range planners are comparing alternative forces in the context of a distant-future, non-nuclear limited war scenario involving countries Y and Z. The specified "task to be done" requires having a future force posture which hopefully will deter Z from attacking Y and which, if deterrence fails, will with high confidence prevent Z from overrunning a specified key portion of Y's territory within, say, a 30 to 60 day time period.[67] Assume now that alternative proposals C and D are being compared, with a view to determining which alternative might do the stipulated task at least cost (that is, the least "total system cost" as defined earlier).

The systems analysts construct a campaign model of the situation and run alternatives C and D through an effectiveness analysis of the problem. It is found that alternative D is considerably more vulnerable to the postulated attack by the forces of country Z, with the result that units of D suffer

---

[65] Here we say "in principle" because estimating wartime consumption rates for conflict scenarios 10 to 20 years into the future is a most difficult (perhaps impossible) task. But this is merely a reflection of one aspect of the problems involved in introducing wartime costs into systems analysis studies concerned with the distant future.

[66] One type of cost that is *not* taken into account here is the cost of replacing wartime readiness reserve stocks once the campaign is over.

[67] The latter specification, of course, has a direct bearing on the probability of success of deterrence.

a higher combat attrition rate than those of C. This means that a much larger force size of D would be required to do the specified task than the force sizes of C to do the same job. Suppose the force sizes of C and D are 20 and 50, respectively. Suppose further that the estimated total system costs for C and D are as portrayed in Fig. 8.5. On the basis of these data, C would be preferred over alternative D.

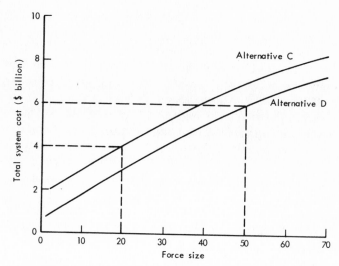

Fig. 8.5 – Total system cost versus force size for C and D

Let us now pose the following question: Do the "peacetime costs" used in comparing C and D contain elements of "wartime cost" over and above those for wartime reserve stocks and manning referred to previously? The answer would clearly seem to be "yes," because the *force sizes* of C and D were determined on the basis of the campaign analysis (including estimated wartime attrition) of the stipulated wartime task to be performed. This in turn has an impact directly on the "peacetime" acquisition and sustaining costs of the war-deterrent capabilities of C and D. Thus, the so-called "peacetime costs" currently used in systems analysis comparisons of alternative distant-future military capabilities usually contain substantial elements of "wartime costs." They are far from being "pure" peacetime costs, as some analysts have maintained. This is especially bound to be the case when the systems analysis is conducted in a "fixed-task-to-be-performed" type of analytical framework.

The preceding argument, however, does not mean that the costs used in systems analyses reflect the full costs of possible distant future conflicts.

The *costs of wars* and peacetime costs containing *elements of wartime cost* are clearly two different things; and total system or force costs typically used in long-range planning studies do not measure the cost of wars.[68] While in principle including all wartime costs seems desirable, in practice it seems infeasible when dealing with the very distant future. The question still remains, however, as to whether or not omission of incremental wartime costs[69] tends to bias the comparisons among alternatives made in systems analysis studies. There can be no general answer, of course. But it is not difficult to think of situations where the outcome might be different if incremental wartime costs were somehow taken into account.

As an example, let us consider the case of a high-intensity, limited nonnuclear war. Here, one of the key variables determining full wartime cost is the length of the conflict. Allowing for variations in this factor (and the associated wartime costs) may or may not change the ranking of the alternatives being compared.[70] But the possibility of such differential effects is what the systems analysts should try to explore.[71] Admittedly this is most difficult to do, and certainly we cannot *predict* the duration of future wars. However, some sort of crude sensitivity testing might be done, as shown in Fig. 8.6.

Here, for a stipulated task to be done the cost of alternatives E and F is plotted as a function of days of war, beginning with D-day (the day war begins). The costs include conventional total system costs plus a rough estimate of the incremental wartime costs after D-day. Here, the incremental wartime costs as a function of time *do* impact differentially on E and F, with the result that a cross-over point occurs at $D + N$ days. For the specified task to be done, alternative F is preferred prior to $D + N$; alternative E is preferred thereafter.

This is an example of the sort of testing that might be done to help assure the analysts about the wisdom of suppressing incremental wartime costs

---

[68] One of the very real costs of wars is, of course, casualties. Total system costs, as we have defined them, do not reflect casualties in an explicit way. However, the effectiveness part of a systems analysis very often contains explicit attempts to estimate casualties. For example, in comparing alternative mixes of future air and ground forces for use in limited wars, one of the measures of effectiveness might be infliction of casualties on the enemy forces and potential for avoiding casualties to friendly forces.

[69] By "incremental" we mean wartime costs over and above those typically taken into account.

[70] Our ability to measure full wartime costs of possible distant-future conflicts may, for example, be so crude that differential effects cannot be detected, with the result that the impact on alternatives is essentially proportional.

[71] An example of a case in point is where the best force mix for the initial stages of the conflict is not the same as the preferred mix for later stages. The characteristics of combat requirements very often change as a function of time.

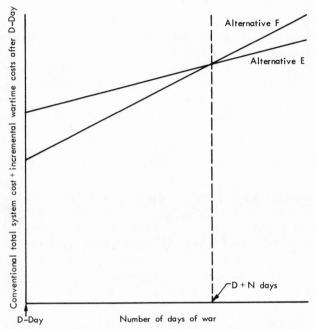

Fig. 8.6 – Cost versus war duration for alternatives E and F

in a given comparison. In those cases where differential impacts on the comparisons of alternatives are detected, the results of the sensitivity analysis should be presented to the decisionmakers in an explicit fashion. Such information could help them in making final judgments about the alternatives under consideration.

## Summary

*Uncertainty*

Cost analyses of distant future military capabilities are typically subject to many uncertainties. These uncertainties may be categorized under two main headings:

1. Requirements uncertainty (analogous to "state-of-the-world uncertainties"),
2. Cost-estimating uncertainty (analogous to "statistical uncertainties").

Requirements uncertainty is by far the more important in most cases.

How the cost analyst treats uncertainty in any given instance is very much a function of the design of the systems analysis study of which the cost analysis is a part. This a especially true in the case of *requirements uncertainty*. Here, imaginative sensitivity testing on the part of the cost analyst can be very useful to the systems analysts in their unending search for dominances and for ingenious ways of hedging against major uncertainties of the distant future. To do this effectively, however, cost analysis methods and models must be parametric in nature. That is, they must be "open-ended" with respect to key cost-generating explanatory variables such as major equipment performance characteristics, operational concepts, force size, and the like.

In dealing with *cost-estimating uncertainties*, the hope in most systems analysis studies is that these uncertainties may safely be suppressed – for example, by using "expected value" cost estimates. One of the main tasks of the cost analysts, therefore, is to determine whether or not such a suppression is appropriate. The following may be helpful in forming judgments in this regard: (1) examination of the measures of reliability (for example, standard errors or prediction intervals) for key estimating relationships used in the cost analysis; (2) sensitivity testing, particularly with respect to the more important categories making up total system (or force) cost; and (3) use of Monte Carlo techniques.

*Problems Associated with Time*

Because of the importance of the subject of time in systems analysis studies, it should always be taken into account specifically, preferably through explicit time-phasing of effectiveness and cost. Nevertheless, this is not often feasible in all stages of the analysis.

Particularly in the early phases of an investigation of a wide range of alternatives, "static" indexes of cost are often used. These indexes usually contain implicit (frequently unrecognized) assumptions about discounting of future costs. Cost analysts have the responsiblity to make these assumptions explicit.

Later in the study, when the most interesting set of alternatives has been uncovered, time-phasing considerations should be treated definitively. When time-phasing is introduced explicitly, usually the best way to compare alternatives is to specify a desired pattern of effectiveness or capability over the period of interest and to seek that alternative which meets the stipulated capability at least cost.

Here, the "base case" cost streams should be computed using a zero rate of discount for the period of time under consideration. In addition, the cost analysts should conduct sensitivity analyses to explore the implications of a relevant range of discount rate assumptions. The objective is to determine whether the ranking of the alternatives is sensitive to the discount rate.

Another topic related to problems associated with time is the matter of "residual value." It arises when possible uses of future military assets beyond the initial planning time horizon are taken into account. One proposed solution used in some past systems analysis studies is to subtract costs from the initial planning period and assign them to the follow-on period ("residual value costing").

This solution is not recommended as a general procedure. The residual value problem should be considered primarily as an effectiveness or benefit issue. If in a particular case definitive arguments can be advanced regarding possible military value of future assets in the follow-on period, the information should be presented to the decisionmakers explicitly – not in terms of arbitrary transfers of cost from one period to another.

*Wartime Costs*

The issue of "peacetime" vs. "wartime" costs is troublesome for a number of reasons. One is that so-called "peacetime" costs generally used in systems analysis studies typically contain important elements of "wartime" cost. Another is that in considering alternative proposals for military capabilities in the distant future, it is very difficult in practice to assess full wartime costs in a meaningful way.

Particularly in analyzing limited war, the key question is whether or not the relative comparisons of alternatives may be biased because of omissions of key elements of wartime cost. Systems analysts will rarely be able to answer this question definitively. However, when it is feasible to do so, the analysts should conduct sensitivity tests in an attempt to shed some light on the matter. For example, the analysis might be carried out for several assumptions regarding the duration of the war. If there are significant differential impacts on the alternatives being considered, this information should be presented to the decisionmakers.

**Suggested Supplementary Readings**
1. Albert Madansky, "Uncertainty," Chap. 5 in E. S. Quade and W. I. Boucher (eds.), *Systems Analysis and Policy Planning: Applications in Defense* (New York: American Elsevier Publishing Co., Inc., 1968). A good general discussion of the problem of uncertainty.
2. Charles J. Hitch and Roland N. McKean, *The Economics of Defense in the Nuclear Age* (Cambridge: Harvard University Press, 1960), Chap. 10, "Incommensurables, Uncertainty and the Enemy"; Chap. 11, "Problems Associated with Time."
3. Harry P. Hatry, "The Use of Cost Estimates," Chap. 4 in Thomas A. Goldman (ed.), *Cost-Effectiveness Analysis* (New York: Frederick A. Praeger, Publishers, 1967).
4. Saul Hoch, "Cost Criteria in Weapon Systems Analysis and Force Studies," published in *Applications of Operations Research to Military Resource Allocation and Planning*, Proceedings of a Conference held at Sandejford, Norway, 23–26 Aug. 1965, Sponsored by the NATO Advisory Panel on Operations Research. Published by: Forsvarets Forskningsinstitutt, Norwegian Defence Research Establishment, P.O. Box 25, Kjeller, Norway.
5. John McClelland, "Peacetime and Wartime Costs In Cost-Effectiveness Analysis," published in T. Arthur Smith (ed.), *Economic Analysis and Military Resource Allocation* (Washington, D.C.: Office, Comptroller of the Army, 1968), pp. 55–64.

# Chapter 9

# SYSTEMS ANALYSIS EXAMPLES

From time to time throughout this book we have presented brief examples of systems analysis studies. At this point, it seems appropriate to probe systems analysis – and its attendant problems of cost analysis – in more depth through the use of several fairly detailed illustrations of actual, and recent, studies. Of course, because we will be concerned with examples, and not the studies themselves, we shall be at a rather high level of generality. Yet this should be adequate to the achievement of our objective, which is to give the reader more of a grasp of the total systems analysis process in terms of (1) conceptual and methodological considerations and (2) some of the practical problems encountered in actually doing a systems analysis study. Here, our point of view will be primarily that of the project leader who must assume the key role in the design and conduct of an analysis pointed toward assisting long-range planning decisionmakers. This means that the cost considerations *per se* are not emphasized more than any of the other aspects of the total process. Cost analysis matters, therefore, are discussed as only one component of an integrated whole and in the context of the particular questions to which the total analysis is addressed.

Let us consider the following three studies:

1. *An analysis of the possible roles of long-endurance aircraft in future military force postures.* This example is based on a 1963 study of the potential uses of long-endurance aircraft in a variety of mission areas. However, to keep the illustration relatively simple, primary emphasis is placed on one mission area (strategic bombardment), and the main focus is on intersystem comparisons and the analysis of critical subsystem components. Another purpose of this example is to indicate some of the types of analyses that can be carried out when the time available to assist the decisionmakers is relatively short – a very likely situation for many analytical staffs in government agencies.

2. *A consideration of trade-offs between ground and air forces in a non-nuclear limited war.* Here again the illustration is based on past investigations. However, the analytical problems involved in this case are in many respects much more complicated than in the first example. For instance, force mixes must be considered explicitly, and an attempt must be made to

deal with the many complexities of limited war scenarios. A particularly troublesome problem pertains to establishing appropriate criteria for assessing the effectiveness of alternative force mixes, and special emphasis is given to this question in the discussion of the example. The basic analytical framework is a "fixed budget" type of comparative format – that is, the air-ground force trade-off problem is examined in the context of equal-cost alternative force mixes.[1]

3. *An exploratory investigation of new approaches to complex problems of choice involving interactions among technological, military, and political considerations.* Unlike the previous cases, the third example is based on the results through 1968 of a continuing exploratory effort which is even now still in its early stages of development. Because of this, our discussion must of necessity be less definitive than we would like. However, those readers who are especially concerned about possibilities for new analytical approaches to complex problems of choice under conditions of uncertainty should find the example interesting and hopefully conducive to further thought. The study which serves as the basis of our example is focused on distant future strategic offensive, defensive, sensor, and command forces in an operational sphere whose diameter is 12 earth radii.[2] That portion of the scenario spectrum of particular interest is the initiation, management, and termination of general war at levels *less than* full counterpopulation exchanges.

The remainder of the chapter is divided into three self-contained parts – one for each of the illustrative cases – so that the reader may select the combination of cases he wishes to examine in detail.

## CASE 1:
## THE LONG-ENDURANCE AIRCRAFT EXAMPLE[3]

The view is often expressed that analytical effort of real value to a decision-maker dealing with complex planning problems may prove exceptionally difficult, perhaps impossible. Two reasons in support of this belief are: (1) an extremely complex environment, along with a host of nonquantifiable variables; and (2) a short deadline to do a study.

---

[1] This is a frequently employed framework of analysis. It has been used, for example, in examinations of force mixes of land-based and sea-based tactical airpower; force mixes of airlift, sealift, and prepositioning; force mixes of Regular and Reserve Forces; and so on.

[2] That is to say, a substantial volume of outer space is part of the assumed operational environment. The time horizon extends out to 1980.

[3] This example is based on G. H. Fisher, "Illustrative Example of Cost-Utility Considerations in a Military Context," Appendix to Chap. 4 in David Novick (ed.), *Program Budgeting: Program Analysis and the Federal Government* (Cambridge: Harvard University Press, rev. ed., 1967), pp. 106–119.

No doubt there are such instances. However, we take the position that even in rather severe cases, *something* can be done, and that this something may often be very useful in spite of the lack of extensive calculations of utility and cost. In the present section, an example having such character-istics is selected deliberately in order to illustrate the kind of analysis that might be done. It is based on an actual study conducted at The Rand Corporation in 1963. In order to avoid security-classification, much of the substantive detail has to be suppressed. However, it is hoped that enough of the essential content of the problem is preserved, so that a few of the more important points can be illustrated.

**General Statement of the Problem**
Basically, the problem may be stated as follows:

1. Investigate the possible role of long-endurance aircraft (LEA) for use in new weapon (or support) systems to perform a variety of U.S. Air Force missions in the 1970–1975 time period.[4]
2. In each mission area compare LEA type systems with alternative possibilities, including missile as well as aircraft systems.
3. Investigate the possibilities for *multipurpose* use of the LEA; that is, of developing a basic aircraft and adapting it to several mission areas. What are the cost savings? What, if any, degradations in utility (system effectiveness) might be incurred in a given mission area by using a multipurpose vehicle rather than one "optimized" to that particular mission?
4. Time to do the study: about *6 weeks.*[5]
5. Assess the implications for possible new development programs to be initiated in the near future, with a view to initial operational capability in the early 1970s.

**Further Consideration of the Problem**
On the face of it, the statement of the problem outlined above appears fairly straightforward, although the short time period for doing the study

---

[4] A long-endurance aircraft is one designed specifically to remain airborne in unrefueled flight for a prolonged period of time – in some cases several days. Usually the emphasis on long endurance involves compromises in certain of the other performance charac-teristics, especially speed and cruise altitude.

[5] It should be pointed out that The Rand Corporation had in previous years done a considerable amount of work on the technical and design aspects of LEA. However, work on *system* applications of LEA was somewhat more limited. In any event, 6 weeks was a short time to do a study of this type, at least to Rand standards. But time to do a study is relative. In a military staff environment in the Pentagon, 6 weeks would no doubt be considered a relatively long time.

imposes a significant constraint. Even preliminary thinking about the problem soon leads to the conclusion that the problem is a difficult one. Some of the more important reasons why are outlined in the following paragraphs.

A wide range of possible mission area applications might be considered; for example, strategic bombardment, limited war, defense against sub-marine-launched ballistic missile attack, air defense of North America (against the air-breathing threat), command and control, satellite launching platform, anti-satellite missile launching platform, air transport, and intelligence or reconnaissance patrol applications.

The future environment (1970–1975) in practically all the mission areas is very uncertain. In limited war, for instance, what kinds of limited war scenarios should we consider?[6] Obviously, we cannot single out one that is "most probable." A range of scenarios must be considered, and this range should not necessarily be chosen on the basis of likelihood, but rather to illustrate possible roles for the LEA.

Within most of the mission areas there is a wide range of alternative systems to be considered – even including the Navy's proposals for an advanced Fleet Ballistic Missile (Polaris) system in the strategic area. (Some of the more relevant alternatives are discussed later.)

After only slight initial examination, it becomes obvious that the most critical considerations do not concern the LEA vehicle itself, but rather the *payload subsystems* that have to be developed and procured to give a LEA system its capability in a given mission area. There are exceptions: command and control is probably one of them, for example. But in general, the payload subsystems pose the more interesting and difficult technical problems; and preliminary cost analysis indicated that the develop-ment cost for a subsystem in a given area (like strategic bombardment) would be considerably greater than for the total development program for the LEA itself. In short, what initially is specified as mainly an aircraft problem rapidly turns primarily into problems concerning subsystems.

The main characteristics of a long-endurance aircraft are extended air-borne capability (endurance), large payload, and long range.[7] These are so-called "positive" characteristics. The main negative ones are low speed and possible constraints on altitude capability. So immediately the analyst should think about mission applications where the positive characteristics

---

[6] Here "scenario" essentially means the context or setting within which the particular type of war is assumed to take place; for example, the geographic area; the political environment at the beginning of the conflict; the political objectives to be attained; the constraints on weapons (nuclear weapons or not?); the sanctuaries, if any; and so on.

[7] There are trade-offs among these, of course.

are desired and where low speed is not a handicap or perhaps is even desirable (for example, in certain types of intelligence/reconnaissance operations). One example is a mission area where airborne patrol operations are important. Another is a situation where vulnerability on the ground to an initial enemy attack is a problem, and an alternative basing scheme is required. The LEA used as an airborne platform provides one such alternative. But there are still other possible alternative basing concepts: ground mobility, water-based platforms (surface), water-based platforms (submersible), and so on. These alternatives would have to be taken into account in the analysis.

From this partial list of considerations, it is clear that the problem is indeed a complex one. The real question is what can be done with it in the short time available for analytical effort. For illustrative purposes, let us take one mission area – strategic bombardment – and consider some of the more relevant factors in this area.

### Some Considerations in the Strategic Bombardment Area

In considering whether the strategic systems being planned in 1963 for the early 1970s should be supplemented, two major uncertainties involving military intelligence were paramount:

1. Whether the enemy was likely to achieve technological advances such that his offensive capabilities would render U.S. fixed base (hardened) missile systems vulnerable on the ground to a first strike.
2. Whether the enemy was likely to achieve a reasonably effective defense against intercontinental ballistic missiles (an ABM capability) during the early 1970 time period.

While the analyst cannot *resolve* these uncertainties, he can and should trace out their implications, enumerate the relevant alternatives that might be used to meet them, and possibly suggest ways to hedge against them.

Regarding the first uncertainty, it is clear that the LEA would be of interest if the problem is one of seeking alternative basing schemes to avoid or reduce vulnerability on the ground. The LEA could be used as a standoff missile-launching platform in a system having a substantial part of the force on continuous airborne alert. Regarding the second uncertainty, the LEA offers no *unique* features; but it could be used as an airborne platform from which low-altitude penetrating missiles (to avoid ABM defenses) could be launched. When the two types of uncertainty are combined, however, it could be that a LEA system (with low-altitude penetrating missiles) might be attractive. But such a system would have to be compared with the alternatives.

What are some of the relevant alternatives? The following is an illustrative list.

For the case where the prime objective is to reduce initial vulnerability to a surprise attack:

1. LEA used as a standoff platform for launching airborne ballistic missiles (ALBMs) in a system having a substantial part of the force on continuous airborne alert.
2. Land mobile (truck or rail) ballistic missile systems.
3. Water mobile (barge) ballistic missile systems.
4. Incremental Fleet Ballistic Missile (Polaris) force. (Incremental to the currently planned Polaris force.)
5. Additional Minuteman missiles (to try to compensate for their ground vulnerability by having a bigger force.)

For the case where the main purpose is to have a system that can penetrate enemy ICBM defenses:

1. Low-altitude penetrating missiles launched from an airborne platform – an LEA or some other aircraft.
2. Land based (fixed) ballistic missile systems with low-altitude penetrating reentry devices.
3. Land based (fixed) ballistic missile systems with multiple warhead (possibly including decoys) reentry devices to confuse the enemy ICBM defense.
4. Sea based ballistic missile systems with low-altitude penetrating reentry bodies or with multiple warhead capability.

For a combination of the above two cases – that is, where the main concern is about the initial vulnerability of U.S. strategic systems and about the enemy having an AICBM capability:

1. LEA used as a standoff platform for launching low-altitude penetrating missiles in a system having a substantial fraction of the force on continuous airborne alert.
2. Land mobile (truck or rail) ballistic missile systems with low-altitude penetrating reentry devices or with multiple warhead reentry bodies.
3. Water mobile (surface) ballistic missile systems with low-altitude penetrating reentry devices or with multiple warhead reentry bodies.
4. Same as (3) except that the launching platform is *below* the surface (for example, submarines or submersible barges).

The main problem is to conduct an analysis to compare such alternatives on a cost-effectiveness basis, with a view to determining preferred alternatives under certain assumed scenarios. Ideally, this would proceed somewhat as follows. (Here, we assume a fixed effectiveness conceptual framework; a fixed budget context could be used instead.)

An enemy target system is specified to be destroyed with some probability of success (say, 90 percent). Campaign analyses are conducted in order to determine the size force that would be required for each alternative to do the specified task. This involves determination of the number of U.S. weapons surviving a postulated initial enemy attack, determination of the force that is successfully launched to make the responding strike on the specified enemy target system, assessment of losses to the enemy defenses, calculation of target destruction, and the like.[8] Given the resulting force size calculations, we then proceed with a resource analysis to determine the *total system cost* (research and development, investment, and operating cost) for each of the alternatives required to do the job. These system costs can then be compared to try to determine which alternative is likely to accomplish the given task at the lowest cost. Finally, the analyst might repeat the analysis for varying levels of initial enemy attack and varying types of U.S. responses, and then conduct a qualitative analysis to supplement the quantitative work.

This approach to the problem would lead to a "hard core" cost-effectiveness analysis – something that is not easy to do and certainly very time-consuming. Since only 6 weeks were available for the entire study, something far short of a complete analysis had to be done. The real question is what *can* be done, if anything, within such limitations. Our position was that a great deal could be done, far short of a type of analysis involving a relatively complete set of calculations of utility and cost.[9] For one thing, a mere *enumeration* of all the relevant alternatives may be very helpful; better yet would be to furnish data and information bearing on effectiveness and cost of these alternatives.

### Summary Analyses of Cost and Effectiveness

One thing that can be done is to develop summary analyses of cost and effectiveness and present them along with a qualitative statement of some of the key implications. Examples are given in Fig. 9.1 and Table 9.1.

---

[8] It should be emphasized that these campaign analyses are very difficult and time-consuming.

[9] Recall that our objective in analytical work is *not* to "make the decision," but rather to provide a better basis for the decisionmakers to exercise their judgment.

TABLE 9.1

**Selected Data Bearing on Effectiveness Considerations
for Alternative Systems A, B, C, D, and E**

| | | | Alternative System | | | |
|---|---|---|---|---|---|---|
| Description | | A | B | C | D | E |
| Quantitative Inofrmation | | | | | | |
| Effective range (n mi) | | | | | | |
| Cruise speed (kn) | | | | | | |
| Penetration speed (kn) | | | | | | |
| Warhead yield (MT) | | | | | | |
| Circular error probability (CEP) | | | | | | |
| Single shot kill probability | | | | | | |
|    Against soft targets | | | | | | |
|    Against hard targets | | | | | | |
| Extended strike option time (days) | | | | | | |
|   . . . etc. | | | | | | |
| | | | | | | |
| Qualitative Information[a] | | | | | | |
| "Show of force" capability | | | | | | |
| Multidirectional attack capability | | | | | | |
| Ground vulnerability | | | | | | |
| In-flight vulnerability | | | | | | |
| Controlled response capability | | | | | | |
|   . . . etc. | | | | | | |

[a] Some of these items have quantitative aspects to them; but they are
very difficult to assess in a study with a short time deadline.

Figure 9.1 shows total system cost vs. force size for several alternative systems. In this example, "force size" means number of missiles in position ready to go. In the case of a system like Minuteman, it means number of missiles in silos ready to fire. In the case of a LEA system carrying airborne air-to-surface missiles, it means number of missiles continuously airborne on station and ready to go. Used in conjunction with data pertaining to effectiveness (as in Table 9.1), curves that indicate system cost vs. force size can be useful.

For example, equal-cost cases can be generated ($F_1$ of Alternative A, $F_2$ of Alternative C for cost level $B_0$ in Fig. 9.1). These can in turn be compared in terms of the data bearing on effectiveness, with a view to reaching judgments about which alternatives might offer the most capability for the given level of cost.

In any event, the decisionmaker is clearly in a better position to exercise his judgment if he has the benefit of Fig 9.1 and Table 9.1 than if he did

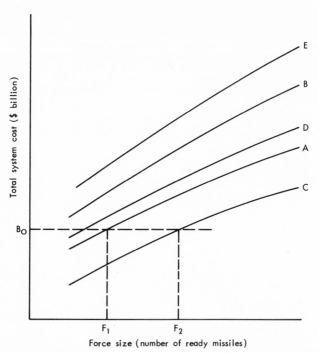

Fig. 9.1 – Total system cost versus force size for alternative systems A, B, C, D, and E

not have them.[10] This is an example of what can be done between the extremes of no analysis whatever, on the one hand, and "hard core" cost-effectiveness analysis, on the other. The results are certainly far short of a detailed quantitative analysis; but they nevertheless may be useful.

### A Purely Qualitative Analysis

Quite often a purely qualitative comparison can be very helpful, especially when used to supplement the kind of analysis presented above. An example is presented in Table 9.2.

Here, the various alternatives are listed in the stub of the table, and in the body various qualitative comments are made regarding the characteristics of certain key capabilities of the alternative systems. In cases where a large number of alternatives are under consideration, such information can be useful in weeding out those cases that are likely to be of little interest from those that appear worthy of further and more detailed deliberation.

---

[10] It is assumed, of course, that the decisionmaker also has the benefit of any interpretive comments that the analyst may have.

TABLE 9.2

**System Comparison**
(Illustrative Example)

| Alternative System | Invulnerable to | | | Useful for | | | Time on Station (days) | Alert Capability[a] |
|---|---|---|---|---|---|---|---|---|
| | Improved Enemy ICBM's | AICBM Defense | Air Defense | Hitting Known Hard Targets | Penetrating for Recce-Strike | "Show of Force" | | |
| A | No | No | Yes | No[b] | No | No | Unlimited | No |
| B | No | Somewhat | Yes | Possibly | No | No | Unlimited | No |
| C | Yes | Yes | Somewhat | Yes | No | Yes | 2–3[c] | Yes |
| D | Yes | No | Yes | No | No | Yes | 2–3[c] | Yes |
| E | Yes | Yes | Yes[d] | Yes | Yes | Yes | 2–3[c] | Yes |
| F | Yes | Yes | Somewhat | Yes | No | Yes | 2–3[c] | Yes |
| G | Yes | No | Yes[d] | No | No | No | 90 | Yes |
| H | Yes | Yes | Yes[d] | Yes | No | No | 90 | Yes |
| I | No | Yes | Yes | Yes | No | No | Unlimited | No |

[a] Number of missiles on station can be increased in times of tension.
[b] Poor CEP and low yield.
[c] Assuming no refueling on station.
[d] With existing enemy defenses.

**A Subsystem Example**

Subsystem considerations are often of paramount importance in decision problems, particularly when uncertainties are present. In our present example, assume that one of the alternatives under consideration is a long-endurance aircraft (LEA) system utilizing a chemically fueled low-altitude penetrating missile (LAPM) launched from the LEA airborne platform located in a standoff position outside enemy territory. Assume further that we are somewhat uncertain about the gross weight vs. low-altitude range relationship for this new LAPM, which is not yet developed and which, if developed, would not be operational until some six or more years from now. Upon examining the system characteristics of the LAPM, suppose that the analyst finds that its gross weight is very sensitive to low-altitude range, and that this relationship can be graphed for two cases: an "optimistic" and a "conservative" relation between weight and range. (See Fig. 9.2.) We note that a rather severe weight penalty is incurred in moving from a range permitting coverage of 70 percent of the enemy target system ($R_0$) to one permitting a 95 percent coverage ($R_1$).

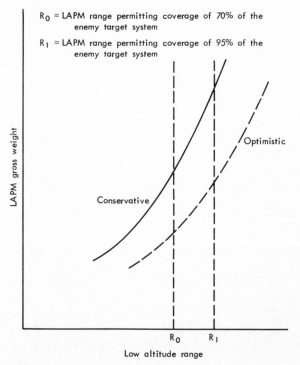

Fig. 9.2 – LAPM gross weight versus low-altitude range

It may be instructive to explore the consequences of the relationships portrayed in Fig. 9.2. For example, let us consider a sensitivity analysis of total system cost as a function of the key variables in Fig. 9.2 and two additional variables: force size (defined as the total number of missiles in the system which are continuously airborne on station) and the average fly-out distance from base to station.[11] The results may look something like those given in Fig. 9.3.

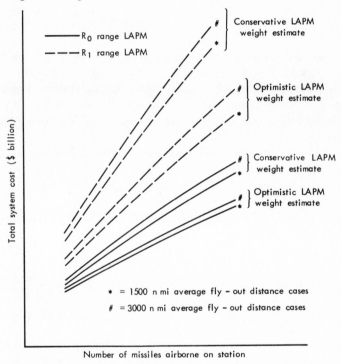

Fig. 9.3 – Total system cost versus force size for various cases

From the figure it is clear we have examples of both sensitivity and relative *in*sensitivity. Total system cost is *very* sensitive to LAPM range (and hence gross weight), and it is fairly sensitive to whether the optimistic or conservative estimate of the weight vs. range curve is used. Moreover, these sensitivities seem to increase as total force size increases. On the

___

[11] The importance of average fly-out distance from base to station (U.S. bases are assumed) depends upon the strategic scenario being considered. If a quick response to an initial enemy first strike is desired, a long fly-out distance would be required. If not, a short fly-out distance might suffice.

other hand, total system cost is relatively insensitive to average fly-out distance from base to station.[12]

The marked sensitivity to low-altitude range (and hence missile gross weight) is not surprising. As missile weight increases, the number of missiles that can be carried by each LEA decreases. This means that to obtain a given total force of missiles continuously airborne on station, a larger number of LEAs must be procured. The total system cost spirals upward not only because of increased aircraft and missile procurement, but also because of increased number of personnel, facilities, supplies, and so on.

Here we have an example of how a relatively simple analysis of subsystem characteristics can illuminate key influences on the total system. In this case it might suggest certain research and development programs on components of the system – such as the propulsion system – that would result in a more favorable relationship between LAPM gross weight and low-altitude range.

Research and development in component areas may be significant. Where major uncertainties (or other reasons) make difficult compelling arguments for immediate initiation of development for the *total* system, the analysis may suggest relatively inexpensive *component* development programs which will in effect provide hedges against some of the major uncertainties in the problem.

**Summary Comment**

The LEA example illustrates a number of the main points made in previous chapters: for example, how system cost as a function of force size relationships can be used in analyses involving intersystem comparisons among alternatives for a given level of budget.

However, one of the main reasons for presenting this example is to illustrate more concretely the analysis of *subsystem* problems in the context of a complex total system proposed for the distant future. In so doing, we again illustrate many of the key points made in earlier chapters; for example:

1. *Important cost considerations are not always measured in dollars.* In Fig. 9.2 the cost of an increment in LAPM low-altitude range is the penalty incurred in terms of LAPM gross weight. This cost

---

[12] This is not always the case. Here we are assuming a relatively efficient LEA platform from the standpoint of endurance. For less efficient LEAs, total system cost may be more sensitive to average fly-out distance.

tends to increase at an increasing rate – that is, marginal costs (in terms of gross weight) with respect to LAPM range are increasing. The impact of these increasing marginal costs on the total LEA system is very significant. (See Fig. 9.3.)

2. *Use of sensitivity analysis.* From Fig. 9.3 we see that for a specified task requiring a certain number of missiles airborne on station and a certain LAPM range, the determination of the least-cost LEA system configuration is not very sensitive to fly-out distance, but is very sensitive to LAPM gross weight.

3. *Dealing with uncertainty.* The results of the sensitivity analysis have important implications for dealing with uncertainty. If we are indeed very uncertain about what LAPM gross weight is likely to turn out to be, then an additional increment of resources spent for exploratory development on, say, LAPM propulsion technology might have a high payoff in terms of reducing uncertainty.

## CASE 2:

## TRADE-OFFS BETWEEN GROUND AND AIR FORCES IN A NON-NUCLEAR LIMITED WAR[13]

### Introduction
The main purpose of Case 2 is to illustrate certain major conceptual and methodological problems of systems analysis, especially those pertaining to the examination of trade-offs among equal-cost future force mixes.[14] We shall attempt to do this by: (1) defining an approach to making a trade-off analysis, and (2) illustrating the application of the approach in the context of mixes of tactical air and land combat forces in a tactical non-nuclear conflict situation. Our interest is solely in how one force mix might be compared with another, and not in whether any of the mixes we will consider will actually exist at the time our hypothetical conflict takes place.

### Establishing a Point of View
The analyst's first obligation, if not his first task, is to recognize that several approaches to a trade-off analysis may be possible, each of which can be

---

[13] This example was prepared by L. H. Wegner and M. G. Weiner as Chapter 21 in E. S. Quade and W. I. Boucher (eds.), *Systems Analysis and Policy Planning: Applications in Defense* (New York: American Elsevier, 1968), pp. 388–417.

[14] Recall that we discussed this problem briefly in Chapter 4.

supported rationally. He knows, of course, that none of them can be free of uncertainties or the difficulties they imply. There are, for example, the uncertainties introduced by the sheer diversity and complexity of tactical operations, which encompass political, technological, and economic as well as military considerations. Moreover, the variety of possible conflict situations that may develop; questions about the size, disposition, and effectiveness of enemy forces; questions about the size and nature of the forces of our allies; the very fact that neither national policies nor the capabilities of military forces remain static in or out of battle – all of these and other factors combine to the analyst's disadvantage.

In view of these considerations, the analyst has to make decisions on the scope of the analysis. To compare the military effectiveness of different mixes of air and land combat forces in a hypothetical campaign some years hence, we need to decide, first, on a level of analysis. Should we limit our attention to, say, the ability of these mixes to attack specific targets? Should we take a more comprehensive point of view? What criteria apply on each level? What measures of effectiveness? Second, having decided on a level of analysis, we have to specify the force mixes to be compared. What forces will be available and should be considered? How can we estimate the cost of these forces? Third, we should specify the nature of the threat. What contingency might call these forces into play? Is there a range of possible threats? Fourth, we want to define the model we intend to use to study the possible forces and threats on the various levels. What are its restrictions? What are its capabilities?

Now, the basic purpose in comparing the combat capabilities of combat forces is to determine the effectiveness of different combinations, or mixes, of forces in implementing national policy. But the extent to which forces can be mixed is limited by the necessity for balanced forces, capable of appropriate responses not in one crisis, but across a spectrum of different military situations. A complete substitution of the forces of one service for those of another is unreasonable. It would contradict the history of warfare, which demonstrates an increasing interdependence among the services; and it would overturn the present posture, organization, and employment of general purpose forces, which for many situations are crucial. Thus, between the present force posture on the one hand and the requirements for balanced forces on the other lies the area in which trade-offs may be considered. And within this very broad area, trade-offs can indeed be considered on a number of different levels. Let us examine three of them, and something of the basic methods of analysis that might be used on each.

## Levels of Analysis and Criteria
### Level 1. Trade-offs Between Different Forces to Accomplish the Same Specific Task

Analysis on this level – the "task" level – would aim at assessing the effectiveness of various combinations of air-delivered and ground-delivered weapons in achieving a variety of particular missions, as, for example, destroying an enemy artillery emplacement or denying the enemy a hill position. At its simplest, the analysis might proceed by first defining a series of such tasks, from which a list of targets involved in accomplishing the task could be identified. A matrix could then be drawn, as in Fig. 9.4,

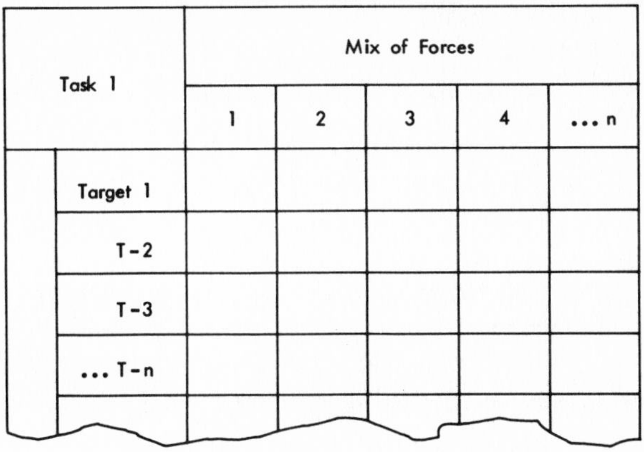

| Task 1 | Mix of Forces | | | | |
|---|---|---|---|---|---|
| | 1 | 2 | 3 | 4 | ... n |
| Target 1 | | | | | |
| T-2 | | | | | |
| T-3 | | | | | |
| ... T-n | | | | | |
| | | | | | |

Fig. 9.4 – Basic weapon-target matrix

which would relate mixes of weapons to targets, according to a measure like the number of rounds or bombs required to achieve a specified level of damage. Data on the cost of producing this damage could then be developed. In turn, the results appearing in the matrix and the cost data could be used to provide either an "equal-effectiveness, different-cost" comparison or a "different-effectiveness, equal-cost" comparison, against which the various mixes could be weighed.

One way in which we might make the analysis more valid would be by introducing a "distance measure." A list of targets likely to be found at various distances from the forward edge of the battle area (hereafter,

FEBA) could be constructed. The addition of distance would introduce different types of fire missions, such as close fire support for targets near the FEBA, close support for those farther away, interdiction for those still farther away, and so on, as indicated by the matrix of Fig. 9.5. The same

| Mission          Target | Mix of Forces | | | |
|---|---|---|---|---|
| | 1 | 2 | 3 | ... n |
| Close fire support (0-3 km) | | | | |
| Target 1 | | | | |
| T-2 | | | | |
| T-3 | | | | |
| Close support (3-12 km) | | | | |
| T-1 | | | | |
| T-2 | | | | |
| T-3 | | | | |
| Interdiction (12-75 km) | | | | |
| T-1 | | | | |
| T-2 | | | | |
| T-3 | | | | |
| Deep interdiction (over 75 km) | | | | |
| T-1 | | | | |
| T-2 | | | | |
| T-3 | | | | |

Fig. 9.5 – Weapon-target matrix with a distance measure added

procedure as in the simpler analysis could be carried out, and the relative cost and effectiveness of different mixes of air- and ground-delivered weapons could be established. But the addition of a distance measure would provide several new insights. Of these, the most useful would be the suggestion of a scale that would indicate at one end the unique capabilities of ground-delivered weapons; at the other end, those of air-delivered weapons; and, between these points, various mixes of the two. For example, safety considerations for ground forces could define the minimum distance from the FEBA at which air-delivered weapons are acceptable. Similarly, artillery ranges could define the maximum distance from the FEBA at which artillery can be used. Between the two extremes, cost and other considerations might be used to define the more efficient forms of delivering ordnance.[15]

Analysis at the task level can be carried at least one additional step by adding a time dimension. A series of target lists could be drawn up, with each list representing a target structure at a different point in time. Thus, a hypothetical development of the conflict could be depicted by a changing target structure. In this approach, the changing target structure could be derived from previously played war games or exercises.

In sum, methods *can* be created for analyzing possible trade-offs between mixes of tactical air and land combat forces in terms of their relative capabilities to accomplish specific tasks. But an anlysis on this level would have several serious drawbacks. For one thing, the utility of defining "specific" tasks and analyzing the relative effectiveness of different mixes would be limited, unless such "situational" factors as terrain, tactics, or intelligence were introduced. But even if they were included, task analysis would still be limited because the effect of accomplishing these tasks on the total conflict situation would still have been left out of account. Thus, by themselves, the capabilities of force mixes for achieving specific missions could not be used in assessing the total utility of the forces.

Moreover, it is probably not reasonable to construct a detailed two-sided game situation for use only in a task analysis. Note that an analysis on this level involves essentially only one of the criteria of trade-offs, the potential of different force mixes to destroy enemy targets. But to apply even this one criterion would involve great effort, since an adequate evaluation of the effectiveness of different types of weapons against different targets can be made only when many characteristics of the weapons and targets are incorporated in the analysis. Since this information would also be a significant part of more comprehensive analyses, the construction and play of a game on the task level might better be deferred in their favor.

---

[15] Obviously, not too much should be made of this scale, since it would underrate the flexibilities that have been built into military forces. Land combat forces might, in theory and in practice, attack enemy airfields beyond artillery range by the use of air-delivered assault units. Air forces might stop the movement of enemy ground forces by interdiction of the supplies, reserves, and lines of communication of the enemy.

**Level 2. Trade-offs between Different Forces in the Same Situation**

The step from Level 1 to Level 2 – the "situational" level – brings into the analysis the setting or context in which the military operations are conducted. This incorporates the objective of the military operation, the purpose for which the forces have been committed to combat, and some consideration of specific policy, economic, and strategic goals, as well as a range of purely military goals. On the task level, the connection between national policy and the destruction of an enemy tank may safely be left out of account. On the situational level, where we combine many such tasks and examine their influence on the course of the conflict, this relationship is more important.

Consequently, the analysis of trade-offs on the situational level requires an approach different from that used on the task level. For one thing, it necessitates the use of definite (albeit hypothetical), conflict situations with specific military objectives, since military situations are never independent of military objectives. Thus, a scenario for a specific military situation and its accompanying objective has to be defined. The situation will usually incorporate joint and combined operations of different services, and therefore provide a framework within which the critical interdependence or balance of military forces can be analyzed in some depth. Moreover, the use of specific situations requires the inclusion of a host of interacting factors necessary to trade-off choices – geography, time, enemy actions, attrition, logistics support, and so on. Including such factors will make the analysis more comprehensive. On the other hand, it will also tend to decrease the amount of certainty that can be attached to the conclusions.

There is another difference. On the task level, it is possible to be somewhat confident that the results, although limited, will have a reasonable validity for a usefully long time. After all, such specific military tasks as attacking artillery positions will be part of most foreseeable military operations. On the situational level, the ability to define a military situation that may arise in the future, and the manner in which we will respond to it, involves a good deal of judgment. How might the situation develop? What combat forces would be employed? How would they be employed? How would policy considerations, nuclear options, and other factors influence the conflict? As we have seen, these are just a few of the questions that can appear on this level of analysis. Clearly, therefore, such analyses are infeasible within any reasonable limits of time and effort unless judgment is used to restrict the possibilities that might characterize the situation. In short, the analyst's critical conceptual problem in conducting trade-off analyses on this level is to define an appropriate situation and to identify and define within the situation those factors that contribute to a useful comparison of force mixes.

Figure 9.6 presents a list of basic criteria that could be used at the

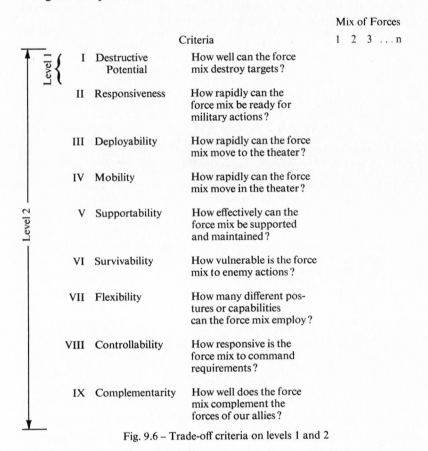

Fig. 9.6 – Trade-off criteria on levels 1 and 2

situational level of trade-off analysis. All of them appear to be directly relevant to the comparison of different mixes of tactical air and land combat forces. We have already discussed how data might be developed so that the first criterion, destructive potential, would be appropriate to the analysis. Let us consider briefly what might be done to provide measures of effectiveness for each of the others.

*II. Responsiveness.* To estimate how rapidly the force mix can be ready for military action, the analyst needs to determine the status of air and ground forces on both sides at some time before the hypothetical conflict is assumed to occur. With that information, he could then develop the requirements – in time, dollars, manpower, equipment, and so on – necessary to bring the various force mixes fully into action. These requirements would thus indicate the "cost" of achieving a specified level of readiness and provide one possible measure of responsiveness.

*III. Deployability.* The simplest measure for this criterion is the time required to move the ready forces of each of the force mixes from their ZI (zone of the interior) and overseas positions to the theater of operations. Estimates could be made for different conditions of available airlift, base posture, sealift, prepositioning, and so on.

*IV. Mobility.* The analyst can represent movement in the theater in at least two ways: movement from the peacetime posture to a military posture appropriate to the conflict situation, and movement of forces during combat operations. The latter can be viewed in terms of the time required to bring destructive potential to bear on the enemy at various times during the course of the conflict. Differences between mixes of tactical air and land combat forces in destructive potential and the rapidity with which it can be brought to bear should be balanced against the ability to maintain this destructive potential over time. Thus, in its usual meaning, "mobility" could include both movement and nonmovement or "stayability" – that is, the ability to maintain destructive potential over time.

*V. Supportability.* The criterion of supportability involves several considerations. These include the ability to *support* the forces in the theater from the ZI or stocks, and the ability to *maintain* the forces within the theater. The former involves the amounts of material, personnel, and carriers needed to conduct combat operations, as well as the time required to provide them. The latter involves the ability to maintain and service the forces in the theater and requires the analyst to estimate the numbers and types of personnel, skills, equipment, and other requirements necessary to repair and service aircraft, to replace land combat personnel and equipment losses, and so on.

*VI. Survivability.* The capabilities to support the forces and to maintain their mobility are dependent on the losses and damage which the forces suffer. Thus, the survivability of the force mixes is an important test of their combat capability. Survivability can be represented in terms of attrition – that is, direct combat losses in such categories as personnel, aircraft, and equipment. It should also include losses of support equipment and limitations in movement due to enemy actions against depots, lines of communication, and support vehicles.

*VII. Flexibility.* The conflict situation should provide an opportunity to examine the ability of different force mixes to modify their combat capabilities as the situation demands. Can the air component operate from different basing postures? Can the ground component operate with different lines of communication? Can the forces develop different combat organizations or procedures to meet specific circumstances? These and other characteristics of force flexibility – such as the ability to move to nuclear operations in both offense and defense – are among the more difficult standards to measure, since they are highly dependent on the particular conflict situation. Nevertheless, in the comparison of different air-ground mixes they can play an important role.

*VIII. Controllability.* Related to the flexibility of the force mixes is their controllability. This can be represented by the timeliness with which the force mix can respond to such command requirements as to change the type or location of the combat operation or to make the transition to nuclear weapons. Controllability can be distinguished arbitrarily from flexibility in terms of the time required to respond to command requirements.

*IX. Complementarity.* In any conflict situation, the size and nature of a nation's commitment will be determined in part by the capabilities that its allies possess to meet aggression. Since these commitments are intended to supplement each other, complementarity can be represented in the analysis of different force mixes by the extent to which the different mixes possess the types of forces that round out those of the allies.

From this very rough description of criteria, it should be apparent that the model used to examine force trade-offs would be most useful if it represented combat operations that change with time; geography, bases, and supply routes; attrition to air and ground forces; logistics and supply of the combat forces; weather conditions; force deployments; the size, composition, and employment of allied forces; command and control; different contingencies, both military and political, that might characterize the conflict situation; and, of course, the alternative force mixes themselves. It is particularly important that the model provide the opportunity to examine variations in contingencies within the same military situation – this can be accomplished with different scenarios – and variations in the manner in which the forces are employed to achieve the same objective. In this way, no force mix would be penalized by being considered in too narrow a framework. Later we shall describe the model that will be used in our illustration.

To sum up the situational level, we should consider these points. Trade-offs between different force mixes can be examined at this level, and will include criteria that cannot be included at the task level. Such analyses will involve greater complexity, judgment, and uncertainty, but will also permit broader comparisons of the effectiveness of different force mixes. The addition of different contingencies within the situation and different force employment policies appropriate to the specific force mixes will provide a more comprehensive basis for choosing between the alternative mixes. The results of a situational analysis, however, can be considered appropriate only to the situation analyzed. If there are major differences in the capabilities of the tactical air and land combat forces between the mixes, the comparisons should be extended to other situations. The approach of Level 3 includes this aspect of trade-off analyses.

### Level 3. Trade-offs between Different Forces to Implement National Policy

National policy is a dynamic process that must consider a variety of actual and possible military situations and contingencies. The tactical force posture, therefore, cannot be exclusively determined by the ability to respond to any one threat, even if one predominates. To repeat something said earlier: The requirement that tactical military forces be capable of employment in a variety of different military situations necessitates that the different mixes of tactical air and land combat forces be compared *in* those situations. But on Level 3 – the "policy" level of trade-off analyses – judgment becomes central. What situations, with what priorities, and what weighting of importance should be examined?

Although the main emphasis in attaining and maintaining a military

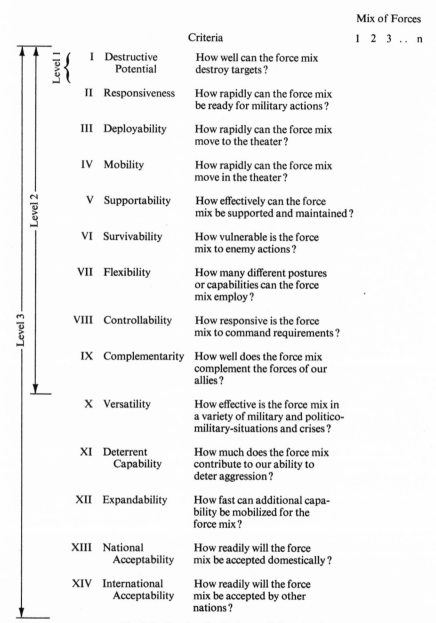

|  | Criteria |  | Mix of Forces |
|---|---|---|---|
|  |  |  | 1  2  3 .. n |

Level 1 {
I  Destructive Potential — How well can the force mix destroy targets?

II  Responsiveness — How rapidly can the force mix be ready for military actions?

III  Deployability — How rapidly can the force mix move to the theater?

IV  Mobility — How rapidly can the force mix move in the theater?

V  Supportability — How effectively can the force mix be supported and maintained?

VI  Survivability — How vulnerable is the force mix to enemy actions?

VII  Flexibility — How many different postures or capabilities can the force mix employ?

VIII  Controllability — How responsive is the force mix to command requirements?

IX  Complementarity — How well does the force mix complement the forces of our allies?

X  Versatility — How effective is the force mix in a variety of military and politico-military-situations and crises?

XI  Deterrent Capability — How much does the force mix contribute to our ability to deter aggression?

XII  Expandability — How fast can additional capability be mobilized for the force mix?

XIII  National Acceptability — How readily will the force mix be accepted domestically?

XIV  International Acceptability — How readily will the force mix be accepted by other nations?

Fig. 9.7 – Trade-off criteria on all three levels

posture rests on selecting the best posture commensurate with military requirements to respond effectively to a spectrum of military conflicts, related considerations of national policy also influence the choice among alternative force mixes. These considerations include a host of domestic and international issues, such as the relation of the tactical forces to the strategic forces, the mobilization capacity required to augment the combat forces, the impact of the forces on the gold flow, and the national and international political responses the military forces might inspire. These issues are frequently difficult to define precisely, and, in many cases, impossible to measure numerically. Nonetheless, their role may be crucial in force-posture choices.

Figure 9.7 extends the list of criteria presented earlier by adding some that are pertinent to the evaluation of force mixes on the policy level. Of these criteria, some are directly related to the multisituational capability necessary for military purposes and some to the broader issues of national policy. Let us look at each.

*X. Versatility.* In part, the policy level can be considered as defining a series of varied situations in different areas of the world with concomitant differences in geography, weather, force size, logistics capabilities, and so on. Versatility – that is, the range of different military or politico-military situations in which the force mixes can be used efficiently – thus becomes the major criterion of trade-off analysis on this level. For the analyst, this multisituational criterion would involve comparing the "utility" of the force mixes in one situation with their utility in others. The measure or measures of utility would include all of the measures used at the situational level. In contrast to the following four criteria, versatility is thus likely to lend itself to quantitative estimates.[16]

*XI. Deterrent Capability.* To estimate the extent to which each force mix contributes to the deterrence of aggressive action by the enemy at different levels is a complex problem. It involves many aspects, such as enemy "risk calculations," and the magnitude and timeliness of response. As such, deterrent capability is one of the criteria which depends heavily on intelligence information, political appraisals, and other considerations with large components of judgment.

*XII. Expandability.* In attempting to determine the extent to which each force mix permits additional mobilization of forces that contribute to its effectiveness – and this is what we mean by "expandability" – the analyst's task is to test such maxims as this: Force mixes involving skills that require an elaborate training base cannot be expanded as rapidly as those with less stringent requirements. He can, for example, assess the cost of having standby production capability available in each force mix.

*XIII. National Acceptability.* This criterion expresses the extent to which there are differences between the mixes in relation to the totality of considerations of the nation's policy, economics, technology, production, manpower, and so on. Among the questions the analyst would want to investigate are the impact of each mix on

---

[16] Of course, even on the situational level, not every factor can be quantified. Some, like leadership or morale, cannot be measured objectively, although in many cases rankings or orderings can be made. In any case, however, a limited or nonquantitative estimate seems preferable to excluding the criteria completely.

the gold flow problem, on the existing crises, and on national attitudes toward military expenditures.

*XIV. International Acceptability.* Here the analyst is concerned to estimate the differences, if any, between the mixes insofar as the various attitudes and postures of the nation's allies, potential enemies, and nonaligned nations are concerned. Although these considerations are certainly not ultimate determinants of military posture, they contribute to its form and nature. The contribution may be direct (for example, through control of the availability of bases or lines of communication) or indirect (for example, through policy reactions).

How significant these policy-level criteria are and the extent to which they should be included in any trade-off analysis are open questions. Without doubt, methods for using them are limited, uncertainty is great, and judgment is crucial. But it is important that the issues they raise be recognized in the creation of any major trade-off analysis. Whether or not they should or can be incorporated in the analysis itself depends, in part, on how comprehensive an anlysis is undertaken. In the illustration to follow, we have purposely restricted our analysis to the situational level in order to avoid some of these difficulties.

## An Illustration

So far, we have said nothing about cost calculations, the model, or the range of contingencies. These matters we will take up in the context of the illustration, highlighting some of the practical problems involved. Since the primary purpose of this example is to indicate that analytic tools for comparing different force mixes can, in fact, be developed, it should be perfectly clear from the start that what follows is intended solely *as* an example. For this reason, what it does or does not accomplish is much less significant than how it goes about accomplishing it. The model, the force mixes, and the results could be different in point of fact (and indeed would be, if the example were not hypothetical), but the methodology would remain basically the same.

### The Force Mixes and Their Cost

Three force mixes will be considered. Mix I is a hypothetical force presumed to exist at the time; it consists of 24 wings of tactical air forces and 16 divisions of ground forces. Using the cost of this mix as a base, we can define two other *equal-cost* alternatives:

- Mix II, which is Mix I less 2 divisions and plus 8 wings of relatively low performance, inexpensive aircraft. (The cost of adding the 8 wings is used to determine the number of divisions to be subtracted.)
- Mix III, which is Mix I plus 4 divisions and less 4 wings of jet aircraft. (These 4 wings are taken arbitrarily as the number to be

subtracted; the money thus freed is used to purchase the additional divisions.)

Because our interest is in outlining a method of analysis, the actual cost calculations required in order to derive these mixes need not be entered into here.[17] But it might be useful to say something about their complexity. Since the basic problem is to estimate the resource changes due to aircraft additions and deletions, translate these changes into costs, and then translate these costs into ground divisions, the first step is to estimate the cost of the first 8 wings of aircraft (Mix II) and the last 4 wings of jet aircraft (Mix III). For the added aircraft, we would want to discover the costs of their RDT & E, initial investment, and annual operation (for either 5 or 10 years). For the 4 wings that are subtracted, only the costs of initial investment (where appropriate) and annual operation need be considered.

Cost-sensitivity analysis is useful at several points in these calculations of aircraft costs, but if we limit our attention to just one – base operating support (BOS) costs – the difficulties involved may be made clear. Base operating costs are of two types: constant costs, which are associated with the base itself, and variable costs, which depend on the level of base activity. In Mix II, the relatively inexpensive aircraft system costs turned out to be sensitive to the inclusion of the constant value. This meant that the cost analysts had to devote further attention to basing considerations for the incremental 8-wing force. Such an investigation was made and it was found that 5 wings could be feasibly tenanted on existing bases, while the remainder would have to be placed on new bases. Therefore, variable BOS costs for 8 wings and constant BOS costs for 3 wings were included in the operating cost estimates for the proposed incremental 8-wing force. Similar considerations were involved in Mix III in estimating the cost decrement associated with the postulated elimination of 4 wings from projected base case tactical aircraft force.

Estimating Army division costs is at least as complicated. The major problem is simply to achieve a consistent cost analysis for the air systems and the divisions, and to include only direct costs and those indirect costs that change measurably with variations in force size. To achieve this consistency in deriving the size of the divisions to be added or subtracted in the present example, it becomes necessary to adjust certain cost categories and add new ones. This done, the next problem is to recompute the investment and operating costs for individual divisions under a variety of costing assumptions, so as to develop the costs of complete divisions of the proper size, type, and number. With this information, we are then in a position to see what forces we can buy in Mixes II and III.

Again, cost-sensitivity analysis is indispensable, even if, as in the tests made for this example, the division costs turn out to be insensitive to the variables examined. For example, one variable is initial training of the division personnel. If we compute this cost at both 100 percent and 50 percent of the cost of *full* training, in order to determine how sensitive the system costs are to the inheritance value of trained personnel, we find that variations in initial training costs are not significant. The explanation is that, while training represents a moderate portion of investment costs, its impact as far as total costs are concerned is diminished because the operating costs are much larger. This is true whether 5 or 10 years of annual operation are assumed. The point to bear in mind, however, is that it is as necessary to discover such insensitivities as it is the sensitivities.

### The Threat

Having specified the force mixes we intend to compare, a next step is to define the situations they are assumed to face. In this example, we will analyze four hypothetical cases – by no means an exhaustive list of possibilities. These four have been chosen solely because they provide some variations for evaluating our three force mixes.

*Case 1: An Intermediate Red Attack.* Here we assume a situation of high tension. The Red forces begin movements to their attack positions on D-3. Blue forces, alerted by the Red movements, adopt their forward defense positions. Forces in the ZI are alerted, and preparations for their deployment to the theater are begun. The Red plan is to attack with a small number of assault divisions and a large part of its air strength, and to commit additional divisions and aircraft if necessary. Blue forces in position at the time of attack consist of fewer divisions and aircraft than Red has available, and the total of Blue divisions and aircraft that could be committed within the first 90 days are assumed to be lower than the total Red forces committed.

*Case 2: A Limited Red Attack.* This Case also assumes a situation of tension. As in Case 1, the Red forces begin moving to their attack positions on D-3. Again, Blue forces are alerted and adopt their forward defense positions. Forces in the ZI are alerted, and preparations for deploying them to the combat theater are begun. The initial Red attack force is the same as in Case 1. Red, however, plans a more limited reinforcement: He commits fewer total divisions to the operation, and plans to introduce them at a slower rate. Blue's response is the same as Case 1. For Red and Blue, the air commitments are the same as in Case 1.

*Case 3: A Major Red Attack.* Case 3 is identical to Case 1, except that we assume an initial Red commitment of 60 divisions, which is greater than the initial commitment in Case 1. The total Red commitment and the augmentation rate is the same as in Case 1. The Blue ground commitment and the Blue and Red air commitments are the same for this Case as they were in Case 1.

*Case 4: An Intermediate Red Attack with Preemptive Air Strike.* Case 4 and Case 1 are identical in forces committed. In this Case, however, Red initiates operations by an air strike against Blue's airfields, defenses, and aircraft prior to beginning ground operations. Red ground forces start their attack with limited close air support for the first few days.

To simplify the force-mix comparisons, we can narrow the list of important influences that we might otherwise want to consider by introducing, for each of these four cases, the following additional assumptions: (1) The major Red attack occurs on one front; (2) neither side is engaged in any major conflicts elsewhere in the world at the time; and (3) strategic balance exists between the sides. The immediate effect of these assumptions (and others made earlier, such as that all the conflicts would be non-nuclear) is to clear away some problems relevant primarily on the policy level. Their deeper effect, of course, is to limit the usefulness of the analytic results, since we are now ignoring some questions a decisionmaker in the real world might well want to have answered.

### The Model

The model (TAGS-II) we shall use for the force-mix evaluation is a substantially modified version of the Theater Air-Ground Study (TAGS) computer model developed by The Rand Corporation in the early fifties for studies of tactical forces.[18] As modified, it is a two-sided campaign model that incorporates the following major conflict elements for both Red and Blue:

- Initial aircraft inventories in the theater for each of three types: a high-payload, high-performance type; a medium-payload type; and a low-payload type

---

[18] See C. P. Siska, L. A. Giamboni, and J. R. Lind, *Analytic Formulation of a Theater Air-Ground Warfare System* (1953 Techniques), RM-1338-PR (DDC No. AD 86022) (Santa Monica, Calif.: The Rand Corporation, September 1954); and J. R. Brom, *Narrative Description of an Analytic Theater Air-Ground Warfare System*, RM-1428-PR (DDC No. AD 86709) (Santa Monica, Calif.: The Rand Corporation, February 1955).

- Initial land combat forces in the theater
- Air augmentation forces
- Ground augmentation forces
- Airfields (subject to attack)
- Airfields (not subject to attack, that is, in sanctuary)
- Aircraft shelters
- Air missions

    1. Counter-airfield
    2. Interdiction
    3. Close support
    4. Air defense
    5. Counter-air defense (radars, control centers, etc.)
    6. Counter-SAM (surface-to-air missiles)

- Allocation policy at different times during conflict for above missions
- Ground missions

    1. Offensive
    2. Defensive
    3. Holding

- Theater stock levels
- Consumption rates for air units in combat
- Consumption rates for ground units in combat
- Line of communication (LOC) capacities
- Capacities required for moving ground units
- SAM inventories
- SAM augmentation
- Antiaircraft artillery
- Terrain

The model, which is shown schematically in Fig. 9.8, involves 300 parameters. Of these, approximately 200 are used for intermediate calculations. Of the remainder, 11 describe characteristics of the initial forces; 22 describe augmentation, repair, and supply; 25 describe force employment; 17 describe offensive operations; 21 describe defensive operations; and 6 describe other ground operations. Values for all the parameters can be fixed for each computer run, can be preset to change on any War Day during the run, or can be set to change when the value of any other parameter reaches a particular point. These are important features, since they allow us to alter such things as air and ground augmentation rates to meet changed conditions.

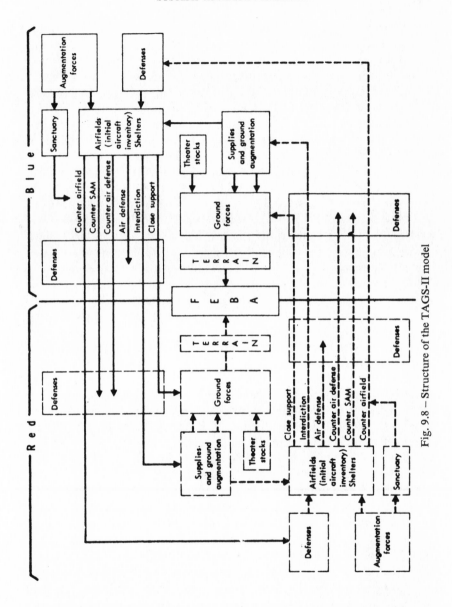

Fig. 9.8 – Structure of the TAGS-II model

To evaluate the performance of our three force mixes, the model incorporates specific measures for each of the nine criteria relevant on the situational level of analysis.[19] The first, *destructive potential*, is represented in various ways. In the counter-airfield mission, offensive strikes are made against aircraft parked on airfields or in shelters. Airfield defenses are attacked by defense suppression aircraft immediately before the primary strike aircraft arrive.[20] In the interdiction mission, which is carried out solely within the theater, aircraft disrupt the flow of men and material by cutting rail lines and destroying bridges on the main transportation routes. In the close air support mission, casualties are produced among ground combat personnel, and the movement of troops is restricted. In the counter-SAM mission, area-deployed SAMs are destroyed in a rollback operation that clears corridors for subsequent deep penetration by aircraft on other missions. In the counter-air defense mission, targets such as air defense radars, command centers, and high-altitude SAMs are destroyed, thus forcing the air defense aircraft into a combat patrol mode of operation. From the ground, aircraft are destroyed by means of antiaircraft fire and SAMs. The ground combat is modeled quite simply, in the sense that casualties are calculated on the basis of planning factors derived from statistical records of World War II and the Korean war. A measure is also obtained of the rate and degree to which the actual commitment of ground divisions approaches the planned commitment.

*Responsiveness* and *deployability* are included in the model by assumption. That is, the ready state of the tactical air and land combat forces in each of our three mixes, and their deployability, are introduced in terms of the time required for the forces to reach the combat theater. Input values for these characteristics are derived for this example on the assumption that each side has a ZI that is outside the tactical theater environs and thus invulnerable to enemy tactical aircraft.

*Mobility* is represented in the model in a limited manner. Maximum rates of movement based on terrain and other factors are included and are modified in light of the combat situation.[21] Similarly, aircraft sorties for different types of aircraft and missions – close support, interdiction, air defense, counter-SAM, and so on – are also included. But differences in

---

[19] See p. 261.

[20] Although aircraft losses through counter-airfield attacks are tallied, the effects of damaged airfield facilities on subsequent operations are not represented.

[21] The FEBA is assumed to move as a unit. The velocity and direction of this movement are calculated as the average movement of the entire theater front, which, in turn, depends upon the ground strengths of each side and the number of aircraft sorties that strike close support targets.

mobility between types of land combat divisions, alternative basing postures for aircraft, or details of the tactical deployments in the combat situation are not included. It should be noted generally that, for use in the model, all the ground forces are considered as homogeneous division slices; that is to say, no distinction is made between armored, mechanized, or infantry divisions.

*Supportability* of both the air and land combat forces is represented in terms of the gross supply requirements for their deployment and combat operations. Such characteristics as the size of theater stocks, the capacity of lines of communication, the daily consumption rate, and the effects of extending lines of communications are included. For the purposes of the example, we assume that aircraft replacements, ground force reinforcements, and supplies are drawn from the ZI. The theater itself contains the ground forces, the supply lines (primarily a rail network), and the tactical airfields.

*Survivability* is represented in several different ways – basically, as the obverse of the results obtained under *destructive potential*. Thus, losses in tactical air and land combat forces from the ground combat situation, from SAMs, from antiaircraft artillery, from air defense interceptor aircraft, and so on are included. The protection afforded by aircraft shelters and "sanctuaries" is taken into account. Losses in supplies and reductions in the capacity of lines of communication because of inter-diction or because of their extension as the FEBA moves are also incorporated.

*Flexibility* and *controllability* of the forces in the different mixes are represented in limited detail. Different allocations of air strikes are pro-vided for, as are changes in these allocations during the course of the conflict. Various basing postures for aircraft, various arrangements of SAM defenses, and various patterns of movement of the land combat forces – including the changes produced by arrivals of land force augmen-tations – are included. But command relationships, differences in flexibility and control, and rules for making a transition to nuclear operations are not included.

**Examples of Output**

Among the outputs of the TAGS-II model are the following:

- Position of the FEBA in miles, plus or minus, from its original position
- Number of Blue and Red divisions in combat
- Number of Blue and Red aircraft, total and by type of aircraft
- Number of SAMs in combat

- Supply capacity available to each side
- Number of divisions lost
- Number of aircraft lost
- Number of SAMs lost
- Number of close support sorties
- Number of interdiction sorties
- Number of counter-airfield sorties
- Number of air defense sorties
- Number of counter-air defense sorties
- Number of counter-SAM sorties
- Losses due to noncombat factors
- Losses due to enemy AAA
- Losses due to enemy air defense
- Losses due to enemy counter-airfield attacks
- Losses due to enemy airfield defenses and SAMs

The list could be extended without great difficulty. But for present purposes, let us focus attention on the results if we take our four cases and the different force mixes and use the model outputs to make explicit comparisons of only a few relevant indices.

One major indicator of the capability of a force mix in combat is the progress of the ground battle. And one overall measure of the progress of the ground battle is the first item on the preceding list: the movement of the FEBA. Although the TAGS-II model can present this information in various ways, we will use only the following five indices:

Index 1: The day on which Red ground forces penetrate approximately 30 miles from their forward position.
Index 2: The day on which Red ground forces penetrate approximately 100 miles from their forward position.
Index 3: The day on which Red ground forces penetrate approximately 150 miles.
Index 4: The day on which Red ground forces penetrate approximately 300 miles.
Index 5: The day on which Red ground forces penetrate approximately 500 miles from the original position of the FEBA.

Another indicator of the ground battle is the number of divisions lost. Considering only Blue's losses, we can call out an additional three indices:

Index 6: The day on which Blue's total ground losses equal approximately 10 percent of his initial strength.
Index 7: The day on which Blue's total ground losses equal approximately 20 percent of his initial strength.
Index 8: The day on which Blue's total ground losses equal approximately 33 percent of his initial strength.

The results of air-to-air action, antiaircraft artillery, and SAMs can be indicated by a number of values, among them these seven:

Index 9: The first day on which air parity is achieved. "Air parity" is arbitrarily defined here as the point at which Blue aircraft in combat are equal to the Red aircraft in combat.

Index 10: The first day that "local air superiority" is achieved. This is arbitrarily defined as the point at which Blue achieves a 2:1 ratio of aircraft in combat over Red aircraft in combat.

Index 11: The day on which "limited air superiority" is achieved – that is, the day on which the ratio of Blue to Red combat aircraft is 5:1.

Index 12: The day on which "air supremacy" is achieved – that is, the day on which the ratio of Blue to Red combat aircraft is 10:1.

Index 13: The day on which the Blue aircraft inventory is approximately two-thirds of total strength. We can also include here the ratio of Blue aircraft to Red aircraft on that day.

Index 14: The day on which the Blue aircraft inventory is approximately one-half of total strength. We also include the ratio of Blue aircraft to Red aircraft on that day.

Index 15: The day on which the Blue aircraft inventory is approximately one-third of total strength. We also include the ratio of Blue to Red aircraft on that day.

The results for these 15 index values are presented in Table 9.3.[22]


**Discussion of Results**

The figures in Table 9.3 indicate that, between the cases, each force mix varies somewhat in limiting the impact and rate of enemy action. Within the cases there are only small differences in the effectiveness of the three mixes, especially as the ground battle is concerned. On balance, both within and between the cases, it would appear that the "more air, less ground" mix, Mix II, is the most successful mix of the three. Why this is so can be seen, perhaps, by looking at the results in Case 2, the contingency in which Mix II's relative superiority seems most clearly indicated.

Case 2, it will be recalled, involved a limited Red attack. It assumed a relatively small initial Red land force and a slow rate of augmentation. In other particulars, including the size of Blue's ground and air forces, the opposing sides were identical to those assumed in Case 1.

---

[22] Since Table 9.3 presents the first comparison of the relative combat capabilities of the three force mixes, it may be appropriate at this point to reemphasize that these results are intended to demonstrate not the value of any one mix, but rather a *way of comparing* the mixes. To avoid any misinterpretation, we have presented no actual values in the table, but have instead indicated only the magnitude and directions of change from the Case 1, Mix I situation. (That is, the capital letters in the Case 1, Mix I column should be taken to represent a particular numerical result; the numbers shown in the other columns are to be read as the difference, plus or minus, from the appropriate base value.)

TABLE 9.3

Force Mix Comparisons Against 15 Index Values (Days)

| INDEX NO. | DESCRIPTION OF INDEX | CASE 1 (Intermediate Red Attack) | | | CASE 2 (Limited Red Attack) | | | CASE 3 (Major Red Attack) | | | CASE 4 (Intermediate Red Attack, with Preemptive Air Strike) | | |
|---|---|---|---|---|---|---|---|---|---|---|---|---|---|
| | | Mix I | Mix II | Mix III | Mix I | Mix II | Mix III | Mix I | Mix II | Mix III | Mix I | Mix II | Mix III |
| 1 | Red ground forces penetrate 30 miles | | 0 | 0 | +1 | +1 | +1 | −2 | −2 | −2 | 0 | 0 | 0 |
| 2 | Red ground forces penetrate 100 miles | | 0 | 0 | +2 | +3 | +2 | −2 | −2 | −2 | 0 | 0 | 0 |
| 3 | Red ground forces penetrate 150 miles | | 0 | −1 | +6 | +6 | +5 | −2 | −2 | −2 | 0 | 0 | 0 |
| 4 | Red ground forces penetrate 300 miles | | +4 | −1 | +20 | +26 | +21 | −7 | −6 | −6 | −4 | −3 | −1 |
| 5 | Red ground forces penetrate 500 miles | | +5 | +2 | +26 | +27 | +27 | −14 | −12 | −10 | −11 | −8 | −9 |
| 6 | 10% of Blue Divisions lost | | 0 | 0 | 0 | 0 | 0 | 0 | 0 | 0 | +2 | +2 | +2 |
| 7 | 20% of Blue Divisions lost | | 0 | −1 | 0 | 0 | −1 | 0 | 0 | −1 | +2 | +2 | +1 |
| 8 | 33% of Blue Divisions lost | | +1 | −5 | 0 | +1 | −5 | 0 | +1 | −5 | +1 | +2 | −4 |
| 9 | Air Parity (1:1) | | −1 | 0 | 0 | −1 | 0 | 0 | −1 | 0 | +5 | +3 | +18 |
| 10 | Blue Local Air Superiority (2:1) | | −2 | +4 | 0 | −2 | +4 | 0 | −2 | +4 | +6 | +3 | +12 |
| 11 | Blue Limited Air Superiority (5:1) | | −5 | +7 | 0 | −5 | +7 | 0 | −5 | +7 | +13 | +6 | +24 |
| 12 | Blue Air Supremacy (10:1) | | −4 | +9 | 0 | −4 | +9 | 0 | −4 | +15 | +14 | +8 | +25 |
| 13 | Blue acft inventory =2/3 | | +1 | 0 | 0 | +1 | 0 | 0 | +1 | 0 | — | — | — |
| | Force Ratio B:R = | | +0.1 | −0.1 | 0 | +0.1 | −0.1 | 0 | +0.1 | −0.1 | — | — | — |
| 14 | Blue acft inventory=1/2 | | 0 | −1 | 0 | 0 | −1 | 0 | 0 | −1 | −3 | −3 | −4 |
| | Force Ratio B:R = | | +0.3 | −0.2 | 0 | +0.3 | −0.2 | 0 | +0.1 | −0.2 | −0.6 | −0.5 | −0.6 |
| 15 | Blue acft inventory=1/3 | | +6 | −3 | 0 | +6 | −3 | 0 | +6 | −3 | −13 | 0 | −27 |
| | Force Ratio B:R = | | +1.9 | −1.0 | 0 | +1.9 | −1.0 | 0 | +1.9 | −1.0 | −2.3 | −0.6 | −2.8 |

Figure 9.9. illustrates the movement of the FEBA in Case 2. Each mix

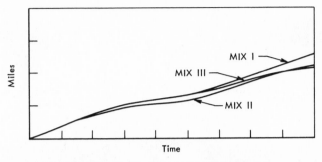

Fig. 9.9 – Case 2: Movement of the FEBA (west)

of Blue forces is considerably more successful in slowing the Red advance than it is in the other cases, but Mix II is slightly more effective. The explanation seems to lie in its ability to generate a large number of close air support and interdiction sorties once the enemy air threat has been substantially reduced. This is indicated in Fig. 9.10, which presents the

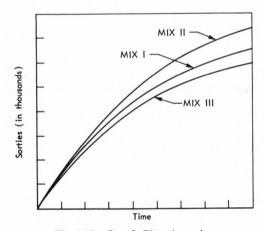

Fig. 9.10 – Case 2: Blue air sorties

cumulative number of sorties flown by each mix. The consequences of this capability are clear: The increased sortie rate not only helps Mix II to lower its own ground losses (Fig. 9.11) and to increase (though very slightly) the rate at which Red aircraft are destroyed in the early phases of the campaign (Fig. 9.12), but it also means that more Red divisions are defeated, or the same number are defeated sooner (Fig. 9.13). Moreover,

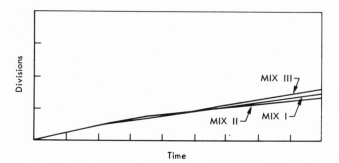

Fig. 9.11 – Case 2: Blue division losses

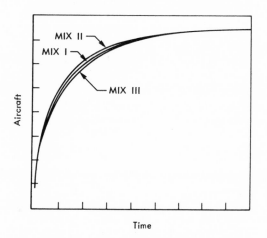

Fig. 9.12 – Case 2: Red aircraft losses

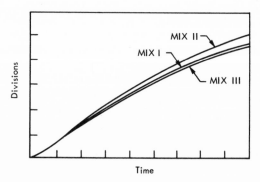

Fig. 9.13 – Case 2: Red division losses

Mix II seems to perform better than its alternatives in slowing the rate of the Red ground commitment (Fig. 9.14) and in permitting the smallest number of Red divisions to survive at the front (Fig. 9.15).

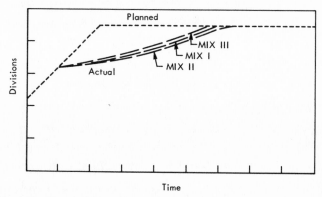

Fig. 9.14 – Case 2: Planned versus actual Red ground force commitments

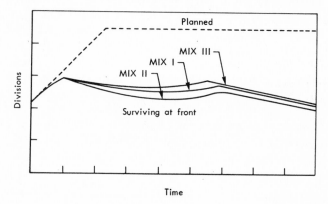

Fig. 9.15 – Case 2: Planned Red ground force commitments, and divisions surviving at the front

On the other hand, the increased sortie rate of Mix II entails a cost to Blue: greater exposure to enemy air, SAMs, and AAA. Thus, as indicated in Fig. 9.16, a greater number of aircraft is lost by Mix II.

From the results of this illustrative "situational" analysis, it is tempting, but inappropriate, to compare the alternative force mixes. We have already considered at length the assumptions that have gone into this example. Simply because we now have a few curves and a table of indices does not

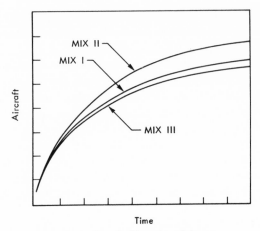

Fig. 9.16 – Case 2: Blue aircraft losses

mean that the assumptions or the uncertainties have magically disappeared. To draw any conclusions, we would need, first, an improved development of the model, the inputs, the costing, the details of the scenarios, the criteria, and the measures of effectiveness. We would need to examine a greater number of situations. We would need a larger variety of sensitivity tests – not merely for reducing the uncertainty in the analysis, but also for identifying the significant parameters and assumptions of the analysis. Without these, the results shown above allow us to say little about the relative capability of our different force mixes.

If, however, we stand back from the details of the example, and reconsider generally the conceptual and methodological problems of producing – through analysis – a basis for comparing alternative force mixes, several broad conclusions present themselves. We might mention five of them.

1. It is unlikely that any single criterion is adequate to compare the relative effectiveness of different force mixes. For the purposes of this discussion, we introduced nine criteria; others could be developed. Moreover, for each of the criteria, no single measure of the relative effectiveness of the mixes seems possible. Although the overall measure of effectiveness used in the example was the movement of the FEBA, this measure showed essentially no difference between the mixes. The use of other measures, such as combat losses, rates of loss, and the time required to gain control of the air, did reveal differences between the mixes. Multiple criteria and multiple measures of effectiveness thus seem necessary in any major force trade-off study to account for the different capabilities of the forces.

2. It is likely that the utility of any force mix will depend on the specific conflict situation. In the illustration, the mixes performed differently in each of the four cases. Within each case, the differences were less pronounced, and no one mix dominated the others in all measures. For any major trade-off study, therefore, it will be necessary to define the situations that are most reasonable or credible in order to "weight" the significance of the results.[23] Defining such situations will require both analysis and judgment.

3. Within any trade-off analysis, there will be important parameters and criteria that cannot be handled quantitatively or by formal analytic techniques. Leadership, morale, the relative controllability of the mixes – none of these was incorporated in the example. Qualitative analysis outside the formal model may be required in such cases.

4. For some trade-off problems, the first step may be to establish the level of the forces required to achieve the military objectives. Then we could vary the force mixes to determine their effectiveness. In the example, none of the mixes was capable of halting the Red advance; the most we could learn, therefore, was the relative effectiveness of the mixes in slowing the advance or in gaining time to implement other options. To establish the utility of different mixes for obtaining a favorable military outcome *in the four conflict situations we postulated*, we would have had to make an initial "requirements" investigation.

5. The results of any trade-off study will be sensitive to the assumptions made in the cost analysis and in the effectiveness analysis. To determine which of the assumptions or parameter values have the greatest effect on the outcome, a variety of sensitivity tests will be needed. An important by-product of such testing can be to identify the factors to which the results are insensitive; these can then be omitted from further consideration.

### Some General Observations

No matter how much time and effort are spent in identifying and defining criteria, developing hypothetical conflict situations, generating various force mixes, or incorporating assessments of other factors important in trade-off analyses on the situational level, the resulting representation of the real world is certain to be imperfect. This sort of imperfection is by no means limited to trade-off analyses. It is likely to appear in virtually all types of systems analysis. Indeed, even the models used by the exact scientist, which are part of a well-confirmed body of scientific knowledge,

---

[23] For example, it might be unreasonable to use a given situation for evaluating the effectiveness of non-nuclear force mixes if it assumes that they will be met with a strategic nuclear response.

may involve this same imperfection and have to be improved through experimentation. The systems analyst, to whom experimentation in national conflict is not available and who has no well-established theory for the phenomena he is dealing with, must construct a model as best he can. As insights accrue from working with the model (the nearest thing we have to experimentation) and more information becomes available, the existing model can be improved or replaced by a more representative model. The goal – and, in some cases, the result – is a model that is fully adequate to handle the questions we are studying.

This process of refining our models through approximation has been born of necessity. Nevertheless, as the basis of operations research, model building has met with some success in industry in coping with the problem of economic choice. It is much more difficult, unfortunately, to make really adequate models of military conflict. The model we have just discussed, for instance, places its stress on such characteristics as weapon effectiveness, gross firepower, and vulnerability, and tends to de-emphasize the human factor – how men are likely to perform, whether at the broad policy and strategy level or at the level of small combat actions – since it is difficult to represent this within an anlytic structure. More important, perhaps, is that not only are many of its existing elements and their interactions imperfectly understood, but they concern a future time period and thus introduce the serious problem of predicting new or altered elements and interactions.

Consequently, we stress the importance that should be given to the structure of the analysis, whether it be in the form of a computer model or a political assessment. Unless that structure represents the salient – and relevant – aspects of the real world as best we understand them, we cannot have great confidence in the resulting predictions. Sheer size or complexity are not guarantees that a model represents the real world in as valid a way as our knowledge permits. To the extent that any model forces us to make explicit the elements of the situation that we are considering and imposes on us the discipline of clarifying the structure we are using (thus establishing unambiguous, intersubjective communication about the problem under consideration), we progress toward greater validity. As a result, the insights and recommendations that stem from this process have a better chance of being appropriate than do those that are produced without the use of an explicit model.

### A Final Comment

Trade-off analysis is an important concept underlying much of the discussion in Chapter 3. As pointed out in Chapter 4, its application to equal-cost future force-mix problems has been particularly important in recent years; hence our reason for including Case 2 among the examples in this chapter.

The example points up once again many of the main ideas presented previously. Some of these are:

1. *The key role of cost considerations in equal-cost force-mix studies.* In a real sense the cost analysis sets the stage for the effectiveness analysis, since it provides the principal basis for generating alternative force mixes that may be obtained from the base case budget level.

2. *The importance of giving careful attention to ensuring that the costs used as a basis for generating the force mixes are relevant costs* (a key point in Chapter 3). This means that only those costs which are a *consequence* of the postulated trade-off decision should be taken into account. For example, certain support costs which are invariant with respect to the range of force size variations being considered should not be included.

3. *Use of sensitivity analysis.* The Case 2 example again indicates how sensitivity analysis can help in dealing with the relevancy problem discussed above. For example, in cases of uncertainty about the relevancy of certain costs in view of the information available initially, sensitivity analysis can assist the analyst in deciding whether or not to probe the matter in greater depth.

## CASE 3:

## ANALYSIS OF DISTANT FUTURE STRATEGIC FORCE MIXES[24]

**Introduction**

Systems analysis, in some form or another, has existed for many years. It could perhaps be traced back to antiquity. However, in its modern form, it is only a little over 20 years old.

Much has happened over this 20-year period; for example:

1. Prior to 1950, most military studies were concerned primarily with systematic examination of the engineering parameters of a particular system. Later the emphasis fell more on investigations of

---

[24] This case illustration is based on a current exploratory research effort at The Rand Corporation under the direction of Dr. E. W. Paxson. Much of the material presented below was taken directly from Paxson's writings about his project.

Before getting to the case illustration *per se*, we present some background material to help put the example in context.

alternative systems to accomplish a specified future mission. Still later, the complementarities of system mixes were found important.

2. Particularly during the 1950s a growing appreciation of the pitfalls of analysis began to evolve. This led to a substantial amount of basic work in such areas as the treatment of uncertainty, the criterion problem and its relation to objectives, the difficulties of dealing with problems associated with time, and so on.[25]

3. By the 1960s, analysis no longer provided merely a one-shot input to the decision process. The analysts and the decisionmakers essentially became dialogists in a continuous sequential decision-making process.

In sum, much progress has been made over the past 20 years. However, a number of systems analysts are beginning to believe that significant further advances will have to be made if analysis is to adequately serve the decisionmaking process in the future. Systems analysis as developed to date is not likely to be as helpful as we would like in dealing with many of the broad-scope national security problems that decisionmakers will have to consider in the future. Let us examine this matter briefly.

**Why Further Advances are Needed**

To help make the discussion concrete, we shall consider a specific area of national security: the strategic mission. It is in the strategic realm that classical systems analysis has been judged most successful in the past (particularly the 1950s). Part of this success, however, may reflect the fact that our standards were lower then, and that possibly an inappropriate case or two were treated extremely well. For example, the type of scenario that was deemed most important as a basis for planning future strategic force postures was full-scale thermonuclear (general) war.[26] Here, the characteristics of the conflict situation are much easier to structure, or to "model," for analytical purposes than is the case for scenarios involving levels of violence below full counter-population exchanges (for example, controlled-response general war cases). In the latter type of scenario, political and other difficult-to-quantify factors are at least as important as the technological and military considerations.

---

[25] For example, see Charles J. Hitch, "Suboptimization in Operations Research," *Journal of the Operations Research Society of America*, May 1953, pp. 87–99; and "An Appreciation of Systems Analysis," *Journal of the Operations Research Society of America*, November 1955, pp. 466–481.

[26] Sometimes referred to under such labels as the "spasm response case" or "massive retaliation."

Thus, in "controlled general war" contexts the focus is considerably more on *joint intent/capability* analyses (multisided) rather than on extreme intent cases where the adversaries use their maximum capabilities. As pointed out in Chapter 2, this implies considering subjects like the following (in addition to assured destruction capability): damage-limiting capability, coercion and bargaining capabilities to be used in an escalation process stemming from a crisis situation (to the extent that this is not automatic from damage-limiting analyses), intrawar deterrence of counter-value exchanges, and war termination.

All of these topics involve complex interactions among military, technological, political, psychological, bureaucratic, behavioral, and other factors.[27] Each is a subset of a complicated total system. The matter of interactions among these subsets is precisely one of the important kinds of considerations that need to be explored more carefully in future analyses of national security problems. These interrelations are, of course, context dependent. An investigation of context may be the most important aspect of future analyses.

Systems analysis as we know it today can shed *some* light on these problems. But a number of analysts feel that new advances in the analytical state-of-the-art are needed for the future if really substantive contributions are to be made to the long-range planning process. What might be done?

## Some Speculations About Future Approaches

From a very speculative point of view, we might envision at some time in the distant future the bringing together of many advanced disciplinary efforts to form a new integrated analytical approach to assist decision-makers in dealing with complicated problems of choice examined *in context* – an approach that E. W. Paxson calls "systems synthesis."

There are major, but for the most part separate, topics in modern research which in principle might themselves form the building blocks in the systems synthesis concept. Some of these, for example, are bureaucratic

---

[27] One example of the interaction among some of these factors (especially the military, technological, and political ones) is portrayed by thinking about the so-called "empty-hole" problem in possible distant-future strategic missile exchanges. E. W. Paxson has described it as follows: "Technologically feasible sensor systems which can determine launch points and predict enemy impact points may mean that he who strikes first partially solves the empty-hole problem for the other. If we are that "other," we have then the option of launching on warning from those systems at risk *in kind*, that is, against his [the enemy's] holdback forces. He has the empty-hole problem when his first strike arrives. Hence concepts such as the advantage of a first strike, defending forces to "ride out" such strikes, and even deterrence itself are subject to reexamination. Major space war may be an initial phase of strategic confrontation buying all-important negotiation time." (From an unpublished talk, November 1967).

behavioral analysis, bargaining theory, n-person game theory, behavioral psychology, new concepts for retrieval and manipulation of information in large data banks, techniques (such as the Delphi technique[28]) for polling systematically the views of experts on individual propositions in the context of chains of argument, and so on.

The notion of systems synthesis does not envision "hard-core" optimization, but rather a partly quantitative, partly qualitative input to all major aspects of a decision process, and not to a monolithic decision-maker. It involves a deliberate examination of context, a matter largely ignored by classical systems analysis. This implies that the human decision process itself must eventually be an important field for investigation and analysis. Here, there would be no intention of replacing the decision process in any mechanistic way; rather the problem is simply to increase our understanding of that process.

The above is admittedly speculative and futuristic. Such research objectives cannot be attained in the near future. However, efforts are currently under way which could provide important foundations for further work at some future time. Let us consider briefly one of these endeavors: an exploratory study of strategic force planning for the distant future, with emphasis on gaining a deeper insight into the decision processes underlying the initiation, management, and termination of general war at levels less than full counter-population exchanges. This study is called Project XRAY.

### A Current Example: XRAY

Past efforts to deal with complex, broad-context decision problems have often used some type of war-gaming as supplement to classical systems analysis. Because of limitations in both gaming and systems analysis, the usefulness of the results of these studies has been limited. Particularly when traditional war-gaming has been the main thrust of the analytical approach, the study activity has been subjected to rather severe constraints, among them the following:

1. Unless the game is overly simplified (and hence perhaps essentially useless or misleading), one run-through takes an inordinately long time, and therefore is very expensive in terms of man-days of effort.
2. In a given "play" of the game, so many key factors vary that interpreting the significance of a single play has been most difficult.

---

[28] See N. C. Dalkey, *Delphi*, P-3404 (Santa Monica, Calif.: The Rand Corporation, October 1967); and Dalkey, *Experiments In Group Prediction*, P-3820 (Santa Monica, Calif.: The Rand Corporation, March 1968).

Repetitions, under controlled conditions, could help solve this problem; but in the past the length of time required for one play made a large number of run-throughs infeasible.

3. It is difficult to make readily available to the players the large body of information (including a kit of analytical tools to utilize this information) required to permit them to assess adequately the relevant range of alternatives before deciding upon a move. Control and evaluation teams experience similar difficulties in recording, assessing, and directing the play. In sum, there are difficulties in getting the desired analytical substance into the games to prevent them from degenerating into a series of isolated plays which are too little subject to meaningful analysis and interpretation.

From the viewpoint of Project XRAY, which is focused mainly on multisided, controlled-response scenarios in the context of a dynamic sequential decision process, these limitations are intolerable. They are just too restrictive to permit attaining the degree of analytical depth desired in Project XRAY. Yet XRAY requires some sort of gaming. Are there alternative approaches?

In addition to classical systems analysis and traditional gaming procedures, we have at the present time several other tools which might help in dealing with analytical problems like those posed in Project XRAY. One such tool is advanced computer technology – particularly on-line, time-sharing, multiconsole computing, using natural languages, verbal and graphic. (In subsequent discussions we shall refer to this as OLTS computing.) Another tool involves an extension of the Delphi method: a procedure for systematizing the interactions of a group engaged in a joint endeavor in the context of a dynamic sequential decisionmaking process. How might these tools help solve our problem?

As an example, let us consider OLTS computing. This advanced computer technology can help substantially in creating an integrated analytical process in which classical systems analysis and conventional gaming techniques can be mutually reinforcing. Classical systems analysis has the advantage of analytical content, but often in practice it suffers from narrowness of context. Gaming, on the other hand, can offer the advantage of rich context, but usually at the cost of foregoing analytical depth.

In Project XRAY we would like a "dominant solution" to this dilemma: the advantages of both systems analysis and gaming, without the disadvantages of either. Obviously this cannot be attained in practice. However, OLTS computing can help considerably in bringing about a partial mutual reinforcement of the two approaches (a small step toward the "systems synthesis" referred to previously).

The following are examples of the ways in which OLTS computing can help:

1. Large data banks of information and numerous submodel routines (modules) can be stored in memory, to be called up and used as needed by the game participants. The adversaries can thus have, via their own respective OLTS consoles, a wealth of information and analytical tools *readily* available. These may be used in making substantive cost-effectiveness evaluations of alternative systems and force mixes before making the next move in game play. One of the modules in XRAY, for example, is a force-mix cost model which computes very rapidly (within minutes) the year-by-year resource implications of a specified mix of strategic offensive, defensive, sensor, and command forces projected 10 or more years into the future.[29] The main point is that having these rapid-response analytical tools available on call can result in:

    a. A much greater amount and depth of analytical activity for a given period of game time than would otherwise be the case, or

    b. A shorter period of game time for a desired (or hoped for) level of analytical activity.[30]

2. Much of what has just been said pertaining to the adversary participants also applies to the game control and evaluation team participants. The evaluation and control team must, among other things, structure the game play, issue directives to the players, control the play, assess the consequences of moves by the adversary players, keep track of the "history" of the play as it unfolds sequentially, and conduct post-game evaluations and analyses. The data bank and analytical tools made readily available via the team's own OLTS console help immeasurably in the conduct of these duties – both in terms of time saved and in terms of contributions to the richness and analytical depth of the game.

---

[29] At certain stages of the XRAY game the players have to engage in a planning exercise to structure their respective strategic forces for the distant future. Numerous alternative systems and mixes of systems are available for consideration, and the force-structure choices have to be made subject to a budget (resource) constraint. This means that the players have to engage in a considerable amount of cost analysis activity in the process of trying to arrive at the most effective force that might be obtained from the stipulated overall cost level. Using conventional cost analysis methods and techniques would take an inordinate amount of time. The OLTS computer cost module essentially solves this problem. (The cost module will be discussed in more detail later.)

[30] This in turn might have the important result of increasing the chances for obtaining time-limited senior personnel as exercise participants.

3. Implicit in these first two points is a most important consideration that we must make explicit and emphasize. In addition to contributing substantially to the analytical content of a *single* game play, the OLTS computing system makes it possible to conduct such a game several times within a relatively short period. This has far-reaching consequences. While increasing the analytical content of an *individual* game play is vitally necessary, much of the type of analysis sought in Project XRAY can only be attained by systematic examination and evaluation of a body of data and information generated by *numerous* game plays (some of which may be repetitious of certain important scenarios using different adversary participants in successive plays). To attempt to conduct a long series of plays of a rich-context game using traditional gaming procedures would be out of the question. In sum, by shortening the time of an individual game play without sacrificing context richness and analytical content, OLTS computing makes it feasible (in terms of time and cost) to generate the broad data base of game histories which is necessary for deep analysis of the set of problems under consideration. OLTS computing can also help significantly in facilitating this kind of game history analysis.

Let us now consider the XRAY gaming procedure in more detail. We shall do this in two ways, by presenting the initial "memorandum to participants," and by discussing briefly the force-mix cost module.

### The Memorandum to Participants

At the beginning of an XRAY exercise, the participants are given an initial "memorandum to participants" which provides general orientation regarding the nature of the XRAY game and a summary of the procedures to be followed in the play of the game. In this section we shall present an example of such a memorandum, so that the reader may gain a better understanding of Project XRAY.

The content of a typical memorandum to participants is as follows. Here, the reader should imagine that he is one of the adversary participants, and that the memorandum is addressed to him.

"As a major part of our examination of alternative future strategic force postures, we are trying to get a deeper insight into the decision processes underlying the initiation, management, and termination of general war at levels less than full counter-population exchanges. Our purpose is to study how the political options and courses of action for this decision process are conditioned by the size, composition, and technological capabilities of opposing strategic offensive, defensive, and sensor systems; and conversely, what demands would be placed on technology by politico-military actions.

"XRAY is a series of exercises designed to elicit your actions and your reasons for them, were you part of the highest decision level of either the BLUE, RED, or YELLOW blocs, in a crisis situation which could well lead to some form of general war.[31] You are not an actor, but rather a playwright attempting to construct, illuminate, and perhaps explain behavior at these decision levels.

"Your commitment will be approximately ten 3-hour sessions on consecutive working days, preceded by a small amount of preparatory reading and followed by an introspective recording of what you think you learned from the exercise.

"There is one more color – XRAY GREEN. This team will, among other things:

1. Calculate the results of all military actions you order.

2. Maintain your force status files and intelligence files on your opponents.

3. Tell you what you are entitled to know at appropriate times.

4. Act as an advisor and discuss your proposed actions with you.

5. Provide inputs, whether you want them or not, from the concerned sectors of your society outside your core position (for example, the rest of your bureaucracy, Congress, press, population).

6. Provide inputs from allied and neutral countries.

"The overall structure of the exercise follows:

1. Your team will decide on a Chief (BLUE 1, RED 1, YELLOW 1), who has final say on all actions. (Opposing team members may not be known to you by name.)

2. You will read a synopsis of world events from 1945 to 1967 (Section B).[32]

3. You will be given as a base posture the forces now planned for the period 1968–1980. Working from this base and a menu of feasible new weapon systems, you will prepare a complete posture of strategic offensive, defensive, and sensor forces for this period whose year-by-year cost must

---

[31] Here, the general context is similar to that in crisis exercises conducted by the Joint War Game Agency in the Pentagon. (The color codes refer to the adversary teams. BLUE and RED are the major adversaries. YELLOW represents a "third area" bloc whose behavior might well influence actions taken by BLUE and RED, and whose behavior might also be influenced by the major adversaries.)

[32] Lettered sections refer to additional packages of written material made available at the beginning of, or during, the course of game play.

not exceed an assigned level.[33] The nature, effectiveness, and pros and cons of all systems are given in the vignettes notebook.[34]

4. At this point you should dictate, tape-record, or write a résumé of your reasoning in choosing the posture balance you did.[35] GREEN will consult with you during steps (3) and (4).

5. Section C is now issued. It is a script of world events through 1972, but as seen and interpreted from the viewpoint of the bloc you represent (RED, BLUE, YELLOW).

6. Based on intelligence provided by GREEN, you may now modify your force posture for 1972–1980 within the constraints of lead times and budget.[36]

7. A new script (Section D) for a specified future time period is now issued.

8. You next receive a detailed description of a crisis or confrontation (Section E).

9. Section F contains discussions of the OLTS computer programs for penetration and fallout and mortality calculations used in XRAY. This is for your information and background only.

10. Section G contains instructions for logging on and off the OLTS computer system, and details on the composition of frag orders (orders initiating a military operation in game play). Also, there are instructions for the operation of the TWX machine.[37]

11. At this point, actual interacting exercise play begins. Within the previously described constraints imposed by GREEN, you may exchange freely political or military blows of any intensity. Political actions may be offers, threats, demands. Military actions can be exemplary, punitive, or major counterforce, and need not be against opposing homelands. They may occur in space, in the air, at sea, or overseas.

---

[33] Here is one of the key points in the exercise where the force-mix cost module is an indispensable tool in providing analytical content within a reasonable period of time.

[34] This notebook contains descriptive and analytical information on all weapon and support systems to be considered in the exercise. Many of these are proposals for distant-future capabilities which are currently only in the conceptual stages of development: advanced strategic missile systems, new sensor systems which would operate in outer space, advanced ballistic missile defense systems in various basing modes, advanced command and control systems, and so on. The menu of systems is interservice; that is, Army, Navy, and Air Force capabilities are all represented.

[35] A statement of objectives must also be included.

[36] Here again, the force-mix cost module is an important aid to the participants.

[37] This is an independent circuit in parallel with the OLTS lines. Primarily, it handles the large message volume during an exercise. But should the OLTS system fail temporarily, the exercise can be kept running on the TWX circuits.

12. At the point of each major decision, you *must* dictate or tape-record your reasoning with regard to courses of action open to you, expectations about enemy response and intentions, expected developments or branching possibilities, how you related your acts to national objectives, and the like. Note that you can call on GREEN for advice and for "what if" calculations – what would be the estimated physical results of proposed military actions.[38] In fact, at the termination of each session you can ask GREEN to do this and perform similar staff actions, giving you the results at the beginning of the next session.

13. Play will be stopped if (a) the situation has led naturally to termination, (b) a major escalation seems likely, (c) protracted low-level exchanges or stalemate can be estimated, (d) time available for the exercise has run out. Play is stopped by mutual agreement among all colors.

14. If physical contiguity permits, there is now a face-to-face debriefing or post-mortem session attended by all hands.[39]

15. Each team prepares in writing its analysis of the exercise. If requested, past participants will receive digests of subsequent exercises. In any event, all participants will be asked to comment on the final overall review and analysis of the entire XRAY series."

### The Force-Mix Cost Module

As indicated in the previous discussion, at various points in an XRAY exercise the adversary participants have to plan their respective future force mixes of strategic offensive, defensive, sensor, and command forces. Since this has to be done subject to a time-phased resource (cost) constraint, a considerable amount of cost analysis work is called for in an iterative process of arriving at a force mix which meets the national security objectives established by each of the blocs (BLUE, RED, YELLOW).

The XRAY force-mix cost module is one of the key tools available to the participants to facilitate their long-range, force-planning activities. Since the XRAY cost module is reasonably well developed, and since this book emphasizes cost considerations in defense planning, we might spend a moment to examine the main features of the cost module.

Basically, the XRAY cost module represents the formalization of a

---

[38] Here, information (in many cases precomputed results) contained in the data bank may be called up and used. Also, certain "damage assessment" computer programs can be called up and exercised through the OLTS computer console.

[39] The participants in a given XRAY exercise need not all be at the same physical location. OLTS consoles can be stationed at various locations around the country, but still be connected to the central data bank and computer facility. The capability to conduct an XRAY exercise by "remote control" offers the distinct advantage of being able to tap a reservoir of desired game participants who would otherwise not be available.

procedure for assessing the time-phased resource impact of alternative future strategic force mixes (strategic offense, defense, sensor, and command and control forces). It is programmed for an OLTS computer system,[40] and is designed to assist XRAY game participants in the iterative process of selecting a future force mix that will best meet a particular bloc's objectives, subject to a stipulated cost constraint.

The starting point is the "base case": the assumed currently planned strategic force mix for the next decade for a particular bloc team, and the associated year-by-year costs[41] for a 12-year period into the future. As indicated in Chapter 4, and as shown by curve AB in Fig. 9.17, the base case is in effect a "spendout" projection.

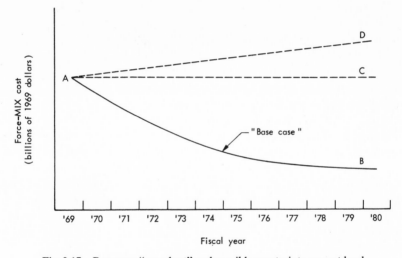

Fig. 9.17 – Base case "spendout" and possible constraints on cost level

The bloc team then receives from XRAY GREEN information regarding its stipulated year-by-year resource constraint. This amount may be at a constant level over time (curve AC in Fig. 9.17), or at an increasing level (curve AD in Fig. 9.17), or possibly a decreasing level over the planning period. Given its initially formulated national security objectives, and given

---

[40] This was done by H. G. Massey of the Resource Analysis Department, The Rand Corporation. The program is written for Rand's on-line, timesharing computer system, JOSS.

[41] Costs are expressed in terms of total obligational authority (TOA) measured in constant dollars. The base year is the first year in the planning period. By altering the lag factors in the model, expenditure estimates, instead of TOA, could be obtained. The model can also measure resource impact in terms of manpower requirements.

294 COST CONSIDERATIONS IN SYSTEMS ANALYSIS

the menu of new weapon and support system possibilities for the future, the bloc team must then go through an iterative planning process of adding to or subtracting from the base case force structure to arrive at a projected (12-year) strategic posture which is likely to best meet the bloc's objectives within the imposed cost constraint.[42] Oftentimes the initially desired projected force postures will not be within the cost constraint, and they will have to be pared down. Or sometimes the originally specified bloc objectives may have to be modified.

In any event the XRAY force-mix cost model must be structured so that the bloc participants can input the base case and then readily make modifications to it in an iterative fashion. This is accomplished by making an OLTS computer console available to the bloc team and by providing for an extremely simple input procedure.

Suppose, for example, that weapon systems $S_1$, $S_2$, $S_3$, and $S_4$ make up the force mix in the base case. This force mix and its time-phased total cost are stored in the computer memory and can be called up at any time. Suppose further that the bloc team wishes to add new system $S_5$ to the base case posture. The basic building blocks and cost-estimating relationships for $S_5$ (as well as all other systems contained in the game menu of systems for the bloc) are stored in memory. The result is that all that need be done to add $S_5$ to the basic mix is to call up the base case and input the following items for system $S_5$:

1. The code number for system $S_5$.
2. The total force size (peak buildup) of $S_5$ in terms of number of units. For a missile system this might be, for example, the total number of unit equipment (U.E.) missiles.
3. The year of initial operational capability (IOC).
4. The number of years to complete the change (in this case the number of years from IOC to peak buildup).[43]

The resulting output can be called for in various alternative formats. One frequently used output is the following (in which all quantities are time-phased year by year over a 12-year period):

---

[42] The cost constraint cannot be met precisely, of course. Overages of about 5 or 10 per cent may be allowed in a given 1 or 2-year period if similar amounts "below budget" appear in subsequent years. The control team (XRAY GREEN) makes the final judgment regarding whether or not a certain bloc's planned force posture is acceptably within the stipulated resource constraint for that bloc.

[43] The model has built-in constraints on inputs 2 through 4. For example, if the bloc team specifies an IOC which violates the development and production lead time for $S_5$, the OLTS computer program will reject the input. However, as will be discussed later, development cost-time tradeoff options are available for certain weapon systems in the menu of new systems.

1. The total cost of the base case force mix.
2. The cost profile of the overall cost constraint imposed upon the bloc's force planning deliberations.
3. The force structure of system $S_5$ expressed in terms of number of units at the end of each year in the planning period.
4. The total cost of system $S_5$.
5. The total cost of the new force mix $(S_1, S_2, \ldots, S_5)$.[44]

The bloc team may now formulate a second change, which may be treated as a modification of the first iteration. Then a third change may be postulated and treated as a variation of the second iteration, and so on. At each point along the way various output options are available. For example, only the aggregate results of the proposed change may be called for. Or, if desired, the detail of the base case and all iterations to date may be called up.

A postulated change may take numerous forms, in addition to adding a new system as in our example above. Among the more frequently used ones are the following:[45]

1. Phase-out of a system contained in the base case force mix.
2. Modification of the phase-in schedule of a new system in the base case: rate of phase-in, IOC date, and so on.
3. Modification of the phase-out of a system in the base case.
4. Modification of the phase-in schedule of a new system added to the base case in a previous iteration.
5. Cancellation of development and phase-in of a new system ordered in a previous iteration (provided the decision has not become "locked in").

Let us now illustrate some of the preceding points through the use of a hypothetical example. In Table 9.4 we start with the total cost of the base case force mix of systems $S_1, \ldots, S_4$ (row A), and the year-by-year cost constraint (row B). In this instance the constraint is increasing slightly as a function of time.

Iteration 1 illustrates the modification of system $S_3$ in the base case force mix. The steady state force size is increased from 80 to 120 units, beginning

---

[44] An alternative to (5) is to ask the computer to supply the *difference* between the stipulated cost constraint (2) and the total cost of the new force mix (5).
[45] Most of these are subject to automatic constraints built into the computer program. For example, the computer would reject an input calling for an increase in the force size of an aircraft system in the base case, when that particular aircraft has been out of production for a considerable period of time. It will also reject inputs which violate development and production lead time constraints.

TABLE 9.4

**Example of Output from the XRAY Force-Mix Cost Module**
(Hypothetical Numbers)

| Item | 1969 | 1970 | 1971 | 1972 | 1973 | 1974 | 1975 | 1976 | 1977 | 1978 | 1979 | 1980 |
|---|---|---|---|---|---|---|---|---|---|---|---|---|
| (A) Base case total force-mix cost[a] | 1427 | 1592 | 1602 | 1372 | 1385 | 1321 | 1325 | 1197 | 1072 | 1035 | 999 | 977 |
| (B) Force planning cost constraint[a] | 1427 | 1650 | 1700 | 1751 | 1803 | 1857 | 1913 | 1970 | 2029 | 2090 | 2153 | 2218 |
| *Iteration No. 1:* | | | | | | | | | | | | |
| *Input:* Change peak buildup force size of system $S_3$ in base case from 80 to 120 units, beginning in 1972 and completed in 1978. | | | | | | | | | | | | |
| *Output:* | | | | | | | | | | | | |
| (C) Adjusted force size of $S_3$ (No. of units) | 45 | 50 | 55 | 60 | 70 | 80 | 90 | 100 | 110 | 120 | 120 | 120 |
| (D) Adjusted cost of $S_3$[a] | 99 | 128 | 146 | 156 | 165 | 178 | 172 | 162 | 151 | 153 | 160 | 160 |
| (E) Adjusted base case total force-mix cost[a] | 1427 | 1618 | 1639 | 1413 | 1437 | 1391 | 1395 | 1255 | 1117 | 1081 | 1053 | 1030 |
| *Iteration No. 2:* | | | | | | | | | | | | |
| *Input:* Add new weapon system $S_5$ to results of Iteration (1), beginning in 1976 and completing phase-in by 1978. Force size = 50 units. | | | | | | | | | | | | |
| *Output:* | | | | | | | | | | | | |
| (F) Force size of $S_5$ (No. of units) | 0 | 0 | 0 | 0 | 0 | 0 | 0 | 17 | 34 | 50 | 50 | 50 |
| (G) Cost of $S_5$[a] | 0 | 0 | 23 | 220 | 584 | 491 | 262 | 154 | 32 | 23 | 27 | 27 |
| Difference between the force planning cost constraint and the total force-mix cost for Iteration (2).[a] (Negative numbers mean force-mix cost is less than the "ceiling.") | 0 | -33 | -38 | -118 | 218 | 25 | -257 | -562 | -881 | -986 | -1073 | -1160 |
| *Iteration No. 3:* | | | | | | | | | | | | |
| *Input:* Add new system $S_6$ to results of Iteration (2), beginning in 1977 and completing phase-in by 1979. Force size = 50 units. ($S_6$ is a missile system employing the same booster as $S_5$.) | | | | | | | | | | | | |
| *Output:* | | | | | | | | | | | | |
| Force size of $S_6$ (No. of units) | 0 | 0 | 0 | 0 | 0 | 0 | 0 | 0 | 17 | 34 | 50 | 50 |
| Cost of $S_6$[a] | 0 | 0 | 0 | 0 | 0 | 59 | 261 | 220 | 165 | 48 | 40 | 47 |
| Force size of $S_5$ (No. of units) | 0 | 0 | 0 | 0 | 0 | 0 | 0 | 17 | 34 | 50 | 50 | 50 |
| Cost of $S_5$[a] | 0 | 0 | 23 | 220 | 583 | 486 | 256 | 149 | 31 | 23 | 27 | 27 |
| (H) Difference between the force planning cost constraint and the total force-mix cost for Iteration (3)[a] | 0 | -33 | -38 | -118 | 217 | 79 | -1 | -346 | -716 | -938 | -1034 | -1113 |
| and so on to Iterations 4, 5, . . . , $N$. | | | | | | | | | | | | |

a In millions of 1969 dollars (total obligational authority).

in 1972 and ending in 1978.[46] In this case the output appears on the OLTS console in the form of: (1) the new time-phased force size for system $S_3$ (row C), (2) the new time-phased cost stream for $S_3$ (row D), and (3) the new (increased) aggregate cost stream for the modified base case force mix (row E).

Iteration 2 portrays the addition of new system $S_5$ to the force mix obtained as a result of iteration 1. The inputs are as shown in Table 9.4. The form of the output is the same as in the previous example, except that here we exercise the option to call up the aggregate result in terms of the *difference* between the new total force-mix cost and the force planning cost constraint. The time-phased results are shown on row G. (Here, negative numbers indicate that total force-mix cost in a particular year is less than the cost constraint for that year.)

Iteration 3 illustrates the ability of the cost model to take certain interrelations among systems into account. In this instance, system $S_6$ is added to the force mix obtained as a result of iteration 2. $S_6$ is a missile system utilizing a major component (a booster) which is also employed by $S_5$. Because of the cost-quantity relationship (the "learning curve") for the common booster, the system costs of $S_5$ and $S_6$ should be computed simultaneously. The XRAY cost model does this automatically. Thus, in Table 9.4, notice that the output for iteration 3 contains results for both $S_5$ and $S_6$. Notice also that because of the model's treatment of the booster commonality problem, the cost of the same configuration of $S_5$ in iteration 3 (see row H) is lower than in iteration 2 (see row F).[47]

In an actual XRAY exercise, further iterations (4, 5, ..., $N$) would no doubt take place as the bloc team planners attempt to generate that projected force mix which best meets the bloc's objectives, subject to the given resource constraint. The final aggregate result might look something like that shown in Fig. 9.18. Notice that in the distant future years of the planning horizon we get the so-called "bow-wave" effect – the tailing off of the total force-mix cost curve. This, of course, is inevitable, given a truncated planning horizon. In order to fill the gap (the shaded area in Fig. 9.18) the force planners would have to consider force postures for the decade of the 1980s.

The system or program element detail of a strategic force-mix cost analysis may be presented in a number of alternative ways. One convenient format is portrayed in Table 9.5. Here, the various systems are

---

[46] The following inputs are entered on the OLTS computer console: (1) The code number for system $S_3$, (2) the postulated change in force size of $S_3$, (3) the year in which the change is to be started, and (4) the year in which the steady state level is to be reached.
[47] Note especially years 1974–1976.

TABLE 9.5

Illustrative Format for Presenting Results of a Strategic Force Mix Cost Analysis

| Program Element | Force Structure (No. of Units) | | | | | | | | | | | | Total Obligational Authority ($ Billions)[a] | | | | | | | | | | | | |
|---|---|---|---|---|---|---|---|---|---|---|---|---|---|---|---|---|---|---|---|---|---|---|---|---|
| | '69 | '70 | '71 | '72 | '73 | '74 | '75 | '76 | '77 | '78 | '79 | '80 | '69 | '70 | '71 | '72 | '73 | '74 | '75 | '76 | '77 | '78 | '79 | '80 |
| *STRATEGIC OFFENSIVE FORCES:* | | | | | | | | | | | | | | | | | | | | | | | | |
| Manned Aircraft Bomber System | | | | | | | | | | | | | | | | | | | | | | | | |
| Land-Based Ballistic Missile System | | | | | | | | | | | | | | | | | | | | | | | | |
| Sea-Based Ballistic Missile System | | | | | | | | | | | | | | | | | | | | | | | | |
| Satellite Bombardment System | | | | | | | | | | | | | | | | | | | | | | | | |
| etc. | | | | | | | | | | | | | | | | | | | | | | | | |
| Total Offense | | | | | | | | | | | | | | | | | | | | | | | | |
| *STRATEGIC DEFENSIVE FORCES:* | | | | | | | | | | | | | | | | | | | | | | | | |
| Defense Against Manned Bombers | | | | | | | | | | | | | | | | | | | | | | | | |
| Ballistic Missile Defense (Hard Point) | | | | | | | | | | | | | | | | | | | | | | | | |
| Ballistic Missile Defense (Area) | | | | | | | | | | | | | | | | | | | | | | | | |
| Defense Against Submarine-launched BMs | | | | | | | | | | | | | | | | | | | | | | | | |
| etc. | | | | | | | | | | | | | | | | | | | | | | | | |
| Total Defense | | | | | | | | | | | | | | | | | | | | | | | | |
| *STRATEGIC SENSOR SYSTEMS:* | | | | | | | | | | | | | | | | | | | | | | | | |
| SS System No. 1 | | | | | | | | | | | | | | | | | | | | | | | | |
| SS System No. 2 | | | | | | | | | | | | | | | | | | | | | | | | |
| etc. | | | | | | | | | | | | | | | | | | | | | | | | |
| Total Sensor Forces | | | | | | | | | | | | | | | | | | | | | | | | |
| *COMMAND SYSTEMS:* | | | | | | | | | | | | | | | | | | | | | | | | |
| System No. 1 | | | | | | | | | | | | | | | | | | | | | | | | |
| System No. 2 | | | | | | | | | | | | | | | | | | | | | | | | |
| etc. | | | | | | | | | | | | | | | | | | | | | | | | |
| Total Command | | | | | | | | | | | | | | | | | | | | | | | | |
| *GENERAL SUPPORT* | | | | | | | | | | | | | | | | | | | | | | | | |
| GRAND TOTAL | | | | | | | | | | | | | | | | | | | | | | | | |

[a] Provision is also made for displaying the manpower requirements of a postulated force-mix.

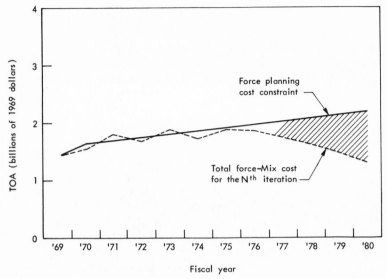

Fig. 9.18 –Results of the *N*th iteration

grouped according to major function: offense, defense, sensor, command, and so on.

So far, we have focused on the major input and output features of the XRAY force-mix cost module. Let us now outline briefly some of the other characteristics of the underlying cost model:

1. All of the weapon and support systems contained in the menu of systems for a particular game play are stored in memory. These may be called up at any time, and their costs estimated for varying force sizes, IOCs, and the like. However, for some systems numerous other "system configuration" options are provided. In the case of offensive ballistic missiles, for example, the following are available:

a. Numerous payload alternatives.
b. Several booster options.
c. Variations in basing: fixed bases, land mobile, water mobile (barge basing), and so on.

Other examples include new manned bomber aircraft systems (basing, alert level, and air-to-surface missile options), and space systems (on station in orbit, or on ground alert options).

2. As indicated previously, certain intersystem interactions are taken into account in the model. One of the most important pertains to cost-quantity effects when one item of major equipment is used in more than

one weapon or support system in the force mix under consideration. For example, the C-5A transport aircraft may be used in several different systems. If so, a postulated change in any one can induce cost changes in the others in a given force mix, because of the cost-quantity relationship for the C-5A aircraft. The XRAY cost model takes these iterations into account automatically.

3. Development and production lead times are taken into account in the model. These vary according to the type of major equipment being considered and are essentially average lead times for each case. However, in many instances the players have the option (within limits) of shortening the average development lead time for a particular system by trading off time and cost. For example, if an additional amount of development cost is incurred, the IOC date for the system would be $N-1$ instead of future year $N$.

4. Support costs are treated in accordance with the principles set forth in Chapters 3 and 4. That is to say, for a given postulated change in the strategic force mix, only those support costs which are a direct consequence of that particular decision are included in the estimated incremental cost of the change.[48] General support costs which are not a function of force mix are computed separately and included as a line item in the total cost of the base case force mix.[49]

5. The present XRAY cost model is designed primarily with a "fixed budget" framework of analysis in mind. However, with only slight modification it could be useful in helping the force planners deal with "fixed capability over time" situations. With this context in mind, a special routine is contained in the OLTS computer file which permits the analysts to compute very rapidly the present value of time-phased future cost streams for any discount rate assumption, including cases where the rate is assumed to vary year by year.

**Summary Comment**

The XRAY force-mix cost module contains an anlytical model which is explicitly designed to help attain the objectives of the broad analyses being attempted in the total XRAY project. By the utilization of OLTS computing, and by the precomputing and storing of a wide range of alternatives and options in the OLTS computer data bank, the resource impacts of numerous alternative strategic force mixes can be computed within

---

[48] For example, a new system using nuclear propulsion would require special depot maintenance facilities. The incremental cost of these support activities would be included as part of the cost of the decision to develop and procure such a system.

[49] An example of this type of support cost is the operating cost of Headquarters, Strategic Air Command.

minutes. This helps in a major way to attain one of the most important objectives in Project XRAY: To make possible a significant amount of analytical depth in XRAY exercises and to do this within the time constraints established for a particular exercise.

Like the other two cases presented in this chapter, the XRAY example serves to illustrate a number of the main points contained in previous chapters. Some of these are:

1. The usefulness of short "turn-around time" force structure cost models in studies and analyses of broad-context planning problems.

2. The importance of tailoring the cost model to the requirements of the overall analysis.

3. The importance of building the cost model in such a way that the key concepts discussed in Chapters 3, 4, and elsewhere in this book are taken into account; for example:

   a. Provision for explicit treatment of time-phasing by fiscal year, including techniques for dealing with time preference problems.
   b. Provision for proper assessment of the incremental (decremental) resource impact of postulated decisions involving marginal changes to a projected base case force mix. (These may pertain to changes in force-mix composition, changes in force size of weapon systems in the force mix, changes in the configuration of individual systems in the force mix, changes in assumed IOC dates, and so on.)
   c. Provision for explicit treatment of key interactions among weapon systems in a projected force mix. (This is necessary to avoid double counting, and to enable the proper assessment of incremental costs referred to in (b) above.)
   d. Provision for assessing the consequences of postulated force-mix decisions in terms of dollars *and* other measures of resource impact – e.g., manpower requirements.

**Suggested Supplementary Readings**
1. E. S. Quade, "The Selection and Use of Strategic Air Bases: A Case History," Chap. 3 in E. S. Quade, *Analysis for Military Decisions* (Chicago: Rand McNally & Company, 1964), pp. 24–63.
2. Richard B. Rainey, Jr., "Mobility: Airlift, Sealift, and Prepositioning," Chap. 9 in Stephen Enke (ed.), *Defense Management* (Englewood Cliffs, New Jersey: Prentice–Hall, Inc., 1967), pp. 150–163.
3. Lt.Colonel R. S. Berg, "Armed Forces' Use of Cost-Effectiveness Analysis," Chap. 6 in Thomas A. Goldman (ed.), *Cost-Effectiveness Analysis* (New York: Frederick A. Praeger, Publishers, 1967), pp. 91–103.
4. Murray Kamrass and Joseph A. Navarro, "An Analysis of Tactical Air Systems," Chap. 8 in Thomas A. Goldman (ed.), *Cost-Effectiveness Analysis* (New York: Frederick A. Praeger, Publishers, 1967), pp. 116–130.

## Chapter 10

# SUMMARY AND CONCLUDING REMARKS

Books written about highly developed and well-disciplined subjects usually do not contain a chapter devoted to a summary and concluding remarks. If the author has done his job properly, there is no need for it. This is particularly true when, as in mathematical text books, the presentation involves starting with certain postulates or axioms and then working out in great detail the implications of these initial premises. But this volume is in quite a different category. It is a subset of a larger subject (systems analysis), which is itself only a partially developed art form at the present time. Changes in concepts and techniques occur frequently. Writing definitively about systems analysis is, therefore, a difficult, perhaps impossible, task. Those who attempt it are particularly aware that their treatment of the subject is unavoidably apt to suffer from varying degrees of incompleteness, outdatedness, disjointedness, and the like. Because of these difficulties, most authors of books on systems analysis feel a special obligation to the reader to attempt to sum up the leading points of the discussion in a final chapter.

For example, the last chapter in *Systems Analysis and Policy Planning*[1] presents such a summary by commenting generally on the following topics:

1. Precepts for the systems analyst:

   a. Pay major attention to problem formulation.
   b. Keep the analysis systems oriented.
   c. Never exclude alternatives without analysis.
   d. Set forth hypotheses early.
   e. Let the question, not the phenomena alone, shape the model.
   f. Emphasize the question, not the model.
   g. Avoid overemphasizing mathematics and computing.
   h. Analyze the enemy's strategies and tactics.
   i. Treat the uncertainties explicitly.
   j. Postpone detail until late in the analysis.
   k. Sub-optimize with care.

---

[1] E. S. Quade and W. I. Boucher, *Systems Analysis and Policy Planning: Applications in Defense* (New York: American Elsevier Publishing Co., Inc., 1968).

2. Principles of good analysis:

    a. Efficient use of expert judgment is the essence of analysis.

    b. Choice of the right objectives is essential.

    c. Sensitivity testing is important.

    d. The design of alternatives is as important as their analysis.

    e. Interdisciplinary teams are usually necessary.

    f. The analysis of questions of R & D should not emphasize optimization.

    g. For broad questions, comparisons for a single contingency are not enough.

    h. Partial answers to relevant questions are more useful than full answers to empty questions.

    i. Estimates of cost are essential to a choice among alternatives.

    j. The decisionmaker by his actions can compensate to an extent for partial analysis.

    k. A good new idea is worth a thousand evaluations.

3. Nature of the decisionmaker and his responsibility.

4. Some dangers of analysis.

5. The future of systems analysis.

E. S. Quade's discussion of these topics[2] is excellent and should prove to be rewarding not only to readers of the Quade–Boucher book, but also to readers of the present volume. Indeed, this material is highly recommended as a general background supplement to what is said in the following paragraphs.

## Some Summary Points

In general, this book has dealt with the concepts and procedures of military cost analysis in a systems analysis context. By way of overall summary, the main points developed in the preceding nine chapters may be outlined as follows:

1. Systems analysis is concerned with helping long-range planners make difficult choices among alternatives in the face of real uncertainty. In providing this assistance the analysts attempt to identify and clarify objectives and the range of alternative means of achieving them. The analysts also attempt to assess the probable consequences of the alternatives in terms of their benefits, costs, and risks, and to make comparisons among these alternatives.

---

[2] Quade and Boucher, *op. cit.*, pp. 418–429.

2. To be effective, the cost analyst must function as an integral part of the systems analysis interdisciplinary study team. He must be on hand from the start to help in the difficult task of structuring the problem to be analyzed, and to assist in the formulation of questions and hypotheses to be examined. Only then will his input to the total analytical process be relevant. Cost estimates can be relevant only when they reflect the consequences of an appropriately defined decision or choice.

3. What do we mean by "cost?" In its most fundamental sense, cost is the value of benefits forgone. Costs, like benefits, are the consequences of decisions; and costs, or consequences, can only be identified by clearly specifying the decision and comparing it with its alternatives. An indication of costs can be provided to the decisionmaker by enumerating required resources, or by determining alternative uses of these resources, or by estimating the value of these alternative uses. In using dollars to estimate costs, the cost analyst is attempting to accomplish all three of these steps concomitantly. However, dollar expenditures will rarely be a full and completely valid measure of total costs. Although dollars are an especially useful measure of costs, other measures can sometimes be simpler and more useful.

4. While it is vitally necessary that the cost analyst utilize appropriate concepts of cost and focus on the output-oriented decision context of the problem at hand, other conditions must be fulfilled before he can effectively perform his job in practice. For example, a great deal of work must be done on the input side of the cost analysis process. Specifically, input structures must be developed to serve as a framework for assembling all the elements (for example, categories of resources) making up the various output-oriented packages of military capability; a historical data base must be built up and maintained to provide the empirical foundation for the cost analysis activity; this basic data base must be processed and analyzed continually with a view to development of estimating relationships; and, finally, all of the forgoing must be put together in the form of procedures or models which can be used in addressing cost analysis problems.

5. Cost models are important because they are, in effect, integrating devices designed to facilitate the analytical process by bringing together a wide range of factors on the input side and relating them to specific types of output-oriented military capabilities in the future. In terms of the problem the model is designed to help solve, four types of cost models are particularly important:

    a. Resource requirements submodels.
    b. Individual system cost models.

c. Mission area force-mix cost models.

d. Total force cost models.

6. As integral participants in the total study effort, cost analysts must stand ready to assist in solving troublesome special problems that typically arise in systems analysis. Perhaps the most important is dealing with the problem of uncertainty. How the cost analyst treats uncertainty in any given instance is very much a function of the design of the systems analysis study itself; generally speaking, however, imaginative sensitivity testing on the part of the cost analyst can be very useful to the systems analysts in their unending search for dominances and for ingenious ways of hedging against major uncertainties pertaining to the distant future.

Problems associated with time represent another area where special difficulties are likely to arise. The timing of future capabilities and costs is especially important in military planning problems. In conducting planning studies of such problems, time phasing should be considered explicitly wherever possible, even though doing so complicates the analysis considerably. When time phasing is introduced explicitly, usually the preferred way to compare alternatives is to specify a desired pattern of effectiveness or capability over the period of interest and to seek that alternative which meets the stipulated capability at least cost. Here, the time-phased cost streams should be computed on the basis of at least two assumptions regarding time preference: (a) a zero discount rate for the period of time under consideration and (b) a positive discount rate which is an approximate measure of the opportunity cost potential rate of return on the resources that would be utilized by the project.

**A Comment About the Future**

What can usefully be said about the future direction or roles of cost analysis in systems analysis? In particular, what are some of the more important areas where work should be done to improve cost analysis?

Anyone who is familiar with the present situation can provide a number of answers to these questions. While these may seem immediately obvious, they are nonetheless important. Some examples are:

1. Improved data and information systems (not all of which have to be complete enumerations on a periodic basis), and hence improved cost analysis data banks.

2. Given (1), further work on development of estimating relationships, particularly in areas that are currently deficient – avionics equipment, space vehicles, numerous areas of support activities in all three military services, and so on.

3. Further development of analytical cost models – especially inter-service force-mix cost models, including provision for explicit treatment of time phasing.

4. Development of improved methods and techniques for dealing with uncertainty: for example, further exploration of the possibility of using ideas from modern decision theory.

With the possible exception of the fourth problem, these topics are straightforward in principle, although making significant advances in any one of them will involve hard work. Other areas where improvements or changes might be needed in the future are much less obvious, and therefore any attempt to discuss them must of necessity be somewhat speculative. One of the main reasons for this is that the subject of cost considerations in systems analysis is intimately tied to the future directions of systems analysis as a whole.

We have already said something about systems analysis in the future in the background discussion for the Project XRAY example presented in Chapter 9. Other authors have also offered thoughts on the matter. Quade, for example, has written as follows:

> In recognition of the profound need for clarity and informed judgment, systems analysis will no doubt see a greater use of scenarios, gaming, and techniques for the systematic employment of experts, along with a growing use of quantitative analysis for problems where it is appropriate.
>
> Moreover, new approaches and techniques are being proposed constantly. Many of these are primarily mathematical in nature, but increasing attention is being devoted to systematic methods for taking into account the various organizational, political, and social factors heretofore so poorly understood but often so critical to national security problems. In the computer field, the trend toward a better union of man and machine through personalized, on-line, time-sharing systems that use natural language and graphical input and output, and store submodels on discs, will be a great boon to the systems analyst. It will give him the capability to change his program instantly, to experiment, and to perform numerous excursions, parametric investigations, and sensitivity analyses. In mathematics, new advances in game theory are giving us insight into the many-person and nonzero-sum situations of conflict and cooperation. And, more importantly, for questions not amenable to quantitative treatment, new techniques for the direct use of expertise are giving us a way to grasp these difficult-to-treat aspects of our problems.[3]

One of the common threads that seems to emerge from this statement and our discussion in Chapter 9 is that systems analyses in the future is very likely to be called upon to deal with considerably broader problems than is typically the case today. Or, even in cases where the breadth of the context is the same, the issues involved might be posed in such a way that present-day systems analysis concepts and methods would be somewhat inadequate to the task of assisting the decisionmakers in a substantive way.

---

[3] Quade and Boucher, *op. cit.*, p. 428.

All of this could have important implications for *cost* considerations in systems analysis in the future. Some speculations about the nature of these implications are as follows:

1. Examination of broader problems in the future could mean that cost considerations that are not now a part of a typical systems analysis study might have to be taken into account in some fashion. The analogy in economic theory is found in the subject of "externalities." For example, in the case of the theory of the firm, the real cost or sacrifice, in terms of opportunities forgone, of increasing the production of commodity x would be the sacrificed production of a certain number of units of commodity y. This cost, however, is *internal* to the firm. It does not measure the possible negative effects on other firms, or possible increases in social costs (such as air pollution). The latter are cost effects which are external to the individual firm. A similar situation might prevail for systems analysis in the future. Costs which were external (and therefore not taken into account) in narrow context problems would no longer be external when the context is broadened. This could well mean that cost analysts would have to attempt to face up to difficult issues which are for the most part ignored today.

2. Related to (1) is the question of the use of dollars as a reflection of real cost (benefits forgone). This book has perhaps placed undue emphasis on the derivation of dollar cost estimates. This, however, reflects rather accurately the current state-of-the-art in military cost analysis; and it is also true that in many instances dollars do represent *one* very useful measure of real cost. (On the other hand, we have stressed that in numerous problem areas dollars may be an inadequate, or even misleading, proxy for real costs.) But for the broader problems we might envision in the future – particularly if more emphasis is to be placed on organizational, political, and social considerations – it is not clear that dollar measures of benefits forgone will suffice even as well as they do now. For one thing, "market prices" are just not available as a basis for developing dollar estimates of the consequences of decisions for many of the types of considerations that would have to be taken into account. Markets for these items simply do not exist. And even when market prices are available, the analyst must exercise caution in using them as a basis for estimating the dollar expenditure implications of *very* large government programs. We must not forget that market prices are in effect marginal prices, and that they may be valid proxy measures of alternatives forgone for only relatively small variations in quantities of resources about the market equilibrium point. Massive government programs may require such large amounts of various specific

resources that their current market price, or marginal price, may be a poor basis for assessing future total program cost. Some reasonably convenient method of testing the acceptability of marginal prices as cost estimators, and for adjusting them if they are not acceptable, is one of the challenges facing cost analysts in dealing with systems analysis problems of very large-scale government programs.

3. If systems analysis should move seriously in the direction of "systems synthesis," as discussed in Chapter 9, several important implications for cost analysis would seem apparent. Perhaps the most significant is that a great deal of additional work would have to be devoted to the development of interservice force-mix cost models with a very rapid response-time capability. This task would be difficult for a number of reasons: differences among the military services with respect to organizational structure (particularly in the support activities area), operational concepts, information and data systems, and the like. These differences make it difficult to structure the model properly so that an appropriate degree of internal consistency is attained and at the same time an unacceptable degree of detail in input requirements is avoided. Failure to attain the latter would tend to defeat the objective of having a quick turn-around time in exercising the model.

Another problem that might arise is related to our speculations regarding the use of dollars as a measure of real cost. Most present day force-mix cost models express their primary outputs in terms of dollars, and on occasion in manpower requirements. These, of course, are very useful measures of the cost consequences of postulated force structure decisions. However, for reasons indicated earlier, such measures may not always be sufficient in dealing with complex issues posed by broad force-mix decision problems. What some of the alternative measures might be, and how they might be obtained, is not clear at the present time. And it is certainly not clear how these might be obtained in view of the requirement for quick response outputs from the cost analysis process.

Thus, even though these comments are quite general, it is clear that much remains to be done if the state-of-the-art of military cost analysis is to be advanced significantly beyond what it is today. An important part of this future effort must be devoted to conceptual problems. Equally important is the continuing improvement in specific methods, which must of necessity involve much tedious hard work. And yet, as we hope we have also demonstrated, the effort can be expected to have enormous value to the decisionmaking process, and to the clarity, soundness, and scope of the decisions themselves.

**Appendix A**

# THE OPPORTUNITY COST CONCEPT: AN EXAMPLE FROM THE MICROECONOMIC THEORY OF THE FIRM[1]

To illustrate the concept of opportunity cost, let us consider a simple example from micro-economic theory: the case of the individual firm with all external economies and diseconomies ignored. Here, the *rate of product transformation* (RPT) – the slope of the product transformation curve – measures the *opportunity cost* or the real sacrifice (internal to the firm) of producing an additional unit of a commodity.

To see this clearly, consider a very simple situation where the firm produces two outputs ($Q_1$ and $Q_2$) by using a single input (X).[2] The firm's production function in implicit form may be written

$$H(q_1, q_2, x) = 0, \qquad (1)$$

where $q_1$, $q_2$, and $x$ are the respective quantities of $Q_1$, $Q_2$, and X. Solving explicitly for $x$, we have

$$x = h(q_1, q_2). \qquad (2)$$

That is to say, the cost of production *in terms of* X is a function of the quantities of the two outputs.

We may now define the familiar *product transformation curve*

$$x^0 = h(q_1, q_2), \qquad (3)$$

which portrays the locus of output combinations that can be obtained from a given input of X. The negative of the slope of the product transformation curve is the *rate of product transformation* (RPT):

$$\text{RPT} = -\frac{dq_2}{dq_1}, \qquad (4)$$

which measures the rate at which $Q_2$ must be sacrificed to get more of $Q_1$ (or vice versa). That is to say, RPT measures the *opportunity cost* of getting more of $Q_1$ for the fixed level of input of X.

---

[1] The basic argument in this example is taken from James M. Henderson and Richard E. Quandt, *Microeconomic Theory: A Mathematical Approach* (New York: McGraw-Hill Book Company, 1958), pp. 67–72.

[2] A slightly more complicated case is treated in Chapter 3 (pp. 26–27) where we considered two inputs and two outputs.

We can also express RPT in terms of marginal costs and in terms of marginal products (MPs). Take the total differential of equation (2):

$$dx = \frac{\partial h}{\partial q_1} dq_1 + \frac{\partial h}{\partial q_2} dq_2. \tag{5}$$

But $dx = 0$ for movements along a *given* product transformation curve. Therefore,

$$\frac{\partial h}{\partial q_1} dq_1 = -\frac{\partial h}{\partial q_2} dq_2, \tag{6}$$

$$\frac{\dfrac{\partial h}{\partial q_1}}{\dfrac{\partial h}{\partial q_2}} = -\frac{dq_2}{dq_1}. \tag{7}$$

Substituting (7) in equation (4):

$$\mathrm{RPT} = \frac{\dfrac{\partial h}{\partial q_1}}{\dfrac{\partial h}{\partial q_2}}, \tag{8}$$

which says that at a point on the product transformation curve, RPT equals the ratio of the marginal cost of $Q_1$ *in terms of* X to the marginal cost of $Q_2$ *in terms of* X.

Now let us differentiate equation (2) with respect to $q_1$ and $q_2$:

$$\frac{\partial x}{\partial q_1} = \frac{\partial h}{\partial q_1}, \tag{9}$$

$$\frac{\partial x}{\partial q_2} = \frac{\partial h}{\partial q_2}. \tag{10}$$

Applying the *inverse-function* rule:

$$\frac{\partial q_1}{\partial x} = 1 \bigg/ \frac{\partial h}{\partial q_1} \quad \text{or} \quad \frac{\partial h}{\partial q_1} = 1 \bigg/ \frac{\partial q_1}{\partial x}; \tag{11}$$

$$\frac{\partial q_2}{\partial x} = 1 \bigg/ \frac{\partial h}{\partial q_2} \quad \text{or} \quad \frac{\partial h}{\partial q_2} = 1 \bigg/ \frac{\partial q_2}{\partial x}. \tag{12}$$

Substituting (11) and (12) into equation (8):

$$\text{RPT} = \frac{1 \Big/ \dfrac{\partial q_1}{\partial x}}{1 \Big/ \dfrac{\partial q_2}{\partial x}} = \frac{\partial q_2}{\partial x} \Big/ \frac{\partial q_1}{\partial x}. \tag{13}$$

Here, we have our desired result: RPT expressed in terms of marginal products. Equation (13) says that RPT (which by our original definition measures opportunity cost) equals the ratio of the marginal product of X in the production of $Q_2$ to the marginal product of X in the production of $Q_1$.

Notice that this treatment of opportunity cost has in no way involved any of the firm's revenue considerations. All of the measures of opportunity cost are expressed in terms of physical quantities derived from the firm's production function.

It is informative, however, to bring in the firm's revenue function. We shall show that under certain conditions an explicit relationship between RPT (the measure of opportunity cost in *physical* terms) and market prices (*dollars*) can be derived. This is important to much of the discussion in Chapter 3 because it furnishes an example of how under certain assumptions dollars can reflect real (opportunity) costs.

As a first example, let us consider the same case discussed above, and assume that the firm wants to maximize revenue for a specified level of input of X. We shall also assume that the firm sells its two outputs in a competitive market at fixed prices $p_1$ and $p_2$.

The revenue function is

$$R = p_1 q_1 + p_2 q_2. \tag{14}$$

We want to maximize $R$ subject to

$$x^0 = h(q_1, q_2). \tag{15}$$

We have, therefore:

$$W = p_1 q_1 + p_2 q_2 + \mu[x^0 - h(q_1, q_2)].^3 \tag{16}$$

Differentiating partially, and setting the derivatives equal to zero:

$$\frac{\partial W}{\partial q_1} = p_1 - \mu \frac{\partial h}{\partial q_1} = 0, \tag{17}$$

---

[3] Here, we are using the method of Lagrange, where $\mu$ is a Lagrange multiplier. (See Henderson and Quandt, *op. cit.*, pp. 273–274.)

$$\frac{\partial W}{\partial q_2} = p_2 - \mu \frac{\partial h}{\partial q_2} = 0, \tag{18}$$

$$\frac{\partial W}{\partial \mu} = x^0 - h(q_1, q_2) = 0. \tag{19}$$

From (17) and (18) we have

$$\frac{p_1}{p_2} = \frac{\dfrac{\partial h}{\partial q_1}}{\dfrac{\partial h}{\partial q_2}}. \tag{20}$$

But from equation (8) we know that the right side of (20) is equal to RPT. Therefore:

$$\text{RPT} = \frac{p_1}{p_2}. \tag{21}$$

Thus, in this maximizing situation the firm must operate in such a way that RPT (or the measure of opportunity cost) must equal the ratio of the fixed prices of the outputs $Q_1$ and $Q_2$. Here we see that a very explicit relationship exists between RPT (the measure of opportunity cost in physical terms) and dollars (the market prices of the outputs). This is why economic theory says that under certain market conditions and under certain assumptions about the behavior of the firm, market (dollar) prices will reflect opportunity costs internal to the firm.

The example represented by equations (14) through (21) is a special case involving a specific constraint: i.e., the level of the input factor X is fixed. What happens if the constraint is relaxed? We shall now consider such a case and show that for a firm in a profit-maximizing situation, RPT will be equal to the ratio of the fixed market prices of the outputs $Q_1$ and $Q_2$. Letting $\pi$ = profit and $r$ = the fixed price of the input factor X, we have

$$\pi = \overbrace{p_1 q_1 + p_2 q_2}^{\text{Revenue}} - \overbrace{rh(q_1, q_2)}^{\text{Cost}}. \tag{22}$$

Then,

$$\frac{\partial \pi}{\partial q_1} = p_1 - r\frac{\partial h}{\partial q_1} = 0, \tag{23}$$

$$\frac{\partial \pi}{\partial q_2} = p_2 - r\frac{\partial h}{\partial q_2} = 0, \tag{24}$$

from which we obtain

$$r = p_1 \Big/ \frac{\partial h}{\partial q_1} = p_2 \Big/ \frac{\partial h}{\partial q_2}. \tag{25}$$

Or, substituting from equations (11) and (12),

$$r = p_1 \frac{\partial q_1}{\partial x} = p_2 \frac{\partial q_2}{\partial x}. \tag{26}$$

Therefore,

$$\frac{p_1}{p_2} = \frac{\dfrac{\partial q_2}{\partial x}}{\dfrac{\partial q_1}{\partial x}} = \text{RPT.}^4 \tag{27}$$

What about the "general" case – say $n$ inputs and $s$ outputs? This has been worked out, and it can be shown that when all inputs are held constant, the RPT (the measure of opportunity cost) for every *pair of outputs* (all other outputs being held constant) must be equal to the ratio of their prices.[5] Thus, the general case is a straightforward analogy to our simple two-output case. However, all inputs must be held constant and the outputs taken in pairs.

The above discussion applies only to the individual firm. Similar results can also be derived for the entire consuming and producing sectors of an economy in a state of perfectly competitive equilibrium. To discuss this subject in detail would be beyond the scope of this book. We shall outline only some of the main points.[6]

The key assumptions are:

1. Perfect competition among consumers, producers, and in the commodity and factor (productive services) markets.

2. Subject to their individual budget constraints, consumers seek to maximize their satisfactions (i.e., maximize their utility functions). For any two commodities $Q_j$ and $Q_k$, this means that the consumer's *rate of commodity substitution* (RCS) is equal to the market prices ($p_j$ and $p_k$) of the two commodities.[7]

---

[4] See equation (13).
[5] See Henderson and Quandt, *op. cit.*, p. 73.
[6] For a complete treatment see Henderson and Quandt, *op. cit.*, pp. 202–208.
[7] See *ibid.*, pp. 11–13. RCS for consumers is analogous to RPT for producers. In effect RCS measures the consumer's "opportunity cost" of exchanging more of one commodity for less of another.

3. Producing firms seek to maximize their profits.
4. Externalities are absent.

Under these conditions, competitive equilibrium will result in the following:

$$\text{RCS} = \frac{p_j}{p_k} = \text{RPT}.$$

Here we have an example of a situation where market prices reflect directly the opportunity costs of both consumers and producers. This, however, is a very special case which is never generally attained in reality. That is one of the reasons why in Chapter 3 we are very cautious in making statements about how well dollars measure real costs. In an economic and political society like the United States, dollars do in fact serve as a *reasonably good "proxy"* for opportunity costs in a great many economic sectors. In others, however, dollar expenditures may be a very poor measure of economic cost, because assumptions 1–4 outlined above are only very inadequately fulfilled.

## Appendix B

# THE CONCEPT OF COMPARATIVE ADVANTAGE

The concept of comparative advantage is applicable to many types of problems and contexts. It is usually illustrated in economic texts with examples drawn from international trade, although its significance pervades all levels of economic activity from the international to the individual. Let us start out by considering its application to international trade.

To illustrate the principle of comparative advantage, consider the following simple example:[1]

|  | Production Cost | |
| Product | In America | In Europe |
| --- | --- | --- |
| 1 unit of food | 1 day's labor | 3 days' labor |
| 1 unit of clothing | 2 days' labor | 4 days' labor |

At first blush one might conclude that trade would never take place because of America's overwhelming *absolute* efficiency in the production of both commodities. However, the principle of comparative advantage says that even if one of two countries is absolutely more efficient in the production of every commodity than is the other country, trade will still be mutually advantageous to both if each specializes in the production of products in which it has the greatest *relative efficiency*.

In our example, America has the *comparative* advantage in food and Europe in clothing. Why? Because:

$$\frac{\text{Food cost in America (1)}}{\text{Food cost in Europe (3)}} < \frac{\text{Clothing cost in America (2)}}{\text{Clothing cost in Europe (4)}}$$

$$\frac{\text{Clothing cost in Europe (4)}}{\text{Clothing cost in America (2)}} < \frac{\text{Food cost in Europe (3)}}{\text{Food cost in America (1)}}$$

Let us now return to the B-52/fighter bomber example in Chapter 3 (pages 26–27). We may set up the following matrix, which is analogous to the one in the international trade example:

---

[1] This example is based on Paul A. Samuelson, *Economics: An Introductory Analysis*, 7th ed. (New York: McGraw-Hill Book Company, 1967), pp. 649–651.

|                    | No. of Units Required |    |
|--------------------|:---------------------:|:--:|
| Task               | B-52                  | FB |
| Attack an air base | 1                     | 10 |
| Destroy a bridge   | 1                     | 2  |

If the principle of comparative advantage is applied to this situation, the result is that B-52s are relatively more efficient in attacking air bases, and FBs have the comparative advantage in attacking bridges. Why? Because:

$$\frac{\text{B-52 attack A.B. (1)}}{\text{FB attack A.B. (10)}} < \frac{\text{B-52 attack bridge (1)}}{\text{FB attack bridge (2)}}$$

$$\frac{\text{FB attack bridge (2)}}{\text{B-52 attack bridge (1)}} < \frac{\text{FB attack A.B. (10)}}{\text{B-52 attack A.B. (1)}}$$

Recall that in our analysis in Chapter 3 (see page 27) the cost benefit ratio of using B-52s to destroy a bridge was $10/2 = 5$. This factor (by which costs exceed benefits) is precisely the same factor that measures the B-52s comparative *dis*advantage in attacking bridges (relative to air bases): i.e., $0.5/0.1 = 5$. It is also the factor that measures the FBs comparative advantage in attacking bridges (relative to air bases): i.e., $10/2 = 5$. Thus we see that there is an equivalence between our cost-benefit analysis in the text in Chapter 3 and our solution to the problem in terms of comparative advantage in this appendix. That is to say, the concepts of comparative advantage and opportunity costs are closely related.

**Appendix C**

# THE THEORY OF MAXIMIZING BEHAVIOR
# AN EXAMPLE FROM THE THEORY OF THE FIRM

The main points made in the discussion of marginal analysis contained in the section on "Minimizing Costs or Maximizing Benefits" in Chapter 3 may be illustrated from topics in economic theory. Basically, the "marginal conditions" used by economists in discussing optimization behavior refer to the mathematical conditions for a maximum (or a minimum) of some specified functional form. We shall illustrate this briefly by an example from the theory of the firm.

Suppose that a firm's gross revenue $(R)$ and total cost $(C)$ may be related to the firm's rate of output $(x)$ for some period of time. Profit $(\pi)$, then, may be defined as the difference between the firm's revenue and total cost functions:

$$\pi(x) = R(x) - C(x). \qquad (1)$$

How should the firm behave if it is to maximize profit? How does the firm choose its optimum rate of output? Assuming that (1) is differentiable, we can readily determine the answer:

$$\frac{d\pi}{dx} = \frac{dR}{dx} - \frac{dC}{dx} = 0, \qquad (2)$$

or

$$\frac{dR}{dx} = \frac{dC}{dx}. \qquad (3)$$

Since by definition marginal revenue and marginal cost are, respectively, the first derivative of the total revenue function and the first derivative of the total cost function, equation (3) represents that familiar theorem in economics for the necessary condition for maximum profit:[1] i.e., the firm must operate at a rate of output such that marginal revenue equals marginal cost.

We may also treat the profit maximization problem in terms of utilization of the input factors. Suppose we have the following:

---

[1] The second order condition for $\pi(x)$ to be a maximum is $d^2\pi/dx^2 < 0$, which implies $d^2R/dx^2 < d^2C/dx^2$. (At the optimum output the marginal revenue curve has to intersect the marginal cost curve from above.)

A. The firm's production function relating quantity of output ($q$) to quantities of the two variable input factors ($x_1$ and $x_2$):[2]

$$q = f(x_1, x_2).$$

B. The firm's cost function relating cost of production ($c$) to quantities of the two productive factors ($x_1$ and $x_2$):

$$c = r_1 x_1 + r_2 x_2 + \alpha,$$

where $r_1$ and $r_2$ are the (given) market prices of the input factors and $\alpha$ is the cost of the fixed inputs.

C. The firm's output is sold in a competitive market at a fixed unit price ($p$). Total revenue, then, is price ($p$) times quantity ($q$) = $pf(x_1, x_2)$.

D. Given A through C, the firm's profit function is

$$\pi = pq - c$$
$$= pf(x_1, x_2) - r_1 x_1 - r_2 x_2 - \alpha.$$

The first order conditions for $\pi$ to be at a maximum are

$$\frac{\partial \pi}{\partial x_1} = p \frac{\partial f}{\partial x_1} - r_1 = 0.$$

$$\frac{\partial \pi}{\partial x_2} = p \frac{\partial f}{\partial x_2} - r_2 = 0,$$

or alternatively

$$p \frac{\partial f}{\partial x_1} = r_1$$

$$p \frac{\partial f}{\partial x_2} = r_2.$$

That is to say, for profit to be at a maximum, the firm will utilize each input factor up to the point where its marginal benefit (value of its marginal product) is equal to its marginal cost. For the first productive factor, for example, the marginal product is $\partial f / \partial x_1$. The marginal cost of the first factor is $\partial c / \partial x_1 = r_1$. Therefore, the first factor will be employed such that:

$$p \frac{\partial f}{\partial x_1} = r_1.$$

---

[2] For simplicity we assume only two input factors. The results can easily be generalized to the $n$ factor case.

Notice that in the process of deciding how to operate the firm so that profits will be maximized, the cost of the fixed factors ($\alpha$) dropped out of the calculations (the derivative of a constant is zero). This is an example of what economists mean when they say that for decisionmaking purposes "bygones are forever bygones."

Samuelson puts the matter this way:

> The economist always stresses the "extra," or "marginal," costs and advantages of any decision. . . . Let bygones be bygones. Don't look backward. Don't moan about your sunk costs. Look forward. Make a hard-headed calculation of the *extra* costs you'll incur by any decision and weigh these against its *extra* advantages. Cancel out all the good things and bad things *that will go on anyway*, whether you make an affirmative or negative decision on the point under consideration.[3]

We stress this because focusing on the cost and benefit implications of *the decision* is a fundamental point in Chapter 3, and for the remainder of this book.

---

[3] Paul A. Samuelson, *Economics: An Introductory Analysis*, 7th ed. (New York: McGraw-Hill Book Company, 1967), pp. 477–478.

# AUTHOR INDEX

Numbers set in *italics* designate the page numbers on which the complete literature references are given.

Abert, J. G., *235*
Asher, Harold, *137, 173*

Baumol, William J., *221*, 226, 227
Berg, R. S., *301*
Berman, E. B., 228
Bonini, Charles P., *121*, 125, 127, *142*, 146, 149, 150, 151, 152, 154, 159, *165*
Boren, H. E., Jr., *130, 191*
Boucher, W. I., *6*, 8, 15, *23, 99*, 302, 303, 306
Breckner, Norman V., *98, 116*
Brom, J. R., *269*
Buchanan, James M., *63*

Christ, Carl F., *165*

Dalkey, N. C., *18, 126, 286*
Davis, Dale S., *154,* 155, *165*
Dienemann, Paul F., *211*
Dixon, W. J., *154*
Drew, Elizabeth B., *21*
Duesenberry, James S., *155*

English, J. Morley, *99*
Enthoven, Alain C., *7, 8, 13, 22*
Ezekiel, Mordecai, *154*

Fisher, G. H., *99, 243*
Fox, Karl A., *154*
Fromm, Gary, *155*

Giamboni, L. A., *269*
Graver, C. A., *130*

Hatry, Harry P., *213*, 227, *241*
Helmer, Olaf, *18*
Henderson, James M., *63, 309*, 311, 313
Hicks, J. R., *89*
Hitch, Charles J., *4, 5, 11*, 19, 20, *23, 202, 212*, 228, 229, 234, *241, 284*
Hoch, Saul, 241

Johnston, J., *165*

Kahn, Herman, *12, 16*, 17
Kain, J. F., *21*

Kamrass, Murray, *301*
Keynes, John Maynard, *220*
Klein, Lawrence R., *155*, 156, *207*
Kroeker, Herbert R., *173*
Kuh, Edward, *155*

Lind, J. R., *269*

McClelland, John, *241*
McKean, Roland N., *5, 11*, 20, *23, 221, 222*, 223, 228, 229, 234, *241*
McNamara, Robert S., *7, 16*
Madansky, Albert, *12, 202, 207*, 215, *241*
Mann, Irwin, *12*
Marshall, A. W., *205*
Meckling, W. H., *205*
Meyer, J. R., *21*
Mooz, W. E., *102, 119*

Navarro, Joseph A., *301*
Niskanen, William A., *4*, 227
Noah, Joseph W., *98, 116*
Novick, David, *20*

Peck, Merton J., *203, 204*
Peterson, Robert E., *173*
Petruschell, R. L., *190, 200*

Quade, Edward S., *6*, 8, 12, 14, 15, *23, 99, 211, 301, 302*, 303, 306
Quandt, Richard E., *63, 309*, 311, 313

Rainey, Richard B., Jr., *301*
Rudwick, Bernard H., *23, 99*

Samuelson, Paul A., *10, 31*, 34, *62, 63, 315*, 319
Scherer, Frederic M., *203*, 204
Siska, C. P., *269*
Smith, T. Arthur, *4, 191, 200*
Specht, R. D., *9, 200*
Spurr, William A., *121*, 125, 127, *142*, 146, 149, 150, 151, 152, 154, 159, *165*
Staats, Elmer B., *57*
Summers, Robert, *203*, 214

321

# SUBJECT INDEX

# Selected Rand Books

ARROW, KENNETH J., and MARVIN HOFFENBERG, *A Time Series Analysis of Interindustry Demands,* North-Holland Publishing Company, Amsterdam, Netherlands, 1959.

BAKER, C. L., and F. J. GRUENBERGER, *The First Six Million Prime Numbers,* Microcard Editions, Washington, D.C., 1959.

BELLMAN, RICHARD E., *Dynamic Programming,* Princeton University Press, Princeton, New Jersey, 1957.

—— (ed.), *Mathematical Optimization Techniques,* University of California Press, Los Angeles, 1963.

—— and STUART E. DREYFUS, *Applied Dynamic Programming,* Princeton University Press, Princeton, New Jersey, 1962.

——, HARRIET H. KAGIWADA, R. E. KALABA, and MARCIA C. PRESTRUD, *Invariant Imbedding and Time-Dependent Transport Processes,* American Elsevier Publishing Company, Inc., New York, 1964.

—— and ROBERT E. KALABA, *Quasilinearization and Nonlinear Boundary-Value Problems,* American Elsevier Publishing Company, Inc., New York, 1965.

——, ROBERT E. KALABA, and JO ANN LOCKETT, *Numerical Inversion of the Laplace Transform,* American Elsevier Publishing Company, Inc., New York, 1966.

——, ROBERT E. KALABA, and MARCIA C. PRESTRUD, *Invariant Imbedding and Radiative Transfer in Slabs of Finite Thickness,* American Elsevier Publishing Company, Inc., New York, 1963.

DANTZIG, GEORGE B., *Linear Programming and Extensions,* Princeton University Press, Princeton, New Jersey, 1963.

DEIRMENDJIAN, D., *Electromagnetic Scattering on Spherical Polydispersions,* American Elsevier Publishing Company, Inc., New York, 1969.

DORFMAN, ROBERT, PAUL A. SAMUELSON, and ROBERT M. SOLOW, *Linear Programming and Economic Analysis,* McGraw-Hill Book Company, Inc., New York, 1958.

DRESHER, MELVIN, *Games of Strategy: Theory and Applications,* Prentice-Hall, Inc., Englewood Cliffs, New Jersey, 1961.

DREYFUS, STUART, *Dynamic Programming and the Calculus of Variations,* Academic Press, Inc., New York, 1965.

FISHMAN, GEORGE S., *Spectral Methods in Econometrics,* Harvard University Press, Cambridge, Massachusetts, 1969.

GALE, DAVID, *The Theory of Linear Economic Models,* McGraw-Hill Book Company, Inc., New York, 1960.

HEARLE, EDWARD F. R., and RAYMOND J. MASON, *A Data Processing System for State and Local Governments,* Prentice-Hall, Inc., Englewood Cliffs, New Jersey, 1963.

HIRSHLEIFER, JACK, JAMES C. DeHAVEN, and JEROME W. MILLIMAN, *Water Supply: Economics, Technology, and Policy,* The University of Chicago Press, Chicago, 1969.

HITCH, CHARLES J., and ROLAND McKEAN, *The Economics of Defense in the Nuclear Age,* Harvard University Press, Cambridge, Massachusetts, 1960.

JORGENSON, D. W., J. J. McCALL, and R. RADNER, *Optimal Replacement Policy,* North-Holland Publishing Company, Amsterdam, Netherlands, 1967.

JUDD, WILLIAM R. (ed.), *State of Stress in the Earth's Crust,* American Elsevier Publishing Company, Inc., New York, 1964.

MARSCHAK, GLENNAN, JR., and ROBERT SUMMERS, *Strategy for R&D,* Springer—Verlag New York Inc., New York, 1967.

McKEAN, ROLAND N., *Efficiency in Government through Systems Analysis: With Emphasis on Water Resource Development,* John Wiley & Sons, Inc., New York, 1958.

McKINSEY, J. C. C., *Introduction to the Theory of Games,* McGraw-Hill Book Company, Inc., New York, 1952.

MEYER, JOHN R., MARTIN WOHL, and JOHN F. KAIN, *The Urban Transportation Problem,* Harvard University Press, Cambridge, Massachusetts, 1965.

NELSON, RICHARD R., MERTON J. PECK, and EDWARD D. KALACHEK, *Technology, Economic Growth and Public Policy,* The Brookings Institution, Washington, D.C., 1967.

NOVICK, DAVID (ed.), *Program Budgeting: Program Analysis and the Federal Budget,* Harvard University Press, Cambridge, Massachusetts, 1965.

QUADE, E. S. (ed.), *Analysis for Military Decisions,* North-Holland Publishing Company, Amsterdam, Netherlands, 1964.

——— and W. I. BOUCHER, *Systems Analysis and Policy Planning, Applications in Defense,* American Elsevier Publishing Company, Inc., New York, 1968.

SHARPE, WILLIAM F., *The Economics of Computers,* Columbia University Press, New York, 1969.

SHEPPARD, J. J., *Human Color Perception,* American Elsevier Publishing Company, Inc., New York, 1968.

THE RAND CORPORATION, *A Million Random Digits with 100,000 Normal Deviates,* The Free Press, Glencoe, Illinois, 1955.

WILLIAMS, J. D., *The Compleat Strategyst: Being a Primer on the Theory of Games of Strategy,* McGraw-Hill Book Company, Inc., New York, 1954.